CAVALRY ON SERVICE

CAVALRY ON SERVICE

ILLUSTRATED BY

THE ADVANCE OF THE GERMAN
CAVALRY ACROSS THE
MOSEL IN 1870

TRANSLATED FROM THE GERMAN OF

GENERAL v. PELET-NARBONNE

BY

MAJOR D'A. LEGARD
17TH LANCERS

The Naval & Military Press Ltd

Published by

The Naval & Military Press Ltd
Unit 5 Riverside, Brambleside
Bellbrook Industrial Estate
Uckfield, East Sussex
TN22 1QQ England

Tel: +44 (0)1825 749494

www.naval-military-press.com
www.nmarchive.com

In reprinting in facsimile from the original, any imperfections are inevitably reproduced and the quality may fall short of modern type and cartographic standards.

TRANSLATOR'S PREFACE

THIS translation was undertaken with the object of putting before cavalry officers of the Army some pages of actual cavalry history.

If it induces them to make a further study of military history in general, and cavalry history in particular, it will have fulfilled its object.

I have inserted an additional map in order to show comprehensively the positions of the German cavalry on every second day.

Certain notes and references in the original text, which are of historic interest only to the regiments concerned, have been intentionally omitted.

I must express my sense of deep obligation to Herr Karl v. Donat, who kindly consented to go through, and carefully revise, the proofs for me, and to Colonel Lonsdale Hale, who gave me both encouragement and assistance; also to Messrs. Smith, Elder & Co., for kindly allowing the use of the map from their publication, "Problems in Manœuvre Tactics."

D'ARCY LEGARD.

STAFF COLLEGE
September, 1906.

PREFACE

AN attempt has been made in this work to discuss the action of cavalry on service in an applied form based on the actual events of a war. A detailed description of a period of the Franco-German war has been attempted, as it seems specially adapted to fulfil this object.*

The endeavour is made to depict real warfare; to trace the actual course of events, even of apparently unimportant events, if they throw light on the subject, and thus to provide as far as possible a basis founded on facts.

We can scarcely hope to meet with complete success, although use has been made of every possible source of information, as well as of much private correspondence.

If we attempt to describe the course of events in detail as far as possible in accordance with facts, there will yet remain gaps which we shall be unable to fill in. Many written reports have been lost, while the verbal ones are perhaps not mentioned in the records. It is as impossible to give an absolutely accurate account of the service of reconnaissance of a large mass of cavalry, as I have tried to do here, for the first time, in regard to the course of the 1870 war, as it is to give a

* A glance at the index at the end shows the most important of the duties discussed and the amount of instruction that can be gained from the events of that period.

complete description of any great battle which every historian knows the difficulty of.

It has certainly been possible to follow the most important events in detail, particularly the experiences of many interesting patrols, so that the gaps are unimportant, and do not seriously affect the object.

On the other hand, it has not been considered necessary to quote all the events, orders, and reports; and incidents have been omitted which were neither of general interest nor affecting the end in view.

The book is not intended primarily to serve as a history, but as the best practical instruction which well-ascertained facts can afford.

The advance and the reconnaissance of the cavalry form the basis of the work. The author only deals *en passant* with the service of outposts and security.

In the second part of the book, which will appear later, the action of the cavalry in the service of security and in the fight, during the operations near Coulmiers, 1870, will come under consideration. The course of events in war must be contrasted with the ideas entertained by our officers in peace-time. It must, however, be emphasized that the almost complete inaction of the French cavalry rendered this service far easier than it is ever likely to be in future.

A great point has been made of giving the orders and reports as far as possible verbatim, as these are often most important.

It is, moreover, interesting for young officers to read reports which have often been written under difficulties, in the presence of the enemy, and even under fire.

In a criticism of the leadership of the great

bodies of cavalry in 1870–1871, we must bear in mind the views then in vogue of their use and the want of experience of the leaders in their employment.

The way in which the cavalry would have been employed, if our modern views had then been established, is therefore the keynote of instruction in this discussion.

One must always recollect, in a subsequent criticism like this, how much easier it is, sitting at table with ample time, to decide on the right course, than under the circumstances prevailing in the presence of the enemy.

There are, nevertheless, faults of omission which are inexcusable even from this point of view, and which must be criticized accordingly.

The time has come when these topics may be fearlessly subjected to candid criticism; the army has a right to gather instruction from these events of the past; and the supply seems all but inexhaustible.

Events have been carefully described with absolute impartiality, and the negative side of the action of the cavalry has been ruthlessly exposed where it seems necessary for purposes of instruction.

Comments are made on events where the lessons are not already apparent from the description of what happened, and where the reader cannot easily gather them for himself.

As regards the action of the German cavalry in the great war, the reader will discover from the accounts given that the higher leading of that arm proved unsatisfactory throughout, and that the training was also at fault.

The following were the chief points the want of which resulted in the work of reconnaissance not being satisfactory on occasions :—

1. The cavalry lacked any higher leaders experienced in their employment.

2. No practice in strategic reconnaissance had ever taken place, and the grasp of it was therefore lacking in the cavalry divisions which were improvised on mobilization.*

3. The commanders rarely gave definite instructions to the patrol leader. This is always necessary, if good work is to be expected, and nowadays the general custom.

4. The men were not brought up to keep touch, once established, with the enemy, without further order.

Squadrons and patrols considered their duty done when they had reached the enemy. They then returned to their commander and made their report.

It was only when it was expressly stated in orders that parties continued their task for several days, but their advanced patrols were not supported by formed bodies in rear—an evil which the inactivity of the enemy rendered less noticeable.

5. This want in training was, however, not at all a serious one; in it we may include perhaps a want of practice in composing written messages, and wherever any special demand was made on the German cavalry, as the reader will learn, they always answered gamely.

Since then the cavalry has endeavoured to repair these omissions in their training with the most satisfactory results. Their efforts in future will be still more productive if more and more attention is paid to conditions possible only in time of war. During a long period of peace this is too easily lost sight of.

The gravest error was that the higher leaders

---

* Improvising in war-time is always a disadvantage as compared with an established organization in peace.

PREFACE

made little or no use of their cavalry, either in reconnaissance work or in the fight.

Consider the influence of General v. Steinmetz, who held the opinion, and openly expressed it, that cavalry should be kept in rear!

It is therefore unjust to hold the German cavalry responsible in this campaign for their frequently unsatisfactory performances.

Their spirit was admirable, and was proved to be so whenever they were employed. Their claims to gallantry and disregard of life are undeniable. Where the most favourable opportunities demanded action they often thirsted in vain for employment.

But how can action be expected of troops of which no use is made?

Let us demand great exertions of the cavalry and they will assuredly perform them. We must learn to regard the life of a cavalryman as not so especially precious; we must expect the cavalry to suffer losses, when the situation requires it, just as much as the infantry do on many occasions, without being affected, and without making much ado about it.

In any criticism on one's own performances the enemy's measure must be taken into consideration; and here we are compelled to admit that the French cavalry proved far from competent in their duty.

The reason lay in their insufficient, or rather, absolute want of training in the service, both of reconnaissance and of protection. Cavalry patrols were practically never sent out by the French, and if they were, they scarcely went beyond the outposts. Measures of protection, if there were any, as a rule, were entrusted solely to the infantry.

The half-trained cavalry of the Republican army, however, began to show signs of improvement in the right direction.

Further reasons for the ill success of the German cavalry lay in their faulty distribution, for, on the one hand, no cavalry was permanently set apart for the infantry divisions, but only as occasion demanded, and then in insufficient numbers; and, on the other, in the wrong use which was made of the cavalry divisions, as they were always kept back behind the infantry, and retained as reserve cavalry, or kept for use on the battlefield.

In equipment the French cavalry were superior to the German, by reason of the longer range of their carbines, and because they were more accustomed to act dismounted.

Their training with sword and sabre was perhaps better than that of the Germans.

Their education in employment in large bodies on the battlefield was wanting just as much as that of the German cavalry. The French leaders were even less enterprising than the Germans in their use of cavalry.

The *cauchemar Prussien*, which clung even to the French cavalry after the first few misadventures, had a decided influence on their behaviour; but they still fought with the old dash when they were led into action.

The French cavalry, too, badly trained as they were, would yet have done better work if they had been better handled, as good leaders and a proper comprehension of their use are more vital even than careful training. *L'homme est tout*, and for him dash and enterprise are more valuable assets than any amount of theoretical knowledge.

Among the higher leaders who commanded cavalry Prince Frederick Charles was the only one who stood out as capable of handling cavalry; so it is with all the more pleasure and satisfaction that we follow the early efforts of officers in the lower

PREFACE

ranks, who afterwards gained great credit and will always be held up to future generations as bright examples of cavalry officers.

The action of the 15th Uhlans, under Colonel v. Alvensleben, from the 8th to 12th of August must be placed in the front rank. Their performance was indeed ideal. Other patrols, too, afforded brilliant examples of quick wit and prudence. The 15th Uhlans during those days were properly only a large patrol, whose duty was to observe and not to fight. I may mention among many others the names of Stumm, v. Ramin, v. Thiele, v. Hymmen, Graf Itzenplitz, Brix, v. Leipziger, v. Ebart, v. Podbielski, Brauns, v. Rosenberg, v. Kotze, v. Trotha, v. Hirschfeld, v. Vaerst. From them the young officer may gain instruction.

The maps for each day mark the furthest point which the advanced patrols and main bodies of the German cavalry reached on that particular day, but their quarters for the night are not always shown. *Explanation of maps.*

In the description of the service of reconnaissance it is clearly less important to show where a party passed the night than to point out how far the advanced points reached during the day. The maps, therefore, refer to no particular hour of the day. It was impossible to ascertain the situation so exactly as that (for the smallest parties are referred to), since information is wanting. The position of the patrols has been ascertained both from German and French sources. If the unit is not marked, it shows that it is not mentioned in the German sources of information (*i.e.* reports and records of the higher commands), or in the accounts of French historians, where we often find an accurate description, as to time and place, of the appearance of German patrols.

As a clear appreciation of the services of the

German cavalry is impossible without including the divisional cavalry, which on some occasions contributed very materially to success, the advance of individual regiments of the divisional cavalry are also described.

The French troops are shown in large masses on arrival at their destination, or still on the march at the end of each day.

If the situation of the German cavalry on any one day is compared with the enemy's position on the same, or the previous day, it will be clearly seen where the German cavalry kept touch with the enemy and where they lost it. The reason for the latter event will appear in the text. German units of the other arms could not be shown without making the map too complicated, but the regiments of divisional cavalry are marked with a lighter sign than those of the cavalry divisions.

The reader will be able to make out the advance of the other units with the aid of the text and of the distribution given at the end of the book, especially as the divisional cavalry usually remained in close touch with their divisions.

TABLE OF CONTENTS

	PAGE
Translator's Preface	v
Author's Preface	vii

INTRODUCTION

Review of the general situation—Comments on German cavalry before the battle of Spicheren—Events of August 6—Explanation of Map 1—3rd Cavalry Division—Ramin's patrol—Hymmen's patrol—The 19th Dragoons—Stumm's patrol—11th Hussars—12th Dragoons and 3rd Uhlans—6th Cavalry Division—Ebart's patrol—15th Cavalry Brigade—Colonel v. Schmidt—Lachmann's patrol—Brix's squadron—12th Cavalry Brigade—Reconnaissance on Rohrbach—The 13th Dragoons—Patrol with Bavarian Jägers—Loss of touch . . . 1–29

CHAPTER I

Duties in pursuit—Head Quarters of First Army—Prince Frederick Charles—Employment of cavalry during concentration on the frontier—Comparison of Steinmetz's with the Prince's views on the employment of cavalry—3rd Cavalry Division—Ramin's patrol — Hymmen's patrol—Stumm's patrol — Steinmetz's views for the 7th—Pursuit by the 6th Cavalry Division—Grüter's Brigade before Forbach—Colonel v. Unger with the 12th Dragoons and 15th Hussars—Steinmetz intervening—Reconnaissance in a thick mist—Captain Haelmigk's reconnaissance—On outpost duty at Merlenbach—Comments on Grüter's action—Orders of Duke William—Concentration of the 5th Cavalry Division towards the left wing—Occupation of Saargemünd—König's patrol—Lieut.-Colonel v. Rauch at Saargemünd—Comments—News from Royal Head Quarters about the enemy's retreat from Wörth—Measures of Prince Frederick Charles—Orders to the Fourth Army Corps and the 12th Cavalry Brigade—Reconnaissance of the 5th Dragoons on Bitsch—Movements of the French—Results of the German reconnaissance 30–84

CHAPTER II

The First Army—The 3rd Cavalry Division—Ramin's patrol—Papen's patrol—Outpost reports—12th Dragoons—Thiele's patrol—Krell's patrol—The 6th Cavalry Division—Orders to the 15th Uhlans—Colonel v. Alvensleben at St. Avold—Leipziger's squadron—The 5th Cavalry Division—Attachment of Cavalry Divisions to Army Corps—The 7th Cuirassiers on their errand to gain touch with the Third Army—Comments on Prince Frederick Charles's arrangements—Movements of the French 85–114

CHAPTER III

Measures of General v. Steinmetz—Moltke's telegram—The 3rd Cavalry Division—Ramin's patrol—Wallenberg's patrol—Balthasar's patrol—Hymmen's patrol—Papen's patrol—Skirmish at Bolchen—Itzenplitz's patrol—Measures of the Third Army Corps—The 15th Uhlans at St. Avold—Major Graf Haeseler's reconnaissance—Oppenheim's patrol—Schmiesing's patrol—Skirmish at Gross-Tänchen—Czettritz's patrol—Captain v. Cramm—The 5th Cavalry Division—The 12th Cavalry Brigade—Orders for reconnaissance—Comments and suggestions—Captain v. Rochow—Destruction of the railway at Saarburg—French movements . . 115–142

CHAPTER IV

Order to the First Army and its orders for the cavalry—The 3rd Cavalry Division—The 1st Cavalry Division—The 14th Uhlans—Wallenberg's patrol—Hymmen's patrol—Asseburg's patrol—Head Quarters of Second Army—The 6th Cavalry Division moving to the front—The 15th Uhlans at St. Avold—Attitude of the French outposts—Orders to the 5th Cavalry Division—Lieutenant v. Podbielski's report—Comments on General v. Rheinbaben's measures—The 12th Cavalry Brigade—French measures 143–164

CHAPTER V

Measures by the First Army—The 1st and 3rd Cavalry Divisions—Ramin's, Papen's, Voigts-Rhetz's, Hymmen's, Asseburg's patrols—Prince Frederick Charles's action—Action of Cavalry Divisions when opposing armies meet—Order to the 6th Cavalry Division—Results of placing Cavalry Divisions under Army Corps—Duke William's orders—The 15th Uhlans—Captain Brix's reports—Orders to the 5th Cavalry Division

—Lieut.-Colonel v. Caprivi's letter to General v. Redern—
Rheinbaben's order—Redern's order—Rosenberg's recon-
naissance—Rheinbaben's reports—The 17th Hussars—
Hirschfeld's patrol—Lieutenant Neumeister's report—
Captain v. Kotze's report on the enterprise against Dieulouard
—Comments on it—The 12th Cavalry Brigade—Movements
of the enemy 165–194

CHAPTER VI

The Cavalry Divisions of the First Army—Reconnaissance by
Colonel v. Lüderitz — Hymmen's report — Lieutenant v.
Voigts-Rhetz before Diedenhofen—The 1st Cavalry Division—
Reconnaissance by the 9th Uhlans—Comments on the Cavalry
Divisions of the First Army—Itzenplitz's patrol—Head
Quarters of Second Army—Order to the 6th Cavalry Division
—Duke William's order—Reconnaissance on Ars Laquenexy
—The Duke's reports—Army Corps Head Quarters' views on
these reports—The 2nd Dragoons—Order to Rheinbaben—
Criticism of the order—Order or general instruction—Order
to Redern—Enterprise against Frouard—Comments on its
execution—Raid on Pont à Mousson—Rosenberg's recon-
naissance—Rosenberg's reports—Vaerst's squadron—Kleist's
squadron—Garnier's detachment—Order to the 12th Cavalry
Division—The 3rd Guard Cavalry Brigade—Measures taken
by the French 195–238

CHAPTER VII

Order of Royal Head Quarters—Order of General Steinmetz—
Measures taken by the 3rd Cavalry Division for crossing the
Mosel—Comments thereon—Report of Graf Groeben—The
3rd Cavalry Division—The 8th Uhlans' attempt to charge
French cavalry—Reconnaissance by the 4th Uhlans—Order
of the Third Army Corps—Formation of a Corps Cavalry
Brigade—Orders to the 6th Cavalry Division—Duke
William's orders—Measures by the Head Quarters of Second
Army—Occupation of Pont à Mousson—The Light Guard
Cavalry Brigade at Dieulouard—The 12th Cavalry Brigade
rejoins its Division—Measures of the enemy . . 239–264

CHAPTER VIII

Order from Royal Head Quarters—Order of General Steinmetz—
The Cavalry Divisions of the First Army on the day of the
battle of Colombey—Reconnaissance by the 4th Uhlans—
Stumm's patrol—The 1st Dragoons—The 6th Cavalry

xviii TABLE OF CONTENTS

PAGE

Division—Colonel Graf Groeben's reconnaissance—Leipziger's squadron—Colonel v. Alvensleben—Werthern's patrol—Orders to the 5th Cavalry Division—Rheinbaben's measures—Vaerst's and Salm's squadron—The 13th Uhlans—Rosenberg's reports—Comments on the actions of the 5th Cavalry Division—The Brigade of Guard Dragoons—Patrols on Frouard—Trotha's squadron before Toul—The enemy's position 265–288

CHAPTER IX

Order of H.M. the King—Measures by General Steinmetz—The Cavalry Divisions of the First Army—Bassewitz's patrol—Wilamowitz's patrol—Orders to Colonel Graf Groeben and Major v. Hessberg—Groeben's reconnaissance—Hessberg's reconnaissance—The 6th Cavalry Division—Contradictory reports at Head Quarters of Second Army—Order to advance on the left bank of the Mosel—Orders to Rheinbaben—Orders to Bredow—Rheinbaben's measures—Comments thereon—Vaerst's and Salm's squadron—Salis's patrol—Redern at Xonville—Action of the enemy—Redern decides to attack—Rheinbaben's arrival—The attack given up—Comments—The 5th Cavalry Division places outposts—Kotze's report—Wulffen's squadron on Jarny—An artisan seized who gives important information—Comments—Rheinbaben's despatches—Lyncker's detachment at Novéant—Blumenthal's report—Studnitz's report—The Guard-Uhlan Brigade—Platow at Commercy—Rosen before Toul—The Brigade of Guard Dragoons—Kleist's squadron—Movements of the French—Review 289–329

APPENDIX

I. Disposition of the Cavalry of the First and Second German Armies in the war of 1870-71 331

II. Examples of a few schemes which may help to a further study of the duties of cavalry on the basis of the accounts and criticisms given in the book 335

INDEX of the most important of the duties of cavalry discussed in this book 347

CAVALRY ON SERVICE

INTRODUCTION

To explain the general situation of the opposing armies on those first August days of 1870, the following brief summary must be made.

The First Army had been concentrated on the line Losheim-Wadern by August 3; strong detachments had been pushed forward towards the Saar, and in particular to Conz, Saarburg, and Saarbrücken; the fortress of Saarlouis had its armament and war garrison.

No further event had followed the French attack on the 2nd at Saarbrücken.

The German Head Quarters had drawn the conclusion from this attitude that no serious offensive movement on the part of the enemy was to be expected for the present, and that the Second Army, which was still on the far side of the mountains, could be concentrated in front of the wooded district of Kaiserslautern, without fear of being exposed to attack from the enemy before it had completed its passage through the defiles.

The Second Army therefore continued its advance through the Haardt, and on August 5 removed its Head Quarters to Kaiserslautern.

Of its cavalry divisions which were operating in front, the 5th, with the 11th and 13th Brigades, on this day reached on the right flank the neighbourhood of Einweiler-Guichenbach; with the 12th Cavalry Brigade and the 10th Hussars, separated from these brigades by the 6th Cavalry Division, Einöd; the 6th Cavalry Division the country between St. Ingbert and Bliescastel.

The First Army had continued its advance, and on August 5 its Corps had reached the line Ottweiler-Lebach, while the 3rd Cavalry Division, the only one available at this time, and which had been kept back in rear, reached the neighbourhood of St. Wendel.

The Third Army on August 4 had already assumed the offensive, had gained the first victory at Weissenburg, and on the 5th stood on the Sauer in close touch with the enemy.

The positions of the French Army after its successful deployment can be summarized in groups as follows:—The main body, the 2nd, 3rd, and 4th Corps, in Lothringen on the Mosel; the 2nd Corps pushed forward as advanced guard; the 1st and 7th Corps in Elsass, about Strassburg and Belfort; between these groups, the 5th Corps at Bitsch; the 6th Corps in camp at Chalons, as a general reserve, and the Imperial Guard in Nancy.

On August 5 the 1st Corps (4 Divisions) and the 1st Division of the 7th Corps lay on the French right wing on the Sauer, facing the German Third Army; the 5th Corps at Bitsch, Rohrbach, and Saargemünd; the 2nd Corps at Forbach; the 3rd Corps behind it, about St. Avold; the 4th Corps about Bolchen, and the Imperial Guard about Kurzel.

On August 6, at the points where the opposing armies came into immediate touch, took place the battles of Wörth and Spicheren, which were victories for the Germans.

INTRODUCTION

Although our descriptions and comments only begin on August 7, yet since the employment of the German cavalry on the subsequent days in reality develops from their distribution on the previous ones, we must connect them by a brief account.

By the German Head Quarters the battle had not been intended; a great decisive blow had been planned, so the events of Spicheren came as a disturbing element in between.

Comments on the German cavalry before the battle of Spicheren.

In spite of the mistakes of the higher leadership, the battle proved a victory, owing to the admirable courage of the troops and the impulse which animated all the leaders to march towards the sound of the guns; but specially in consequence of the totally inexplicable action of the French generals.

If these had supported the commander of the Second Army Corps by only a simple forward movement, the battle could not have been won by the Germans.

The battle may be characterized as a complete tactical surprise to the Germans. That this was so must be attributed absolutely to the improper use which already, on the days preceding, had been made of the numerous cavalry of the First and Second Armies.

At Head Quarters it had long been known that large masses of French troops were going to be concentrated at St. Avold; the presence of the 2nd Corps in advance at Saarbrücken had confirmed this by the engagement on August 4. It was known that Saargemünd was also occupied, so that the presence of a large army behind the line of the Saar in the triangle Saarbrücken-St. Avold-Saargemünd could be conjectured.

Opposite to it the deployment of the armies advancing from their detraining points was to be protected* and concealed, and information to be obtained about the distribution, movements, and intentions of the enemy's forces.

These duties, which fall to the cavalry, were of both an offensive and defensive nature, and must be separately carried out to attain a successful result—*i.e.* the duty of observation must be fundamentally separate from that of protection.

Only the first of these duties properly belongs to the Army Cavalry, in this instance the Cavalry Divisions; the second belongs to the divisional cavalry, if these, as in this case, are available in such quantities, otherwise they would be strengthened for the purpose by the Cavalry Divisions.

A reconnaissance, to find out what is going on in rear, can only be successful if carried round the flanks of the enemy's army.

This rule holds good in general, but here, is particularly applicable, owing to the configuration of the country where the Saar and the hidden ground on the opposite bank divided the armies.

On the other hand, this river-course assisted the German cavalry in their defensive task, which between Saarbrücken and Saargemünd, as well as farther east towards Bitsch, could well have been allotted to the divisional cavalry, if, after successfully detraining, these regiments, leaving one squadron with each division, had been pushed forward, placed as army corps cavalry under unified control, and had their employment regulated on general lines by Army Head Quarters.†

In this way the Cavalry Divisions of both armies would have been free to undertake their

* It was specially necessary, as was explained on p. 1 to render possible the deployment of the Second Army on the other side of the wooded district of Kaiserslautern.

† Compare the corresponding measure adopted by the Third Army Corps Head Quarters on August 13.

proper *rôle*—the strategic reconnaissance, for which purpose it was desirable to combine them into Cavalry Corps, as was done provisionally by the Second Army with the 5th and 6th Cavalry Divisions.

It would then have been the business of the Divisional Cavalry to secure the army in front.

The concentration of the group of the right wing of the First Army had to take place at Saarlouis and north of it, where as a matter of fact the 3rd Cavalry Division assembled.

The line of operations of this group was marked by the valley of the Nied, where the 3rd Cavalry Division soon found very suitable ground for cavalry beyond the frontier in the first few days, where it had already located the extent of the French left, cleared up the situation at St. Avold, and threatened the enemy's communications with Metz. This was the more important task; but the isolated 3rd Cavalry Division was certainly too weak to solve it fully, and it would have been necessary to reinforce it by the 1st Cavalry Division as soon as possible after it had joined the Army.

The Cavalry Divisions of the Second Army could have been concentrated on the Blies, in order to operate later on against St. Avold by Rohrbach-Saaralb, after the Guard Cavalry Division had joined.

Employing the masses of cavalry in this way for strategical reconnaissance, the various tasks for which should have been detailed by Royal Head Quarters, from a comprehensive point of view, was bound to lead to a complete insight into the general state of affairs with the enemy; it would have prevented tactical surprises and secured for the German leaders complete freedom of action, and this is, after all, the most important task of all reconnaissance by cavalry.

On the other hand, it should have been the duty of the divisional cavalry, which was pushed forward to the Saar, to take up the tactical reconnaissance, to push their reconnoitring detachments for this purpose as far forward as possible over the river; and, supported by an army advanced guard, establish themselves on the far bank, as a sort of bridge head.

Map No. 1 gives the positions reached by the cavalry on August 6; further down we will also give details of some important exploits in reconnaissance which show further developments during succeeding days.

The following remarks will serve to further explain the map :—

Explanation of Map No. 1. On the extreme right wing, halfway between Lebach and Saarlouis, about Saarwellingen, is the 3rd Cavalry Division, with outposts on the Saar on the line Roden-Derlen, and advanced points at Rehlingen, Busendorf, and Ueberherrn. In touch, on the left, is part of the 5th Cavalry Division, the 4th Cuirassiers, and 13th Uhlans, with the staff of the 11th Brigade about Heusweiler, whilst the third regiment of the brigade, the Oldenburg Dragoons, is pushed far forward, split up into single squadrons at Ludweiler, Ham unter Varsberg, and in front of St. Avold. The staff of the 5th Cavalry Division had gone to Saarbrücken.

Of the regiments which belong to the division, the 11th and 17th Hussars have arrived on the battle-field.

Of the first regiment one squadron has been pushed forward to Carlsbrunn, half a squadron to Schöneck, while the 17th (Brunswick) Hussars have sent the 2nd squadron to Arnual. The 3rd regiment

INTRODUCTION

of the 13th Brigade, the 10th Hussars, is still separated, far in the south-west, with two squadrons between Rheinheim and Medelsheim, and the 3rd and 4th in front of Rohrbach; the Brigade Staff being still in Heusweiler.

On the extreme left wing stands widely extended the 12th Cavalry Brigade, separated from the two other brigades of its division by the 6th Cavalry Division; its staff with the 7th Cuirassiers and two squadrons of the 10th Hussars are making a reconnaissance towards Rohrbach and Guisingen. The 16th (Altmark) Uhlans are on outpost on the line Eppingen-Wolmünster-Breidenbach, and yet further on the left about Busweiler are the 13th Dragoons, with an advanced point pushed forward to within 2200 yards from Bitsch. The 5th Dragoons are in Zweibrücken.*

The 6th Cavalry Division, which separated the units of the 5th Division, we find about Ensheim and Eschringen.

The 6th Cuirassiers, belonging to the 14th Brigade, has hurried to the field of battle, while the 3rd and 15th Uhlans are united in the brigade; a squadron of the latter regiment has gone forward to Neunkirchen and cuts the Saargemünd-Bitsch railway, by a patrol at the place marked south-east of the town. A squadron of the 3rd Uhlans has been pushed forward on St. Johann, and a patrol is at Oettingen. The 15th Brigade has reached the neighbourhood of Habkirchen, with one troop of the 16th Hussars as

---

* This regiment belonged to the 4th Cavalry Division, and since July 26 had had severe work on duty on the frontier; it had already on this day sent patrols into French territory, and since August 5 had attached itself to the 12th Cavalry Brigade. It wished to rejoin its division in the advance, as otherwise this was practicable only by a very circuitous route. From August 8 it was attached to the 8th Infantry Division until it marched off on the 12th to rejoin its division.

far as Neunkirchen, which is still held by the enemy.

The main portion of the 1st Cavalry Division is still on the railway journey; the Guard Cavalry Division has been concentrated at Hauptstuhl.

The distribution of the divisional cavalry, marked by a different conventional sign, is also given on the map. We will call particular attention to only a few of their regiments, as, for instance, to the 8th Hussars at Forbach, which have pushed an advanced patrol far forward to Buschborn; the 12th Dragoons, which have two squadrons at Stiring and also one in front of Arnual and another in front of Saargemünd, with advanced points at Gross-Bliedersdorf and Karlingen. The 9th and 15th Hussars are on the field of battle.

The distribution of the French troops, as shown by the map, depicts the general situation after the battle.

The 2nd, Frossard's Corps, beaten at Spicheren, is on its nocturnal retreat to Saargemünd-Püttlingen, with the infantry divisions of Vergé and Laveaucoupet, and Valabrègue's Cavalry Division, whilst Bataille's Infantry Division, in a position at Oettingen, is covering this withdrawal.

Of the 3rd Corps, Bazaine's, Metman's Infantry Division, which had gone forward from Marienthal on Forbach, is nearly two miles south of Forbach; Marshal Bazaine himself, with Decaen's Infantry Division and two brigades of Clerembault's Cavalry Division, are at St. Avold. Reconnoitring parties of one regiment of this division towards Buschborn, and one of the Marshal's on the high-road to Karlingen, are marked.

Juniac's Cavalry Brigade, sent towards Forbach

to support Frossard, has reached Beningen on its retirement to Püttlingen. Castagny's Infantry Division is on its retreat from Folklingen to Püttlingen, whence it had advanced in the morning; whereas Montaudon's Division, which had advanced from Saargemünd, occupies a strong position at Cadenbronn.

The 3rd Reserve Cavalry Division (Forton's) belonging to the Army of the Rhine, has reached Folschweiler near St. Avold, from Pont à Mousson *viâ* Falkenberg.

At Saargemünd is Lapasset's Brigade of the 5th Corps, which effected the subsequent retreat on Metz in conjunction with the 2nd Corps. Maussion's Brigade of the 5th Corps is at Rohrbach; Goze's 1st Division camped at Bitsch, with it the Corps Head Quarters; and the 3rd Division, Lespart, is on the march towards Wörth. Ladmirault's 4th Corps, on the left wing, has marched from near Busendorf, crossing the Metz-Saarlouis main road, to the neighbourhood of Bolchen, and camped as follows: Lorencez's Infantry Division near Kuhmen, Cissey's Infantry Division near Teterchen, Legrand's Cavalry Division at Bolchen. A cavalry regiment and two battalions have been pushed forward to the heights of Tromborn.

The 3rd Cavalry Division sent out from their rendezvous south of Lebach two strong patrols into the enemy's country, namely, thirty picked men and horses from different squadrons under Captain v. Hymmen, 5th Uhlans, and twenty-five under Lieutenant v. Ramin, 14th Uhlans. *[margin: Patrols of v. Ramin and v. Hymmen.]*

These two officers received instructions to ride together as far as Saarlouis, and gain information from the commandant as to the situation in front of the fortress.

Lieutenant v. Ramin had then to take the

direction of Busendorf, while v. Hymmen was to reconnoitre towards St. Avold.*

The officers reached Saarlouis, and left that fortress at midday. The information given by the commandant, who had his outposts at Ittersdorf, had been previously sent back.† This report, dated Saarlouis, 3.30 p.m., gave information that Busenweiler and Tromborn were occupied by the enemy, who since the day before had been moving southeast.

Lieutenant v. Ramin, as he rode through Ittersdorf, learnt from the outposts that the wood in front was held. The wood had to be passed if he was to reach his objective.

To make certain that the wood was occupied, v. Ramin left his patrol under cover, and, accompanied by only two orderlies, rode at a fast pace straight up to the wood. Contrary to expectation, no shots were fired from the wood, but the smoking embers and scattered surroundings gave ample proof that it had only just been evacuated.‡ Along the high-road to Busendorf, with the great wood always

---

* The Division Commander had personally given instructions, as he very often did later on, to both officers before they set off.

† According to the War Diary of the Head Quarters of the First Army, news of the enemy, up to this time, depended really on the communication from the Commandant of Saarlouis, who had on August 5 reported the presence of strong hostile bodies of troops on the line Busendorf-Tromborn-St. Avold. Apparently the despatch of the patrols was for the purpose of obtaining more details of this information, which probably had been furnished by spies. It will very often, in war, be the task of officers' patrols to ascertain the truth of unauthenticated information, which even, if it is indefinite, is of value, as indicating the direction in which the reconnoitring should be carried out.

‡ A reconnaissance in this way is often the only means of ascertaining whether localities, places, and forests which cannot be gone round are occupied. A single mounted man thus dashing forward does not run much risk, but it is recommended against a line occupied with shooters, not to ride straight at it, but, on account of the grazing fire, to ride in an oblique direction, and thus also to withdraw from it.

a hundred and fifty paces on the flank, the patrol went forward at a fast trot. Northwards the wood checked the view; southwards the high plateau, over which the road bore, afforded, however, a magnificent range of vision. The left flank patrol very soon also reported a large camp on the left flank. Ramin dismounted to use his glass better, and now, himself under cover, watched a large bivouac at Tromborn, in which the horses were off-saddled and covered with white blankets. The troops camped there were estimated at two battalions and one cavalry regiment. Neither outposts nor patrols were visible. As v. Ramin was anxious to find out as soon as possible whether Busendorf was clear of the enemy, he left a N.C.O.'s post behind to keep the camp under constant observation from a suitable place, and trotted with the patrol on to Busendorf. Near that place he found on the main road a lately deserted camp, with fires still smoking and articles left behind by the troops.* In the middle of the camp stood a waggon, covered with a red, white, and blue flag, and laden with two very large casks of wine.

The patrol entered Busendorf at a gallop; all exits were occupied; vedettes and patrols were sent out in front, whilst the leader discussed matters with the Burgomaster in the market-place. The Uhlans found the church full of Frenchmen, nominally sick, but some of them apparently malingerers; they did not dare to make any show of hostility. In front of a large forage store two large four-span waggons laden with oats were found and commandeered.

* In the abandoned French bivouacs were generally found a considerable number of small articles of equipment left behind, which is always a proof of want of discipline.

Since the little party could not remain in the place under the very eyes of the enemy at this advanced period of the day, and wanted to bring their booty into safety, they slowly withdrew on Ittersdorf; the captured oats as well as the wine was handed over, and Lieutenant v. Ramin in person reported to the divisional general. He had done so in writing to the commandant of Saarlouis.

In consequence of the return of the patrol, the French camp remained unwatched, and the touch, which had been gained, was lost.

If up till now the action of the leader can be called exemplary, his return must be characterized as an error. Apparently he was anxious to safeguard the booty, so welcome to his regiment, yet that was a side issue compared with the highly important duty of not again losing touch with the enemy now found. The patrol ought to have searched for a suitable position to rest in, from where the camp at Tromborn and Busendorf could be kept in observation. A few Uhlans, as escort, could have taken back the captured waggons. We shall see how far better this smart and capable officer acted on the days that followed.

Captain v. Hymmen separated from v. Ramin soon behind Saarlouis, turning southwards. He reached Ueberherrn, crossed the frontier there, and turned back by a circuitous route to Alt-Forweiler. Unfortunately, no official report of his ride on this day is to be found. According to a private letter from the patrol leader, he encountered some African mounted Jägers, who fired on the patrol without result.

The 19th Dragoons. Also some squadrons of the 19th Dragoons are shown by the map as pushed far forward into French territory.

INTRODUCTION 13

The regiment had received its mission by a brigade order of August 5, which ran as follows:—

"The regiment will be at Völklingen to-morrow at 8 a.m., cross the Saar, advance to Ludweiler; from there send a squadron to Kreutzwald, and, leaving a squadron in support at Ludweiler, march with two squadrons by Lauterbach towards Karlingen, to see how far the enemy has retired.

"The enemy, with a pretty strong force of all arms, was to-day still at Karlingen, also at Forbach, Morsbach, and Rossbrücken, without any outposts at these latter places. The 11th Hussars will undertake the protection against this latter position. Should the regiment, contrary to expectation, be unable to carry out its retreat by Wehrden and Völklingen, it must retire by Saarlouis."

In accordance with the order, the regiment advanced to Ludweiler, left the 4th Squadron there, whilst the 1st and 2nd Squadrons pursued their way under the colonel to Karlingen; the 3rd Squadron marched on Kreutzwald. The colonel with his two squadrons rode through Karlingen without seeing anything of the enemy. According to the War Diary, when the advanced point was already approaching St. Avold, it struck "on the bivouac of a hostile brigade of all arms, exchanged a few shots with some mounted Jägers, and retired," etc.

From the account of Dick de Lonlay the interesting fact can be gleaned, without any doubt, that the hostile mounted troops with which shots were exchanged belonged to Marshal Bazaine's escort. The Marshal was then with Decaen's Division in St. Avold.

Prussian patrols had already that morning been seen on the St. Avold-Saarlouis main road;* the

* These can only have belonged to the 1st Squadron 11th Hussars, which got as far as Carlsbrunn on this day.

thunder of guns from Forbach could be heard over here An attack from the direction of Saarlouis was expected, so entrenchments were thrown up and occupied.

About midday the whole of Decaen's Division stood to arms, but the Marshal decided to ride forward along the road from Saarlouis to reconnoitre, with only a N.C.O. and four mounted Jägers with him as escort. When he was inspecting the position of the troops near St. Avold, according to Dick de Lonlay, a couple of shots fell amongst his staff, and were at once answered by a shot from the escort. "Those are Prussians," exclaimed the officers. "No, no," cried the Marshal, amid the first confusion, "those are our own dragoons sent out on patrol, who have made a mistake." In point of fact, they were Prussian dragoons, who had halted about 220 yards off the road, and, after firing, turned round and disappeared, followed in vain by the Jägers.

The German horsemen had naturally never dreamt that they had a French Marshal in front of them, and till now this interesting fact has remained unknown even to the regiment.

Had the Marshal carried a distinguishing pennant behind him, as is now the custom also in France, the Dragoons would have been apprised of the fact; one sees that the use of these pennants can thus have their disadvantage. The pursuit by the Marshal's escort must, besides, have been very unproductive, since the two squadrons were apparently never discovered. The French account, after describing this episode, says, "The Marshal is under the impression that the enemy is near."

With a whole cavalry division near him, and more under his command, this general sat in this hole of St. Avold as if blindfolded. It can be

INTRODUCTION 15

seen what an extraordinary impression these few Prussian dragoons and hussars, in conjunction with the sound of the guns, had created.

The Marshal's opinion, strengthened also by a report received from Imperial Head Quarters, that he would be attacked from the direction of Saarlouis, was confirmed, and he therefore omitted to provide any real reinforcement for the 2nd Corps.*

His Cavalry Division sent the 2nd Mounted Jägers between 2 p.m. and 5 p.m. to reconnoitre in the valley towards Buschborn. Why this direction, away from the enemy, was taken, cannot be explained; false reports which found their way into St. Avold may have been the cause. The regiment returned without having seen anything, but the division kept their horses saddled all night.

The 3rd Squadron had found Kreutzwald unoccupied; but Ham unter Varsberg was held, and on the road from Gertingen to Ham an infantry column of three or four battalions had been seen on the march to the latter. When the enemy had noticed the squadron, two or three hostile squadrons appeared out of Ham, which sent out some scouts, but did not venture on an attack. To the west of Ham no enemy was seen, only empty bivouacs.

These troops belonged to Grenier's division of the 4th Corps, which had been on the march since 4 a.m. from Teterchen, by Kuhmen, Gertingen, and Ham, to Buschborn. The cavalry belonged

* As the French were not accustomed to patrol far to the front, they believed at that time that there were strong forces behind every Prussian patrol that appeared; only thus can the impression that the mere sight of patrols had on the enemy in the days that followed be explained. In any future campaign this influence cannot, of course, be reckoned upon; but in an enemy's country the first appearance of hostile patrols often makes a stronger impression on the population, and if it occurs unexpectedly, on the army leading, than is generally assumed.

to Gondrecourt's brigade of dragoons. Dick de Lonlay relates that, when Ham was reached, a Prussian squadron evacuated the place at a gallop, and that the march was observed by " Uhlans."

The 4th Squadron had, in the mean time, reported from Ludweiler that hostile infantry columns were moving from Forbach and Klein-Rosseln on Ludweiler. As it was consequently possible for the 3rd Squadron to have lost its direct line of retreat, the colonel sent it the order to return by Saarlouis. This order did not reach the squadron, and it safely rejoined the regiment at Ludweiler.

The regiment, which considered its task accomplished, and was returning in accordance with its instructions into cantonments at Saarwellingen, heard the sound of the guns at Spicheren on its return march, when nearing Völklingen. Although thirty-eight miles had already been covered, the colonel obeyed this call, and hurried to the battlefield, where the regiment arrived at 4 p.m. The 2nd squadron had been attached to Glümer's division, which had been met on the return march at Völklingen, and which lacked any cavalry.

The regiment had this day rendered remarkably good service in reconnaissance, and the method of its employment, which, indeed, the brigade had laid down in very exact detail, was in complete accordance with the situation. Only is it to be regretted that the retirement of the regiment had been ordered, as the choice of the shelter for the night should have been left to it.

We shall often see that at this period of the war a similar view is entertained, which has the disadvantage, not only of breaking off touch with the enemy, but also of causing an extraordinary waste of power, because the march forward has

INTRODUCTION

frequently to be undertaken again on the following day.

As a rule, the advanced reconnoitring patrols considered their task completed when they had established touch with the enemy; but this touch was also immediately afterwards broken off.

In the middle of the enemy's troops at Buschborn the map shows us a patrol of the 8th Hussars. The adventures of this patrol are of such uncommon interest that they merit a detailed description. The 8th Hussars formed the divisional cavalry of v. Glümer's 13th Infantry Division. Major-General Baron v. der Goltz, commanding the advanced guard of the division, which on April 6 was on the march from Hüttendorf to Völklingen, gave Lieutenant Stumm of that regiment about noon the order "to start at once with one N.C.O. and twelve picked men of the 3rd Squadron on a reconnaissance to the left bank of the Saar. He was, so to say, to form a small independent party, march as quickly as possible to St. Avold, where the enemy's main forces were conjectured to be stationed, in order, as far as possible, to clear up the situation on the rear and the left flank of the enemy's positions. He was free to remain out two or three days according to need, perfectly independent, to act on his own initiative, and merely send back speedy and frequent reports to the rear."

Lieut. Stumm's patrol.

In truth a glorious mission, with the objective clearly defined. It gladdened the young officer's heart. Indeed, who would not be inspirited by such a task? Sad to relate, as we shall presently see, he did not meet with quite such good fortune as the far-seeing general had anticipated.

About midday the patrol crossed the Saar. It had been on the move since 5 a.m., having marched with the advance guard to Völklingen.

Its action will be best understood by the officer's reports, which are to be found in the confidential war records—

> "Report No. 1.—I have arrived within an hour's ride of St. Avold, and have not discovered anything of the enemy. They all appear to have moved off to Forbach, whence artillery fire can be heard. In Karlingen the last French patrols were seen this morning at 7 a.m. Some hundreds of men are said to be camped in front of St. Avold. I am about to ride thither. All the troops from Kreutzwald, Ham, and Diesen have gone away to Forbach and St. Avold. [Time? Author.] In my rear in Karlingen I have destroyed the telegraph apparatus, or rather I have deposited it with the inhabitants of the town. I most humbly beg the General to send a patrol after me along the St. Avold road, to bring me information as to the position of the troops on the Saar.
>
> "*In front of St. Avold,*
> "August 6, 1870.—6.15 p.m.
> "STUMM, Lieutenant."

Lieutenant Stumm had apparently ridden through Karlingen after the squadrons of the 19th Dragoons, many hours before, had left the highroad, without having heard anything about them. The French made hardly any reconnaissance. This explains why he had been able to get on so far without meeting the enemy. The contents of his report depend evidently, as should have been noticed, entirely on the assertions of the inhabitants, who, as it turned out, had given him entirely inexact and involuntarily misleading information. Truth is mixed with untruth.*

---

* Here we have proof of how little value is often to be attached to the statements of inhabitants. If it is often difficult even for the military observer to ascertain the direction of a movement of troops

INTRODUCTION

He also appears to have placed rather too much reliance on the inhabitants of the village of Karlingen, which lies on the far side of the frontier, as the fact of his handing over to them the telegraph apparatus seems to point out.

It appears from the concluding sentence of the report that the officer felt the need of being informed of the position of the forces of his side, obviously to arrive at a correct understanding of the enemy's dispositions.

This shows how needful it is for a patrol leader, before he starts, to obtain sufficient information, which in due course must be supplemented as much as possible by further intelligence.

How little his first report concurred with the truth the officer was to experience as soon as he had sent it off, when he continued his ride towards St. Avold.

He had scarcely trotted half an hour on the way to St. Avold down the high-road in the wood which begins immediately beyond Karlingen, when a commercial traveller came along the road alone. He was at once made to stop, and, terrified, gave the information that an infantry party lay scarcely 400 paces behind him, that St. Avold was strongly held, and that several generals of high rank, with their staffs, were quartered there. To circumvent that party, which were assumed to be outposts, was for the time being impossible, because the thick wood shut in the road on both sides. So the patrol went on at a quick trot to meet the reported enemy, with an advanced point in front, and carbines at the advance.

The horsemen had scarcely rounded the corner

which he has observed, in particular whether it is a question of an advance or a retreat, or a lateral movement, how much more must this apply to a non-military one who has no idea of the general situation.

when they were received by rapid rifle-fire at under 400 paces, which slightly wounded one horse, and damaged Lieutenant Stumm's saddle. The enemy deployed, about a company strong; and a further advance on St. Avold appeared impossible. Covered by the fire of his own advanced point, Lieutenant Stumm wheeled quickly about, and, riding back a few hundred paces, disappeared into the wood on the right side with his little troop.

He safely reached the southern edge of the wood, and as he halted, hardly 800 paces east of the party he had got round to the left of, he suddenly saw St. Avold lying below him. He gazed at an animated hostile camp of infantry, cavalry, and artillery between himself and the little town. On the opposite heights there was another camp, and apparently also artillery positions, and at the station stood a long troop-train, which appeared to have come in from the east.*

In the twilight Lieutenant Stumm hurriedly scribbled a few words on a message-form, which briefly gave the situation in front of St. Avold, and sent it by his smartest corporal, by a bridle-road *viâ* Karlingen and Lauterbach, to General v. der Goltz. In such an important situation a second man should have been sent with the despatch rider. Now Lieutenant Stumm started off again to reconnoitre a strong position of the enemy beyond Buschborn, which had been reported by the country people.

The patrol dashed through Karlingen at full gallop, and disappeared in the wooded country east of Diesen.

* In point of fact, Decaen's Division was camped on the heights between the town and the station, and it had pushed a battalion north of the town as an outpost line facing north. Near the main road St. Avold-Karlingen, about a mile from St. Avold, a cavalry brigade was camped.

INTRODUCTION 21

It was beginning to get dark. The patrol had now been fifteen hours in the saddle without a break, and covered 45 to 55 miles as the crow flies. The men had had nothing to eat since 5 a.m. beyond what they had carried on the saddle, and the horses had not been watered or fed.

As Lieutenant Stumm emerged from the Diesen wood, he noticed a little mill down in the valley. [The Porcelette mill probably: see map No. 1.]

The patrol halted at the edge of the wood, and the lieutenant, with three of his most trustworthy men, rode down. The miller was pulled out of bed and brought up to the edge of the wood with one of his waggons filled with hay, corn, water, bread, and milk. (The miller was brought along with it, probably to avoid risk of treachery.)

This small night raid was hardly completed, and the waggon hidden behind the protecting shelter of the trees, when a strong hostile patrol of the enemy's cavalry trotted past the mill from the Saar, that is, from the rear, and rode on towards Ham unter Varsberg.

The enemy noticed nothing, and at last the exhausted men and horses could enjoy a short rest, without, however, off-saddling.

While some of the men fed their horses, Lieutenant Stumm rode forward to the border of the wood to reconnoitre.

Close in front of him on the opposite heights he unexpectedly saw, one after another, large and far-stretching bivouac fires appearing. In an endless line fully twenty to thirty rows of bright gleaming fires were blazing up.* He could clearly

---

* Grenier's Division (4th Corps), on the march from Busendorf to Buschborn, who were following the main road by Porcelette, owing to the bad state of the direct road.

distinguish the noise of a camp at night, and signals and words of command.

At 1 a.m., by the light of a lantern carefully concealed under a cloak,* Lieutenant Stumm wrote a short report of the events—the third—and sent it at once by two corporals to Forbach.

He remained the whole night here in the Diesen wood, close in front of the main position of the enemy, who must have been more than one division strong, right inside his outpost line.

Not a man dared leave his horse for a moment or close his eyes. Seldom can horsemen have gone through hours of such excitement as this patrol.

Amid almost superhuman excitement and tension, the long-wished-for daylight approached very slowly. The few hours appeared an eternity to the men.

In the description of the events of August 7 we shall find them here again.

11th Hussars.

As previously mentioned, when speaking about the employment of the 19th Dragoons, the 11th Hussars had received instructions from the brigadier to secure the left flank of the dragoons in their advance. Accordingly the 1st Squadron was to advance by Gross-Rosseln, and send a couple of troops into the wooded district due north of Forbach. Captain v. Knobelsdorf in addition was sent with two troops through the ford of Bockershausen on Schöneck.

While the 1st Squadron arrived thus directly in rear of the French at Forbach, the half-squadron at Schöneck found itself scarcely two and a half miles from their left at Stiring. Patrols from the 1st Squadron had in this way evidently reached the St. Avold-Saarbrücken main road, as already

* A lantern, suitable for carrying on the saddle, should be included in the indispensable equipment of every cavalry officer.

INTRODUCTION 23

mentioned, and somewhat disquieted the Head-Quarters in St. Avold by their appearance.

They reported large columns retiring in the direction of St. Avold. Whether this observation was quite accurate cannot be ascertained.

The 12th Dragoons had been amply employed on reconnaissance by General v. Stülpnagel (commanding 5th Division). The 1st Squadron had been sent to Saargemünd, and had pushed forward a troop beyond Arnual. The squadron reported a considerable number of troops, estimated at 20,000 men, between Saargemünd and Neunkirchen.* [12th Dragoons.]

The 2nd Squadron watched the country on the left of the infantry engaged in the Gifert Wood, and sent to Gross-Bliedersdorf one troop, which met some French cavalry there.†

An officer's patrol rode forward west of the battle-field to Karlingen; there it was attacked by a party of mounted Jägers, and had to retire by Lauterbach. The 3rd and 4th Squadrons had gone into action with the division.

The 6th Cavalry Division had put out outposts on the Saar, and a troop patrolled on the far bank. From this outpost position the development of the action at Saarbrücken, on the French right, could be clearly watched. Captain v. Leipziger, commanding the 5th Squadron of the 3rd Uhlans, sent a report to his colonel, who came at once and supported his view, which was that the attack of the 6th Cavalry Division on this wing, where the batteries were completely exposed, would prove greatly effective. Colonel Graf Groeben made a further report, and even visited the divisional [3rd Uhlans.]

---

* The 1st Division, Montaudon, of the 3rd Corps, which afterwards advanced on Cadenbronn, and Lapasset's Brigade of the 5th Corps.

† The 1st Squadron Mounted Jägers (Rifles).

INTRODUCTION

general in his quarters for the purpose; but the latter considered it sufficient for a troop to be sent across the Saar to reconnoitre.

The 4th Squadron had been heavily fired on in a reconnaissance to Saarbrücken on August 5, and had suffered some loss.

With reference to this reconnaissance, Lieutenant v. Ebart had received instructions " to make a reconnaissance on the far bank of the Saar with a patrol of three horses, and to bring back news of the enemy under any conditions."

Ebart's patrol.

The officer carried out his task in extraordinarily bold fashion. Since all the crossings were sharply watched by the enemy, he turned northwards, and crossed the Saar near Völklingen on the night of August 5-6. With the help of Head-ranger Solf, by way of Nassweiler and Morsbach, close past the French positions, he succeeded from Carlsbrunn in reaching the heights of Oettingen, which lie to the south of Forbach, by 6 a.m. Here the French infantry division of Bataille was encamped, and he could see the enemy's positions at Forbach.

The patrol, first noticed by individual mounted Jägers, and then followed by a whole squadron, yet succeeded in reaching Völklingen through Gross Rosseln by secret paths, and rejoined its unit on the evening of the 6th.

Owing to all these circumstances, Lieutenant v. Ebart could only forward his report on his return. In the very difficult situation in which the patrol found themselves, a single despatch rider would have had great difficulty in reaching his destination, and it was not feasible to send two despatch riders, owing to the size of the patrol, which was far too weak for the task. A strength of nine horsemen would have been suitable, four of

INTRODUCTION

which could have advantageously been left at Völklingen as relay posts. The weakness of the patrol naturally favoured their slipping through to the rear of the French lines. So weak a patrol pushed far forward can only depend on the safe arrival of its reports, when provided with relay posts not too far behind it.

This officer's report is so instructive that it may serve as an example for the execution of like tasks, and is therefore given word for word—

"Reconnaissance of Lieut. v. Ebart, 3rd Uhlans, from August 5-6 to Forbach, to 5.15 a.m., August 6.

"On the evening of August 5 the line Saarbrücken to Forbach was so strongly held that the crossing of the Saar was only possible at Wehrden. On the road Wehrden-Ludwigsweiler-Carlsbrunn no trace of the enemy was to be seen. Nassweiler, where an entrenched camp had been, was evacuated early this morning. Between Emmersweiler and Rossbrück there were two squadrons of the enemy; at Morsbach some artillery—about 15 guns. Forbach was surrounded on all sides with strong bodies of troops; northwards a camp of tents stretched about 2000 paces along the road.

"South of Forbach, on the Oettinger hills, strong bodies of infantry were visible, apparently in entrenched positions. The reconnaissance of Forbach was checked for some time by a squadron of Chasseurs. The infantry, which have been lately seen on the frontier, belong to the 19th, 41st, 95th, 51st Regiments. From Forbach no retirement of troops has taken place lately; on the other hand, about 15,000 men are said to have retired the day before yesterday from Nassweiler to Puttlingen or Saargemünd. The Kaninchenberg (N.W. Forbach) was entrenched and occupied by artillery, infantry, and cavalry.

"Large masses of troops lay north-west of the Kaninchenberg in the wood of Forbach, 20,000 men, according to the account of the local authorities and foresters of the neighbouring villages, several infantry regiments in Schöneck, and infantry and cavalry in

Stiring. The whole line from Saarbrücken to Emmersweiler was occupied by two divisions. The Second Army Corps (Frossard's) is said to be in the country between Saarbrücken-Saargemünd-Merlenbach.

"v. EBART."

Certainly no experienced officer of the general staff could have carried out the reconnaissance more successfully than this young lancer officer.

Close up to the enemy, we further see the 15th Cavalry Brigade about Habkirchen. This brigade had that day received orders to advance from Assweiler, "to cross the Blies at Rheinheim, to reconnoitre towards Rohrbach and Neunkirchen, and occupy a position on the Blies."

16th Hussars. But having reached the bridge over the Blies at Rheinheim, the brigade again retired, when the approach of strong detachments was reported— two companies from Neunkirchen moving on Rohrbach, one battalion and one squadron from Saargemünd on Frauenberg. In addition to this they had received the erroneous report of the appearance of hostile squadrons of lancers on their right flank.*

In the afternoon the brigade advanced again under orders from the division, and occupied their appointed position. The colonel of the 16th Hussars then personally reconnoitred Neunkirchen, and reported three battalions of infantry and some cavalry behind that place.†

Meanwhile the sound of guns at Spicheren was heard. In order to relieve as much as possible the pressure on those fighting there, Colonel v. Schmidt begged the brigadier to send forward the battery,

---

* It was the 1st Squadron of the 15th Uhlans which had advanced on Neunkirchen.

† About this time only Lapasset's brigade was still in that neighbourhood.

INTRODUCTION

which General v. Rauch, however, declined. A troop of the regiment, under Lieutenant v. Lachmann, had dashed into Neunkirchen. The place was still weakly held, and the troop lost three men, one of whom was killed, and four horses.*

Brix's squadron of Uhlans, which had been the cause of the erroneous report to General v. Rauch, had, in the mean time, reconnoitred towards Neunkirchen, and, in accordance with orders, had cut the railway line in the vicinity of the Neunkirchen-Rohrbach main road, under the enemy's fire.

General v. Bredow, commanding the 12th Cavalry Brigade, had carried out a reconnaissance towards Rohrbach with the 7th Cuirassiers and the 3rd and 4th Squadrons of the 10th Hussars, acting under orders from General v. Alvensleben Sr., commanding the Fourth Army Corps. The hussars got close up to the place, which was strongly held They were received by a hot fire, and had one man killed and one officer (Captain v. Kaisenberg) wounded. *[margin: Bredow's Brigade.]*

A squadron of the enemy was seen on the march to Saargemünd; about one infantry regiment occupied the crest of the hill at Freudenberger Hof, further back near Bitsch a column of waggons, apparently some of them artillery, were noticed, and the strength of the enemy at Bitsch was estimated at 20,000 men. The Cuirassiers got as far as 2000 paces from Guisingen, and came under machine-gun fire, as it seemed, without suffering loss.

A troop of the 13th Dragoons, who were to keep touch with the Third Army, together with a section of Bavarian Jägers on waggons, had *[margin: 13th Dragoons.]*

---

* Diary of the 16th Hussars. It would have been better if the officer, leaving his troop behind, had himself personally reconnoitred in the first instance.

28 INTRODUCTION

moved forward to Bitsch, and got within 2000 paces of the fortress, where a strong hostile detachment, estimated at a division,* was alarmed. Small mixed patrols of this sort have their doubtful advantages.

In a rapid advance, the infantry act as a check on the cavalry, and in the event of serious danger the cavalry, by reason of their lack of strength, can offer no support to the infantry, or else must sacrifice themselves. In difficult country and under special circumstances it may be advisable to send small infantry detachments to specified points, to support the advancing cavalry.

Loss of touch.

General v. Bredow's cavalry had reconnoitred with prudence and success; but touch with the enemy in front was, unfortunately, not maintained. In the night of August 6-7 the 5th Corps disappeared through the mountains in the direction of Lützelstein to form a junction with MacMahon's Army, and for days all touch with the enemy on this flank was lacking.†

The German cavalry must here meet with a definite reproach. It is clear that the want of observation during a few night hours can bring about weighty and irreparable results.

It can also be noticed that our peace exercises in general are but little adapted to accustom our cavalry to active night operations. Cavalry outposts are drawn in at night. The Field Training Regulations certainly lays down that touch with the enemy must be maintained also at night by the cavalry, but, as a matter of fact, patrols are very sparingly employed, and this occurs because want

* Goze's division, the 1st of the 5th Corps.

† The 5th Corps had started at 9 p.m., and reached Lemberg during the night; thence, at first losing its way, it got close to Ingweiler, which had been occupied by German troops (Third Army), and arrived at Lützelstein at 9 a.m. on the 7th. (*Revue Militaire*, 1899.)

of activity does not bring its own punishment. In our peace manœuvres the enemy does not disappear during the night, and the patrols which are sent out at daybreak can almost always report as unchanged the position of the enemy, whose outposts, one regrets to say, are usually close to one's own.

The service of patrols by night is not sufficiently practised.

If the cavalry is not trained to more industrious patrolling by night, and this can only arise by their being prepared for a secret retirement of the enemy, which the authorities have opportunely arranged, it is to be feared that it will in the future have the same experience as Bredow's Brigade had in the night of August 6–7, 1870.

Should the enemy escape the cavalry responsible for keeping touch, the troop certainly merits reproach; but the higher commanders are culpable, equally with the outpost commander.

If proper active measures are not taken, and suitable instructions not given, a certain amount of inertness will occur within the squadron, without giving proof of inferior training.

CHAPTER I

<small>Aug. 7.
Headquarters of First Army in the morning.</small>

AFTER the conclusion of the battle of Spicheren the following tasks were incumbent upon the cavalry: *i.e.* the pursuit of the beaten French 2nd Corps, the location of its line of retreat, and the observation of the other forces of the enemy, announced as at Tromborn, St. Avold, Saargemünd, and Bitsch. The results of the battle of Wörth were first known during the course of the 7th.

As the cavalry stood on the 6th (see the map for this day), there were available for the pursuit of the enemy several divisional regiments of the First and Second Army, together with the 11th Cavalry Brigade, the greater part of the 13th Cavalry Brigade, and the 6th Cuirassiers of the 6th Cavalry Division, all ready immediately on or near the battle-field, while the remainder of the 6th Division were in a position to operate by Gross-Bliedersdorf and Saargemünd against the right flank of the enemy. As regards the 3rd Cavalry Division in the neighbourhood of Saarwellingen, they could have made themselves felt on the left flank, but only as the evening advanced; and portions of the units named as ready on the battle-field were also immediately available for movement against this flank.

In a fight which arose on the Bitsch road, apart from the divisional cavalry, only the 12th Cavalry Brigade, the 10th Hussars, and the 5th Dragoons * were able to take part.

---

* Belonging to the 4th Cavalry Division. (Trans.)

We will now see what orders were issued for this pursuit at Spicheren. _{Aug. 7.}

The General Officer Commanding First Army had never contemplated any pursuit of the defeated enemy. Concerning the views prevailing in this quarter, von Schell, in his " Operations of the First Army," says the following :—

> " Any profit to be wrung from the victory by an energetic pursuit was precluded all the more by the fact that the 3rd Cavalry Division, pushed forward towards Saarlouis on the 6th, had, late in the evening, announced formidable hostile forces to be still at St. Avold and Tromborn.* An isolated advance would have possibly led to defeat, especially as a great part of one's own troops were still too far behind."

We grant that the circumstances rendered an energetic pursuit with large mixed forces very difficult. On the day of the battle darkness had only put a conclusion to the contest; the enemy drew off in good order under cover of a strong rear-guard, which up till the morning of the day following still occupied Forbach and the heights of Oettingen; the German troops, especially those in the first line, had suffered heavily, with the exception of the 13th Division, which had advanced by Rosseln, and was intact. It was absolutely necessary to establish order among the different units; in addition to all this, a thick fog on the morning of the 7th hindered all view. Circumstances differed entirely at Wörth, where the retreat of the French developed into a flight. Another fact that counselled prudence was, that fresh and very superior hostile forces (some less than one day's march away) were ready for action.

---

* Ramin's and probably Hymmen's reports.

Aug. 7.

At the same time, all the superior commanders of the First Army were not of this way of thinking. General v. Goeben, writing on the 9th from Spicheren to his wife, said, "I am dissatisfied with our still remaining here. If we had marched the day before yesterday, it is apparent that the fruits of the victory would have been immense."* It does not lie within the scope of this work to find out whether Goeben's conclusion was not too optimistic But this much may be maintained, that no sort of objection can be raised to a more energetic use of cavalry with horse artillery, and therefore on this score the dispositions of the General Officer Commanding First Army must be estimated as quite insufficient. Only "reconnaissances" were arranged for the morning of the 7th, and with regard to these it still remains doubtful how far Army Head Quarters were concerned in the issue of these orders from the battle-field (see p. 48). It was not even arranged to move the 3rd Cavalry Division to the front, in order to ensure its employment on the 8th, and only a slight advance towards Saarlouis took place, having for its object the reconnoitring of the roads leading to Metz. The 1st Cavalry Division was not yet available; it was beginning to assemble about Lebach. The insufficient use which was made of the 3rd Cavalry Division is the less to be understood, as the General Officer Commanding First Army looked upon his force from the first as an offensive wing for the Second Army,† and the Headquarters-in-Chief had described its task as an offensive one against the enemy's left flank, in particular, "to most decisively intervene in battle against the enemy's

* "Life of the Royal Prussian General August von Goeben," by Zernin.
† Steinmetz's telegram of August 4, 3.35 p.m.

left flank."* One should think that, as an offensive arm *par excellence*, the 3rd Cavalry Division would therefore have been pushed forward as soon as possible on the outer wing. Instead of which their movement of the 5th to Lebach was ordered still solely with defensive intentions "to cover the right flank," and this brought it from its position straight in rear to one in the right rear.† Quite a different idea as to the disposal of the cavalry animated the leader of the Second Army. Prince Frederick Charles had already, during the concentration of his army, arranged for the employment of his cavalry right out on the frontier with the aim of concealing the movements of his forces from the enemy, ascertaining their positions, dispositions, and measures, and estimating, according to their true value, the incursions upon German territory. Already for July 30 the 6th Cavalry Division had been ordered to move from their cantonments, in the region of Sprendlingen-Gaualsheim, on a broad front by Meisenheim, Kosel, Neunkirchen, to the frontier. The 5th Cavalry Division was from the first divided into two columns, owing to the position of the places where the army corps detrained, to which its regiments belonged. The northern of these two columns (11th Brigade, 11th and 17th Hussars of the 13th Brigade, and a horse artillery battery), assembled on July 31 between Bingen and Kreuznach, was to proceed by Baumholder and St. Wendel on Völklingen; the other column (12th Brigade, with the 10th Hussars and a horse artillery battery) was to march from Dürkheim-Oggersheim by Kaiserslautern on Bliescastel, with a detachment going to Pirmasens. It therefore happened that the 6th

Aug. 7.

Employment of cavalry by Prince Frederick Charles.

---

* Letters from Moltke to Steinmetz of August 5, 6 a.m., and 12 noon.
† Compare sketch of August 6.

D

Aug. 7. Cavalry Division moved in the centre, and the 5th, divided, on both flanks.*

By reason of the common task before them, it appeared advantageous to the Prince to place this large mass of cavalry—56 squadrons (8000 men and 18 guns) for the moment under undivided control; this was entrusted to Lieut.-General Baron v. Rheinbaben. The force was to reach the frontier on the 3rd, and gain touch with the enemy simultaneously on the whole line from Völklingen on the Saar to Pirmasens. They were not to gain this touch in masses, but rather to appear "everywhere" and to commence harassing the enemy's frontier guards.

As support for the cavalry, the 5th Infantry Division was to move behind its right wing into the vicinity of Neunkirchen, the 8th to Homburg. The aim of this arrangement is clear. The army was to effect its concentration behind the screen of the advanced cavalry, but the latter, without seeking battle (putting large bodies into action would not correspond at the time with the object in view), was to display great activity, that is to say, find out the intentions of the opponent whilst veiling their own measures. It was the Prince's particular wish not to push beyond the mountain defiles the vanguards of the army which had advanced into them, and not to begin the march through them with the main bodies until he could feel himself secure, by information sent back that

---

* What views General v. Steinmetz had concerning the disposal of the cavalry appears from an utterance of his on this forenoon in Saarbrücken to the then General Staff Officer of the 5th Cavalry Division, now Lieut.-General v. Heister (retired). According to what the latter told the author, Steinmetz said to him, in the course of conversation, "Tell your general that the cavalry's proper place is in rear." Heister rightly refrained from delivering this message to his superior, already known as unenterprising.

he need expect no attack during the march—for a battle in the mountains would not have allowed the army to take advantage of its numerical superiority.

Aug. 7.

When it was known for certain on August 3 that the enemy had no intention of advancing further, and, above all, that the fight at Saarbrücken was simply a demonstration, the advance to the line of the Saar began on the 5th.* The Third Army, after completing its task in Lower Alsace, was designed to reach that line above Saargemünd on August 9, and the Second Army made dispositions which would enable them to attack on the same day.

But by the victory on the 4th at Weissenburg, and much more so by the victory on the 6th at Spicheren, the circumstances were completely changed. Already on the 5th the Prince had ordered his cavalry to hang on to the opponent, and to find out what effect the affair at Weissenburg might exercise on his attitude.

The dissimilarity in the employment of their cavalry by the General Officers Commanding First and Second Armies is at once apparent. Whilst General v. Steinmetz held his cavalry divisions behind the other troops as a reserve of cavalry of unhappy memory (*i.e.* like the cavalry corps in the beginning of the '66 campaign), where they could effect nothing, and yet were much knocked about and (at least in 1866) badly cared for, Prince Frederick Charles, who, as a French journal put it, " had seized the new ideas with ardour," took his cavalry from the first to the front. Certainly General v. Steinmetz had ordered reconnaissances for the 3rd Cavalry Division, but as the patrols of

* See remarks about the general situation in the Introduction and the comments on the use of Cavalry, pp. 3, 4, etc.

Aug. 7. that division had to be brought up from far to the rear, and received no support from the division which remained stationary, the measure seems really somewhat absurd. As the circumstances were, these few patrols might have been better furnished by the divisional cavalry, these being at hand. Prince Frederick Charles, however, had recognized how important it is that the reserve of whatever force is furnishing the advanced detachments also follows at a suitable distance, if one wishes to count upon lasting results; and this point specially held good here, when the advanced parties were encountering everywhere along the frontier formed hostile bodies. For this reason, therefore, the Prince had on the 3rd already ordered the main bodies to move further forward, in order to give timely support to the advanced squadrons, which had been told off to hang on to the enemy. On the same day the divisions were also again placed directly under the command of the General Officer Commanding the Army, and the establishment of relay-posts ordered. Already, on August 4, the outpost service had been assigned to the cavalry divisions.

This retrospect was necessary in order to show the originally and fundamentally different comprehension as to the employment of cavalry in both armies. We shall see later how the ideas of the General Officer Commanding First Army continued unchanged, to the disadvantage of the whole; indeed they were so deep-rooted, that only with hesitation and almost reluctance was any effect given to the later and urgent general instructions from the Headquarters-in-Chief.

How, on the contrary, Prince Frederick Charles continually tended to a proper employment of his cavalry is apparent from a letter of Captain v.

Heister, General Staff Officer of the 5th Cavalry Division, addressed to the 12th Brigade on August 6, in which he says that he had just come from the Prince, who "counsels the division under all circumstances to keep touch with the enemy and to keep forward as much as possible."

Aug. 7.

It was quite in the spirit of his previous measures that Prince Frederick Charles on the night before the 7th sent, through General v. Rheinaben, orders to the 6th Cavalry Division to march at once to the battle-field of Saarbrücken. This put the division on the right wing, and thus the former separation of the 5th Division into two columns was at last done away with.

If we examine the doings of the cavalry on this day in detail, we see Lieutenant v. Ramin's patrol again moving to the front on the extreme right wing by orders from the 3rd Cavalry Division, and, as before remarked, it is only to be regretted that the whole distance covered on the preceding day had to be done anew. The reconnaissance was again to be made in the direction of Bolchen. When the patrol reached the place from which it had on the previous day observed the enemy's camp, the latter was found unchanged, and in a most unconcerned state of repose. Without being disturbed, the patrol succeeded in getting to within 500 paces of the camp, and only here in the immediate vicinity of the bivouac was a hostile patrol of six hussars encountered :* this, in spite of eager pursuit, was not overtaken. Although now discovered, Lieutenant v. Ramin was able to establish himself opposite the bivouac and report every change, which took place, to the division.

Ramin's patrol.

---

* Probably from the 7th French Hussars, which encamped at Teterchen. Endeavours should have been made to avoid this patrol and escape discovery by the enemy if possible.

38 CAVALRY ON SERVICE

Aug. 7.

Cissey's French division left their camp between Tromborn and Teterchen on this day at 5 a.m., and began their retirement to Bolchen. "Scarcely," says Dick De Lonlay, "was Teterchen left, when the enemy's vedettes arrived!" Bravo! According to the regimental diary of the war, Lieutenant v. Ramin announced "that the troops reported to be yesterday at Tromborn drew away to the S.W." His observation was consequently quite accurate.

Hymmen's patrol.

Captain v. Hymmen on this day proceeded with his patrol from Alt-Forweiler by Kreutzwald to Karlingen, thence by Lauterbach to Ludweiler, and then by Gross-Rosseln to Forbach. Unfortunately his special object is not known. He had (drawing a conclusion from a private letter) the opportunity of observing the retreat of the French.* In a message from Forbach before departure, August 8, sent early on that day, he only says what he had learnt from Duke William of Mecklenburg's staff concerning the position of the Second Army, while the reports furnished on the day before are unfortunately missing.

In the message just quoted he announced his decision of advancing on that day again upon St. Avold, and then westward.

Conduct of Lieut.-General Count Groeben.

Lieut.-General Count v. der Groeben sent on this day to Army Head Quarters (by wire from Saarlouis) the contents of the reports of v. Hymmen's and v. Ramin's patrols, adding the remark, "Large cavalry masses on the other side of the Saar, for the present, of no use." This remark was certainly calculated to strengthen the General Officer Com-

---

* Captain v. Hymmen says, among other things, "No; this is a fabulous, almost incredible picture of a flight—everything left behind. They have here, again, a following like they had at Rossbach. At the station I have seen trunks and chests of ladies' toilettes, damask—bedclothes, etc." It may also be observed that the spoil after Wörth contained similar articles.

CAVALRY ON SERVICE

manding First Army in his endeavour to hold the cavalry back. Upon what the divisional commander supported his view is not clear. The enemy were reported so far away that, for the moment, they could certainly not hinder the passage of the Saar, especially as the information had clearly demonstrated that a further withdrawal from the vicinity of Saarlouis had taken place. The country in the vicinity of the fortress is certainly rather wooded and enclosed; but before arriving at Tromborn the map shows an open, undulating country, which up to the Nied and beyond quite favours the employment of cavalry.

Aug. 7.

It must of course be taken into consideration that not one of the four regiments of the division carried carbines, and that this considerably increased the difficulty of an independent employment of this force in a country which, after all, was not an easy one.

In this war a certain shyness of using cavalry in difficult country is apparent; a shyness which is also to be noticed at Head Quarters of the Third Army—after Wörth, for instance, when it was a question of carrying on the pursuit into the Vosges. The insufficient armament of the cavalry may partly account for this. But training and habit can here also do much; let the cavalry no longer dread in peace to act in a mountainous country, and we shall soon find it more daring in war in this respect.

We left Lieutenant Stumm of the 8th Hussars the previous evening in the forest near Buschborn, right among the enemy's outposts.* At 3 a.m. he despatched a patrol of three men to slip away and investigate the country between Porcelette and Buschborn. It would have been better if the officer himself had led this patrol, adhering to the

Stumm's patrol.

* See the map, "Country between the Saar and Nied."

Aug. 7. principle to "see for yourself" whenever possible. At 4 o'clock it returned. It had seen a large French camp on the high ground behind Porcelette and Ham, and it had appeared as if fresh troops were continually coming up from behind the hostile position. It had been debarred from further advance south-west by strong patrols prowling about. Towards 4 o'clock the patrol moved away towards a farmhouse south-west of Diesen, the so-called Grünhof, to water and requisition. This was reached unmolested, the foraging carried out in great haste, the necessary corn bound up in small portions in empty sacks and thrown over the saddle. Suddenly some shots were heard, and the hussars on look-out posts dashed in at the gallop. A squadron of hostile dragoons, followed by some infantry, came on at a rapid pace. In wild haste everybody rushed for Diesen, and up to the old hiding-place. From here Lieutenant Stumm saw the enemy moving up into position, in the strength of several divisions. The hostile squadron had, however, remarked the patrol up on the edge of the wood, and disposed itself to cut it off, so Lieutenant Stumm, at a sharp trot, rode back on the road to Karlingen. On the other edge of the forest, right in front of the last-named place, he observed a column of the enemy's cavalry, of at least two squadrons. Again back into the forest, but now in a northerly direction on Kreutzwald. It was high time for the patrol to return, for hostile troops were again seen marching from Diesen upon Karlingen. Doubtless the foraging at "Grünhof" had alarmed the enemy!

In riding back, the patrol reached a clearing high up in the forest in front of Kreutzwald. Opposite this was a broad stretch of high ground extending, within view, to a great distance. It was strongly occupied by the enemy, and more and more of their forces were drawing thither from the west.*

Aug. 7.

How important must the knowledge of this state of affairs be to the Army Head Quarters at Saarbrücken at this moment! In excitement scarcely to be described, Lieutenant Stumm sprang out of the saddle, and wrote down the following message:—

Message from Lieut. Stumm's Patrol (8th Hussars).

"The patrol bivouacked during the night near Diesen, the enemy in front, right, and left of us. This morning cavalry patrols discovered in Karlingen coming from St. Avold.

"When we advanced about 5 a.m. towards the camp of Buschborn (opposite and not far distant from which we lay the whole night, and which contains quite three divisions and several cavalry regiments), in order to reconnoitre it, we were surrounded on our right and left near Ham by strong cavalry patrols, and obliged to retire on Kreutzwald. There we met the two orderlies from the brigade.

"We are now trying to come back by Spittel. I viewed the camp at Buschborn quite plainly in detail, and at this moment clearly see how the infantry and cavalry are taking position on the height to the right of Buschborn. I remain for the present on the high ground at Karlingen in order to observe the enemy's infantry divisions. It appears at this moment as if they are preparing to march.† Buschborn and Schloss-Varsberg lie on a dominating ridge commanding the roads to Metz.

"(Sd.) STUMM.

"P.S.—Please send back bearer with note saying where I may find the brigade."

* Grenier's division (see sketch of August 6) and the Guards Corps advancing during the night upon the "Lubeln Berg" (see map, "The Country between the Saar and the Nied").
† Start of Grenier's Division.

Aug. 7.

This message was immediately transmitted by a N.C.O. and man at the quickest pace by Ludweiler to General v. d. Goltz. This report arrived by wire at the King's Head Quarters at Homburg on the morning of the 8th, and read as follows:—

Telegram to His Majesty the King.
"Homburg (in the Palatinate).
"Report of Lieut. Stumm's patrol (8th Hussars).

"Patrol bivouacked on the night 6/7 near Diesen (4½ miles north of St. Avold) between hostile detachments. Observed at Buschborn a camp of three divisions and several cavalry regiments. It saw on the morning of the 7th the infantry and cavalry deployed, artillery taking position on the height to the right of Buschborn.
"(Sd.) v. STEINMETZ.
"Völklingen, 8th August, 10.30 a.m."

As the date and time show, this message unfortunately arrived at general Head Quarters very late.

According to the records of the First Army, the report reached the 13th Division at 9.30 a.m., August 7, the Head Quarters of the Seventh Army Corps at 12.30 p.m., and was therefore despatched to his Majesty as much as twenty-two hours later. An unwarrantable mistake seems to have occurred on the part of one of the staffs concerned. Such a delay in the channel of communication could have been avoided if the first recipient of the intelligence had given information of the contents direct to Royal Head Quarters. In future, officers' patrols will, on an important occasion, have to report direct to the supreme authority at the same time as to the intermediate commanders. This will naturally be feasible only when the patrol leaders know where their Head Quarters are, and these must therefore, as far as possible, be notified to them on their departure. Reports such as the last of Lieutenant

Stumm's are of more vital importance to the Army Commander, and sometimes even more so to the Commander-in-Chief, than to the intermediate commanders. In such cases, therefore, it must be considered right to forward the information first and with utmost despatch to the highest authority.

Aug. 7.

Lieutenant Stumm, immediately after despatching his last messenger, received, by a hussar who was returning from orderly duty, the unexpected command to return at once and report himself to the divisional commander.

This strict order could not be disregarded. Quite dispirited, the patrol started at a trot to Forbach by Ludweiler, crossed the battle-field of the previous day, and arrived in the afternoon at divisional Head Quarters in the crowded and burning town of Forbach.

Lieutenant Stumm, after the mental excitement of his independent little expedition was finished, and half dead from exhaustion and tension, could only with great labour, and supported by a staff officer, give to the divisional commander his information, frequently interrupted by shots which fell from the neighbouring houses into the middle of the staff collected in front of the inn.

Only by the greatest exercise of his last remaining strength was he able to compose a written account of his ride. After the last stroke of the pen he sank to the earth in a deep, death-like sleep near the bench, on which he had spasmodically kept himself erect.

The account, written at about 11.30 a.m., was as follows:—

Report from the Patrol of 2nd Lieut. Stumm (8th Hussars).

"Yesterday, August 6, about noon, I received from General v. Goltz orders to proceed to St. Avold with a

Aug. 7.

patrol of ten hussars and a N.C.O. as an independent party, to discover whether the troops at Forbach were retiring towards Metz or towards Nancy. I might remain out two or three days, according to circumstances. I received the order in Völklingen, and rode at once at a long trot over the Wehrden bridge and by Geislautern, Ludweiler, Lauterbach, Karlingen, on my way to St. Avold. Near Ludweiler my advance was checked by the fight going on in front of Gross Rosseln. I at once turned back to Wehrden, and reached the Saarlouis-St. Avold road by Differden and Kreutzwald. About 4 p.m. I reached Karlingen, after finding out for certain that during the daytime and night of August 5/6 the French troops (one to two regiments infantry, one regiment cavalry, and some artillery) had retired from Kreutzwald, l'Hôpital, Karlingen, Diesen, and Ham to St. Avold.

"Yesterday afternoon I found the bivouacs at Ham and Porcelette just lately abandoned. After I had discovered, by means of the telegraph in Karlingen, that the line from Karlingen to Bening was clear of the enemy, I rode forward between 4 p.m. and 5 p.m. at the fastest pace towards St. Avold.*

"I knew that one or two regiments of infantry, one regiment of cavalry, and some artillery were in St. Avold, and also that an advanced post of some two hundred infantry stood on the main road just this side of St. Avold. I rode close up to the outposts, who levelled their rifles at me and began firing. I satisfied myself as to their numbers, and took sufficient note of the general situation, and then, in the dusk, retired along the main road to Karlingen, followed by strong infantry patrols. During the whole of the cannonade at Saarbrücken the camp remained absolutely quiet. It may therefore be assumed that these troops formed a separate corps. I had learnt in the afternoon that the hills of Buschborn and the villages of Porcelette, Bisten, and Lubeln were strongly held, so I retired on Diesen and formed my picket, hidden in the wood. I lay

* An attempt like this to gain information through the telegraph can be most effective, and even in the enemy's country can, with a little ruse, have excellent results.

exactly opposite the camp of Buschborn, scarcely an hour's distance away, and could see their bivouac fires very clearly. I estimated the camp at two divisions, exclusive of cavalry and artillery. On our flanks, in front and behind, bodies of the enemy's troops were stationed, and patrols came and went during the night. No one disturbed us, although we lay right in the enemy's lines, and had commandeered food and forage as far as Ham. We encountered cavalry patrols, and they (cuirassiers) always retired at once. At 4 o'clock in the morning we rode forward by Diesen to Porcelette, after requisitioning oats in the Grünen Hof, near Diesen, under the enemy's eyes at Buschborn. My intention was to slip away to Buschborn and Lubeln, and to watch the road to Metz. I had got halfway to Buschborn when I was forced by strong parties of cavalry, which appeared to my flank and rear, to draw back by Diesen on Kreutzwald. I had already observed that the troops encamped at Buschborn, which were on the crest, had been increasing ever since 7 o'clock in the direction of Niederwiese and Oberwiese, and that therefore more divisions were gradually deploying on the heights of Lubeln-Buschborn-Varsberg, and Niederwiese. Towards 8 o'clock I thought I could make out three or four divisions, which could be clearly distinguished in columns of regiments on the sides of the hills. Northwest of Buschborn were disposed artillery and a quantity of cavalry. At 8 o'clock the whole heights were occupied in a continuous line of nearly five miles, keeping in touch with St. Avold, where this morning the same troops were as yesterday. The whole line, therefore—Niederwiese, Bisten im Loch, Oberwiese, Buschborn, Kleinthal, Lubeln, St. Avold—is thus strongly held by four or five divisions, not counting cavalry and artillery, and likewise the hills of Werdel, Deckenberg, and Budenloch.* It is quite certain that the two or three new divisions, which are now north-west of Buschborn, only arrived there at 6 or 7 o'clock this morning. The bivouac fires of the two divisions in Buschborn were clearly distinguishable till 3.30 a.m. The adjacent ground was quite dark. It appears that the camp at

Aug. 7.

* On the ordnance map these hills have different names.

Aug. 7.

Buschborn consisted of the 2nd Corps (Frossard's), and was later increased by portions of the 4th Corps from Thionville and the 3rd (Bazaine's) from Metz. When I was certain that the whole line was stationary, and was not advancing, I rode off (followed by cavalry patrols as far as Kreutzwald and Karlingen) by Lauterbach and Ludweiler to Forbach, where I reported to the General Officer Commanding Division. I was much surprised that the division was moving on Saarbrücken, and not towards St. Avold. All that I have reported I have exactly ascertained myself. The actual strength of the troops holding the line Lubeln-Buschborn I naturally cannot judge to a thousand. Towards the frontier the range, on which the troops were standing, is a remarkably commanding one, and runs parallel with the frontier at a distance of four to nine miles.

"Educated inhabitants, who took me for a French officer on patrol,* assured me that this hill was strongly occupied and defended even in 1813–1814. They said that the Prussians could never get up there. Forage and supplies are very scarce. The French inhabitants are obliging, but terrified of Prussians. The most amusing proclamations by Napoleon are posted up everywhere. Altogether I rode over nine miles into France, have looked into seven or eight French villages, and made requisitions on payment in several of them.

"(Sd.) HUGO STUMM,
"Lieut.

"*Divisional Staff, Forbach,*
7, viii., 70."

Lieutenant Stumm had been in the saddle thirty-four hours without break, and without any nourishment except a cake of chocolate and a gulp of brandy and water.

The horses, in the excitement of short halts and insufficient watering, had only touched a small quantity of oats. Bread soaked in brandy had with difficulty kept them on their legs. The patrol had covered seventy-five miles in a direct line, besides

* Lieutenant Stumm spoke French fluently.

the work of the various flank and detached parties, the continual riding to and fro in the forest and when meeting the enemy.

Aug. 7.

All honour to the memory of this young officer. The manner of carrying out such work as here depicted cannot be surpassed. In Lieutenant Stumm were united all qualities which should distinguish the leader of a patrol. Calm deliberation in the first place, then the greatest dash in execution, quick resolve in difficult situations, the toughest endurance and at the same time accurate observation. The messages were clearly composed (if not so classically put together, as is now the custom)* and cleverly transmitted, so that none appear to have gone astray. How far all the details as reported proved correct cannot be ascertained, owing to the imperfect French accounts; but the reports on the whole were absolutely correct. If we were to criticise that the events on the French side had not been quite accurately stated by Stumm, we would commit the error of so many commanders at manœuvres, who demand from cavalry patrols performances which cannot be executed in the face of the enemy. Let us therefore beware of armchair criticism! especially if we have to deal with such strenuous exertions as those rides of Stumm. The order to him to turn back appears quite incomprehensible, and we can imagine the chagrin of this intelligent leader when he was recalled from a duty so important and interesting. The divisional commander ought to have considered himself lucky in having such an officer in that important position. The strength of the men and horses after their exertions might certainly not

* Perhaps in carrying out the prescribed "Form" too much time occasionally is spent at the expense of the real "matter," to which the "Form" is, of course, really subservient.

Aug. 7.

have sufficed to do much more in continuation of the task assigned, and in such cases it will sometimes be the duty of the responsible officer to consider whether reliefs should not be sent with returning messengers, although this may not be immediately asked for.

We will come across Lieutenant Stumm again during the next days.

Steinmetz's views for the 7th.

General v. Steinmetz had on the evening of the battle reported by telegraph to the king the storming of the heights of Spicheren and the driving back of the enemy on Forbach. He then continued—

> "I have, as the senior, taken over command of the troops engaged here belonging to the two armies. Tomorrow I will rearrange the troops which are to stay here, and order only cavalry patrols to follow, to see whether the enemy has altogether retired."

Two points arise from this despatch. Firstly, Steinmetz on the 7th still had command of all the troops on the battle-field; and rightly, because his command, taken over on the day before, must naturally last until the action which the troops under his orders had brought together came to an end; and that was certainly not the case in the early hours of the 7th. Secondly, he had no idea of having fought out a victorious battle, which might, perhaps, demand a pursuit, but was far more under the impression that the battle would be continued, and that preparation should be made for an attack by the enemy, by standing still for the moment.

The troops, too, felt that the battle was not decided. Major-General v. Damnitz (Lieutenant of the 2nd squadron, 19th Dragoons, in 1870) told the author from his notes, that when the squadron which had accompanied Glümer's division had left it about 6 p.m., and was looking for its regiment, the squadron leader, Captain v. Gristede, as he rode through Saarbrücken, heard from other officers " that the battle was indecisive, and that the French might advance again at any minute."

Aug. 7.

During the night touch was evidently lost with the main forces of the enemy, who made use of the darkness to withdraw. Further discussions on the subject, as they concern the events of August 6, do not come within the scope of our description.

Touch lost.

It must, however, be emphasized that the cavalry must always be blamed for such an occurrence, and that in default of orders from the higher commanders it can never be exonerated.

As this frequently occurs, it is not sufficient in explanation to throw the responsibility simply on the leaders concerned. A proper understanding is better arrived at by mentioning what circumstances have caused this omission, without palliating them.* In this case it can be stated that the fight did not end till dark, that many thought it would be renewed on the following day, that above all Forbach, as we shall see, was occupied during the night by the enemy, that this place, at any rate from Spicheren, was difficult to outflank, that a retreat of the enemy to Saargemünd was improbable, and that the country was extremely difficult for cavalry.

The 13th Division was far more favourably placed. Patrols from the Kaninchenberg could easily feel their way forward past the south-west exit of Forbach.

General v. Steinmetz issued no orders to the cavalry early on the 7th to clear up the situation

* Compare the explanations given on p. 29.

E

Aug. 7.

in front, though other leaders recognized the necessity of taking measures for that purpose.

6th Cavalry Division.

The 6th Cavalry Division started to the battlefield at 2 a.m., in accordance with instructions received from the headquarters of the Second Army. The 6th Cuirassiers had already arrived there the evening before by Rheinbaben's order.

Grüter's Brigade arrived at the Exerzier-Platz at 4 a.m., Rauch's Brigade, with the batteries, at 6 a.m. In the morning there was a thick mist, which limited the view to a few paces, and did not clear off till 11 o'clock. At the instigation of Major v. Schoenfels, the officer on the General Staff, Duke William of Mecklenburg directed the 3rd and 15th Uhlans, under their brigadier, Major-General Baron v. Grüter, to advance on reconnaissance towards Forbach.

The 15th Cavalry Brigade, with three squadrons of the 6th Cuirassiers, was left behind "in reserve" on the bivouac-ground; only the 4th squadron of the latter regiment was, during the advance on Forbach, sent to reconnoitre on the left flank towards Esslingen.

It found 500 of the enemy's wounded there, but otherwise no enemy.

The 3rd Squadron of the 15th Uhlans was not sent forward till midday (the order reached the brigade at 12.30 p.m.) to reconnoitre towards the enemy and to seek for communication *via* Behren with the 19th Dragoons in the neighbourhood of Lixing and Gross Blittersdorf.

Connection was not established, since the 5th Cavalry Division, as we shall see, had been led across the Saar.

On the evening of the battle General v. Stülpnagel had withdrawn the 1st and 2nd squadrons of the 12th Dragoons which he had sent off to the left flank; and, apparently to replace them (by whom the order was given cannot be ascertained), the 2nd and 4th squadrons of the 17th Hussars, under Major van Semmern, were pushed forward by St. Arnual to discover whether Saargemünd was still held by the enemy.

Aug. 7.

The 2nd and 4th squadrons, 17th Hussars.

The leader of the squadrons reported—

"St. Arnual, 6 a.m.

". . . Saargemünd is said by the inhabitants to be still occupied, and in fairly strong force. There are supposed to be no more of the French in Gross Blittersdorf."

The 40th French Regiment, which, according to Dick de Lonlay, had rested at Alsting, southeast of Spicheren, till 1.30 a.m., had probably marched through that place at 2.30. This report gives no information of the action of van Semmern's detachment, and scarcely admits of the assumption that patrols were actually sent as far as Saargemünd.

According to the account given to the author by the leader of the advanced guard squadron (the 2nd),* the squadrons left the battle-field at 8 p.m., and advanced noiselessly, without taking notice of the isolated bodies hidden in the villages, who kept very quiet. Behind Gross Blittersdorf the advanced guard squadron halted, and sent patrols to Saargemünd, who reported the place occupied.

The squadrons rejoined Redern's Brigade at 7 a.m. in Gross Blittersdorf, and made their report. This was probably verbal, amplifying the previous written message. It seems impossible to obtain a clearer idea of this expedition, as there were no written memorandums available. The advanced squadron seems to have gone considerably further forward than the rest of the detachment.

* Captain v. der Mülbe, now Lieut.-General (retired).

52 CAVALRY ON SERVICE

Aug. 7.

It is incredible that the squadrons can have missed the spoor of the retreat of such large masses of the enemy as must have moved in this direction. The action of the other two squadrons sent to the left flank is certainly not satisfactory, especially that of the 3rd squadron, 15th Uhlans, which was directed immediately on to the line of Laveaucoupet's retreat.

3rd squadron, 15th Uhlans, and 4th squadron, 6th Cuirassiers.

His (Laveaucoupet's) division had retired by Behren, Buschbach, on Cadenbronn, and thence had reached the great Forbach-Saargemünd road, with Vergé's Division on the left, on the line of whose retreat the 4th squadron of 6th Cuirassiers must have been moving. [See map, August 6.]

As the French marched partly across country, owing to the block on the roads, their tracks must have been specially easy to see; and it must be considered out of the question that the cavalry did not light on them, and did not send messages, even though they are not mentioned in the records. But it was unlike cavalry not to follow their spoor.

If the cavalryman finds a track such as that, he must, without further orders, follow it untiringly, as the pointer follows the game, till it is located.

Itzenplitz' patrol.

The records of the 13th Division contain only one report, evidently sent in early in the morning by Graf Itzenplitz, 8th Hussars, which expressly stated that the French had retired on Saargemünd. He had had to seek for communication with the 14th Division, according to the account he gave to the author, and had ridden forward by Stiering.

The 13th Division had apparently not forwarded the report. The officer doubtless never came across the enemy again. The report was made on signs that were unmistakable, and had thus the value of establishing an absolute fact.

Cavalry

The troops left "in reserve," who had been

hoping at least to reach the enemy, were sadly depressed by their employment in this fashion. [According to the account given me by Colonel v. Spalding, then a lieutenant in the 6th Cuirassiers, the regiment was kept back on account of unsuitable arms and equipment; and their colonel, Graf Lynar, charged him with collecting the French chassepot rifles on the battle-field. This was done, and gradually twenty-five Cuirassiers per squadron had these arms, which came in very useful in the course of the campaign.]

Aug. 7.
"in reserve."

This measure of the Duke's cannot be understood; the advancing Uhlan regiments required no reserve, as the numerous units of all arms east of Forbach offered sufficient support. The division should have moved to the front, united. This was one of those occasions when it was clearly expedient to hand over to the commander of the 6th Cavalry Division all the divisional cavalry regiments within call with the object of employing them in common action.

Grüter's Brigade moved off at 5.30 a.m.* Bothe's squadron (2nd) of 3rd Uhlans formed the advance guard, and Lieutenant Lange led the advanced troop. The latter describes the events that followed in a letter he sent home—

Grüter's Brigade.

"I led the advanced troop forward in a mist, so thick that I could not see twenty paces in front of me. I trotted along the high-road with the advanced point, and the troop in rear, into the village,† and was suddenly fired on with a volley, although I could not see a single Frenchman, and they could not see us in the thick

* The description of the events at Forbach is not only based on the records of war and the history of the 3rd Uhlans, but also on notes of the then Captain Bothe, and on letters sent home by First Lieutenant Lange of the same regiment.

† Lange remembers having ridden past a church on the left of the main street; he therefore must have been right in the centre of the town.

Aug. 7.

mist. The bullets passed all above us. We sought cover in a side street, and I ordered the rest of the troop to scatter and search the place. The French still stood at the exit, otherwise all the streets were empty and the windows closed. It was only after our infantry had from the opposite side driven the enemy out that we could proceed."

This information is supplemented by some notes of the squadron leader—

"It was not only a single volley; the road to Saarbrücken was repeatedly swept by fire; and a Frenchman who had been firing was brought out by the patrols. I sent patrols round Forbach on both sides, which took some time in the impenetrable mist; and it was difficult country on the south side.* The Uhlans found the exit towards Rossbrücken occupied by the enemy, and had ridden up to it within a few paces. It was not till perhaps three-quarters of an hour later that we heard a violent fusillade in Forbach, and recognized the Prussian 'Hurrah!' This came, as we found out, from the troops of Glümer's Division. I went forward at once with the squadron, right through Forbach, and sent a verbal message to the regiment that the place was in our possession, and that I was following the enemy towards Rossbrücken."†

There occurs in the records of the 13th Division the following message from the advance guard dated 4.45 a.m. :—

"Forbach is occupied. The outposts are stationed mostly on the eastern exit, on the far side of a stream. Firing went on intermittently towards the south-east both last evening and during the night.

"v. DER GOLTZ,
"Outpost camp in front of Forbach."

* The Schloss Berg, with the Kleinwald, comes close up to the place, which on the north is bordered by some meadows cut up by wet ditches; so to make a circuit of the town in such foggy weather was extremely difficult.

† This message seems to have been delayed on its way to the brigade, and thus have caused the late start of its main body.

The garrison appears, according to their regimental history, to have consisted of the 10th Jäger Battalion, which belonged to Laveaucoupet's Division.

Aug. 7.

The troops, which seem to have been isolated, stayed the night at the station, which lies near the eastern entrance, in its front a stream that flows into the Rossel.* The battalion, warned by the inhabitants, did not wait for the German's attack, but withdrew towards Püttlingen, but, as it appears from the above-mentioned reports, not without having hotly fired on and delayed the advancing German cavalry. That the German infantry, in their advance on Forbach afterwards, imagined the place still occupied is apparent from the fact that they were prepared for a serious engagement, and advanced in attack formation. It is natural that when stragglers were only encountered later (though in considerable numbers), that the mistaken idea arose that Forbach had not been occupied at all. In short, the outposts of the 13th Division had sent in correct information, and it may be inferred that the 8th Hussars participated, from the fact that the next battalions to arrive, the 55th Regiment, noticed a dead hussar horse close to the village.

The 55th Regiment had moved at 6.15 a.m. from the Kaninchenberg towards Forbach, and took it half an hour later, after a small engagement, in which also formed bodies of troops offered some resistance in the streets. About 100 slightly wounded and 50 unwounded men were taken.

To reconnoitre towards Forbach, also the 12th Dragoons and the 15th Hussars, the latter with a horse battery, were sent forward respectively by the General Officer Commanding 5th Infantry Division and the Commander of the Eighth Army

Colonel v. Unger reconnoitring with the 12th Dragoons and 15th Hussars.

* Compare the wording of the report just quoted.

Aug. 7. Corps independently. Colonel v. Unger, Chief of the Staff of the Seventh Army Corps, accompanied the latter regiment. In front of Forbach he met General v. Grüter and his brigade, who told him that it was still held by French infantry. Two officers sent on by Unger to reconnoitre found the place occupied, not by the enemy, but by Prussian infantry. The explanation, from what has been stated, is that Bothe's squadron had passed through in the mean time, but his report had not by then reached General v. Grüter.

This follows from the fact, as we shall see, that this squadron had kept at the head of the cavalry the whole morning, and no other cavalry troops had overtaken it.*

Colonel v. Unger gained no direct information of subsequent events, as he did not accompany the hussars beyond Forbach.

General v. Grüter had reported to the Divisional Commander that he had been obliged to halt in front of Forbach. The Divisional Staff officer, Major v. Treskow, conveyed this message to General v. Steinmetz, whom he met in Saarbrücken towards 7 a.m. [This mention of the time is interesting, as it is $5\frac{1}{2}$ miles from Forbach to Saarbrücken.]

Steinmetz intervening in the cavalry movements.

The General gave v. Treskow a somewhat unfavourable reception, and requested the Duke "not to provoke the enemy, as it is not intended to move the First Army forward on the 7th, but first of all to collect and put in order the troops which are mixed up with the Second Army."

The cavalry were thus to some extent fettered;

---

* Bothe has told the author that, when Colonel Cosel later in the day wished to form the van with the 15th Hussars, he seriously remonstrated by saying, "No, Colonel; I am advanced guard, and shall stick to it."

and this fact must be borne in mind, if we wish to judge their action fairly on this date. The fact of the Duke having instructions from the Second Army "to keep touch with the enemy" could not release him from bearing in mind the later order of the General, under whose command he actually was at the time. But the Duke was not thereby hindered from keeping at the enemy's heels and adopting all possible measures for reconnaissance. He was only requested to avoid any serious or disadvantageous engagement. The General's instructions were not to be taken in any other sense. The Duke could have protested, and a "General v. Schmidt" would certainly have done so, especially when the enemy had evacuated Forbach.

Aug. 7.

If a cavalry leader finds the situation different to what his superiors anticipated in their instructions, he must act independently and on his own initiative as the altered circumstances dictate.

Initiative of leaders.

Special permission is not required in that case. Duke William, however, unhappily possessed little enterprise, and took very kindly to a passive *rôle*.

It is plain that events would have taken a very different course if there had not been so thick a mist on the morning of the 7th. It will be interesting to consider how cavalry ought to act under such conditions. Opposed to a demoralized enemy, the action of the 4th Cavalry Division on the morning of August 31, the day after the battle of Beaumont, when they advanced in pursuit on the left bank of the Maas, seems to be well worthy of imitation.

Reconnaissance in a thick mist.

The illustrious leader of the division, Prince Albrecht of Prussia — the elder — ordered the advance guard to move forward at a fast trot along the great high-road, without waiting for reports from

Aug. 7. the flank patrols, and without paying any attention to the numerous stragglers in the villages, who, however, offered no resistance. Even advanced posts were ridden through, and disappeared hastily in the mist. There was hardly a halt till the mist cleared and Frenois had been reached, when the advanced squadron (1st) of the 6th Uhlans, commanded by the author, attacked the enemy opposite (infantry) and scattered them. It was quite impossible, even with the numerous patrols that had been sent out, to ascertain the numbers and composition of the enemy; the patrols pushed close up to their detachments, and suffered some loss, without being able to find out their strength.

The method of action adopted was, moreover, highly successful. The cavalry division had been able to gain ground, and had brought in hundreds of prisoners. The success must be attributed to the demoralization of the enemy, the country was favourable, and nowhere serious opposition was met with.

At Forbach the conditions were different. In such a case there is nothing else to do but make flank reconnaissances—as was done—with patrols, feeling their way slowly forward, which naturally takes a great deal of time.

Attack on a French supply column. The advance guard of Grüter's Brigade had meanwhile pressed through Morsbach, overtaken the enemy, and captured a supply waggon. The advanced troop then attacked a formed body of infantry. Captain Bothe now perceived for the first time that his regiment was following, and also that the battery attached to the 15th Hussars was shelling a supply column which was hurrying away under a strong escort. Between Rossbrücken and Merlenbach, soon after the squadron had galloped through the former place, several waggons fell into their hands. But at this point the squadron was heavily fired on from the front and from the station at Cochern, and compelled to halt.

The 5th squadron, v. Leipziger's (the 1st had remained at home at the depôt), had received orders in Morsbach to proceed to the station at Cochern, in order to hinder the departure of a train that was reported to be loading there. The train started as the advanced troop reached the station, and it was the more impossible to stop it, as several companies, which had extended along the road west of Rossbrücken, had opened fire. The squadron, anyhow, captured several waggons, and seized a large quantity of provisions abandoned at the station.

The transport column, which lost a large number of waggons—thanks to the Uhlans—belonged, according to Dick de Lonlay, to Metmann's division of the Third Corps, which had not taken part in the battle, and from August 6 to 7 had camped behind Forbach, close to the Prussian outposts.

It had left its camp equipment in Marienthal, had ordered it up for the night, and was now sending it back again.

According to the French story, when the column had reached Rossbrücken, some Uhlans galloped up to it (the advanced troop of the 3rd Uhlans), and, firing a few shots, attacked the many isolated detachments which were marching with the transport, whereupon a panic took place. In spite of the artillery fire directed on them, the majority of the 500 waggons escaped, and with them the war chest. Only 30 waggons and about 150 stragglers were taken by the Uhlans.

The French losses amounted, in addition, to one man killed, one officer and three men wounded.

Aug. 7.   It was the 5th Squadron, by the diary of the 14th Cavalry Brigade, which seized the fifty waggons of the French supply column, while the 2nd moved against a column retreating on a road beyond Rossbrücken, the column being also fired on by artillery. But the squadron was unable to accomplish anything, as two battalions of the enemy's infantry advanced to cover the retreat.

The Uhlans, according to Dick de Lonlay, also seized the baggage waggons of the 4th squadron, 5th Dragoons (Juniac's Cavalry Brigade), and captured the leader, Lieutenant Moinet, after a severe struggle.

One cannot now judge from an armchair whether a greater success could have been achieved here. A fuller knowledge of all the conditions, and of the extremely difficult country, would be needed for the purpose than is now available. Could it have been seen that, as a matter of fact, they had to deal with a large column of transport, the escort of which was, according to the above-mentioned French records, moreover, 1200 men?

Placing outposts.   On arrival at Rossbrücken, the 15th Hussars and the 12th Dragoons rejoined their divisions, while the cavalry division took over the outpost line facing Merlenbach, which was still occupied by the enemy. A further advance was impossible, according to the impression conveyed to me by the officers concerned, and which was quite in accordance with the situation, as we shall see, without putting in far stronger forces, which were not available, since an engagement was not intended. Captain Bothe had been ordered to put out outposts where he was, but could not comply till the enemy had retired on Merlenbach and Beningen, where he confined himself to occupying these places.

CAVALRY ON SERVICE

The 2nd squadron of the 8th Hussars, Captain Haelmigk, had already scouted to the right flank of the 13th Division by General v. der Goltz's order, and had reconnoitred by Carlsbrunn towards Emmersweiler. The squadron did not meet the enemy. For practical common-sense reasons they left the extensive woodlands of that country, and, leaving out patrols, went into bivouac at Ludweiler.* From here the squadron leader intended to move forward the next morning. He started very early to Carlsbrunn, and from there despatched a troop, under Lieutenant Welter and Ensign Samman, to Nassweiler and Merlenbach respectively, to watch the great Metz-Saarbrücken road. Both troops were hotly fired on by infantry, and had to retire out of range. They found a position well under cover close by, kept watch, and sent their patrols far forward, at the same time maintaining communication with Bothe's squadron of the 3rd Uhlans.

Captain Haelmigk had ridden forward himself on the report from the advanced troops, convinced himself of the enemy's resistance, and sent in the following message:—

[Time omitted; probably after 10 a.m.]

"Report of 2nd Squadron, 8th Hussars.

"Enemy has received considerable reinforcements, especially of cavalry and artillery, apparently from St. Avold and Metz. It seems as if he means to take up a position between Merlenbach and Nassweiler.† All the enemy's movements are watched by a troop at

---

* Such a procedure is absolutely justified, provided patrols remain in touch with the enemy.

† As Castagny's Division and Forton's Cavalry Division, which had followed the former as far as Marienthal, apparently moved into the position of Bettingen at a later hour, it is here more likely only an advanced guard pushed forward to the Siel-Berg. French accounts have meanwhile confirmed that about this time troops of that division had made their appearance there. (*Revue de Cavalerie*, May, 1901.)

Aug. 7. Merlenbach. The squadron is moving on the flank, and was this morning near Carlsbrunn and St. Nicholas."

Upon this, according to a memorandum on the despatch signed v. Werder, the officer of the general staff with the 13th Division, two battalions of the 15th Infantry Regiment and a battery were sent forward. From the Diary of the Division it appears that this detachment, with the addition of a squadron, all under Colonel v. Delitz, was directed to advance from Morsbach by Rossbrücken, to take up a position facing St. Avold, one report even having mentioned "that these troops seemed bent on advancing."* The Diary then continues to say "that the existence of the enemy's troops on this side of St. Avold has been ascertained, and that considerable forces were said by the inhabitants to be near that place."

Meanwhile, Captain v. Haelmigk had been brought an order by a N.C.O. (it could not be ascertained from whom this order emanated) to continue to reconnoitre on the right flank, and he sent in this message—

"Carlsbrunn, 11.30 a.m.

"Under-officer Lœw brought me the order all right, and I will try to carry it out at once, as soon as the two troops watching the enemy on the road to Metz come in. This is a shocking country—nothing but narrow paths through woods. I sent General Goltz a message this morning that the enemy seemed willing to accept battle. They have received reinforcements from St. Avold and Metz, especially of cavalry and artillery."

A third report from the squadron, received "in the afternoon," ran as follows:—

"Afternoon. Place (?). I have been in Lautherthal (ought to be Lauterbach,—author). Scheele has

* The enemy's advance to occupy the position at Beningen could not now be explained otherwise.

gone to Karlingen and Spittel, and not yet returned. Merlenbach is strongly held by the enemy. One of my troops was hotly fired on by infantry from there. Under-officer Blum and six men has gone out to bring in a supply waggon left behind near Merlenbach, has come under fire from infantry, and has not yet returned."*

It cannot now be ascertained what the late Lieutenant v. Scheele, who had ridden on to Karlingen and Spittel, had said in his report. This, like many other reports, has been lost.

It is indubitable, from the short distance between the two places (about two miles), that he reached Karlingen and reported it clear. Probably he went on further in the direction of St. Avold.

He is, perhaps, responsible for the information as to the existence of hostile troops on this side of St. Avold, which is entered in the Diary of the 13th Division; anyhow, he was prevented from reconnoitring the town itself by the enemy, who was still on this side of it.†

The squadron had evidently been in an extremely favourable position near Carlsbrunn, and certainly exceedingly active. Unseen to the enemy, it kept the two main roads to St. Avold under observation (the one from Wehrden by Lauterbach-Spittel, and the other from Saarbrücken by Merlenbach), and, through a broad opening in the woods, which runs from Carlsbrunn by St. Nicolas and Nassweiler to Merlenbach, was easily able to watch the movements of the enemy there and on his left flank, while its patrols kept pushing forward.

Captain Haelmigk had performed his task most

* The enterprise of this smart N.C.O. did not succeed, owing to the hot fire of the enemy.

† These roads, according to French records, were watched by the 2nd and 4th Dragoons. (*Vide*, p. 82.)

64   CAVALRY ON SERVICE

Aug. 7. excellently, and received orders in the evening to return to the bivouac at Forbach.

It would have been better to have sent him orders to reconnoitre further south and south-west the next morning; yet it is quite natural that the divisions should wish to keep their squadrons in hand, leaving the strategic reconnaissance to the cavalry divisions.

Haelmigk obeyed, and started in the dark on the great road to Rossbrücken.

There he struck an infantry picket under a sergeant-major. How easily excitement may be fatal on service is shown by the following incident, which I quote from the account of the squadron leader:—

> "As I was riding quietly along with my trumpeter, thirty paces ahead of the squadron, and the Hussars were singing lustily, I suddenly heard the order, 'Fire!' and a volley was fired by twenty to thirty rifles, the bullets whistling over our heads. I shouted, 'Prussians!' at the top of my voice, and received for answer the second volley. The matter was getting serious. I spurred my horse forward, and was close to the sergeant-major before he could give the order a third time to fire. (His men were standing behind stacked wood near the main road.) It appeared that the young man had already reported to the rear, 'Enemy's cavalry are attacking!' and that upon this the reserve of the outposts had got under arms, and a further alarm had taken place even in the camp at Forbach. That the squadron escaped without any loss must be attributed to the agitation of the infantry, to the darkness, and to the close range, which caused the bullets to fly too high."

Measures of the 13th Division. There is in the records of the 13th Division an indication of how Haelmigk's report affected the measures which were adopted, since the following pencil memorandum is to be found at the bottom of Lieutenant Stumm's original report:—

"Shortly before receipt of this report, written down by my order, a second one arrived from the squadron at Emmersweiler, to the effect that the enemy had been considerably reinforced at Merlenbach and the neighbourhood. I have formed front facing Merlenbach, occupied Morsbach with two battalions, one squadron, and a battery, and moved with the remainder to Forbach, with the exception of the squadron which remains in Emmersweiler."

Lieutenant Stumm's report had left no doubt that St. Avold was still occupied in the morning. That patrols were unable to push forward in front of the place on the afternoon of the 7th can be gathered from the details given above. The following report from Captain v. Schütz, leader of the 1st Squadron, 8th Hussars, shows that the patrol pushed far to the west this day:—

"Place (not given). 3 p.m.

"Under-officer Gabriel has searched Kreutzwald and Ham, and found nothing. There were proofs that the enemy bivouacked there shortly before. From information, 8000 men of all three arms are said to have withdrawn southwards.* The squadron halted on the right of the road leading to Porcelette."

The 4th Squadron of the same regiment had acted as personal escort to General v. der Goltz's staff in the mist that morning in front of Forbach; in the afternoon it was sent to reconnoitre towards Saargemünd, and announced the retirement of the enemy from there to Metz.

The existence of large bodies of the enemy at Beningen and Nassweiler had also been known to the 3rd Uhlans' outposts opposite Merlenbach, as their regimental history shows.

The French outposts at Merlenbach stood so

* These troops may have belonged to Grenier's Division of the Fourth Corps, which had moved south to St. Avold to join the Third Corps.

Aug. 7. close to the vedettes of the 2nd Squadron, 3rd Uhlans, that its captain made a hussar patrol, which was just to hand, fire their carbines at them, upon which they retired to the entrance of Merlenbach. The vedettes were pushed up to within 600 paces of this strongly-held village, so the closest contact was established.

A Uhlan patrol, which later on had been ordered to ascertain whether the place was perhaps clear, had reached the middle of the village all right, when infantry suddenly appeared in the windows and gardens and opened a brisk fire.

The patrol leader, Corporal Remuth, jumped a garden fence and seized an infantryman by the collar to drag him away, but had to let him go, to go to the assistance of his three men, who were hard pressed. One of them was severely wounded in the stomach, and another by a shot in the thigh.*

Soon after, a squadron of chasseurs appeared on the left of the road, that is, from Bettingen; the Uhlan squadron went to meet it. The former, however, retired without waiting—" to an infantry camp in rear."

The squadron commander reported the affair to Major v. Moellendorff of the Staff, who had just then arrived at the outposts, and also to his colonel, for he was soon afterwards relieved by the 15th Uhlans. It may be mentioned here that Admiral Prince Adalbert of Prussia, accompanied by the squadron leader, had watched for some time the most advanced posts of the enemy, who now and then sent the German vedettes a salute from their chassepots.

* A report from the outposts of this affair, timed 6 p.m. and signed by Major v. Moellendorff, is in the War Records of the 14th Cavalry Brigade.

Duke William of Mecklenburg, the commander of the cavalry division, had not deemed any personal observation necessary, and had on this day only reached Morsbach. What a contrast!

Aug. 7.

Meanwhile General v. Grüter had reported:—

"Rossbrücken, 10.15 a.m.

"Brigade reached Rossbrücken. The enemy occupies the opposite hills weakly. In accordance with orders received through Major v. Schoenfels, I shall put outposts on the Rossel at Rossbrücken, and bivouac the brigade at Morsbach."

Order to Grüter to halt.

Simultaneously with this report, the General Officer Commanding Seventh Army Corps through the 14th Division received the following report from Colonel v. Cosel, commanding the 15th Hussars:—

"9.15 a.m.

"The 15th Hussars, the horse battery, and Grüter's Uhlan Brigade are on a level with Morsbach. Strong, hostile columns are withdrawing from Rossbrück on the St. Avold road, and are being fired at from here."

General v. Grüter, in halting here, simply obeyed the clear orders of his superior officer. The general, too, was probably personally convinced that this order accorded with the situation (*vide* p. 60). It is of interest, all the same, to consider whether other action could have been taken.

Comments on Grüter's action.

At the moment when the order arrived to halt, after 10 a.m., the opposite hills were apparently "only weakly held," but yet held by infantry.

These hills command the long defile from Oberhomburg to St. Avold, which it is impossible to turn, and with the strongly held village of Merlenbach situated in front of it. It was anyhow next to impossible to discover exactly the

Aug. 7. strength and position of the enemy in that wooded and hilly country. What steps was the general to take to make an advance here with his squadrons, while at the same time—see Haelmigk's reports—the enemy advanced with both an infantry and a cavalry division, and took up a strong position just opposite the outposts? The pursuit was bound to end here; even a "Gneisenau" or a "York" would have been compelled to halt.

It was only by a fresh and serious engagement, which was not intended, and by bringing up stronger forces, that the enemy could be forced to renew his retreat.

If the further advance of the isolated brigade, detailed for outpost duty, was thus certainly impossible, the duty of further reconnaissance yet remained. Every effort should have been made to gain information about the enemy that had newly arrived. If that enemy prohibited an advance of the patrols to the front, nothing prevented their moving round his right wing by Genweiler. The blocked defile of Marienthal could also be circumvented by way of Karlingen-Spittel.

Whether the brigade did everything that could be done, it was impossible to ascertain, and must remain questionable. Many patrols were sent out, says the official diary, and brought in many prisoners. These patrols will certainly have given the leader information about the enemy immediately in front, even though the records give no account of it.

Cavalry into bivouac. The retirement of the main body of the brigade to Morsbach cannot be found fault with, because it is the regular procedure for cavalry, which take their turn of rest, to do so by placing a reasonable distance between themselves and the enemy; otherwise they do not obtain the necessary repose.

CAVALRY ON SERVICE 69

Touch is to be kept by patrols, specially officers' patrols, who are to be pushed up as close as possible to the enemy, and conform to his every movement.

If these do their duty, touch is maintained, and the troops may be proportionately spared.

Duke William entered Forbach at 2 p.m., and took up his quarters there. Here he gave orders for General v. Grüter to send a well-mounted officer by Lixing to Saargemünd, to discover whether, and in what strength, the place is occupied. A report on the subject was to be sent by 6 p.m., both in writing and personally, to Prince Frederick Charles at Bliescastel. General v. Rauch, in Saarbrücken, was directed to secure at once information on the same subject, and to telegraph it to Bliescastel that very night.

This general was ordered at the same time to march at 6 o'clock to Forbach with the part of the division that stood at Saarbrücken.

General v. Grüter was further directed to have patrols sent at dusk on Karlingen, St. Avold, and Farschweiler.

These orders from the duke were issued very late, and were occasioned less by his own anxiety to clear up the situation than to satisfy an urgent demand from Prince Frederick Charles, who had sent orders that the Forbach-St. Avold road was to be followed by the division, and that a report was to be sent him very early on August 8, whether Saargemünd was still held by the enemy.

Lieutenants Reimer and v. Wasner rode to Saargemünd together, and reported to the General Officer Commanding Second Army direct that the town had meanwhile been evacuated. The 15th Uhlans sent to St. Avold, Karlingen, and Farschweiler patrols, who reported, even on the 7th

Aug. 7.

Orders of Duke William.

Aug. 7. according both to the official account and the regimental history, that Karlingen and Farschweiler were clear, but that hostile troops comprising all arms were assembled at St. Avold.

It is not known whether patrols had also reconnoitred Püttlingen and Cappel on the 7th.*

The 6th Cavalry Division never received a report to that effect, as can be gathered from an order on the following day to Grüter's brigade (see p. 96). Anyhow, the Burgomaster of Cappel, according to Dick de Lonlay, had only reported on the evening of the 7th to Püttlingen that Cappel was being occupied by a battalion of the enemy. This was certainly not the case, but would point to the appearance in the neighbourhood of hostile patrols, who produced a great effect on the nervous mind of the chief magistrate.

Concentration of the 5th Cavalry Division.

To turn to the action of the 5th Cavalry Division.

In order to concentrate towards the left wing, the division marched as follows:—the 13th Brigade, with the 11th and 17th Hussars, and Schirmer's battery, moved by Brebach to the line Bliesbolgen-Bliesbrücken, joining up on the left with the 1st and 2nd squadrons of the 10th Hussars, thus once more with their own brigade; while the other two squadrons of the 10th, further to the west, still remained with the 12th Brigade.

The most direct way to cross the Saar led by Arnual, over a ford, and this was allotted to the squadrons, the battery being assigned the longer route by Saarbrücken.

---

* Sergeant-Major of the Reserve, v. Saldern, who led the patrol on St. Avold, lost his way, however; his report is dated 8.10 a.m., August 8th. It was certainly not right to employ a young N.C.O. of the Reserve on such an important mission; and it cannot be wondered that, without a map, he lost his way in the large forests about Karlingen, and wasted so much time.

CAVALRY ON SERVICE 71

As the ford could only be crossed in single file, much time was lost before the other bank was reached, and the battery had long ago arrived when the regiments were at last able to continue the march on the other bank. From this we see that the shortest way is not always the quickest.

In the case of fords in particular, they should only be accepted as a means of passage in the arrangements for the march if they have been previously reconnoitred. If, in this case, the ford had been examined, the other road would certainly have been chosen for the brigade.

The 11th Brigade followed to the line Klein Blittersdorf-Bliesbolgen.

The 19th Dragoons had been ordered "to leave Saarbrücken at 8 a.m., reconnoitre by Spicheren on Forbach, and from there to patrol the left bank of the Saar, gain touch with the 6th Cavalry Division, and then rejoin the division."

This mission was completed without incident. At Auersmachern the 13th Uhlans took up the outpost line. The late Captain Schlick (3rd Squadron) had command of the outposts, according to memoranda left by him. A strong patrol led by him on Saargemünd, and accompanied by Lieutenants v. Kotze and Graf Königsmarck, caused the French garrison there great perturbation, and the party were hotly fired on, though without result. "A bivouac close by the town was alarmed, cavalry and artillery trotted back, and numerous patrols despatched in all directions ascertained that the enemy had retired on the road to Metz." According to the regimental diary, the patrols reported the enemy had retired to St. Avold. There is a report without date from the same day, or perhaps the next morning, which came from Captain v. Rosenberg, of the 13th

Aug. 7.

13th Uhlans before Saargemünd.

Aug. 7. Uhlans, who encountered half a division of the enemy in front of Wustweiler.

The 11th and 17th Hussars had also sent patrols on Saargemünd and Wölferdingen, and had found them occupied.

König's patrol.

In reference to this, the notes of the then Lieutenant Baron v. König, of the latter regiment, are of special interest, given from his diary and letters home to the author. I will quote the following:—

> "When the regiment reached Fechingen, Lieutenant v. König received the following order from his commanding officer:—
>
> "'Your object is to ascertain whether Saargemünd is occupied, as one of our main lines of advance runs through this place. Ride off with three men.'"

On his way, perhaps an hour short of Saargemünd, König met the 11th Hussars, who had found the town occupied. About midday he arrived close to the town, keeping under cover. The Saar bridge was barricaded, numbers of infantrymen were seen in the streets. König let his men fire on a squadron of chasseurs who apparently rode down to water; this caused the horsemen to beat a hasty retreat.

Since it was impossible to enter the town, he rode back some 1200 yards, and resolved to summon the town to surrender. He did so by writing on a message-card—

> "As the town of Saargemünd is barricaded, I cannot consider it open, and I will therefore bombard it, unless it is cleared within an hour.
>
> "König."

A landowner who was promised a good reward, or, on the other hand, a confiscation of his property, took the message into the town, and returned an

CAVALRY ON SERVICE 73

hour later with the burgomaster's assurance that the barricades should be removed, and that the French troops were leaving the town.

Aug. 7.

On this, König, taking the countryman with him as hostage, and leaving one man on the right bank of the river, went into the town, where the burgomaster, Baron de Geiger, soon appeared, and handed over his card as a sign that the town was taken.

Hundreds of men surrounded him in a threatening attitude; a further advance on the part of these few horsemen was impossible; he was lucky to be able to leave the town unhurt. König rejoined his regiment about 1 p.m. His commanding officer wrote on the card, "The Brunswick hussars place the town of Saargemünd at your Royal Highness's feet," and sent König, who had also reported to General v. Rheinbaben, off to Prince Frederick Charles, where he arrived towards 5 p.m.

General v. Rheinbaben sent the following telegram to Army Headquarters at 5.45. p.m. :—

> "In consequence of Lieutenant v. König's (Brunswick Hussars) report, I have ordered Lieut.-Colonel Rauch to occupy Saargemünd at once, and push vedettes towards Püttlingen and the railway line."

With reference to Rheinbaben's command of cavalry, it is noticeable that evidently no measures were initiated by him to discover where the enemy went to. Lieut.-Colonel v. Rauch took up his task very differently. At 11.30 p.m. he was able to report to Army Head Quarters from Saargemünd "that the enemy had retired on Püttlingen, followed by patrols," * and added that the inhabitants

17th Hussars before Saargemünd.

* The appearance of patrols near Ernstweiler, about 6 miles from Saargemünd, is testified by Frossard's book. In a report to the 13th Cavalry Brigade, Rauch expressly mentions the sending out of an officer's patrol.

Aug. 7. were talking of the approach of the French Guard Corps. Everything was by no means done that ought to have been done by the hussar colonel after the occupation of the town, else Rauch's reports would have been more detailed. The regiment formed the advance guard of an army, and its commander had thus important duties to fulfil.

The action of the commander of an advance guard cannot be better described than Napoleon has done in his " History of the Campaigns in Italy "—

> "General Steingel, a native of Alsace, was a distinguished Hussar officer; he had served under Dumouriez in his northern campaigns, and was skilful, intelligent, quick, combined the qualities of youth with those of a ripe age, and proved himself a real leader of advanced troops. Two or three days before his death he was the first to enter Leregno. The French general who followed him a few hours later found all arrangements that were necessary already prepared.
>
> "The defiles and fords had been reconnoitred, the messengers placed under supervision, the parson and the postmaster interrogated, communication with the inhabitants arranged, spies sent in various directions, the letters at the post-office seized (those which contained military intelligence translated and discussed), all measures taken for the formation of the supply magazines and for feeding the men " (vol. i. p. 394).

First of all it should have been ascertained what regiments had been quartered in and near Saargemünd. This could easily have been done by examining the inhabitants, and information would have thereby been acquired as to what units had retired here.* It may be taken for granted certainly that the letters, etc., were seized.

The German vedettes on the far side of Saargemünd, where the 1st Squadron had taken up the

* Compare, for example, the reports of the 15th Uhlans on August 8 and 9.

outpost line, were fired on at first by the mounted Jägers, who had been left behind; so the patrols could only advance after some time, which explains Rauch's late report on the direction of the enemy's retreat.

Aug. 7.

But these chasseurs, who obstructed the reconnaissance, ought to have been driven off, and this unimportant impediment cleared away. *Reconnaissance, after all, means fighting.*

The Germans found an abundance of stores in Saargemünd, as well as a whole railway train and four locomotives, which the French had abandoned in their hurried retreat.

Graf Droste, 11th Hussars, had also reported the retreat of the enemy to Püttlingen that same afternoon.

The reports of the enemy's retreat from Saargemünd had stated " on the road to Metz," " to Püttlingen," and " to St. Avold," thus hitting off the essential always correctly; for the army commanders wished above all to learn whether the enemy was moving westwards on Metz or perhaps southwards to join MacMahon's defeated corps.

It is surprising, if we consider the measures of the 5th Cavalry Division, that the leader, though he had collected the main portion of his command on the battle-field on the 7th, entertained no idea of following the beaten foe. He knew that two regiments of the 6th Cavalry Division had taken up the pursuit, and seems to have considered this sufficient, for at 8 a.m. he began the appointed march with the regiments assembled at the bivouac, " with the object of concentrating the division towards the left flank."

Comments on Rheinbaben's measures.

From a cavalry point of view, these measures are beyond comprehension.

The concentration was certainly desirable but

Aug. 7. by no means urgent, and should have been effected by a forward movement.

Moreover, there was no question of a concentration that evening, in order to make a combined advance the next day [see map], as the division was extended along a line of about nineteen miles, as the crow flies, and the commander had his quarters on the left flank. The division was left with a stream (which would certainly have to be crossed next day) between itself and the enemy, known to be still at Saargemünd.

The most pressing necessity was to hang on to the enemy, and do him as much injury as possible, instead of which the division turned away from him. That Prince Frederick Charles assumed that General v. Rheinbaben would himself also join in the pursuit on the 7th with his regiments is apparent from a communication sent from Army Head Quarters at Homburg to the Fourth Army Corps the same day, in which the victory at Spicheren is mentioned, and the following added: " The right wing of the 5th Cavalry Division and the 6th Cavalry Division, which advanced during the night. are consequently following the enemy."*

The concentration of the 5th Cavalry Division, to effect which efforts were made at such an inopportune moment, was not therefore based on

* Compare also Baron v. d. Goltz's "Operations of the Second Army, etc.," where it is stated: "The pursuit after Spicheren was to be carried out by the four brigades of General v. Rheinbaben, which had been assembled on the battle-field, etc., etc." It is further stated in a letter of the Prince to Moltke, dated the 7th, in which he refers to the victory of Spicheren: "Four cavalry brigades of the Second Army are pursuing the enemy to-day in that direction." The Prince also says in a postscript to a letter addressed to the 10th Corps: "I am, up to one p.m., without news about Saargemünd, as well as without news of the 3rd Corps and the four cavalry brigades under General v. Rheinbaben, which are pursuing the enemy by Forbach." What the revelation of the lamentable issue of this "pursuit" must have been to the Prince gives one food for thought.

some possibly "antiquated" order from superior authority. Aug. 7.

The Prince took it for granted that the cavalry divisions would play their part according to the situation, and was unfortunately in this case again the sole superior commander who thought as a cavalryman should think. The most effective measure would have been an advance of the brigades forming the right wing of the 5th Cavalry Division towards the line Püttlingen-Saargemünd, with the main strength moving by Cadenbronn; while the 6th Cavalry Division operated towards the line Püttlingen (exclusive)-St. Avold.

As the latter division was still under General v. Rheinbaben, the combined movement could have been directed by him. Such an operation would not have failed to produce its effect on the retreating enemy.

Even if, with our present knowledge of the situation, the 6th Cavalry Division was likely to come to a standstill opposite Castagny's Division, in its position at Bettingen (compare p. 68), the 5th Cavalry Division would, at any rate, have seriously threatened the retreat of the enemy's forces withdrawing from Saargemünd on Püttlingen, would have considerably increased the enemy's disorganization by an energetic pressure, and could have achieved great results.

The 3rd Cavalry Division (*vide* map) should, however, have been pushed forward to the line Bolchen-St. Avold.

Unity of purpose was unfortunately wanting in the operations of the cavalry, and this will always be wanting, in cases where such cavalry masses are not subordinated under an individual control.*

* It may be asserted that uniting cavalry divisions in this fashion temporarily under one commander can never produce the same results as would a permanent organization of this kind.

Aug. 7.

We need only allude to the measures adopted for the reconnaissance of Saargemünd, which was undertaken by the various commanders independently, and therefore involved a waste of strength, which was out of all proportion to the results obtained.

Measures of Royal Head Quarters and of Prince Frederick Charles.

Towards midday the General Officer Commanding Second Army had meanwhile received the news of the victory at Wörth. To the telegram announcing the victory General v. Moltke had added the remark that strong hostile forces were still remaining on the Saar, about the intentions of which the cavalry should bring news. A communication came in later from the Third Army saying that masses of the beaten French troops had, it was alleged, turned towards Bitsch, and that, if they did go there eventually, they would arrive on the 7th, and could come in touch with the left wing of the Second Army on the 8th.

Prince Frederick Charles immediately set himself to think of how he could deal a blow at these forces. He had at his disposal for this object the Fourth Army Corps as well as the 12th Cavalry Brigade, with the regiments which had temporarily joined the latter. The 12th Cavalry Brigade, which, as we have seen, had till now been separated from its division, had been during this period under the orders of the General Officer Commanding Fourth Army Corps for purposes of quartering, supply, etc.;* and it had, since its arrival at the frontier, been attached to the corps for this reason. It was now by Army Orders of the 7th expressly placed, till further orders, under the corps

---

* The 5th Cavalry Division, by order of July 22 from General Officer Commanding Second Army, had been attached to the Fourth Army Corps for supply, quartering, etc.; but the General Officer Commanding reserved for himself the right to dispose the Cavalry Division when operations were going to begin.

commander. The latter attached the 5th Dragoons to the 8th Division. The Prince had so early as on the morning of the 7th (in the letter from Homburg, quoted above) requested the General Officer Commanding Fourth Army Corps to direct General v. Bredow to extend his existing outpost line (Bliesbrücken-Schweigen) as far as Bliesbolgen.* He was frequently to send reports to Bliescastel, the new Army Head Quarters, and establish relay-posts thither. At 1 p.m. the Prince notified that—

Aug. 7.

> "A portion of the enemy beaten at Wörth is said to have gone back by Bitsch. An advance on Rohrbach, with cavalry and artillery on Lemberg and Lorenzen, is therefore intended. With this object the IVth Corps will advance to-day to the south of Wolmünster, and be at Rohrbach at latest by 8 a.m. to-morrow, the 12th Cavalry Brigade pushing beyond that place. The 2nd Guard Infantry Division will protect the corps from attack from Saargemünd, and be at Gross Rederching at 11 a.m., whilst the 12th Infantry Brigade † will be requested to co-operate with the corps on the left."

The march commenced at 5 p.m. The 8th Division reached Busweiler, the 7th Urbach, the advance guard (7th Dragoons) being pushed forward on Rohrbach. Bredow's brigade, leaving its outposts in their position, concentrated north of Rohrbach, and watched towards Saargemünd. The country around Bitsch proved to be free from the enemy, but strong forces had moved away in a southerly direction. The Bitsch-Saargemünd railway was broken up at Rohrbach, but it is not

---

* From this arrangement, by which the Saargemünd-Bliescastel high-road should be included in General v. Bredow's outpost line, it again appears that the Prince was far from assuming that General v. Rheinbaben, with his other brigades, would advance on the right bank of the Saar.

† Was in the vicinity of Landau.

Aug. 7. apparent with what aim this was done, for the enemy, being in such close proximity to strong hostile forces, would surely not think of using the line.

Useless destruction of railways.

In the beginning of this campaign railways were frequently destroyed, when, in the state of affairs prevailing, no inconvenience was caused to the enemy; while, on the contrary, disadvantages would accrue later to one's own people when the lines were wanted for their use. In this respect definite regulations, such as now appear in the "Field Service Regulations," paras. 518 and 519, were then wanting. A railway was often destroyed quite at will without any order. If a patrol came upon a railroad, then, without any further reflection, it generally tried at once to destroy it. At that time the cavalry had no suitable tools for the business, and no practice in carrying it out, and though these were really serious drawbacks on many occasions, one might almost call them extremely fortunate ones on others.

Touch is not regained.

As regards re-establishment of touch between Bredow's brigade and the enemy, nothing apparently was done on the 7th, and no attempt was made to rectify the past mistake, which would certainly have been possible.

The 5th Dragoons.

The 5th Dragoons had accompanied the artillery of the Fourth Army Corps, and when close in front of Hornbach they, as well as the 13th Dragoons, received the order to reach the Bitsch-Weissenburg road as soon as possible, and report quickly if any of MacMahon's troops were approaching, as it was anticipated they would do. Both regiments reached the road by Hanweiler without meeting any enemy, and three squadrons of the 5th reconnoitred Bitsch, going close up to the fortifications. They were shelled, and lost three men and four horses killed, six

CAVALRY ON SERVICE 81

men wounded. Only pickets were encountered in front of Bitsch. _{Aug. 7.}

As regards the enemy's movements, the map shows what points were reached by them at the end of the day. A few remarks will suffice to explain the general situation. _{Movements of the French.}

The Emperor Napoleon, upon the news of the loss of the battles at Wörth and Spicheren, had determined on the general retreat of the army from Lorraine upon Chalons. The 1st Corps (MacMahon), 5th (Failly), and the 7th (Douay), were to join there. The 2nd Corps, according to explicit French accounts, had, followed by some "Uhlan patrols," reached Püttlingen between 3 and 4 p.m. by Saargemünd, where it had rested awhile. Frossard had chosen this line of retreat in order to clear the front of the 3rd Corps, and in the hope that Bazaine would threaten the Germans in flank, while he did the same in front. The news reached him at night in Saargemünd of the loss of the battle of Wörth, and now, apprehensive of his retreat, he gave orders for the march on Püttlingen, and told Lapasset's brigade * to follow him and take up the rearguard duties. The brigade had apparently halted between Wustweiler and Ernstweiler, and occupied the former place—Rosenberg's report. Prussian patrols (4th Squadron, 8th Hussars? see p. 65) followed meanwhile to Ernstweiler, presumably coming from a northerly direction.† Juniac's Cavalry Brigade also arrived during the course of the day in Püttlingen. Montaudon's

---

* Belonged to the 5th Corps, which latter had given way to the south of Bitsch, leaving the brigade behind in Saargemünd.

† Frossard and Dick de Lonlay. In the first edition of this book it was assumed that these patrols had belonged to the 4th Cuirassiers; this, however, appears not to have been the case, as the report from the Cuirassiers is dated the 8th. The main thing, though, is that Prussian patrols did appear at Ernstweiler on the 7th.

Aug. 7. division, starting from near Cadenbronn, reached Püttlingen already between 9 and 10 a.m., observing as well at Gebenhausen enemy's patrols following them up.* Metmann's Division, which, as already shown, had lost part of its train at Rossbrücken, arrived at Püttlingen towards 2 p.m. Castagny's Division, which had left their baggage at Püttlingen the day before, moved there in the night to pick it up, marched forward again, and then occupied, as we saw, the heights by Bettingen, in front of St. Avold, in order to cover the retirement through the defile of St. Avold, as well as the trains of the 2nd Corps moving back on Püttlingen.†

The Germans did not disturb this further retreat, " but their patrols hastened to occupy the points vacated by the French." Decaen's Division had remained in St. Avold. The 2nd and 4th Dragoons watched the roads to Kreutzwald, Spittel, and Karlingen. Forton's Reserve Cavalry Division had moved to Marienthal ‡ in support of Castagny's Division, and towards evening returned to its bivouac at Folschweiler.

Of the 4th Corps, Cissey's Division reached Bolchen at 2.30 p.m., followed by Prussian patrols, and Lorencez's Division Helsdorf. Grenier's Division, in order to join the 3rd Corps, to which it had been temporarily attached, was directed on St. Avold, and at 8 p.m. occupied the heights on the other side of the town and Klein-Ebersweiler. The Guard Corps marched from near Bingen to Lubeln.

Results of the German Reconnaissance.

The events depicted as happening on the 7th and a glance at the map clearly show that touch had been established, even that forenoon, with

* Montaudon and Dick de Lonlay.
† *Revue Militaire*, 1900.
‡ *Vide* p. 61, note.

strong bodies of the enemy at the defiles of Marienthal and Ober-Homburg, also that the march of Castagny's and Forton's Divisions had been reported. The further occupation of St. Avold, as well as the retreat of the enemy in the morning, on Saargemünd, and from there towards Püttlingen in the afternoon, had become known; and further, that Karlingen, Spittel, and Ham were clear, and Püttlingen and Cappel occupied.

Aug. 7.

Much hard work had been done. Patrols had pushed far to the west and south; and apart from the failure of the higher leading which we have discussed, real exception, as far as can be seen, can only be taken as regards the action of a squadron each of the 15th Uhlans and 6th Cuirassiers, which reconnoitred from Spicheren on the left flank.

The furthest points that can be proved to have been reached by German patrols on the 7th were: in front of Buschborn and Porcelette, in Karlingen-Spittel, Merlenbach, Farschweiler, in front of Cappel, Gebenhausen, Püttlingen, and Ernstweiler.

Our account has shown that the critic of the performances of the cavalry on this day finds much to take exception to with good reason. The causes must be looked for, generally, in the training, as was emphasized in the Preface.

The failures of Bredow's brigade on the extreme left wing have already been alluded to, and it will be seen that the re-establishment of touch was not effected with Failly's corps till many days later—a fact which proves how difficult it is in reconnaissance to repair mistakes once made.

If even only the written communications entered in the records had reached the higher commanders, they would have had sufficient information of the rest of the French corps to come to the proper conclusions, but the transmission of the

Aug. 7. reports shows the greatest defect. For is it not a fact that the 13th Infantry Division, which had been most excellently informed* by its cavalry regiment, did not forward the most important of them at all?

So it naturally follows that the General Officer Commanding Second Army was far from satisfied with the reports that had reached him.

Blame attaches to the authorities concerned, not to the arm, which those authorities did not understand the use of, and which, nevertheless, when they did use it, performed its work in a satisfactory, and, in some instances, even in an admirable manner.

* The Division knew that the enemy had retired on Saargemünd and thence on Metz, that columns were moving on St. Avold, that this place was still occupied, and it heard of the advance of Castagny's and Forton's Divisions, and of their occupying a position.

The performances of the 8th Hussars on August 7 indicate what could have been expected from the German Cavalry.

CHAPTER II

A GENERAL advance of the First and Second Armies might have been expected on this date. But the information which had reached their Head Quarters—as we have seen, many important reports never came in—was not sufficient to establish a clear view of the enemy's dispositions, and, moreover, certain circumstances had caused the mass of the troops to halt, or had led to their employment in a direction in which no enemy was encountered.

Aug. 8.

Expectant attitude of the First and Second Armies.

The First Army received instructions to remain halted, to occupy the heights of Spicheren, and to guard against a possible attack. Since no proper use of the cavalry had been made—the 3rd Cavalry Division in particular remaining absolutely inactive —that freedom of action which only cavalry can assure to the commander had been lost, and the result was anxious hesitation; for it is only full knowledge that begets bold determinations (compare note 1 on p. 86). Nothing had been done towards keeping the enemy's forces in observation at St. Avold, or in gaining accurate information about the arrival of fresh hostile bodies from Metz. Amongst the populace general rumours were current of the arrival of the corps of Guards (see p. 74). A further advance of the First Army was moreover not projected at headquarters, for the reason that a general right wheel of the three German armies was to be carried out, and the First Army was to form the pivot of it.

Aug. 8.

General v. Steinmetz was naturally not restricted in any way in the use of his cavalry. On the contrary, the remark in Moltke's telegram that had come in—"Orders for the further advance can only follow when the cavalry have rendered more definite information about the enemy's situation"—ought to have been an inducement for an energetic employment of the numerous cavalry available.*

But a comparison of the maps of August 7 and 8 shows that no forward movement of the cavalry occurred, although meanwhile the 1st Cavalry Division had arrived, with the exception of the 9th Uhlans, who still were further in rear.

The officers' patrols in touch with the enemy from the 3rd Cavalry Division, however, did their duty.

Lieutenant Ramin's patrol.

Lieutenant v. Ramin, 14th Uhlans, had not let the enemy's camp at Tromborn out of his sight. He noted how camp had been struck in the morning, and that the French had marched off in the direction of Metz. The Uhlans followed at once to Bolchen, where they saw a large supply column halted in the streets. As sufficient infantry were with it, no attempt could be made to seize it, and, moreover, the limit fixed for their advance was now reached.

We often see, during these days, patrols capture spoils such as these and get them safely home.

The attempt to capture trophies which form a more tangible proof of bold enterprise than the best information, is an alluring one, but it must be

* In a letter of Royal Head Quarters to those of the Second Army of 11 p.m. August 7, it is said: "As the cavalry has not yet ascertained whether the enemy has marched from Forbach and Saargemünd on Metz, or to the south, the First Army has received orders to remain in its position to-morrow and to occupy the heights of Spicheren.

remarked that it diverts the patrol in most cases from its important objective, and at least involves a weakening of it by the men who escort the booty back. Lieutenant v. Ramin, as related already, was induced, two days previously, to lose touch with the enemy, merely in order to bring back a few waggons.

Aug. 8.

Lieutenant v. Ramin reported at 3 p.m. from Ittersdorf, whither he had retired and thereby given up touch with the enemy, as follows:—

> "Marched this morning early to Bolchen. The order to advance on Busendorf was brought to me in Teterchen by Lieutenant v. Papen. I rode by Wolwingen, Brettnach, Alzingen, to Busendorf, commandeered here 57 cwt. of oats, 3 casks of wine, some bacon and sausage. Large camping grounds of the enemy empty. They are said to have marched to Metz. Patrols who had gone straight to Bolchen reported that a supply column with infantry escort stood in the streets. Must rest to-morrow. Will go to Thionville the day after."

A strange combination of patrol and foraging party seems to have occurred here. He makes particular mention, too, of the intention of having a rest-day. Now, for a patrol there is *no* rest-day. The men will need one in the most exceptional cases only; besides, as already remarked, if necessary the men can be relieved, and even should a few horses succumb to exhaustion, they will have been paid for over and over again. The divisional commander sent on Lieutenant v. Ramin's report at 5.30 p.m., same date, to Army Head Quarters, with the remark that this officer had received instructions to proceed further on the Busendorf-Metz main road, and Lieutenant v. Papen, 5th Uhlans, with fifteen horses, to advance on the Bolchen-Metz road. Ramin's report was telegraphed at 8 p.m. to his Majesty.

Aug. 8.

Papen's patrol.

Lieutenant v. Papen-Koenigen had received orders from the divisional commander—

> "To advance with 15 horses from Derlen on Bolchen, to watch the Metz-Bolchen road, and reconnoitre as far as possible towards Metz."

He reported at 4.30 p.m. from Teterchen—

> "I met Lieutenant v. Ramin about 2 p.m. between Tromborn and Teterchen, and learnt from him that French troops had retired south-east towards Ham. When I reached Bolchen, where two divisions * had camped for the night, my advanced point met at the exit of the village a hostile cavalry patrol of 12 men, which retreated at full speed to Buschborn, after firing their carbines at us. I followed them for a good distance, but could not overtake them, as they had a considerable start. According to the accounts of the country folk, the troops are said to have departed for that place at 11 o'clock. [The account was not correct.] From Bolchen to Tennschen I found nothing of the enemy except a few small, deserted camping grounds. Owing to the tired state of the horses, I went back to Teterchen, and had the men and horses fed. I shall spend the night in Ober-Felsberg. I have sent to Saarlouis three waggon loads of hay, which I found in the market-place at Bolchen, and which were probably intended for the French troops."

Comments on Papen's patrol.

On this report the following comments must be made:—

1. It is strange that in v. Ramin's report there is no account of the march of French troops on Ham which v. Papen mentions.

2. The account besides is very indefinite; even days and *dates* are wanting.

Probably August 6 was meant, the day on which Grenier's Division had taken that direction. It can be taken as certain that on August 8 no

---

* They were Cissey's and Lorencez's Divisions.

French troops of any importance marched in that direction.   Aug. 8.

On the night of the 7th–8th, however, Cissey's Division had marched on the road from Bolchen to Tennschen, and at 6 a.m. on the 8th had arrived east of Tennschen, where it camped.* We may take it for granted that this tallies on the whole.

3. The obvious error in the report, that the patrol had found nothing of the enemy at Tennschen, can only be explained by either the patrol leader being mistaken as to the place, or else that he personally had not ridden so far forward, and that a smaller party went on and made the mistake.

4. The fact, reported by him, that two divisions had camped at Bolchen till the evening of the 7th, is correct. That the patrol failed to determine in what direction these divisions had retired must be held as an omission of duty, as such large bodies of troops leave behind them unmistakable traces of their march.

5. In the pursuit of the enemy's patrol the officer seems to have allowed himself to be completely diverted from the direction assigned to him, which was a mistake. Every patrol must keep their main objective in view under any circumstances whatever. They must never let the direction assigned to them drop out of their mind. Any chase of an enemy's patrol is reprehensible; a few men should be sent after it, to ascertain what becomes of it, and to find out whether any stronger bodies of hostile troops are in its neighbourhood. If the patrol leader finds important traces of the enemy which lead in a different direction to that assigned to him, he must, of course, follow it, but must split up his patrol, and let the remainder follow the original direction.

* Acording to Rousset and Dick de Lonlay.

Aug. 8.

I have already laid stress on the fact that the bringing in of supplies is calculated to divert the patrol from their duty, and this may occur to a still further degree in the pursuit of the enemy's patrols, especially when, as in this case, the patrols are turned aside from their proper direction.

Such a proceeding seems correct only in very special circumstances, where it is of peculiar importance to make prisoners, and where such a duty is specially notified.

6. Altogether it must be regarded as certain that the patrol did not get much beyond Bolchen in a westerly direction. It is also out of the question that, in face of the enemy's division camped closely behind the Nied, it should have crossed the river and have reached Tennschen.

7. The distant retirement to Ober Felsberg to take up quarters for the night must be regarded as wrong, not only from the point of view of reconnaissance, but also on account of sparing the horses.

On the other hand, it stands to reason that a patrol in touch with the enemy must look out for a suitable resting-place for the night where it can be as safe as is possible, and that a slight retreat may be made for that purpose.

In Graf Groeben's minute, 8.30 p.m., forwarding Lieutenant v. Papen's report, the following occurs :—

> ". . . Captain v. Hymmen proposes to advance to-day to the right of St. Avold. All the same, I am sending another officer to-morrow at daybreak by Lauterbach towards Buschborn, to gain definite information of the whereabouts of the divisions. The Uhlan who will bring the report has been within four hours of Metz, and can possibly give further verbal information."

Papen's report was telegraphed to His Majesty at 11 p.m.

CAVALRY ON SERVICE 91

The error in this despatch had this very serious result, that General v. Steinmetz, as well as Royal Head Quarters, assumed the enemy's left flank to be at Buschborn,* as is shown by the sketches in the war records, drawn out by Moltke, of the positions of the French corps on August 7, 8, and 9.† {Aug. 8.}

The outposts had reported at 12.45 a.m. from Karlingen as follows :— {Outpost reports.}

> "Patrols sent to Diesen and Ham report that, according to the accounts of several inhabitants, an enemy's camp at Ham was evacuated at 4 a.m. this morning. Patrol saw the place of the camp. It pointed to infantry and cavalry; and several regiments had clearly camped there." ‡

From Lauterbach [no time given]—

> "St. Avold is occupied by the enemy. An outlying picket stands on the high-road this side of St. Avold. East of the town lies a camp, in which there appear to be two infantry regiments. Single cavalrymen have also been seen. Town is said to be barricaded. Inhabitants may not go in or out;—this the report of a patrol which was near St. Avold."

It can be seen from all these reports that the patrols, sent out by the General Officer Commanding 3rd Cavalry Division in the right direction, had only partially learnt the enemy's dispositions. How much more thorough would the information have been if the division had followed in support of these patrols. Its leader

---

* Every young officer will recognize from this incident the importance of his reconnoitring duties, and the high responsibility he incurs.

† *Vide* Moltke's "Military Correspondence," Part III. vol. i. p. 207.

‡ Grenier's Division, on its march from Teterchen to Buschborn on August 6, had halted for some time at Ham unter Varsberg, in order to let its trains pass through, and had cooked and fed there; hence these traces of a bivouac. (Compare also the report of Corporal Gabriel, p. 65.) The accounts of the inhabitants, as here reported, must have referred to stragglers only, unless deception was intended.

Aug. 8. had certainly received no order to do so, but it was his business to take the initiative. Our Regulations now lay it down clearly *that the cavalry leader must never wait for orders.*

Thiele's patrol.

Of the divisional cavalry regiments two reconnaissances of the 12th Dragoons are specially worthy of note. Major v. Thiele, a squadron leader, went out in the direction of St. Avold. He had been given personal instructions by Lieut.-General v. Stülpnagel, who explained to him in giving him the situation, 11 p.m. on August 7, that Prince Frederick Charles had not received sufficient intelligence from the 6th Cavalry Division, and that the Prince had specially directed that he, v. Thiele, should reconnoitre, and render a report by 7 a.m. on the 8th on the direction in which the enemy was effecting his retreat.

Thiele chose the fifteen best horses from his own squadron, while the other squadrons each provided five picked ones; and with these thirty horses he started away at 2.30 a.m. from the bivouac at Saarbrücken towards St. Avold. His route led by Forbach, Rossbrück, where he passed through the outposts of the 6th Cavalry Division, and then by Cocheren to Bening-les-St. Avold (the German " Beningen "). Arrived here, the major, who had lost his map during the night's ride, saw that this was not the St. Avold he was looking for; he had, besides, found no traces of the enemy, so turned back to the great main road to reach the town of St. Avold. Had he kept on his way to Bettingen, he would shortly have struck on the enemy; in fact, he would have met Castagny's whole division, which was camped between Genweiler and Bettingen on the top of the Siel-Berg. [See the General Staff map, and map for August 7.]

The darkness of the night, and the fact of the

French outposts being probably pushed out a very short way to the front—the pickets were probably in the Bettingen valley and some sentries on the hill—explain how he failed to discover the proximity of the enemy. He was unwilling to take along with him a few captured stragglers, as they were a hindrance to him in his expedition; but he ascertained that the retreat of the large mass of the enemy had followed the great northerly road.

He now went on at highest speed by Merlenbach to Niederhomburg. On the way from here to Oberhomburg an enemy's cavalry post burst suddenly out of a farm—Bach-Mühle most probably —and retired in the greatest hurry towards St. Avold. Major v. Thiele describes his further advance as follows:—

> "As I was fired on, on my left flank, out of the woods, I intended to reconnoitre in that direction; but I suddenly heard numerous cavalry calls after the hostile cavalry party had passed under the railway crossing. I was now convinced that a large bivouac—perhaps on the Mittenberg—had been alarmed.
>
> "I hurried forward with the patrol, and, as soon as I had crossed the railway, saw, on the northern slopes of the Mittenberg, what appeared to be a large body of cavalry in the act of moving off. Its outposts had been placed close to the road, above it, so that they could not harm me, owing to the steepness of the slope and the masonry work.
>
> "My task was not yet finished. It was broad daylight, and I knew that here strong bodies of the enemy were just moving off.
>
> "I had as yet obtained no view of the west and south slopes of the Mittenberg. To get this, I hurried, after having arrived about 400 yards west of the level crossing, up to some infantry battalions, which were moving at the double towards Neumühle, along the Saargemünd road. They had apparently not yet noticed my party. Three of the enemy's guns moved into

Aug. 8.

94 CAVALRY ON SERVICE

Aug. 8.

position on the hill south of Neumühle; and now at 200 paces the infantry wheeled into line, and opened a rapid but ineffectual fire, as they fired too high. My party now, on my word of command, hastened back at the fastest pace, and it was only at the longest range that the enemy's fire became dangerous. My horse was wounded, and several dragoons lightly scratched.

"On approaching Oberhomburg, I saw a large number of men close to the road, and at once made my men walk, in order that my retirement might not appear to be a flight. I called out in French to my own men [N.B.—None of them understood a word of French], 'Look above there, at the head of our main body, and there (pointing north over Oberhomburg) are our Uhlans already coming!'

"It had the desired effect, and I soon had left the difficult country behind me, without any further trouble. Then I handed over the command to a sergeant, to bring the patrol quietly back, while I, to report, finished my ride at top speed with one orderly. At 7.45 a.m. I handed my report in, personally, to his Royal Highness, Prince Frederick Charles. I myself counted 13 French battalions, as far as I remember, while the sergeant and a dragoon said that they counted 17. The position of the cavalry on the northern slope of the Mittenberg could not be clearly made out."

A short written report is to be found in the records of the Head Quarters of the Second Army.

The official "History of the War" mentions this clever and successful reconnaissance ride in very favourable terms in Part I., p. 414.

According to Dick de Lonlay's account, the infantry, against which the patrol advanced, appear to have been the 15th Jäger battalion. The map for August 7 gives information of the enemy's troops which v. Thiele met, and confirms the accuracy of his report.

Comments on Thiele's patrol.

The patrol is instructive in many points. It shows how names that sound alike—and in France

CAVALRY ON SERVICE

there are many exactly the same, which have some addition which distinguishes them—can easily cause mistakes, and need particular care in this wise.

To get a view of the enemy's forces, the patrol dashed boldly forward, instead of making a flank movement, as our doctrines lay down.

In this case, however, a turning movement was impossible, owing to the deep cutting of the road, as shown in the map, and owing to the heights too, being partially held. The fact of the patrol coming out with so little loss in their advance, shows that surprise greatly lessens the danger. The French cavalry, too, were apparently so taken in that no pursuit was thought of. Retreat through so easily barred a defile was risky; and, if the bluff employed had not been successful, might have been attended by serious loss. The loss of touch after the reconnaissance had been carried out, was such a common occurrence during these days, that I will say no more about it. This state of things was caused by the want of instruction at that time with regard to the requirements of reconnaissance. The patrol had to, as it did, escape in a hurry, out of range of the enemy's effective fire; but, as it had not been followed, it could have faced about in the neighbourhood of Merlenbach-Beningen, and continued to observe the retreating enemy from some high point. Such, for instance, was the Siel-Berg, which seems peculiarly suitable.

The patrol of Captain Krell, 12th Dragoons, also thirty strong, had been sent in a southerly direction, and went towards the Blies river by Brebach and Klein-Bliedersdorf. As the bridge over the Blies at Saargemünd had been destroyed, the leader swam the river with half his patrol, and so reached Saargemünd, which the 17th Hussars had just occupied.

Aug. 8.

Krell's patrol.

Aug. 8.

The despatches of Thiele and Krell were sent off to Head Quarters of the Second Army at 8.15 a.m. In their memorandum accompanying these despatches the Head Quarters of the Third Army Corps concluded that the French had retired, part by Saargemünd on Püttlingen, part by Forbach and Homburg on St. Avold, and that the last-named road in particular was crowded with baggage.

Colonel v. Alvensleben's task.

The reports forwarded by the 6th Cavalry Division on August 7, as we have seen, had not satisfied Army Head Quarters.

In order to gain clearer information about the enemy's troops, especially at St. Avold, Duke William of Mecklenburg issued the following order from Forbach early on August 8 to Major-General v. Grüter :—

"1. Colonel v. Alvensleben, with three squadrons, will advance to St. Avold, if possible occupy the place, push forward patrols towards Falkenberg and Lixing, keep touch on the right with the First Army, whose advanced posts are at Kärlingen. If it is of any use, he may cut the railway and telegraph at St. Avold.

"2. The squadron of the 15th Uhlans [the 3rd—Author], hitherto posted between Forbach and Blittersdorf, will advance to Metzingen, keeping touch on the left with the 5th Cavalry Division, which is to be informed of these measures by the nearest regiment, the 19th Dragoons.

"3. To establish communication between Metzingen and St. Avold a squadron of the 3rd Uhlans (the 5th squadron was detailed) will go to Pfarr-Ebersweiler, and push forward strong parties to Cappel and Püttlingen; and towards the latter place the squadron at Metzingen must also patrol. The direction in which the enemy is retiring is to be ascertained, in what strength he is at St. Avold, whether and how strongly the heights there, as well as whether Püttlingen and Cappel are occupied. The remainder of the brigade will remain in bivouac at Morsbach. Relay posts are to be established at short distances on the three roads. The greatest activity is urged, in order to regain the lost touch * with the enemy at all cost, and to keep it."

Aug. 8.

Captain v. Treskow, the adjutant of the division, according to the account which he gave me, had solicited this task for his own regiment, the 15th Uhlans, and had informed Colonel v. Alvensleben, when transmitting these orders, that Head Quarters had news that St. Avold was occupied in strength, but could not yet discern whether the parts of the French army, which were still split up in separate camps, intended to concentrate southwards towards Strassburg or towards Metz.

Since this was the preliminary condition for all further operation orders, it would not matter how many horses the colonel should lose.

The measures must be regarded as answering the purpose, but in the light of to-day we may well ask the question why the entire division was not employed to solve the problem.

The division reported the measures taken to Head Quarters, and added, undoubtedly on account of Colonel v. Alvensleben's report, which we give later on, "that Karlingen was unoccupied, that, on the other hand, the heights of St. Avold were occupied in considerable strength by a hostile force of all arms. That Pfarr-Ebersweiler was unoccupied. That prisoners of the 32nd and 66th Infantry Regiments affirmed that the enemy who had been defeated at Forbach had retired a small part to St. Avold, and the main force to Püttlingen. That traces were found everywhere of the extreme demoralization of Frossard's corps."

* As has already been explained, it cannot be said that " touch was lost" here on August 7, though there was no clear conception about the distribution of the enemy's forces.

H

98 CAVALRY ON SERVICE

Aug. 8.

This report reached Head Quarters of the Second Army at 10.30 p.m., and was calculated to give a pretty clear view of the situation.

The 15th Uhlans.

Colonel v. Alvensleben, immediately on receipt of the order, started away with his three squadrons on St. Avold. Towards 11 a.m., when the regiment neared the point on the direct road to the town, where the Oberhomburg-St. Avold road cuts the railway, the colonel, who had ridden forward, found the road, about 800 yards west of Neumühle, blocked by trenches and occupied, and halted the regiment. [See the General Staff map.] A flank patrol moving by Neumühle to Klein-Ebersweiler found this road also barred, and was turned back by the fire of a "grand-garde." The staff then rode to the slope between the two roads south of Neumühle, just high enough for them to overlook the nearest part of the plateau without being exposed to view. Here they found themselves at once within range of two Grande-Gardes. Having observed all this, it was clear that an advance against the enemy's main position and the turning of its flank could only be attempted from Oberhomburg, and not from here.

So the squadrons returned to that place, while the staff compelled a railway official, whose patriotic objections had to be overcome by a picket rope and the drawing of a pistol, to conduct them to the Mittenberg (marked 320), along safe forest tracks.

Here, on the edge of the wood just east of the railway, the colonel and his staff found themselves right in front of the enemy's outposts, and there gained an extensive view.

Upon this, Colonel v. Alvensleben wrote the first report at 2 p.m.* to the 6th Cavalry Division, which ran thus:—

---

* Considering the general situation, it seems that this message is timed considerably too late, and that it ought to read 12 noon.

CAVALRY ON SERVICE   99

"The heights of St. Avold are occupied for action. Four battalions, in first line, are posted on the Kreutzberg,* from the quarry (Stbr. on map) to the railway at Klein-Ebersweiler. The road to Forbach is enfiladed from the heights of La Carrière by entrenchments, behind which skirmishers are lying. The heights north of St. Avold are similarly occupied.

"A battery is posted south of La Carrière. A squadron is about to turn St. Avold, to reach the roads to Metz and Nancy at Lubeln. A second squadron has been directed on Püttlingen."

Aug. 8.

This report was presented at 8 p.m. to the Head Quarters of the Third Army Corps, to which the 6th Cavalry Division had been meantime attached, as we shall further see, and was sent on by wire to Head Quarters of Second Army.

However, the special task assigned to the various squadrons and their separate advance was not carried out.

Whilst the squadrons were feeding, news came through an inhabitant, who had been brought in, that the French troops had suddenly marched out of St. Avold.

The three squadrons could now remain together in direct touch with the enemy, and close at their heels.

In St. Avold it appeared that Marshal Bazaine, who hitherto had been there with his Head Quarters, was retiring by Lubeln on Metz.

After the advanced squadron, at the Hecken Wald, beyond St. Avold, in a short chase with a few men of the leading troop, had captured the only French patrol †—5 dragoons—which had up till now been seen, they came up to the enemy west of Lubeln at the St. Dominik Hof.

* The heights immediately east of the town; not named on the Staff map.
† According to Dick de Lonlay, it was not a patrol, but a N.C.O.'s post of the 2nd Dragoons, which they had forgotten to relieve.

Aug. 8.

Here the rearguard infantry, step by step, with tiers of fire, had occupied the road which, devoid of any cover, rises in a zigzag, while a cavalry regiment and several batteries crowned the heights above it.

The squadrons of the main body went behind shelter not far from Drei-Haüser, the advanced guard squadron behind the Kastel-Berg, and reconnoitring patrols went forward.

From this hill, where the colonel was watching the enemy, some artillery could have decimated this sadly exposed rearguard in no time, and have chased it away.

According to Dick de Lonlay, it was Grenier's Division which covered the retreat, halted east of Zimmingen, and deployed for action in expectation of attack.* It was only when convinced that nothing but Uhlans confronted them that at 6 p.m. the troops, on Bazaine's order, continued the retreat over the German Nied.

When the enemy evacuated the position of St. Dominik, and retired along the Metz road towards Möhringen, the regimental staff rode over the Finselinger Berg to the Lubelner Berg, while the regiment followed along the road.

On this occasion Colonel v. Alvensleben, who had, as usual, ridden far in advance of the regiment, reconnoitring with only a weak escort, was pounced on from the Bambesch wood by a troop of the enemy's dragoons. They pursued him for a short distance in extended order, and he only escaped by

---

* Probably the intention of allowing the trains to get a start, as they were in peril and always proved such disagreeable impedimenta in these retrograde movements, contributed to this deployment. If the trains are not directed judiciously, it may happen that the troops have to sacrifice themselves for their waggons. In reference to this, it is recommended to study vol. 17 of the "Kriegsgeschichtliche Einzelschriften," *e.g.* p. 466.

jumping a considerable ditch, which the Frenchmen stopped at. The colonel was known as a first-class horseman across country, and mounted, as a rule, on thoroughbreds.

Aug. 8.

The enemy prevented any further reconnaissances beyond St. Gangulf. At 5 p.m. Colonel v. Alvensleben sent the following report to the 6th Cavalry Division, apparently from the Kastel-Berg, on the recommencement of the march of the French rearguard from St. Dominik:—

> "Enemy left St. Avold in the afternoon, and retired towards Metz. I am following with three squadrons. Towards evening I return with two squadrons to St. Avold. The remainder to keep in touch with the enemy. A prisoner from the 4th Artillery Regiment stated that the 3rd Corps (Bazaine's) had been about St. Avold, and in particular the 81st, 95th, 62nd, 51st Regiments. Captain v. Leipziger, 3rd Uhlans, reports from Büdingen that the place is clear of the enemy, also Püttlingen, which was evacuated this morning. The traces of the retreat point towards Metz."

The report reached the 6th Cavalry Division at 6.45 p.m., the Third Army Corps at 10 p.m., and from there was forwarded to Head Quarters of Second Army.

Captain v. Ploetz, of the 3rd Squadron, moving from Metzingen by Lixing, had gained touch with the retreating enemy at Hellimer at 6.45 p.m.; and at 7.35 p.m. had found an extended French camp of all arms at Gross-Tänchen.* He reported direct to the brigade.

* In the camp lay Lapasset's brigade of the 2nd Corps, pushed forward as a rearguard towards Hellimer, and further back still the rest of the 2nd Corps. When the Uhlans appeared the cry was heard, "The Prussians are coming!" Then ensued a *confusion épouvantable*. The corps was afraid of being attacked the next morning, and therefore continued its retreat in the night. The 3rd Squadron of the 15th Uhlans had this day become really enterprising, in contrast to their dilatory attitude on August 7.

Aug. 8.

As darkness came on, and it had been noticed that the enemy had gone into camp on the left bank of the German Nied, the colonel ordered the retirement into quarters at St. Avold of the squadrons which had reached Zwei-Häuser with their advance guard, and Dominik with the main body. St. Avold was reached about 9 p.m., with patrols towards Püttlingen, Gross-Tänchen, and Falkenberg, while the 5th Squadron remained on outpost at Lubeln. The regiment always kept to the same practice, that is, the main body were allowed to retire into quarters at night, so far as it was in the colonel's power, to maintain their strength unimpaired, with the result that the whole regiment was never exposed to the weakening influence of a bivouac, except in a few exceptional cases, during the campaign.

The colonel, while reconnoitring south of the town, had already ridden into it alone from the west, had gained information from the burgomaster, and ordered billets for the regiment.

Captain v. Rosenberg, 5th Squadron, bivouacked between St. Dominik and Lubeln, with vedettes on the line Zimmingen-Baumbiedersdorf, and patrolled towards Memersbronn, Dorweiler, and Trittlingen.

Leipziger's (5th) squadron, 3rd Uhlans.

Leipziger's (5th) squadron of the 3rd Uhlans had received instructions to get communication with the 5th Cavalry Division, to ascertain the enemy's retreat southwards by patrols, and find out in particular if he had already evacuated Püttlingen and Cappel.

Lieutenant v. Ploetz's patrol to Püttlingen came on the enemy just in front of this place as they were leaving camp in a south-westerly direction. It was fired on, and ascertained that two infantry and two [artillery regiments had

stayed about that place as yet in the morning. A Aug. 8.
prisoner was captured.

Lieutenant v. Ebart's patrol to Cappel had found the place unoccupied, overtook the enemy for the first time beyond Büdingen, found Vahl-Ebersing and Lellingen unoccupied, and brought in nine stragglers as prisoners.

Captain v. Leipziger had reported to the 6th Cavalry Division at noon, at 3 p.m., and at 6 p.m.

The 3 p.m. despatch ran as follows:—

> "Place (?). Lieutenant Ebart found Barst clear of the enemy—2 p.m. The French marched away to Metz and Nancy this morning. Two prisoners of the 4th Artillery Regiment taken. According to their statement, they left Püttlingen this morning, which was occupied by two infantry regiments and two cavalry regiments (4th and the 11th)."

The originals of the despatches are no longer in the War records.*

Colonel v. Alvensleben, in a 10 p.m. despatch, which cannot be found, gave the further important information that the 2nd Corps (Frossard's) had not marched by St. Avold, but south of it.

The services of the advanced detachments of the 6th Cavalry Division must be characterized as quite exceptional and worthy of imitation.

In a report of the division, sent in at 9 a.m., which is to be found in the Second Army Head

---

* According to the Diary of the 6th Cavalry Division, Captain v. Leipziger reported at noon, that the country between Saargemünd and St. Avold was clear of the enemy, and that there was a French camp at St. Avold; at 6 p.m., that Lieutenant v. Ebart had reached Vahl-Ebersing and Lixingen south of St. Avold, and that he had found bivouacs which had just then been deserted; at 6.30 p.m., Büdingen is clear of the enemy, the French have withdrawn to Metz; at 6.45 p.m., Lieutenant v. Ploetz gained touch with the enemy at Hellimer; Saaralbe is clear of the enemy; at 7.35 p.m., west of Hellimer, in the direction of Gross-Tänchen, there is a camp of cavalry and infantry. Therefore plenty of reports!

Aug. 8. Quarters records, the result is summarized as follows:—

"1. St. Avold evacuated.

"2. Bazaine's retreat towards Metz.

"3. His rearguard, six battalions and two batteries, once more took up position at dusk at Lubeln.

"4. Colonel v. Alvensleben captured prisoners from the 2nd Dragoons (Ladmirault's corps), from the 19th Infantry Regiment (Bazaine's corps), and from the 98th Infantry Regiment (Ladmirault's corps).

"5. Captain v. Leipziger captured prisoners from 7th Infantry Regiment (Bazaine's corps), 63rd Infantry Regiment (Frossard's corps), 68th Infantry Regiment (Failly's corps), 97th Infantry Regiment (Failly's corps), 15th Jäger Battalion (Bazaine's corps).

"6. Bazaine was still in St. Avold yesterday.

"7. Frossard has not retired on St. Avold."

The attitude of Bazaine's corps on this day produced on the Prussian cavalrymen the impression of a predetermined but intentionally dilatory retreat.

5th Cavalry Division.

Early on August 8 an order from the Army Head Quarters reached the 5th Cavalry Division, in accordance with which the distribution of the 6th Cavalry Division, under the orders of General v. Rheinbaben, was withdrawn. Bredow's brigade was attached to the Fourth Army Corps, and General v. Rheinbaben was directed to advance with the other two brigades by way of Saargemünd towards Püttlingen, and put out outposts on the line Püttlingen-Saaralbe.

The divisional leader had intended this movement previous to the arrival of the order. The division began its advance at 6.15 a.m. The 11th Brigade used the fords across the Saar, that is to say, the 13th Uhlans and 4th Cuirassiers crossed at Wölferdingen, the 19th Dragoons at Gross-

Bliedersdorf. At Wustweiler—about three miles off—the enemy's rearguard were hit on; they had been therefore in close touch. *Aug. 8.*

Lieutenant Cox, 7th Hussars, reported that, facing the wood, thus one and a quarter miles in advance, were two companies of infantry; these went back to occupy Wustweiler; and that cavalry also were noticed, which were covering the retreat.

Further, General v. Redern reported from Saaralbe at 12.45 p.m. that behind Rech, hostile detachments—more definite information was wanting—had been seen marching on Geblingen, apparently also belonging to the 2nd Corps. Lieutenant Schweppe, 17th Hussars, who had gone forward from Saargemünd by Pfarr-Ebersweiler towards St. Avold, reported on the situation there, the same as the 15th Uhlans had found it before the retreat of the French.

The report was not handed in till 9 p.m. The 1st squadron of the 4th Cuirassiers, under v. Wurmb, had reconnoitred from Wölferdingen by Püttlingen, captured ten stragglers beyond that place, and seized six waggons partly filled with supplies, but met no more concentrated bodies of troops. Columns of French infantry were reported on march to Nancy.* From the account in the War Records it is improbable that patrols had remained in touch with the enemy.

At 6 p.m. orders were issued from Head Quarters at Saargemünd, in accordance with which General v. Rheinbaben, with the 11th and 13th Cavalry Brigades, was put under the Tenth Army Corps, and the 6th Cavalry Division under the Third Army Corps. The Prince ordered: "Reports, *Prince Frederick Charles's arrangements.*

---

* At any rate, it is thus made clear that the enemy was continuing his march, *not* to St. Avold, but along the southern road from Püttlingen. The designation of Nancy—50 miles as the crow flies—as the destination of march is not a very apt one.

Aug. 8. however, on all important events are to be sent at once here direct to me by the generals in touch with the enemy. For the day of battle I keep the cavalry divisions at my own disposal." *

Wrong conclusions from reports.
The 5th Cavalry Division reported the position it had taken up at 3.45 p.m. to Head Quarters, and at the same time stated "that the head of the division was in touch with the enemy retiring from Saargemünd. Prisoners were taken from four different regiments. Half a division said to have retreated on the road to Püttlingen and Saaralbe."

This report asserted too much. Lieutenant Schweppe only had met with large hostile detachments, in a direction which was not at all within the divisional reconnaissance area, while no one in the area Saarable-Püttlingen, allotted to the 5th Cavalry Division, had encountered formed bodies, and only stragglers had been captured. Touch cannot be regarded as established, either by the capture of stragglers or by a report on the enemy's line of retreat, without reaching him and locating his position, which in this case was easy, as his rearguard halted just behind Hellimer. It is clear that it would not have been difficult to attain this object on August 8. The indefinite statement at the end of the report shows how fogged the divisional authorities themselves were over the situation.

It is most important to emphasize the point of

---

* The expediency of the arrangement, on the whole, will be examined at the end of the chapter; but we may as well here express a doubt whether it is advisable to issue such an order once for all as in the last sentence, since it is not at all unlikely that the cavalry, in that case, receiving on the day of battle no orders from the Army Corps, to which it was attached till then, may miss the opportune moment for acting independently while waiting for orders from Army Head Quarters. The fate of the 4th Cavalry Division on the day of the battle of Wörth shows, that forgetting to send instructions is also a factor to be reckoned with.

view that the reconnaissance has only attained their *objective* when the main bodies of the cavalry have gained touch with the enemy's columns of all arms. This objective all the operations of the higher commands must strive to reach.

Aug. 8.

As already mentioned, Prince Frederick Charles expected an opportunity would occur of attacking part of MacMahon's army, beaten at Wörth, on the great Bitsch-Saargemünd main road, and made his arrangements accordingly.

The Fourth Army Corps was to be at Rohrbach on August 8. General v. Bredow, with four regiments and a horse battery, had been finally attached to it. The Guard Corps was to support the Fourth Corps, and for this purpose the Guard Cavalry Division and the 2nd Guard Division were to be at Gross-Rederchingen between 10 and 11 a.m. on this date.

Bredow's Brigade.

The Tenth Army Corps was to occupy the attention of the enemy, which was still at Saargemünd at midday on the 7th.

The false information coming from Royal Head Quarters and from the Third Army, about MacMahon's retreat, produced, however, the well-known result that the left wing of the Second Army struck in the air.

The regiments placed under General v. Bredow this day carried out extensive rides, without, however, reaching the enemy, and without bringing in definite information. The desired communication with the Third Army was not very satisfactorily established.

Army Head Quarters had ordered the advance of General v. Bredow on Lemberg and Lorenzen. General v. Alvensleben gave his instructions in person to the brigadier.

He started at 4 a.m. with his regiments, and

Aug. 8. reached Lorenzen at 10.45 a.m., without meeting the enemy. His patrols could only forward negative information. Of the brigade the 10th Hussars reached Herlitzheim, and the 16th Uhlans Saarunion. In the neighbouring places of Mackweiler and Riemsdorf the patrols reported one and a half squadrons of the enemy's hussars, who had disappeared in haste.*

The 13th Dragoons had not joined their brigade, but followed on the next day, as they, by some inadvertence, had not received the order.

The adjutant of the regiment at last found the brigade, and in the evening brought the regiment the order to follow on the next day.

Reconnaissance of the 7th Cuirassiers. The 7th Cuirassiers were given the task of gaining touch with the Third Army by first advancing towards Bitsch, and then bending southwards.

The regiment left a troop under Lieutenant v. Stammer in front of Bitsch. He found the fortress occupied, but no outposts out. He destroyed the telegraph, and carried off from the Lemberg railway station a supply column of sixteen waggons, intended for the fortress.

In Lemberg, Major Graf v. Schmettow, the officer in command of the regiment, found a Bavarian requisitioning party under a captain, who probably belonged to the 2nd Bavarian Corps, and must have gone forward pretty far, as Lemberg was not occupied by the corps till the following day.

Graf v. Schmettow may have thought that, by this meeting, touch with the Third Army had been satisfactorily established.

As a general rule, such a task demands that

* According to the position of affairs, these hussars belonged probably to Failly's (5th) Corps. By such an encounter no *touch* with the enemy is established. That implies seeing formed bodies of troops in some strength, and infantry in particular.

CAVALRY ON SERVICE 109

communication be established with some superior authority, who is in a position to give information of the situation of the neighbouring army. Such information naturally cannot be expected from the leader of a requisitioning party.

Communication cannot be regarded as established if only a few men of the corps concerned have been met with. That proves very little. It can, however, be assumed that the leader of the party can give information of the direction in which the Head Quarters of his corps is to be found. On this date it lay in Egelshardt, only 6¼ miles east of Lemberg. Why Graf Schmettow did not push on in that direction is not quite clear. There must have been special reasons which decided him to go on towards Ingweiler. Perhaps the instruction to take a "southerly direction" from Bitsch was what settled it.

The important thing was the establishing of communication; in what direction this was done was only a secondary consideration.

The regiment certainly found no formed bodies of hostile troops on its road, but was much troubled by the numbers of fugitives, who fired on the regiment from different woods and places, without their being able to keep these bands off, with their inferior arms.

Their advanced party had almost reached Ingweiler, when the order came to go back to Saarunion, where the regiment arrived about midnight. It had started at 4 a.m., and covered more than sixty miles without having attained any real results.

Anyway, the regiment came out of this expedition with serious loss in horses.

By the extension of the left wing by Rohrbach the front of the Second Army had become unusually

Marginalia: Aug. 8. Attachment of cavalry

110 CAVALRY ON SERVICE

Aug. 8.
divisions to army corps.

extended. The Prince thought that it was expedient, for the reconnaissance and pursuit of the enemy, to make each of the large columns advancing on the main roads as strong in cavalry as possible.

The Guard Corps and the Twelfth Army Corps already had their own cavalry divisions at their disposal. The Ninth Corps had the Hessian Cavalry Brigade with it. The different parts of the 5th and 6th Cavalry Divisions, as already seen, were now attached to those Army Corps, in front of which they had been brought by the progress of events.

The Prince did not completely give up the direct employment of these troops, as he reserved to himself their use in the event of an action [see p. 106], and had given instructions that the generals had also to report direct to him all important results of the reconnaissance.

The control of the service of reconnaissance in *unified combination* was thus given up. The opposite principle was adopted, which had induced the Prince in the preceding days to place the 6th Cavalry Division as well as the 5th in conjunction under General v. Rheinbaben.

The employment of the cavalry divisions was not in accordance with the strategical *rôle* which belongs to them. Tasks were allotted them which it should have been the duty of the divisional cavalry to carry out.

Comments on the Prince's arrangements.

I do not think such a mistake would occur to-day in our more enlightened view of the strategic service of reconnaissance. The greater extent of front an army has, the longer time will a concentration of forces require, and therefore the further forward must the cavalry reconnaissances be pushed.

The distance of the cavalry in front of the

CAVALRY ON SERVICE 111

army is in direct proportion to the extension of the latter. Aug. 8.

If this cavalry is allotted to army corps, it is fettered; it becomes checked in its necessary forward movement and in its independence, and the exact opposite of what is wanted is arrived at.

In this case the unduly separated parts of the Second Army naturally needed a sufficient strength of cavalry for their protection, but it was entirely the duty of the divisional cavalry to afford this protection, and it possessed sufficient troops for the purpose. Whatever the number of cavalry which are put under an army corps, it is only in accordance with human nature for the general to use them entirely in the narrow interests of his own strategic action. [See events of August 11, p. 178].

It is necessary for the commander-in-chief of an army to keep in his own hand a force of cavalry as a continuous and active implement, to keep touch with the enemy, and to feel every beat of his pulse, in order to learn all his movements.

The commander-in-chief of an army acts in accordance with a settled plan of operation, the object of which is the enemy's army. He can only learn what the enemy is doing through the eyes of his cavalry, which gains and keeps touch with the enemy, and gives information of his movements. He alone is in the position of giving to this cavalry force the instructions which aid the intentions he has in view.

The Prince, by letting his cavalry divisions out of his hand, denied himself this implement. The army had only a numerous divisional cavalry, too strong a corps cavalry, and no cavalry of the army.

How far also the general commanding-in-chief of all the armies should keep cavalry directly under himself will depend on the particular circumstances.

112 CAVALRY ON SERVICE

Aug. 8. As a general rule, I do not consider it expedient or needful; but to retain direct control over the masses of cavalry allotted to individual armies—as King William did in certain cases in individual army corps—must, at any rate, be kept in view.

If the cavalry divisions had remained as before, directly under Army Head Quarters, it would have been advisable to collect these in a cavalry corps, in the interests of a uniform carrying out of reconnaissance, and to allot to the weak 6th Cavalry Division, as being nearest to the First Army, the country from St. Avold inclusive, southwards to the railway line from Falkenberg to Metz inclusive; to allot to the 5th Cavalry Division the country south of it, with instructions to keep up communication with the Third Army, and to swing their left-wing brigade round from the south towards Metz.

As later events prove, this brigade would have had to operate especially on the flank and line of retreat of the enemy. While the 6th Cavalry Division, which was in touch with considerable forces of the enemy, would have effected a forward movement with its main body, generally speaking, on a single road, the 5th Cavalry Division could have carried out its reconnaissance on a broad front on two or even three lines of advance, a plan involving no risks, as the roads were ample and extremely easy, the country generally open, and the division very strong.

The movements of the French.

As regards the enemy's movements, a short description may be given to supplement the map.

On the French left, Cissey's Division reached Tennschen at 6 a.m. by a night march, and camped east of that place; Lorencez's reached Silly at 4 a.m.; Grenier started 9 a.m., made a long halt at St. Avold, left at 11 a.m. and took up a position on the Lubeln plateau to protect the retreat from the Prussian cavalry, "qui suit de près sur les talons de notre arrière-garde." Aug. 8.

The retreat invariably suffered serious delay through the transport, which had to be sent on in advance and be protected; an impediment which becomes a matter for consideration in a retreat in a very different way to what it does in an advance. The division only reached its bivouac between Bingen and Kurzel at 11 p.m. Legrand's Cavalry Division bivouacked at Landendorf; the 2nd Hussars, up till now detached in advance, had returned to it.

Montaudon's Division started at 4 a.m., and went into bivouac at Falkenberg, where Bazaine also made his Head Quarters. French 3rd Corps.

Metman's Division also started at 4 a.m., and reached Falkenberg at 2 p.m.

Castagny's Division, which had left the entrenched heights at 4 a.m., made a three-hours' halt on the Lubeln plateau, and deployed for action; 3 p.m., marched off. 4.30 p.m., fresh deployment for action at Halleringen, the artillery moved into position on the Möhringer Berg, and the 90th Regiment deployed skirmishers. All this occurred, because Uhlans had appeared above the heights of Buschborn. 8 p.m., bivouac at Füllingen on the left bank of the Nied.

Decaen's Division, the outposts of which during the night had frequently exchanged shots with Prussian patrols, also started at 4 a.m. It took part in the deployment at Lubeln, only left that place at 6 p.m., which was at once occupied by a troop of Uhlans, and bivouacked at Füllingen.

Clerembault's Cavalry Division had marched at 9 a.m., brought its battery into position on the far side of St. Avold, and bivouacked at Bingen.

Aug. 8. Juniac's Dragoon Brigade joined it again there; it had started from Püttlingen at 3 a.m., and left St. Avold at 2 p.m., after burning a large quantity of abandoned stores there.*

The 2nd Corps, as has been stated, also made a night march, and bivouacked at Gross-Tännchen, putting out Lapasset's Brigade as a covering body towards Hellimer. At daybreak, when Lapasset's rearguard left Ernstweiler, Uhlans appeared in the neighbouring woods.

Forton's Reserve Cavalry Division had left Folschweiler at 3.30 a.m., and went into bivouac between Luppy and Solgne.

The Imperial Guard had started at 4 a.m., observed by hostile patrols. Against these it covered itself by infantry skirmishers and scouts from the Guides—heavy cavalry—who, however, did not march more than 250 yards to the side of the road! The Guard bivouacked between Silly and Maizery.

* There were also left behind at St. Avold 40,000 chacos, which the troops had exchanged for caps, as well as 5000 blankets.

CHAPTER III

For this day General v. Steinmetz had issued the following order:—

Aug. 9.

Measures of General v. Steinmetz.

"The 3rd Cavalry Division will push forward detachments to-morrow, to gain information of the enemy's position, especially of the corps which, according to Lieutenant Stumm's report, is at Buschborn."

The First Army Corps was directed "to place a battalion at the disposal of the 3rd Cavalry Division to serve as a reserve and support to the advance of the detachments as ordered to-day." At 11 p.m., after a review of the reports received, the further order was sent to General Graf von der Groeben "to let the battalion placed at his disposal advance at the furthest to Lauterbach, and to direct his reconnaissance chiefly towards St. Avold and its neighbourhood."

General v. Steinmetz had formed the idea from the reports that the troops met with formed the left wing of the enemy. On this point clear information had to be gained by sending out patrols on the 9th.

Thus, "detachments," and not, as hitherto, only "patrols," were at last to be sent out.

To let the division loose was as yet too much for them. The 1st Cavalry Division received orders to remain where it was.

General v. Steinmetz had, in addition, asked Royal Head Quarters whether he could not advance,

Aug. 9. at least with his right wing, in the direction of Buschborn, "as, according to the present state of affairs, the First Army was only in touch with the enemy's left by means of widely advanced cavalry patrols." *

It is clear from this request that General v. Steinmetz severely felt the want of satisfactory contact with the enemy; yet he could not make up his mind to employ his cavalry bodies to suit the occasion. An advance of the army was not at all necessary to gain this touch; the advance of the cavalry would have sufficed for that purpose.

Meanwhile a telegram of August 8 had arrived from Moltke, which ran as follows:—

Moltke's instructions. Delay of Ramin's report.

"Since no intelligence has yet arrived of the enemy having left Bolchen and Busendorf, the army will remain to-morrow in its present position." †

When this order, which reached the First Army at 2 a.m., was issued, the reports of the 8th were evidently not yet known at Royal Head Quarters.

Lieutenant v. Ramin's despatch of 3 p.m., which reported the evacuation of Bolchen and Busendorf, was sent by the division at 5.30 p.m. to Army Head Quarters, and telegraphed by them at 8 p.m. to His Majesty, as already stated.

The transmission by telegraph must therefore have suffered very considerable delay.

If the despatch had reached Royal Head Quarters at the proper time, or if Lieutenant v. Ramin had telegraphed there direct, the measures resolved on for August 9 might have been different.

* As already noticed (p. 91), General v. Steinmetz, through Lieutenant v. Papen's inaccurate reports, had arrived at the conclusion that he had to deal with the enemy's left wing at Buschborn, and that the troops previously reported at Bolchen, had retired there. He knew nothing of the existence of the 4th Corps at Tennschen.

† Knowledge alone begets bold resolutions; ignorance begets anxious delay. [See p. 85.]

CAVALRY ON SERVICE 117

From this it follows how important it is for every link, from the patrol leader to the highest authorities, to make every endeavour that despatches, which have to be sent on, should be forwarded as speedily as possible. The further lesson to be drawn from this incident is, that also the telegraph offices should be properly supervised in rapidly forwarding despatches, insisting that an important despatch should have the preference over any other if the line is not clear.

The 3rd Cavalry Division did not reach the point of pushing out "detachments"—if the parties of thirty strong are not to be called "patrols." The division remained, as the map shows, with its tactical bodies on the right bank of the Saar, and only outposts were pushed across it.

In addition to those patrols, whose activity we have already followed, and who continued their duties, a few others were sent out.

Lieutenant v. Ramin had again gone forward to Bolchen, and reported this place clear of the enemy. The same thing had already been reported the previous day by Lieutenant v. Papen-Koenigen. Ramin turned off from here towards Diedenhofen. No further despatch from him can be found on this date; he seems to have kept his previously mentioned rest-day. Meanwhile, before daylight, Lieutenant Balthasar, 14th Uhlans, with twenty horses, and Lieutenant v. Wallenberg, same regiment, with fifteen horses, had ridden out on reconnaissance.

As far as Lauterbach both patrols were to travel together; from there Balthasar was to turn off to Buschborn to join the patrol of Captain v. Hymmen, who was scouting about there; while Wallenberg was to take the direction of St. Avold. Unfortunately the war records do not give the

Aug. 9.

Patrols of the 3rd Cavalry Division.

Aug. 9. reports these officers sent in. Lieutenant Balthasar met Captain v. Hymmen this day, and the original detachment was thus increased to sixty strong.

Captain v. Hymmen.

Captain v. Hymmen, on this day, had orders to reconnoitre towards Buschborn, and had got in touch with the 6th Cavalry Division. He received from Major v. Schoenfels, the general staff officer of this division, a message, and he reported at 10 a.m. from Forbach—

> "The troops, camped at St. Avold, were Bazaine's corps, which retreated yesterday towards Metz. The 15th Uhlans keep touch with them." Intelligence by Major v. Schoenfels, 6th Cavalry Division: "The Third Corps is pushing forward its advanced posts to-day beyond St. Avold, if not further. According to the reports received by the 6th Cavalry Division, the corps appears to have formed the enemy's left wing." *

He moved by Ludweiler, Lauterbach, Karlingen, and Porcelette, to Buschborn, and in the afternoon sent the regiment a captured French waggon, with supplies of different sorts.

Lieutenant v. Papen.

Lieutenant v. Papen-Koenigen was ordered

> "to ride forward with 15 horses from Derlen † towards Bolchen, to watch the Bolchen-Metz main road, and reconnoitre as far as possible towards Metz.

Skirmish at Bolchen.

As he approached Bolchen, a strong party of the enemy's cavalry appeared from there.

This was a made-up squadron of the 2nd Hussars, which General de Ladmirault had sent out to drive off the enemy's Uhlans, "who were always closely following according to their *habitude ingénieuse.*" ‡

---

* The false view of the extent of the French left was strengthened by this information.

† He had, therefore, the day before returned to the camp of his regiment.

‡ Bonie.

CAVALRY ON SERVICE 119

Papen turned off to the road to Busendorf. Aug. 9. Before he reached it, he had to jump a stream, which three of the horses of the patrol refused.

Owing to this delay, thirty of the enemy's party had come up so close that he had either to leave the three men in the lurch, or else to recross the ditch with the remainder, and attack the superior number of the enemy. He did the latter. In the skirmish the French lost their captain, Juvenot, killed, an officer and three men seriously wounded,* who had to remain in Bolchen.† The Uhlans lost one man and two horses killed.

The French detachment fled to Bolchen, and when the rest of the squadron appeared, Lieutenant v. Papen retired.

The French captain had left half his squadron behind in Volmeringen, and had advanced with the other half to Bolchen.

This little skirmish again gives proof that when in doubt the offensive should always be taken. If the officer had dallied, he would have ignominiously lost three men at least, taken prisoners.

With the personal bravery which the French invariably showed when it came to blows, victory of the small party can, moreover, only be explained by the marked effect of the lance.

Lieutenant v. Papen rode to Ober Felsberg after this incident, left the patrol there, and delivered his report in person.

According to General Graf v. der Groeben's despatch to Head Quarters about this patrol, dated Derlen, 4 p.m., the report ran thus:—

* According to Dick de Lonlay, he had received three lance wounds in the breast.

† This unimportant affair was, according to Rousset, the cause of General Ladmirault deploying his corps for action on the next day, as he thought the enemy, whom he believed to be close to his front, would presently attack.

Aug. 9.

"At 10 a.m. to-day I had an encounter on the main road N.E. of Bolchen with about 30 men of the 2nd French Hussars, and lost one man and two horses killed, while I estimate the enemy's loss at from 10 to 12 men, including one officer. I am bringing back one horse captured; two others were lost again, as a whole squadron came up. I believe this party is a reconnaissance from Metz, as I have seen no troops in the whole country from Bolchen to Tennschen,* and heard from the inhabitants that all have marched off to St. Avold and Metz."

Graf Groeben added the remark that Lieutenant v. Papen would return to-day to Ober Felsberg to his patrol, and would reconnoitre afresh from there towards Metz.

"According to his (Papen's) account, large bodies of cavalry could not be usefully employed in that undulating and hilly country."

There was no information as yet to hand of the existence of the divisions camped at Tennschen, and the French detachment met with by Lieutenant v. Papen was regarded as an isolated one in advance, while in reality it had moved only about four miles ahead of the main body of its force.† Blame cannot be laid on v. Papen's patrol this time. He did what was possible here. But we must not ask too much from such isolated patrols pushed far in advance. Against an active hostile cavalry or inhabitants who resisted, these patrols could never have advanced so far forward.

Our peace conditions lead us in this respect to wrong notions. Under difficult, *i.e.* ordinary service conditions, every patrol must be backed by a body of troops following in support seven to ten

---

* The patrol, we know, never went to Tennschen.

† Von Schell's account, too, of this encounter in his book, "Operations of the First Army under General v. Steinmetz," runs as follows: "This enemy could only have been an isolated reconnoitring party, since all reports agreed that that locality was clear of troops." These reports unhappily were false. The reason has been explained.

CAVALRY ON SERVICE 121

miles behind. Had it been decided to follow up v. Papen's patrol with but a single united squadron, a view beyond the Nied would probably have been gained; but in any case fuller information would have been arrived at, if several squadrons had advanced, as they would certainly have alarmed the French camps.

Aug. 9.

But as it was, the false impression obtained with the present, that the French left flank was to be found at Buschborn.

According to the war diary of the 5th Uhlans, v. Papen reached the regiment in the afternoon, delivered his report, and started again two hours later with fourteen fresh men and horses. If we admire this officer's smartness and staying power, we must also lament the useless waste of energy, which the superior Head Quarter authorities equally failed to recognize as such.

The 8th Hussars, whose patrols had already done such excellent work, sent out another patrol to-day, and, skilfully and boldly led, it brought n good information. It was Lieutenant Graf Itzenplitz, who received orders to advance by Buschborn from the outposts at Lauterbach with two N.C.O.'s and ten horses, in order to regain touch with the enemy.

Itzenplitz' patrol.

Without finding any vestige of the enemy, the patrol rode forward by Buschborn, Zimmingen, and Halleringen, and reached the St. Avold-Metz road near Möhringen about 5.15 p.m., where it met a 15th Uhlan patrol. On this road numerous traces of the march of troops were noticed, and Graf Itzenplitz, as soon as he reached the Möhringer Berg, unexpectedly saw a large camp on the plain below.

"As soon as I arrived on the hill (it may have been about 5.30 p.m.) the camp was alarmed, many bugles

Aug. 9.

sounded, and it was seen that all haste was being made for departure. I now sent my patrol back on Möhringen, and kept by me only a couple of N.C.O.'s to keep a further watch. The French had apparently placed no outposts; so much so that a corporal remarked to me, 'If it were us lying there in camp, we would surely have placed, at least, a vedette up here.' From my post of observation I saw the enemy's columns assemble and set themselves in motion. I could not look far enough into the valley to see in what direction the columns were moving, whether forwards or backwards. [From this it appears again that to decide even this is not always an easy job.] So I rode with the two N.C.O.'s at a quick pace on Füllingen, where I was greeted by a volley at 100 yards range. My horse was hit by four bullets, and the N.C.O., Ullrich's, by three, as was seen next day. Both of us lay pinned under our horses. I was the first to succeed in getting out from under my horse, by leaving one of my boots behind; and I then helped the N.C.O., as the other N.C.O.'s horse had run away with him to the rear. Running round the trees by the wayside, one on the right and the other on the left of the road, and screened by a slight dip in the ground, we soon escaped from the enemy's fire. We were not pursued, although French cavalry stood already mounted only a hundred paces off, and we thus escaped capture, which in open country would have been unavoidable. I soon met my patrol, which had ridden to meet me on hearing the firing. I mounted a hussar's horse, and then sent back a verbal report 'that large hostile camps lay west of Füllingen, but that they had been alarmed.' I kept further watch on it with the N.C.O. Ullrich, who had also been remounted. I told the other N.C.O. to commandeer a waggon in Möhringen for the two dismounted men, and to ride back with the patrol.* I now rode with Ullrich to the hills south of the main road, and from there I clearly saw the French were marching off to Metz. Here I met a vedette of the 15th Uhlans, to whom I pointed out that the enemy were moving off, and that they must report the fact.

* Probably only back under cover.

"On the return journey I met Captain Brix, the squadron leader of the Uhlans, and informed him of the retreat of the enemy, of which he had received no news.

"Having got back to the squadron, I made out the written report with Captain v. Schütz, my squadron leader, and sent it off."

This report, which occurs in the War Records of the First Army, and which was handed in to the Head Quarters of the Seventh Corps at 9.30 p.m., runs as follows:—

(Transmitted by the outposts.)

"Buschborn, August 9.

"I advanced from Buschborn, by Zimmingen, Möhringen, and on the road to Metz, as far as Füllingen. There I found a French camp on the south side of the road, by information as well as on the face of it, 40 to 50,000 strong,* which broke up at once on the appearance of our patrol, and marched away towards Metz. I made sure of this with my own eyes, as I rode right on to the position, and both I and my N.C.O. had our horses shot under us. A squadron of the 15th Uhlans is billetted in Lubeln, and a squadron is on outpost between Baumbiedersdorf and Zimmingen."

The report is clear and full, only, unhappily, any mention of time is wanting.

The 6th Cavalry Division, as we know, had been put under the Third Army Corps by the Army Order of August 8, and the instructions for the corps were to advance on the 9th to a selected position at St. Avold.† By corps orders from St. Johann, 5.30 a.m., the 15th Uhlans were attached to the 6th Infantry Division, which were in

Measures of the Third Army Corps.

---
* The estimate was correct, as Itzenplitz alone had four infantry divisions in front of him. [See map for August 9.]

† The Tenth Corps was to be near Saargemünd on the left bank; the Guard-Corps near Gross-Rederchingen; the Fourth near the road Saarunion-Rohrbach, with orders to reconnoitre with patrols far to the south; the Ninth in second line, near St. Ingbert; the Twelfth, which had its cavalry division advanced to the front since the 8th, near Habkirchen.

Aug. 9. advance. So a fresh office was set up, which reports had to pass through. The question involuntarily arises, why the 6th Infantry Division did not combine with the Uhlans, their own divisional cavalry regiment, the 2nd Dragoons? For this regiment remained behind the Uhlans in close touch with the division. [See the map.] One arrives at the general impression that the infantry divisions were too richly provided with cavalry, and that they made an insufficient use of them, with the exception of the 5th and 13th Divisions.

For the cavalry division the following orders were issued:—

> "The division will start as soon as the rear of the 5th Infantry Division is clear of Forbach, and will billet in Nassweiler, Rossbrück, Morsbach, Cocheren, and Beningen. Squadrons will be sent to Püttlingen and Barst, patrols to Hellimer and Vahl-Ebersing. Reports to be sent by relay posts to St. Avold."

By this order, too, the main body of the division was held back in rear. By putting this regiment, which was in close touch with the enemy, under an infantry division, some of its reports would probably never reach Duke William.

If Prince Frederick Charles had retained direct command over the division, he would doubtlessly have used it in an offensive spirit.

It is clear, however, from corps orders, that the General Officer Commanding, Lieutenant-General v. Alvensleben, jun., who had had news of the enemy's evacuation of St. Avold, had already resolved independently, before the arrival of the above Army Orders, to occupy the town and to advance beyond it.*

---

* Meeting one day Head Quarters of the Third Army Corps, Colonel v. Voigts-Rhetz highly praised the excellent reports of the division,

Orders of the 6th Cavalry Division—

Aug. 9.

Orders of the 6th Cavalry Division.

"Rauch's brigade will send one squadron to Barst, which will keep up communication with the 6th Infantry Division on the right, and will patrol to Vahl-Ebersing on the left. It will send one squadron to Püttlingen, which will keep up communication with the Tenth Corps in Wustweiler on the left, and will patrol by Hellimer on the road to Gross-Tänchen. The squadrons are to report by relay posts direct to Corps Head Quarters. The squadrons of Ploetz and Leipziger, hitherto detached from Grüter's brigade, will rejoin their regiments."

The 15th Uhlans had, meantime, continued their reconnaissance in the neighbourhood of St. Avold.

15th Uhlans.

The terribly rainy weather which had set in for several days had soon turned the country, off the main roads, into a marsh. Rosenberg's (the 5th) squadron had suffered great discomfort on outpost duty at Möhringen. After receipt of the outpost reports, the colonel had them relieved in the morning by the 4th Squadron; but he went with the latter, before they took up their position, on a reconnaissance towards the German Nied, beyond which the last of the enemy had apparently disappeared. French infantry, however, had occupied the Schwalinger Hof, which lay on the left of the main road, and, hiding in there, had shut the shutters. [See the ordnance map.] Suddenly, and luckily too soon, they opened them, and a rapid but ill-aimed fire from the windows of both stories compelled the patrol to give way with a loss of two horses wounded. The enemy soon moved off again from their resting-place, and the advanced squadron at once followed them on Bingen, which was found to be strongly occupied,

which was probably meant for the 15th Uhlans.—(War-Diary of the 6th Cavalry Division.)

Aug. 9. while large columns were seen on the march to Metz.

The employment of the outpost relief, as was done here, is doubly suitable: (1) a fresh and rested body of troops is led to the front, and (2) they are made acquainted with the ground to their immediate front in the simplest manner.

A reconnoitring detachment can hardly avoid such an ambush as was contrived here, since every house on the road naturally cannot be examined to see whether it is occupied, and, besides, houses with the shutters up do not necessarily arouse suspicion, as they are often in war to be found deserted by their inmates.

The following report, sent from St. Avold, 7.30 a.m. to the 14th Cavalry Brigade, was received at 9.45 a.m. :—

> "Captain Brix holds St. Avold with the 1st Squadron, is sending patrols to Püttlingen, Gross-Tänchen, and Falkenberg, and keeps up communication with the First Army and the squadron in Pfarr-Ebersweiler.* Relay posts are formed at Merlenbach, Ober-Homburg, St. Avold (at exit to Forbach), Lubeln (Longeville), and, later, at Möhringen (Marange). I request permission for the squadron in Metzingen to be returned to the regiment."

The brigadier assented to his request. In the morning the following additional report of the regiment went to the Third Corps, and was presented 1.30 p.m. :—

> "Bazaine's corps bivouacked on the night 8th to 9th between Bingen and Rollingen, and moved off to Metz at 4 a.m. this morning."

In the War Records of the Second Army a

---

* Apart from the fact that these duties had to be performed, the colonel wanted to keep a part of his regiment in fresh condition by leaving a squadron behind.

despatch of Captain v. Rosenberg is to be found, Aug. 9. sent from the outposts at Lubeln at 8.30 a.m., which runs thus—

"Enemy moved off from Bingen, 4 a.m. to-day."

The same officer reported from Möhringen at noon—

"Bazaine's corps (3rd) retreated to beyond Füllingen, and is now camped on a front about a mile broad at Bingen and Rollingen. The men are cooking, etc."

At 2 p.m. Colonel v. Alvensleben sent the following report from Möhringen to the First Army:—

"Being directed to keep up communication with the First Army, I am sending this message to their vanguard, with the request to forward it to their Head Quarters, that since yesterday the regiment has been following Bazaine's corps, which retreated yesterday afternoon from St. Avold, on the road from Metz to Lubeln, and last night to Rollingen and Bingen. The corps is cooking at present, and it is not yet certain whether it will spend the night here or will retire further back towards Metz. Füllingen lies to its immediate front, which faces St. Avold. I hear Prince Frederick Charles comes to St. Avold to-day. Outflanking cavalry and advancing infantry are just driving in the outposts." *

The colonel next reported from Lubeln at 7 p.m.—

"Bazaine slowly retired at 4 p.m. along the direct road to Metz, most likely only as far as behind the next position of Kurzel. A brigade remained halted on the left wing at Kombosch; likewise small infantry detachments on this side of Füllingen, which are evidently intended to prevent our cavalry following. The 1st Squadron, on outpost at Möhringen, is to ascertain where these parts of the 3rd Corps are going to.†

* This offensive movement of the enemy soon stopped.
† It appears that the 1st (Brix's) Squadron had been called to the

128 CAVALRY ON SERVICE

Aug. 9.

"It appears as if more than one corps had bivouacked at Füllingen—perhaps still parts of Frossard's corps, retiring straight on Metz."

Contradictory reports and explanation thereof.

A comparison of the contents of these reports shows that they are somewhat contradictory as regards time and places in the enemy's dispositions, since the morning reports of the outpost squadron and the regiment relate the departure of the enemy from Bingen at 4 a.m., while the later reports affirm that the enemy was still cooking at midday, in the position at Bingen-Rollingen, and only started the march on Metz at 4 p.m.

The following explanation of this curious fact was given me by an officer who took a conspicuous part in the events of these days:—

The morning report of the regiment, presented to the Third Corps at 1.30 p.m., was undoubtedly founded on the report of the outposts at 8.30 a.m.

The mistake in the last report can be explained by the fact that the French, on the morning of the 9th, drew in their outposts, which had been left on the right bank of the Nied on the 8th, except the isolated ambush in the Schwalinger Hof.

The advanced troops posted in and near Bingen were first withdrawn, and later on, about noon, those near Füllingen.

Rosenberg was then able, for the first time probably, to get a view of the enemy's main front, and described this in the noon report, as he says, "and is now camped on a front about a mile broad at Bingen . . ." (p. 127).

The point quoted is instructive in many ways. It shows that though a withdrawal of the outposts may be noticed, it is not always sufficient authority

---

front when the enemy's brief counter-stroke, mentioned in the 2 p.m. report, ensued; it then remained on outposts in place of the 4th Squadron.

for deciding that the enemy's retreat has been commenced, and that the report should be limited to stating what was actually certain, without giving deductions as facts, as it probably happened here.

Perhaps Captain v. Rosenberg had also noticed transport columns in the distance moving to the rear, a matter from which the conclusion cannot always be drawn that the enemy is beginning his retirement, as the sending back of transport may happen for many reasons, *e.g.* to refill with ammunition or supplies, or it can be effected very prematurely, especially in a retreat, to let the transport get the necessary start. [Compare p. 100.]

The Army Head Quarters said, notifying these reports, in a memorandum to Royal Head Quarters, dated St. Avold, 8 p.m., August 9—

> "The enemy showed no opposition even to single patrols of Uhlans, and Colonel v. Alvensleben succeeded in imbuing the enemy perpetually with the feeling that they were being pursued."

Truly, no greater praise than this can be meted out to the colonel's energetic action with his three squadrons, which had been able to impose in this way on at least 70,000 men of the enemy's troops, directly opposed to him, and had brought in full information of the situation, which up till then had not been unravelled.

One further report of Captain Brix, who was on outpost duty, dated Zondringen, 9.30 p.m., was forwarded this day to the Head Quarters of the Third Army Corps, where it arrived 7 a.m. on the 10th—

> "Two large hostile camps were noticed this afternoon on both sides of the main road from Füllingen, on the heights of the Pelplinger Hof, in front of Metz. During the afternoon the one south of the main road was broken up, and the troops retired along the Falkenberg road. About 5 p.m. a great explosion, with

Aug. 9.

powerful detonation, was seen in a direction due south of Möhringen. Have watched the enemy's camp till 6 p.m. from the hills north of Baumbiedersdorf, and after that from the hills west of Zondringen, near Kombosch, and placed a piquet at Zondringen.

"I have taken up a position with the rest of the squadron, between Zondringen and Möhringen."

Major Graf v. Haeseler.

On the 9th, too, Major Graf v. Haeseler, from the Head Quarters of the Second Army, had reconnoitred in the country west of St. Avold, and confirmed Colonel v. Alvensleben's report.* He estimated Bazaine's rear-guard at about six battalions, two batteries, and six squadrons.

A report from Graf Haeseler, dated 9.30 a.m., received at Head Quarters at 6 p.m., August 9, somewhat abbreviated, ran as follows:—

"Yesterday morning Colonel v. Alvensleben, who had arrived here with 3 squadrons of the 15th Uhlans, encountered a (weak) rear-guard of the enemy on the hills of St. Avold, which, in the afternoon, followed the corps that retired yesterday on Metz. Colonel v. Alvensleben occupied quarters in St. Avold, and is now following the enemy with two squadrons. Nothing was known of the enemy at General v. Rheinbaben's outposts, which are only as far as Püttlingen. I have sent word to General v. Rheinbaben that St. Avold is occupied by the 15th Uhlans (! author). According to various accounts, a column of all arms is said to have marched, on the 7th, from Püttlingen on St. Avold, and other troops, from Püttlingen, to have taken the direction of Nancy. The troops which retired yesterday are estimated at more than one division (Bazaine). A patrol of the 8th Hussars has just come in from Karlingen, and also one of the 15th Hussars."

Graf v. Haeseler had visited the hospital in St.

* Major Graf Haeseler had reconnoitred St. Avold already on the previous day. The War Records do not contain a report from that day.

CAVALRY ON SERVICE 131

Avold, and reported the numbers of the regiments of all the wounded whom he found there.*

Aug. 9.

Mention must here be made of an incident which a Uhlan patrol experienced in conjunction with a party of the 4th Cuirassiers.

Skirmish at Gross-Tänchen.

A patrol of six Uhlans under v. Oppenheim, a reserve under-officer, had received orders to advance towards the Saargemünd-Metz road, and, if possible, to Gross-Tänchen.

On the road leading from Saargemünd, by Püttlingen, to Metz the patrol found unmistakable signs of hurried retreat. This patrol met a troop of the 4th Cuirassiers at Gross-Tänchen. Lieutenant Graf Schmiesing, the leader, ordered the advanced point to join the Uhlans. The Cuirassiers belonged to the 1st Squadron, and had received orders to reconnoitre from Barst towards St. Avold and south of the Saarbrücken-Metz railroad. The leader was told to advance on the road from Püttlingen by Gross-Tänchen. The stretch as far as Gross-Tänchen was passed without incident. Having arrived in front of that place, the officer remained with his troop halted, reinforced his advanced point by a N.C.O. and four men, who were then to reconnoitre it.

The Uhlan patrol had met him just before, and they also had ridden into the place.

The officer meanwhile rode up to the first house to question the inmates.

Suddenly a rapid fire broke out, and the advanced point, with the Uhlans jumbled up, hurried out of the place.

* The sending out of officers of the general staff from the highest Head Quarters to reconnoitre personally with the most advanced cavalry patrols at important times is recommended, for the reason, if it were for no other, that these officers know the intentions of the directing staff, and are acquainted with the essence of all intelligence received.

Aug. 9. The patrols had been suddenly attacked by a squadron of mounted Jägers.

The enemy was the 2nd squadron of 3rd Mounted Jägers, who had been sent from Montaudon's Division to reconnoitre towards Gross-Tänchen.

The squadron had met Cuirassier vedettes in front of the village—probably the advanced point which, as the regulations prescribed, had just ridden through to the exit on the far side—and had met the Uhlans inside the village.

A French officer was seriously wounded by a Uhlan, and he put the latter *hors-de-combat* by a revolver shot. Of the Uhlan patrol only the leader escaped, slightly wounded; the remainder were either killed or taken prisoners. The Cuirassiers lost one N.C.O. and three men captured. The French asserted that seven Prussians were killed, and four Cuirassiers and three Uhlans taken prisoners. Graf Schmiesing puts the losses at eleven men, two men too much, as he estimated erroneously the Uhlan patrol at eight men.

When the patrol dashed back out of the place, and the officer heard the firing, he led his troop a few hundred paces back.

Turning round again, he saw the enemy's squadron halted near the place, deployed, and was fired on by their carbines without effect. He then had to be a witness to seeing his N.C.O. caught. He wished to proceed to attack to free him, but the enemy now retired, and Graf Schmiesing says he also saw infantry moving towards Gross-Tänchen. It is evident from Graf Schmiesing's letter how seriously this mischance had affected him; and we can understand this. No blame can, however, be laid on that officer. Such things will often occur in minor operations.

Gross-Tänchen is a fairly extensive locality, and it appears that when the Cuirassier patrol rode through it, the enemy reached the other entrance almost at the same moment.

Aug. 9.

If a surprise occurs under such circumstances, we ought not to blame the men; it would only cause discouragement. The leader, too, who will be sure of our sympathy, should not let himself be depressed, but he and all should only think of retribution on the next occasion!

According to Dick de Lonlay, the prisoners were questioned, and seem to have revealed all they knew. This, if it is true, is strongly to be condemned. In training men, stress must be earnestly laid at every opportunity on the duty that obliges any man who has the misfortune to be taken prisoner to give answer to no question which has any reference to our troops, and to make it plain to every man, that if they do, what serious damage they might thus be causing.

If the losses in this skirmish were heavy, yet, by the message sent back, Frossard's retreat to Metz was learnt for the first time (according to the history of the 15th Uhlans), and it was made certain that the country south-east of the Saarbrücken-Metz road at Gross-Tänchen was clear.

There can be no reconnoitring without losses, and these are well paid for if they are in proportion to the advantages gained.

Communication between the advanced patrols of the 6th and 5th Cavalry Divisions was now also established.

The 6th Infantry Division had ordered the 2nd Dragoons to patrol from Lubeln, where the 1st Squadron had taken up the outpost line, on Bolchen, Füllingen, and Landorf. From the last-named

Czettritz' patrol.

Aug. 9. village Lieutenant v. Czettritz-Neuhaus turned off to Falkenberg, which he reached at 11.45 a.m. He had started at 8.15 in the morning from Landorf, and had reached Falkenberg without seeing anything of the enemy. But he had collected important information by questioning the inhabitants, and had made certain that the 11th, 55th, 77th, and 84th Regiments had passed through Landorf from Gross-Tänchen, on their way to Metz, from 8 to 10.30 a.m. on the 9th; that Bazaine and his staff had arrived at Falkenberg at 6 p.m. on the 8th, had passed the night there, and ridden on towards Metz at 11 a.m. on the 9th; that masses of troops had bivouacked around Falkenberg during the night, 8th to 9th, and that the 59th Regiment had been quartered in the town; that Napoleon had arrived by special train from Metz at 10 a.m. on the 9th, had held an interview with Bazaine, and had returned to Metz at 10.30 a.m., after which the railway had at once been cut just beyond the station.*

The despatch is quoted here summarily, because although no direct touch with the enemy was gained, yet it gave very important information, and may be taken as a pattern, from the care with which it was compiled; the information, too, proved correct. That from Falkenberg, as the officer stated, was gained from a notary, who produced a trustworthy impression. The report is made special mention of in the Official History of the War.

Captain v. Cramm, of the same regiment, had apparently before that ridden into Falkenberg, and had found it unoccupied. No report from this officer is to hand.

* The original is to be found in the War Records of the Second Army.

The 5th Cavalry Division, by an order dated 7 a.m., had urged the 11th Brigade

Aug. 9.

5th Cavalry Division.

"to get touch with the enemy by pushing patrols out wide. The brigade should patrol towards St. Avold, Falkenberg, and Nancy, push a squadron to Barst, and watch the Forbach-St. Avold-Falkenberg railway."

The 13th Brigade had to patrol to Finstingen and Nancy. There can only be found in the Records one report from General v. Redern, 13th Brigade, who had despatched patrols to Altdorf, Münster, and Mittersheim, and they could report nothing of the enemy. A few stragglers had been brought in. It was only the 4th Cuirassiers' patrol (11th Brigade), sent towards Gross-Tänchen, which had encountered the enemy, as we have already seen.

Whether the observations made there led to any proper appreciation of the situation is nowhere to be found.

The activity of the two brigades placed under General v. Rheinbaben had little to show this day.

The criticism is contained in the above-quoted report of Graf Haeseler, to which I may point (p. 130).

The outposts of the 5th Cavalry Division this day were about twelve and a half miles further back than those of the 6th Cavalry Division (15th Uhlans); the enemy (2nd Corps), who was immediately opposed to the former, was moving on about the same level as the Third (German) Corps. In that case, one must not be surprised, of course, if no information was gained. I have already shown, in speaking of the measures taken by the 3rd Cavalry Division, that single patrols pushed far in advance do *not* afford a guarantee that reconnaissance will be successful, unless large bodies remain within measurable distance. The same thing

Aug. 9. is again apparent here. General v. Rheinbaben had lost the touch, which he had still retained on the 8th, by his faulty arrangements. [Compare on the maps the position of the regiments on the 8th and on the 9th. It will be seen that on the 9th they were, in part, shifted even to the rear.]

Bredow's brigade.

General v. Bredow, operating on the extreme left with his regiments, did not succeed either in regaining touch, once it had been lost. This, however, can be explained by the fact that, after the enemy had once disappeared, he had, properly speaking, nobody in front of him.

The 7th Cuirassiers only got to Saarunion at midnight on the 8th, after a most exhausting ride; and the 13th Dragoons, who had not received the orders for the 8th, moved to join the brigade only on the 9th (*vide* p. 108). It is therefore easily understood why the brigade did not get further forward on the 9th.

By brigade orders, patrols were to be sent as follows :—

"13th Dragoons—
1. Domfessel - Pfalzburg main road, with small patrols to Lützelstein.
2. Lixheim and Weckersweiler.

16th Uhlans—
1. Saarunion-Pfalzburg.
2. Saarunion-Finstingen, thence in three parties by Lixheim, Barthelmingen, Mittersheim to Dieuze.

"The patrols are to be made so strong, that, after they have split, as ordered, into parties, each remains an officer, or capable N.C.O., and six to eight horses strong. It is left to the regiments to send supports to fixed places."

Comments and suggestions.

Apart from the fact that different patrols were here sent along the same roads, to no purpose, the measures taken do not in the least accord with

CAVALRY ON SERVICE 137

the situation. If the brigade, as a whole, for the reasons given above, could not cover considerable distances beyond Saarunion, yet the 16th Uhlans were available, and the 13th Dragoons were, as the orders show, in the position to provide patrols.

Aug. 9.

The brigade had to carry out two important duties with every means at its disposal: (1) to establish communication with the Third Army which was supposed to be in the passes of the Vosges or just on the far side; and which should be met with by the actively led patrols of the 13th Dragoons by Pfalzburg and Lützelstein; (2) to reconnoitre far in advance towards Dieuze and Noměny.

This duty could have been entrusted to the 16th Uhlans, which could have easily reached Dieuze, twenty-three miles, without undue exertion, as an advanced guard pushed well forward; and could have sent on its vanguards as far as Mörchingen-Chateau Salins, and southwards to the Rhine-Marne canal, nine to ten miles further.

A squadron might have been pushed to the front towards the fortress of Marsal; another squadron to the Rhine-Marne canal, and an officer's patrol to the right flank.

The direction of Solgne, Noměny, and Nancy might have been prescribed for these parties in which to establish further advanced posts.

If the brigade reached Dieuze the next day, the 16th Uhlans could have got to the vicinity of Delme.

In this way the brigade would have carried out the strategic reconnaissance, while, as a matter of fact, they scarcely fulfilled the requirements of divisional cavalry.*

* We may take this opportunity of quoting how Colonel Cherfils theoretically thinks that reconnaissance should be carried out, when it

Aug. 9.

Destruction of the railway.

The next day, at 8 a.m., while on the march to Eschweiler, the general sent a report of the results of the reconnaissance to Corps Head Quarters, which said that "the patrols, sent three hours' distance southwards in a semicircle from Saarunion, had seen no signs of the enemy."

The Corps Head Quarters sent the report on to Army Head Quarters, with the addition that Captain v. Rochow had cut the railway and the telegraph of the Pfalzburg-Lunéville railway at Saarburg, and had left a lance stuck in the place where he had cut it.

Captain v. Rochow, adjutant of the Corps Head Quarters, had been given twenty-five picked

---

becomes a question of pushing patrols forward in a definite direction as far as possible. For purposes of a practical example, we will here assume that it became necessary to push patrols as near Metz as possible on the road by Remilly. As I have already stated (*vide* p. 120), no result can be gained by pushing forward isolated patrols for a great distance. I will further assume that the duty was allotted to the 16th Uhlans under the conditions of August 9.

The regiment puts in the advance guard one squadron, which rejects its weaker horses, about one-quarter of its number, and hands them over to a squadron of the main body. The regiment arrives at Mörchingen, twenty-two miles, without undue fatigue, and the advance guard squadron rides to Holacourt, thirty miles, where the picked horses arrive fit and well. Here two-thirds of the horses remain, and the specially selected one-third get to Remilly, forty miles; from here a well-mounted officer, with six of the best horses of the squadron, arrives in front of the fortifications of Metz, fifty miles.

Any idea of doing more in the presence of the enemy must be given up, since the furthest patrols must preserve a surplus of strength with a view to the movements of the enemy, and the necessity of bringing back intelligence.

If a similar duty were given to a brigade, the most advanced regiment would have to free itself of its weakest horses in the same way, and a further stage could be advanced.

In contrast to the usual mode of finding a selection of very fit horses from a great big mass of troops for a particular job, this method of advance offers the great advantages that the units are not mixed up; that a force, ready to fight, is kept together in a body, in which even the weaker discarded horses can fill the ranks for the fight; that strenuous demands are carried out with the smallest possible loss in horseflesh.

horses from the brigade for the purpose of cutting the railway, and in twenty-four hours had covered fifty-six miles. To support him a strong detachment was held ready at Drülingen, which were to meet him on the 10th. According to the 16th Uhlans' diary, many of the horses succumbed later to fatigue.

Aug. 9.

This action must be regarded as conforming with the military situation, as its object was undoubtedly to check evacuations from Pfalzburg, which was not yet invested.

It is a curious thing that the place where it was cut was marked by a lance, which anybody could have removed. Such a mark, which, by the way, brings the damaged place also to the enemy's notice, should not be employed; but a sketch, in which the place is accurately marked, should be handed in.

It is also a question whether the party could not have been spared such fatigue, which resulted in the loss of many horses, if it had hurried its retirement less, after it had carried out the expedition successfully.

If it is a question of an important duty, the utmost must be demanded of the horses when necessary; but when that duty is completed the saving of horseflesh reassumes its due importance. If a whole squadron had been given the task, and it had proceeded, as explained in the above remarks in the footnote, this loss would probably have been avoided.

How far General v. Bredow's patrols actually went on that day was not ascertainable; the marking of them is therefore omitted on the map.

A memorandum from the Head Quarters of the Third Army reached, moreover, the Head Quarters

Aug. 9. of the Second Army on this date, so the communication between them may properly be regarded as established.

French movements.
The following remarks should be made on the measures taken by the French:—

Supreme Head Quarters had changed their intention of a concentration of the whole army at Chalons. It was decided to face the enemy still east of Metz with the army.

Grenier's and Lorencez's Divisions of the 4th Corps, as well as Legrand's Cavalry Division, had moved off at earliest dawn, and camped on the plateau of St. Barbe, where Ladmirault collected them, and set them to work on entrenchments, to meet the expected attack of the Germans.

Grenier's Division had started at 5 p.m., and reached its camp at Glattigny at 11 p.m.

Bazaine had issued orders for entrenchments at Falkenberg. The events which Lieutenant v. Czettritz related occurred in the morning. The bridge over the Nied was destroyed, as well as the railway, by the explosion which Captain Brix had reported.

Bazaine made his Head Quarters in Kurzel. During the ride through the Remilly wood, horsemen, who watched their march, were noticed on the left flank, some of them dismounted. As Dick de Lonlay mentions, they were thought to be the enemy's advanced guard!

It cannot be ascertained what troops the patrol belonged to. If the French were not mistaken (and they perhaps saw ghosts), these patrols could only have belonged to the 2nd Dragoons or the 15th Uhlans. But it is typical of the state of the French army that nothing was done to gain satisfactory information of the conjectured hostile advanced guard.

CAVALRY ON SERVICE 141

Montaudon's Division left their position at Falkenberg at 10 a.m., and retired to Sanry. During their march through Falkenberg, according to the French account, the rear-guard of 18th Jägers exchanged shots with a troop of Uhlans which followed, keeping them in view. So definite an account as this leaves no doubt of its accuracy. Unhappily the German accounts leave no means of ascertaining to what unit these horsemen belonged.*

Aug. 9.

In any case, it can be taken for granted that touch was maintained here by the German cavalrymen.

The outposts of Castagny's Division had exchanged shots in the morning with hostile patrols on the road to Bolchen.

At 2 p.m. the march began; at 3 o'clock the outposts had again to keep off hostile patrols by opening fire.

The division occupied their bivouac at Kurzel, on the left bank of the Nied, at 11.30 p.m. Metman's Division reached Maizeroy, 9 a.m., followed also by Uhlans, who, partly dismounted, and making skilful use of the ground, watched the march of the column. After repeated halts of an hour or more, to let the transport through, they reached their camp at Pange after midnight.

Decaen's Division had started from Bingen at 3 p.m., and reached their camp at Kurzel at 10 p.m. Clerembault's Cavalry Division had started at the same time, and reached their camp beyond the castle of Urville at 7 p.m.

The 2nd Corps had begun their retreat from

* According to the accounts of an officer, who was in a position to survey the situation on that day, it may be surmised that this troop belonged to the 3rd Squadron, 15th Uhlans, which on the 8th already had advanced by Lexingen, and on the 9th was still employed on the left flank.

Aug. 9. Gross-Tänchen as early as one in the morning, and the rearguard, the 3rd Lancers, could only follow at 7 o'clock, owing to the many blocks and crossings on the way.

"Some hostile patrols appeared." Frossard, arrived at Brulingen, was informed that the enemy was not following any more, but was, on the contrary, taking the direction to the left towards Pont à Mousson.*

The order arrived to reach Remilly as quickly as possible, and, if possible, Courcelles on the Nied, since a Prussian attack was expected. The corps reached its bivouac at Remilly about 7 p.m.

The Guard Corps had started at midday, and camped with its infantry at Sillers and its cavalry division beyond Pange. The previous description shows the enemy's movements were known by the 15th Uhlans, and accurately reported. It was known that the main forces of the enemy had halted. But naturally it could not be at once concluded that the intention to defend the Nied valley was connected with the halt.

* This statement arouses the suspicion that it was formed subsequently, and that it anticipates the events of August 10.

CHAPTER IV

AN order from Royal Head Quarters reached the Head Quarters of the First Army on the evening of the 9th, which said, among other things, that—

Aug. 10.
The First Army and Royal Head Quarters.

> "the cavalry is to be pushed out at some considerable distance, and to be supported by advanced guards well to the front, in order to protect the march and give each army time to concentrate in case of need."

On this General v. Steinmetz made the following dispositions concerning the cavalry :—

> "The 3rd Cavalry Division will march on the right flank of the army either through the ford at Buss, or by Völklingen to Ueberherrn behind the First Army Corps, and will push out parties on Busendorf and Bolchen. The 1st Cavalry Division will follow the army by Völklingen to Ludweiler."

If we compare the instructions of Royal Head Quarters with the measures taken by the Army Head Quarters, we are bound to admit that the Army Head Quarters in its operation orders completely ignored the instructions from Royal Head Quarters, and gave contrary directions to what had been ordered there.

These instructions from Royal Head Quarters let two points be seen: (1) that there was discontent with results hitherto achieved by reconnaissance; (2) that owing to the great extent of front assumed by the whole army, there was felt a need of making

Aug. 10. certain of a timely concentration in case the enemy took up a position or advanced to attack. [Compare with what has been said on p. 111, etc.]

Comments on the tasks to be solved by the cavalry of the First Army.

The First Army on this day had at its disposal the 3rd Cavalry Division as well as the 1st, which was completely concentrated in the neighbourhood of St. Johann.

If it were intended to comply with the order from Royal Head Quarters, this would have best been done by allotting the northern road from Saarlouis by Busendorf to Metz to the 3rd Cavalry Division with the task of sending a strong detachment by Kedingen towards Diedenhofen, and by allotting the Bolchen-Tennschen road to the 1st Cavalry Division with the special duty of reconnoitring the country as far as the St. Avold-Metz road, and keeping up communication with the Second Army, *i.e.* with the 6th Cavalry Division.

The main body of the 3rd Cavalry Division could have reached Busendorf this day, and its most advanced patrols Kedingen and the western edge of the Villers wood.

The 1st Cavalry Division, which could not use the road by Forbach allotted to the Second Army, and had to make a round by Wehrden, would not have got beyond Kreuzwald with its main body, but its officers' patrols could well have reached the German Nied by way of Bolchen and Buschborn, and the advanced squadrons Teterchen and Buschborn.

Considerable exertions should have been exacted from the cavalry divisions on this day to let them get at last the necessary start ahead of the army. They should also have started so early as not to impede the advance of the infantry corps.

Nothing of the sort was done, and we shall see

that the exertions became far more severe when at last the omission had to be repaired.

Aug. 10.

On the 10th, in spite of the cavalry divisions making only average day marches, their fatigues were great.

The march moved forward very slowly, and the day's point was reached very late, on account of the many crossings and the long halts and delays.

Such a method of marching wearies troops out of all comparison with the distance traversed. If the cavalry divisions had been instructed to put their march limit about ten miles further forward, and had been given the chance of riding freely forward, they would have come in fresher than by this procedure.

It is, besides, an old principle that cavalry should never be made to march behind or between other troops if it can possibly be avoided.

The 3rd Cavalry Division had not been able to use the ford at Buss, and had crossed the Saar at Völklingen behind the First Army Corps. The 1st Cavalry Division followed behind the 3rd.

Both divisions had had to wait hours at Völklingen.

In the regimental diaries there are numerous complaints of the fatigues of this march, which was made also in very bad weather.

The bivouac which the 1st Cavalry Division occupied, in a narrow valley at Ludweiler, was completely blocked in front and rear by transport. (It can be seen how a faulty control of transport can call in question the employment of a large body of troops.) Without being obliged by circumstances to do so, the cavalry of the First Army in particular always occupied bivouacs during this advance—a mistake which caused the troops far

Aug. 10. more wastage of strength than if the greatest exertions had been demanded of them.

As a principle, cavalry ought to bivouac *only* when absolutely compelled by circumstances to do so.

14th Uhlans.

The 14th Uhlans formed the advance guard of the 3rd Cavalry Division. It also provided the outposts, and reached its position at a late hour of the night. A report from Colonel v. Lüderitz, commanding the regiment, dated Hargarten, 4 a.m., August 11, is to hand—

> "1st and 2nd Squadrons bivouac at Hargarten-Falk. One squadron west of Hargarten, with a piquet at Teterchen and at Kuhmen. One squadron at Dahlen, with piquet at Tromborn. Piquet at Kuhmen has communication with the outposts of the First Army Corps. No news of enemy. Fifty hussars marched from Bolchen to Metz early this morning."

The source of the last information is not stated. Had a patrol met the hussars, or did the news originate from the account of the inhabitants of Bolchen? It seems certain from the report that patrols had been sent there.

One other report is to hand, from Lieutenant v. Wallenberg, 14th Uhlans, despatched 11 p.m., from Falkenberg to Army Head Quarters, as follows:—

> "The corps hitherto quartered in Chalons is said to have reached the line Kurzel-Pange-Mont, and to have relieved Bazaine's corps, which has moved to Ogy. The bivouacs on this line have been seen at close quarters."

In this report, too, the fault to be found is that the source is not given from which the statement contained in the first sentence originated. It is, therefore, worthless. The actual importance of the report comes from the fact that the leader himself saw a considerable hostile camp on the line Kurzel-Pange-Mont.

Aug. 10.

It was the 3rd Corps which the patrol had in its front, and which maintained its general position during the day. It was probably the Imperial Guard which was taken for the corps that had hitherto been in Chalons.

The composition of the enemy's army was at any rate not known to the patrol leader. It is to be desired that the higher commands should make the leaders of patrols sent to a distance acquainted with what they know from Supreme Head Quarters of the distribution of the enemy.

Captain v. Hymmen had scouted by Buschborn as far as Helsdorf with his strong patrol, and lay up with the enemy's camps at Tennschen opposite him. His vedettes stood in view of the enemy's. As appears from a report from Lieutenant Graf Asseburg, 15th Hussars, of the following day, Captain v. Hymmen had estimated the enemy encamped on the hills on the far side of the Nied —two divisions and the Cavalry Division of the 4th Corps—at 50,000 men, which was rather too high. Hymmen then reached Waibelskirchen, according to a report from Colonel v. Alvensleben (see p. 152). So touch was at last established again with the enemy's left. Unhappily it cannot be found out anywhere what happened to the captain's important reports, which were probably addressed to the 3rd Cavalry Division. Anyway, they never reached Royal Head Quarters, since the following remark occurs in the Official History of the War, p. 427 :—

Hymmen's patrol.

"Since the cavalry divisions of the First Army were not in the front line, direct touch with the enemy here almost entirely ceased. It was only through the

Aug. 10. advance guard of the Seventh Corps that a report from Captain v. Schütz, 8th Hussars, was received in the afternoon, which stated that some corps of the enemy stood west of Füllingen."

The report came from the outposts which the regiment had put out west of Porcelette. It gave no new information, since touch had been gained here on the day before by the 15th Uhlans and by Itzenplitz's patrol, and had been maintained by that regiment.

Here, again, one of the most important reports never reached its destination. It may be remembered that one means of discovering the loss of a report consists in numbering the reports. It is also advisable to recapitulate briefly the purport of specially important reports in a later one, *e.g.*, "Report No. 2, the enemy's camp at Tennschen, reported by me at 5.30 a.m., etc., etc."

The above-quoted order from Royal Head Quarters, referring to a bolder advance of the cavalry divisions, had also been received by the Head Quarters of the Second Army.

6th Cavalry Division. As we saw, Prince Frederick Charles had already constantly given effect on his own initiative to the same idea. It is true, in consequence of the distribution of the cavalry divisions to the Army Corps he had unhappily deprived himself of any influence upon its proper execution. The 6th Cavalry Division had been directed to the rear. As appears from a letter of August 10, from Major v. Schoenfels, general staff officer of the 6th Cavalry Division, to the 5th Cavalry Division, stating what had been ordered, a feeling of being appointed to the Reserve was produced, and this able officer felt it apparently with some bitterness. From the reports sent in of the 15th Uhlans, the Army Head Quarters had concluded that the

CAVALRY ON SERVICE 149

enemy's main forces were on the march from St. Avold to Metz in front of the Second Army's right wing; and that the 2nd French Corps had been induced, by the result of the battle of Spicheren, to retire southwards by Saargemünd. The safeguarding and reinforcement of this wing was therefore ordered, whilst on the left wing considerations of their communication with the Third Army remained all important, as in front of that wing at Saaralbe and Saarunion no traces of the enemy had been discovered.

The 6th Cavalry Division was now pushed forward by the Third Army Corps, probably under the influence of the directions given by Army Head Quarters.

A memorandum was sent this day from Corps Head Quarters to the Army Head Quarters, dated St. Avold, to this effect—

> "I am bringing the 6th Cavalry Division forward to the villages south of St. Avold, with the duty of placing their outposts in touch with those of the 6th Infantry Division on the right, and as far as the Nied, in touch with those of the 5th Cavalry Division on the left. I propose to have them moved further forward to-morrow, towards the Mosel."

On the same day Duke William also received verbal instructions from the Corps Commander.

In accordance with an order of 2 p.m. from Rossbrück, the Duke concentrated the division at 5.30 p.m. at the cross-roads due east of St. Avold, and from there disposed the regiments in the localities south of the town.

The 16th Hussars, furthest on the west, provided the outposts on the line Durchthal-Trittelingen-Tetingen. Active patrolling was ordered by Pange on Metz.

It can be taken for granted that this order, to

Aug. 10.

be found in the diary of the 14th Cavalry Brigade, was accompanied by further verbal explanation, especially as to the patrolling. The 16th Hussars' diary, kept with commendable accuracy, and checked by Colonel v. Schmidt, mentions a patrol to Falkenberg, and remarks, "Still no touch with the enemy, which had been lost since the 6th."

To gain touch with the enemy was certainly not difficult; to regain it had to be striven for by every means, after the division had lost it through being kept back, except its 15th Uhlans, which had been detached to the front.

The object would have certainly been gained if the divisional leader, at the rendezvous of the division, had called up some officers as patrol leaders, and had sent them off with personal instructions. Five patrols—one from each regiment—would have been sufficient. Of these, two by Buschborn-Bolchen, and by Falkenberg-Gross Tänchen should have sought touch with the neighbouring troops, while the three others should have been pushed forward towards the French Nied respectively by Füllingen, Gänglingen, and Falkenberg, and a squadron each sent after them, in support, to the German Nied on Füllingen and Falkenberg.

In the records there are no reports from the 6th Cavalry Division, which only reached their cantonments towards nightfall.

15th Uhlans.

The 15th Uhlans had kept touch with the enemy on this day also. It was made certain that the French were no longer in retreat beyond the French Nied.

At 11.30 a.m. Colonel v. Alvensleben sent the following report from Lubeln, through the 6th Infantry Division, to Corps Head Quarters; it only arrived there at 5 p.m.:—

CAVALRY ON SERVICE 151

"The rearguard of the 3rd Corps retired on the direct road to Metz at 2 o'clock at night (the corps yesterday by Pange). Marshall Bazaine is to-day behind the French Nied, as was anticipated owing to its late withdrawal, in two separate camps at Mont and Sillers on the Nied, with a rearguard at Les Ménils, this side of the wood. Whether other troops are combined with the 3rd Corps, perhaps Frossard's corps, which retired direct from Saarbrücken, can for the moment only be guessed from the size of the camp."*

Aug. 10.

This report was founded on observations of Brix's outpost squadron, which had learnt, from their patrols to the enemy's flanks, of the night march of the enemy's rearguard, which they followed to Bingen, pushing their vedettes forward to the opposite slope within 1100 yards of those of the enemy—a brilliant example of the action of outposts. Of course a report was immediately to be forwarded of the "following up."

At 5.30 p.m. the colonel reported from the high left bank of the Nied valley west of Bingen, which afforded a grand view to the west, close in front of the enemy's posts—

"The enemy is still in the same position at Mont, Pont à Chaussy, and the farm of Plappecourt (Pelplinger Hof), and from there out towards Frécourt. The left of yesterday's distribution of troops, which appeared to belong to another corps, proves to belong to the 3rd Corps as well. The accompanying 'small book' was found there. An inhabitant states that he remembers the 64th, 85th, and 98th in this camp. The regiment learnt from a labourer expelled from Metz that only Gardes-Mobiles and Frontier-Guards mount the guards there, and that on both sides of the road from Metz to the 3rd Corps' camp troops are bivouacking in large bodies. The army thus seems to be making a general concentration there. Marshall Bazaine is therefore

* The observation was correct; only the Guard Corps formed the reinforcement, which the colonel naturally could not know.

Aug. 10.

likely to maintain his strong position there. A squadron, 19th Dragoons,* has arrived in Füllingen, a troop from the 5th and 14th Uhlans in Waibelskirchen." †

Here, therefore, was learnt for the first time the intention of the French to make a stand and fight. The reported halt of the enemy on the previous day did not admit of that intention being established with certainty.

From the notes kindly placed at my disposal, I quote the following example to show the service of the outposts and the activity of the French cavalry :—

> "Bazaine had left strong outposts between the German and the French Nied. In spite of their numbers, these contented themselves with occupying the lower heights on the line Frécourt-Pelplingen-Itzingerhof, with a great number of vedettes and moving squadrons actively behind them, but never in front of them, although the far higher left bank of the German Nied hid from them any distant view. So the 1st Squadron were able to keep their vedettes undisturbed on this most advantageous high ground, overlook every movement of the enemy to his very camp, and rest their main body in safety, covered by the Nied."

5th Cavalry Division.

The following order arrived 3 p.m., August 9, for the 5th Cavalry Division, with whose activity the General Officer Commanding Tenth Army Corps could not possibly have been satisfied on that day :—

> "Lieut.-General v. Rheinbaben will advance with the cavalry division as early as possible to-morrow morning, August 10, in the direction of Metz, and will establish his Head Quarters in Falkenberg. He will send patrols as far as possible towards Metz and Nancy, and provide means of getting his reports to me as quickly as possible."

---

* 3rd Squadron, 19th Dragoons. No mention is made of the advance of this squadron either in the History of the 19th Dragoons or in its War Diary.

† Certainly Captain v. Hymmen's party.

CAVALRY ON SERVICE 153

On the same day this order from General v. Voigts-Rhetz was supplemented by a personal letter of his, timed 6 p.m.— Aug. 10.

> "In consequence of reports * received to-day by me from your Excellency and General v. Redern, I direct you to make every endeavour to-morrow, August 10, to reach the enemy. It will be advisable to send forward a part of the cavalry concentrated under your direct orders, and with the rest to spread out as far as possible in every direction. I have charged Captain v. Alvensleben, orderly officer of the Corps Head Quarter Staff, and Lieutenant v. Podbielski, general staff officer, to report themselves to you this very day, and direct you to employ them at the head of your cavalry."

This letter went to Rheinbaben after the Chief Staff Officer, Tenth Army Corps, had been to see the general, and had recommended him an energetic advance at the request of General v. Voigts-Rhetz, but had not met with any response whatever. This is the explanation of the straight language of the missive.

In a subsequent order of the same day the leader of the 5th Cavalry Division was requested to keep an officer and some orderlies always posted with Duke William of Mecklenburg to report all important events. Such an arrangement is certainly the most effective means of keeping up communication between two bodies of troops. He was also reminded of the forwarding of newspapers, letters from the post-offices, telegrams and prisoners.

These orders and arrangements make it clear that Corps Head Quarters considered it necessary to urge the leader of the 5th Cavalry Division to more decisive action.

General v. Rheinbaben in consequence ordered General v. Redern, at 9.45 p.m. on the 9th,

* *Vide* p. 135.

Aug. 10.
"to send the nearest regiment with the horse battery to Püttlingen on the 10th, so that these troops arrive there at 7 a.m. With the main body he was to reach Landorf, occupy Mörchingen, send patrols on Pont à Mousson, Metz, and Nancy, and make every endeavour to come up with the enemy."

General v. Redern sent the 17th Hussars with the battery to Püttlingen. The regiment was put under General v. Barby's command, and he was ordered by the divisional commander from Barst, 8 a.m., to advance at once to Falkenberg, to send a party to Han an der Nied, and patrols on Pont à Mousson. From the fact of the divisional commander sending this order in writing, it can be gathered that the staff did not accompany Barby's Brigade, but followed it.

General v. Redern reached Landorf with the 10th and 11th Hussars, without meeting any hostile parties, and only a patrol sent to Baronweiler was assailed by some five isolated hostile cavalrymen. A patrol of five, under Lieutenant v. Hirschfeld, 10th Hussars, sent to Château Salins, found the place clear of the enemy. A remark in the brigade diary says, "all reports shewed that the enemy had 24 hours' start."

Schlick's squadron (3rd), 13th Uhlans, had been sent to Han on the Nied; up to there they found no sign of the enemy, but between there and Remilly they took one officer and twenty-four men, wounded and stragglers from different regiments of the 2nd and 3rd Corps, prisoners. Lieutenant Baron Grote, who was given the task of cutting the railway at Remilly, was only very incompletely successful owing to want of tools. (It is not quite clear what object this cutting of the railway was to serve.) The 3rd Squadron, 19th Dragoons, reported, 5 p.m., from Bingen (compare p. 151), that they had

CAVALRY ON SERVICE 155

Aug. 10.

met no enemy, but had learned from the 1st Squadron, 15th Uhlans, that Bazaine lay behind the French Nied.* Captain v. Alvensleben, detailed to the division from Corps Head Quarters, had patrolled to Oron and Château Salins, equally without meeting any parties of the enemy. He reported 12 noon from Landorf—

"Frossard's whole corps going back to Metz on the same road. No touch established yet."

[He accompanied Redern's Brigade. This fact, and the direction of the brigade's advance, may have been known at Corps Head Quarters.]

The first report from Falkenberg was sent by Lieutenant v. Podbielski at 11 a.m.

"Bazaine's corps evacuated Falkenberg 4 p.m. yesterday. An engine stands in the station. Enemy's patrols press up as far as the town. I shall try to get forward, along the railway, towards Metz and Verny. No fresh news from Alvensleben, since communication with Mörchingen is not yet open. A new daily paper herewith."

General v. Rheinbaben sent the following despatch 5.30 p.m. from Falkenberg (abbreviated):—

"The division marched under the divisional commander with four regiments and a battery on the Barst-Val-Ebersing road to Falkenberg. Two regiments under General v. Redern from Saaralbe, by Altdorf and Gross-Tänchen, on Landorf. Large parties reconnoitred on Rollingen, Kurzel, and Han an der Nied, and they were to send patrols to Metz and Pont à Mousson. Large, deserted camps were found, and quantities of provisions at the railway station. It was impossible up till now to overtake formed bodies of men. General v. Redern could not either. Napoleon is said to have inspected Bazaine's corps here the day before yesterday.

* It is strange that the squadron, being at such short distance from that ground, did not itself at once reconnoitre in that direction.

Aug. 10.

According to reports from the outposts of 13th Uhlans, Han a. d. Nied, Remilly, and Chanville are occupied by us, and nothing more of the enemy is to be seen. Reports from Lieutenant v. Podbielski and Captain v. Alvensleben are forwarded herewith."

Podbielski's report.

Lieutenant v. Podbielski sent the following interesting report to his own corps about the same time from Falkenberg :—

"I accompanied twenty of the 13th Uhlans, under Lieutenant v. Treskow, from Falkenberg towards Herlingen. I found the railway bridge blown up at the latter place, so communication to Argenchen was hindered. Small detachments of infantry were marching on the road to Metz, which, according to the inhabitants, belonged to MacMahon's corps. In Argenchen I found out for certain that the last formed bodies of Bazaine's corps had marched at 11.30 last night on the road to Metz. Small parties had remained there till to-day. I followed their tracks by Chanville, and found a man on the far side of the town, a German, who had left Metz early this morning. He said—

"1. Strong columns had moved forward to-day from the town towards Bolchen and Pange.

"2. Gunners had said they were marching eastwards this afternoon.

"3. Great many troop trains had come into Metz from Nancy in the course of the night.

"At this moment the man fled, as a hostile infantry patrol appeared. Sergeant Keck, with a few Uhlans, went out and succeeded in making four prisoners. I then went with Lieutenant v. Treskow, on both sides of the road, towards Pange, and we soon perceived large clouds of smoke in the direction of Pange. We managed to slip through the Berlize wood, and made the following observations :—

"1. A bivouac of at least two infantry regiments on the side of the hill east of Mont.

"2. A camp of the same size behind Mont, and behind it stood a large waggon park.

"3. I saw a vast number of tents at Puche.

CAVALRY ON SERVICE

"4. A bivouac of all arms at Pange.

"5. West of the road to Pange, north of Sanry, lay a battalion only 800 paces from me. I could clearly watch the men's movements cooking.

"6. Heavy columns of infantry and artillery were marching east and south from the hills of Metz towards Kurzel, Pange, and Mont. I carefully watched their direction of march for a long time. I was able to seize an inhabitant of Pange, who verified for me the names of places, and said at the same time that Bazaine's corps was in bivouac at Ogy, and that the advancing troops had been till now in camp at Chalons, and were now going into bivouac behind—that is to say, west of the Nied.

"It was now 4.30 p.m., and I retired with Lieutenant v. Treskow in all haste, so as not to be discovered, by Chanville, to Falkenberg, where I have just arrived. I forward herewith a despatch from General v. Rheinbaben, which gives some explanation of the Emperor's presence in Falkenberg, as well as some letters which I found in a letter-box on the way. I sent the railway time-table for the French troops, which I found in Herlingen, with the prisoners. The railway officials have all left their posts, the points at the stations are destroyed—the bridge at Herlingen too—and the rails torn up in many places. I received the enclosed report about midday from Captain v. Alvensleben, according to which he has not got beyond Mörchingen."

The report affords a brilliant example for the carrying out of such reconnaissances. What General v. Rheinbaben's twenty-four squadrons did not succeed in doing—gaining touch with the enemy and bringing in news of him—Lieutenant v. Podbielski carried out most effectively with a troop of Uhlans.* This fact must, indeed, have been somewhat mortifying to the leader of the cavalry division. The way the officer proceeded deserves special notice. After he had seen the first detachments of the enemy's infantry in

Aug. 10.

* The patrol leader lost his horse on this occasion.

Aug. 10. Argenchen, and had discovered signs of the retreat, the way for further reconnaissance was indicated, the track of the game was found, and it was then stalked in skilful fashion. The questioning of the inhabitants he met had brought in important intelligence. The prisoners sent back were therefore specially useful, because they were not stragglers, and could give information of the latest events. The creeping up to the enemy's camp through the wood north-west of Berlize must have been effected with great boldness and skill.

The coign of vantage of the officers was probably the northern edge of Conroy Holz (wood), because it can be reached by a narrow green valley screened on all sides from view. [See Ordnance Map.]

The patrol itself doubtless remained hidden further back in the wood, while the officers crept forward on foot to within 800 paces of the enemy's camp. It was most important that the leader should verify the names of the places from an inhabitant.

Mistakes are easily made, and may lead to serious results if reported; especially in a country like this, where the villages are so extraordinarily numerous, mistakes can easily occur; it is the same with countries where the appearance of the villages is very much alike—where the church towers, for example, are built all according to one pattern.* It is to be further observed that the patrol leader watched the direction of march of the enemy's columns for some time before he definitely determined its bearing. To determine it thus is often very difficult, as already remarked elsewhere; in

* I call to mind, for example, the Lüneburger Heide, where all the villages are almost hidden in the small cultivated woods, and hardly present any difference in appearance.

order to make sure of reporting correctly, it is absolutely necessary to watch for some time. General v. Rheinbaben attached another letter to Lieutenant v. Podbielski's report, in which he said—

Aug. 10.

> "I consider it no longer necessary to move forward with large bodies of cavalry against the fortress and the strongly held position on the line of the Nied. I therefore propose to remain in Falkenberg with the main body of Barby's Brigade, and to push forward strong reconnoitring parties towards Metz and the Nied, as well as towards Pont à Mousson, and to give General v. Redern a similar order. It appears desirable to occupy the railway station at Falkenberg with infantry from the Third or Fourth Corps."

As the general could not proceed any further to the front, it should not have been difficult for him to see that his way was to approach closer to the Mosel.

Lieutenant v. Podbielski sent a further report to his Corps' Head Quarters the same evening, where it arrived 1.40 a.m. on the 11th, which is remarkable for its grasp of the situation—

Podbielski's suggestions.

> "The position at Falkenberg is regarded by General v. Rheinbaben as very exposed. After having seen the French at large to-day I cannot take this view. The enemy is greatly depressed. I think, on the contrary, that the more we stick to the enemy's heels the more prisoners we shall make. I am very tired to-day, after 20 hours' ride, so that I cannot possibly return to Püttlingen; but I think it would not be a difficult task to cut the railway from Nancy to Metz. It could be done with certainty; but here they want an order for everything, so I humbly beg for instructions for further action."

Captain v. Alvensleben sent another report to Corps Head Quarters at 9 p.m., to the effect that he had ridden from Han on the Nied to Baudrecourt, but had only met stragglers from the 2nd Corps.

If we examine the measures of General v. Rheinbaben for carrying out the order given him on the 9th, we find he had, in accordance with it, taken up his quarters in Falkenberg, whither he had properly directed his main body, while General v. Redern was ordered to take a direction further south in accordance with the situation.

It is not clear whether communication was established with the 6th Cavalry Division—that is, with the 15th Uhlans. If this had been kept on the previous day, the advance of the division would have been based on certain information about the enemy, and could have been directed accordingly. Communication between Püttlingen and St. Avold had to be continuous.

The general remained in Falkenberg with three regiments, whilst the 17th Hussars, which had accompanied Barby's Brigade on the left flank to keep touch with General v. Redern, were cantoned in Chemery and Edelingen. On outpost duty, one squadron 19th Dragoons were in Rollingen, one squadron 13th Uhlans in Chanville, on the far side of the Crown woods of Remilly; so the most important roads to Metz were watched. General v. Redern lay with the main body of his troops in Landorf, with a squadron 10th Hussars pushed southwards to Baronweiler. We have already stated how the patrolling was arranged. Château Salins, Oron, and Remilly were the furthest points to which the patrols had reached that night; Podbielski's patrol was in front of Pange. From Rollingen the patrols of the squadron of Dragoons must have gained touch at Kurzel, and also, as we know, have established communication with the 15th Uhlans. Reports of the enemy from personal observation are, however, not to hand, and anyhow had not been received at nightfall from this wing, as appears from the report of the divisional commander, which we have quoted. This must be regarded as an omission.

Aug. 10.

The measures of the divisional commander on this day appear on the whole to meet the case, but omissions of the previous day cannot be made good quickly. If the enemy has a start of over 24 hours, as particularly here on the right wing, it is difficult to recover the lost ground. The main portions of the division had covered some 19 miles, the furthest patrols between 37 and 44 miles. No care seems to have been taken to secure the uninterrupted observation of the camp discovered at Pange. Had proper measures been taken the divisional leader would probably have mentioned it in his report. The simplest measure would have been to push the squadron in Chanville further forward, perhaps as far as Berlize, with orders to keep the enemy in view.

These observations and these measures should have been brought to the knowledge of the outposts at Rollingen, and these should have been requested to clear up the situation on the other bank of the Nied opposite their own front.

General v. Bredow had received orders from the Head Quarters of the Fourth Army Corps to advance to Eschweiler, to put outposts out on the line Finstingen-Drulingen, and to send patrols, specially in a southern direction, to keep up communication with the Third Army.

Bredow's Brigade.

The 7th Cuirassiers and 16th Uhlans patrolled on Saarburg and Pfalzburg, the 13th Dragoons by Drulingen on Pfalzburg, on Lixheim, and on

M

Aug. 10. Finstingen-Saarburg. So the regimental diaries relate. The patrolling of the regiments, therefore, does not appear to have been subject to a uniform control, since several patrols from different regiments were pushed forward along the same road. The reconnaissance in a westerly direction, particularly on the important road to Dieuze, as well as northwards, to communicate with the 5th Cavalry Division, was not given over to the 12th Cavalry Brigade, and so was probably supplied by the divisional cavalry regiments, and the 5th Dragoons which were still attached to the corps. There is, unhappily, no account whatever of this in the war records.

The patrols found no formed bodies of the enemy anywhere. Only from Lixheim the 13th Dragoons brought one prisoner, two horses, and an officer's kit-cart. A "party of the enemy" had stopped in quarters there the previous night.* Direct communication with the Fifth Army Corps was established in Lützelstein.

The Zabern-Saarburg railway was found cut south-west of Lixheim. Since the general mentions this in his despatch, a cutting of it by the enemy must be meant, for that done by Captain v. Rochow was known to him.

The Fourth Army Corps was unusually strong in cavalry, owing to the attachment to it of Bredow's Brigade and the presence of the 5th Dragoons.

The Head Quarters Staff, however, made practically no use of the cavalry allotted to it. Alas for these splendid regiments! What the regiments of Bredow's Brigade did here, could have

* Report of the brigade. Very indefinite statement. The approximate strength of the party and the troops composing it could at least be ascertained by the patrol in Lixheim. But probably the questions to the prisoners had elicited this.

fitly been done by the divisional cavalry regiments. Aug. 10.
The use that here was made of a considerable
part of the 5th Cavalry Division again arouses
regrets that Prince Frederick Charles had handed
over the direct disposal of them.

As the 5th Dragoons belonged to the Third
Army, and surely were anxious to join their
division, the 4th Cavalry Division, as soon as
possible, it should have been obvious to push
this unit southwards, say, towards Lixheim, to
seek touch with the Third Army as well as to
reconnoitre to the south.

The four squadrons would have fully sufficed
for both duties. While the two divisional cavalry
regiments should have sought to gain touch with
the 5th Cavalry Division by patrolling towards
Falkenberg and Gross-Tänchen; Bredow's Brigade,
united in a body, could have advanced in mass
by Finstingen in the direction of Baronweiler and
Château Salins, and have easily reached Dieuze on
the 10th. As it was, the brigade only marched
about six miles, and in a southerly direction.
[Compare the comments on p. 136, etc.]

On the movements of the French the following French measures.
remarks are to be made:—

The army had been concentrated this day in
the strong position behind the French Nied, and
fortifications had been actively taken in hand. It
was desired to await the enemy's attack here, and
it was thought that it could be expected at any
moment. The position extended from St. Barbe
by Tennschen to Pange. Should the army be compelled to relinquish it, a second position in advance
of the forts of Queuleu and St. Julien had been
decided on.

The movement of the 6th Corps from Chalons
to Metz, begun on the 9th, was continued. On

Aug. 10. the left wing the 4th Corps, to which Grenier's Division had again been attached, took up a position for battle at Glattigny, Cheuby, and on the plateau of St. Barbe, which was strongly entrenched.

The 3rd Corps also remained in its position and worked at entrenchments. A movable barricade was built on the bridge over the Nied at Kurzel. The cavalry division of the corps reconnoitred towards Falkenberg.

"The enemy's Uhlans are pressing right up to the piquets." The 4th Squadron of 2nd Mounted Jägers had a skirmish with Uhlans at Kurzel, who were foraging in a neighbouring farm.*

The 2nd Corps, with Lapasset's Brigade, had retreated by Lemud, Courcelles, to Ars Laquenexy and Mercy le Haut, and these places were occupied and strongly fortified by Lapasset's Brigade, to which a cavalry regiment had been attached; while the 2nd Corps was specially to hold the position of Courcelles.

A night attack of the Prussians was expected. The heights of Mercy were decided on as a second position. The reports make no mention of the appearance on this day of Prussian patrols.

The Guards retired to Lammerberg; their cavalry division remained at Pange.

Forton's Reserve Cavalry Division camped at 6 p.m. at Montigny, on the far side of the Mosel, near Metz. Du Barail's Reserve Cavalry Division, which had started from Lunéville on the 7th, reached Ban St. Martin, near Metz, after forced marches (57 miles in 18 hours).

* German records make no mention of this. The 1st Squadron 15th Uhlans or the 3rd Squadron 19th Dragoons may have been concerned in it.

CHAPTER V

WE have seen from the account of the events of August 10 that the commander of the First Army could not make up his mind to advance the cavalry divisions to the front, in spite of the hints from Royal Head Quarters.

Aug. 11.
Head Quarters of the First Army.

It has also been explained that it was due to the fact that news of the enemy was wanting.

This want was severely felt at Royal Head Quarters. In a memorandum from this staff, dated 6 a.m., the road St. Avold-Falkenberg-Herlingen, Han an der Nied-Nomény was once more distinctly pointed out as belonging to the right wing of the Second Army, as there was still transport of the First Army moving along it; and this distribution was to remain in force until news of the position of the enemy's main army was gained by the cavalry. Moltke, in a memorandum to General v. Stiehle, Chief of the Staff of the Second Army, dated Saarbrücken 10.45 a.m., thanks him for all his information "so much the more, as we have heard nothing from the First Army. I cannot even say where the First, Seventh, and Eighth Army Corps are marching to to-day." But no movement of the First Army was intended on this day, and the cavalry divisions remained in rear in their bivouacs, which were turned by the rain into a morass. An order issued in the morning proposed a forward movement of the corps to the Nied for the 12th, and by this

Aug. 11. the cavalry divisions were still not to be pushed forward, but, on the contrary, were considered as tied to the army, between the corps and on a level with them.

But when, during the course of the day, information had been at last received at Royal Head Quarters of the state of affairs with the First Army, it was thought that decisive intervention could no longer be delayed, and the First Army was therefore the same afternoon ordered to push both the cavalry divisions to the front that very day.

The cavalry divisions of First Army pushed to the front at last.

At 5 p.m. General v. Steinmetz then ordered the cavalry divisions to start forthwith; and the 3rd Cavalry Division was to reach Teterchen to-day, and the 1st Division Buschborn. So the word that freed them was given at last. To comply with the order the divisions had to carry out a very exhausting night march.

The 1st Cavalry Division started at 8 p.m., reached Buschborn late in the night, where the regiments waited a long time for orders, and at last bivouacked behind the outposts of the Seventh Army Corps to get a short rest.

The 3rd Cavalry Division did not leave their bivouac till 10 p.m.; the 14th Uhlans formed the advance guard, and had orders to watch the passages of the Nied from Tennschen to Hollingen. The main body of the regiment remained in Bettingen, furnished outposts on the Nied, and sent the 4th Squadron to reconnoitre towards Bolchen.

4th Squadron, 14th Uhlans, gets in touch with the enemy.

Near that place the squadron met a hostile patrol of dragoons, which was hotly pursued towards Tennschen, but could not be overtaken. In the pursuit the Uhlans reached the neighbourhood of a large camp on the far side of the Nied, in which great activity reigned. Strong columns of all arms were soon seen to leave the camp, and take the direction of Metz. The Uhlans followed at once, and were able to report that the enemy's rearguard halted but within four miles of Metz, at Bellecroix.

Aug. 11.

Lieutenant v. Ramin, who was reconnoitring, as we know, towards Diedenhofen on the extreme right flank, reached Dalstein in the morning, and there joined Lieutenant v. Papen, who was also patrolling in this neighbourhood in a combined advance on Diedenhofen.

Reconnaissance of Diedenhofen.

The two officers took in hand the reconnaissance of that fortress. They got near the gates, made certain that the fortress was occupied, and were able to retire without being fired on or pursued. On the morning of the 12th these two daring officers joined their regiments again.

Lieutenant v. Voigts-Rhetz, 8th Cuirassiers, had been sent with a troop to Busendorf, on the right flank, by divisional orders, in order to observe Diedenhofen and bring in information.

Captain v. Hymmen, who had gained close touch with the enemy the day before at Tennschen, had not let them out of his sight. As early as 5 a.m. he noticed that the enemy's corps, camped there,—"the same that had previously camped at Buschborn,"—struck their tents, and that the roads from St. Avold and Bolchen to Metz became covered with deep columns of all arms, which were marching in the direction of that fortress. He estimated the infantry on the road from Bolchen at 20,000 men.*

Hymmen's patrol in close contact with the enemy.

Captain v. Hymmen followed by Tennschen, and saw that the enemy's rearguard halted, 11.30 a.m., at the junction of both roads at Bellecroix.

This important report, unfortunately, did not

* The estimate—two divisions of the 2nd Corps—seems to have been pretty accurate.

Aug. 11. reach Head Quarters of the First Army till early on the 12th. As it is dated the afternoon of the 11th, it seems to have been delayed in its despatch. Here, again, it must be urged that quick observation in reconnaissance must find its completion in the immediate and certain transmission of the report.

A report from Lieutenant Graf v. Asseburg, 15th Hussars, who only reached the Nied at 2.45 p.m., and had observed the same as Captain v. Hymmen, had been telegraphed on to Royal Head Quarters at 8.45 p.m. This appears to have overtaken Hymmen's report.

So, close touch with the enemy had again been established by the First Army.

Head Quarters of the Second Army.

From the reports of the cavalry received on the 10th, the Head Quarters of the Second Army were bound to conclude that the enemy were preparing to accept battle on the French Nied. To this end pointed the fortification and occupation of the position, and the march of numerous columns eastwards from Metz. The Prince resolved to carry out a right wheel with the army, and to deploy on the line Falkenberg-Herlingen for an offensive battle. The Third Army Corps was to form the pivot of the wheel, and to find a suitable position for the purpose near Falkenberg, which could at once be occupied and strengthened by entrenchments. The advance guard was not to be pushed far forward; only weak cavalry patrols. Everything that might lead to isolated engagements was to be avoided before the general attack of the First and Second Armies should take place on the 16th. The Ninth Army Corps was to be in position on the 12th between Falkenberg and St. Avold, the head of the Tenth was to reach Chemery. The order to the Third Army Corps was issued 10.15 a.m.

CAVALRY ON SERVICE 169

If the presumption in regard to the attitude of the French proved correct, the cavalry divisions would have arrived at that stage which always occurs when opposing armies have approached so close to one another that there is no room for them in front, and when they are obliged to withdraw to the flanks.

Aug. 11.

Action of cavalry divisions when opposing armies meet.

Strategic reconnaissance to the front then comes to an end, but patrols will observe, by pressing round the enemy's flank, whether any change in the situation is occurring, or whether troops are being advanced or withdrawn.

This observation will not always be practicable with the wide extension of front of armies as will in future take the field, and will only be successful if the patrol leaders succeed in obtaining an undisturbed view from some commanding point, and establishing themselves there as standing patrols. The most vital point is to remain there undiscovered, and where necessary to take care by the organization of relay posts that reports arrive with speed and accuracy. In addition to these standing patrols, others will press further round the flanks, to the rear of the enemy.

Since too much reliance cannot be placed on the timely arrival of reports from these patrols, whose squadrons should try to follow at a reasonable distance of five to seven miles, special importance must be attached to the gaining of points suited to continued observation.* Reconnaissance to the front can now be left to the divisional cavalry.

The Second Army, which expected to engage in close touch with the First Army, had only, in

---

* For example, Château St. Blaise was just such a point, as we shall see later, which played an important part as a look-out post in the days that followed, and served the same purpose even during the investment.

Aug. 11. consequence of this, an opportunity for an enveloping movement with one cavalry division, the 5th, on the left wing, which was free.

The 6th Cavalry Division probably would have had at first to fill up the gap between the First and Second Armies, and would then have been withdrawn and placed ready to co-operate in front.

New duties for the cavalry.

But the movements of the enemy on the 11th introduced conditions other than what had been reasonably anticipated in the morning, and other duties developed for the reconnoitring cavalry. The Head Quarter Staff of the Third Army Corps had issued the following order to the 6th Cavalry Division from St. Avold, 11.30 p.m., August 10:—

> "The 6th Cavalry Division will advance to-morrow at 8.30 a.m. by Falkenberg and Steinbiedersdorf on Armsdorf and Brülingen, will occupy these places, and also Thonville, Diedersdorf, and Argenchen; push the advanced guard forward on Herlingen and Holacourt, and send patrols on Chanville, Béchy, Delme, and Baronweiler."

By this order the Corps Head Quarter Staff took the division over to the left flank, where it was at the earliest in a position to reconnoitre on the enemy's flank.

Since the Ninth Army Corps was to be in position on the following day between St. Avold and Falkenberg, the gap that existed through the movement of the Third Corps to the left, in front of the enemy, was soon filled up, and the disposal of the 6th Cavalry Division can be regarded as meeting the case, from the point of view of the Corps Head Quarters. Yet the assumption seems justified that if Army Head Quarters had still retained control of the division they would have

CAVALRY ON SERVICE 171

employed it differently, perhaps in a similar way to that suggested above. Aug. 11.

The Prince had, indeed, expressly reserved the disposal of the cavalry divisions in his own hands in the event of battle, but the method of their disposal naturally depended essentially on the point to which they had been previously directed; and therefore, if their effective co-operation in battle as contemplated by the commander of the army was to be relied upon, he should have determined their position.*

By the distribution of the cavalry divisions to various army corps, as previously mentioned, not only was their combined employment in reconnaissance renounced, but their co-operation on the battlefield, as the army leader had in view, was rendered very doubtful as well.

Duke William had issued the following order from Folschweiler for August 11:— 6th Cavalry Division.

> "The division will be concentrated at 9 a.m. on the 11th at the eastern exit of Tetingen, the 3rd Hussars in advance towards Falkenberg. The division will march by Maiweiler, on the line Herlingen-Holacourt. The 3rd Hussars will find the outposts on the line Argenchen-Holacourt. Patrols to be pushed forward on the right towards Chanville, to connect up with the First Army; on the left to Baronweiler, to connect up with the Tenth Army Corps, as well as to the Béchy-Luppy road; and by Mesnilhof towards Delme. The enemy is said to have retreated behind the Seille. On this point information as accurate as possible is to be collected. The outposts will report in writing, stating hour of despatch."

These orders for reconnaissance appear insufficient. It is, first of all, to be noticed that it is left entirely to the outposts to collect information, and

* Compare note, p. 106, and the explanations, pp. 110 and 178.

Aug. 11. the patrols are not pushed far enough to the front. According to the views obtaining to-day, the strategical reconnaissance (and here it was such in the first instance) would not have been left to the outposts. The divisional leader would immediately, on receipt of the orders from Corps Head Quarters, have ordered four officers to his quarters. These would have been given instructions by him; they would have been made to start at daybreak of the 11th in the directions indicated by corps orders, and to send back their reports to a news-collecting station established at Falkenberg. By some such method the division would have already been informed of the situation on their arrival in the area allotted to them, and could have sent on reports at once. But if the patrols only went out when the division marched off, or even, as it appears, on the arrival of the division in its area, it would be evening before reports could reach the superior authorities. Besides these patrols, one squadron, at least, ought to have been pushed forward on the right flank of the advancing division towards Kurzel-Pange, perhaps on Maizeroy, which, in addition to reconnoitring in that direction, could maintain connection with the First Army.

A patrol, under Lieutenant v. Arnim, Ziethen Hussars, observed on this date two squadrons of Chasseurs d'Afrique between Luppy and Béchy, and brought in a prisoner. The man, who had only arrived from Africa two days before, had taken the hussars for Spahis, and came so near them that he was caught. The incident shows how important it is that the men should be instructed in peace time in the uniforms of their probable enemies.

15th Uhlans. The 15th Uhlans, which on this day had to rejoin their division, meanwhile continued in their successful observations of the enemy in front of them. Specially noteworthy are the reports of Captain Brix, who had followed the enemy by Bingen, as stated on p. 151.

Aug. 11.
Brix's reports.

From there, at 10 o'clock on the morning of the 11th, he sent the following report, which was presented to the Head Quarters of the First Army at noon; and so had been further forwarded on to this command:—

"*French retreated from the position behind the French Nied at Mont and Sillers, in the night of the* 10*th to* 11*th August, further along the road to Metz.** There is a hospital in Kurzel, in which are—

"(1) Two wounded men of the 63rd Infantry Regiment,† reservists de deuxième portion, but two days with the colours. They know only that they were wounded at Forbach.

"(2) One of the 1st Garde-Voltigeurs and one of the Garde-Zouaves, from whose statements, combined with those of the inhabitants, it appears that the united Guard Corps reached Volmeringen (S.W. Bolchen) and Möhringen on the 6th, and then retired to Metz.

"(3) A corporal and two men of the 15th Infantry Regiment.‡ They insist on belonging to a division of the 4th Corps, which is made up of the 2nd Jäger Battalion and the 15th, 33rd, and 54th Infantry Regiments, and has a mounted Jäger Regiment and a Dragoon Regiment attached to it. They came last Sunday from Busendorf to Bolchen, and retired on Monday on Metz.

"(4) A corporal of a regiment stationed in Africa, who went sick on his way to his home."

Brix sent a further report from Kurzel, 9 p.m.—

"At 5 p.m. I moved forward from Kurzel along the road to Metz. The bridge at Pont à Chaussy was

* Italics by the author. The prompt report of this important movement shows how well the Uhlans were watching.
† Lavcaucoupet's Division, 2nd Army Corps.
‡ Lorencez's Division of the 4th Army Corps.

Aug. 11. strongly barricaded, and the walls of the houses were loopholed. After clearing the bridge, I went as far as north of Puche (N. of Ogy). Everywhere I found signs of an intended defence, then of hastily evacuated bivouacs and hurried retreat. I have seen no more of the enemy. Only one hussar piquet stood on the great main road somewhat north of Coincy. From the statements of inhabitants and the wounded and sick prisoners, the enemy's troops, consisting of Bazaine's corps, the Guard Corps, and at least part of Ladmirault's corps, have retreated right under the guns of Metz. According to the inhabitants, the troops are much fatigued by the continual marches backwards and forwards, and make loud complaints."

Copies of both reports were sent, 1 p.m. on the 12th, to Royal Head Quarters.*

These reports can serve as a pattern for procedure in similar cases.

According to the oft-quoted notes placed at my disposal, Captain Brix made not only use of the hospital in Kurzel and the statements of the inhabitants to determine the distribution of the French troops which were retreating to Metz, but he also examined the camping grounds for objects left behind, among which account books, addresses, etc., rendered valuable assistance. [An envelope left behind can sometimes prove to be a valuable find. Care must therefore be taken in such cases, particularly in orderly-rooms, that such, especially rough copies or notes, should not be left behind.] Nothing was found at the Kurzel post-office.

Captain Brix got to about seven miles from the fortress this day.

If we now see coming to an end the action of

---

* In the records of the Third Army Corps there is only *one* report from 9 p.m., which repeats the substance of both the above-mentioned reports. This can only be explained by the fact that Brix must have reported to two different authorities, and to each in a different form.

the regiment after these few days in the country west of St. Avold, on the two branches of the Nied, every reader of the description will feel that the regiment could not have carried out the task allotted to it more completely or with more circumspection, and that the procedure of Colonel v. Alvensleben must be considered exemplary.

Aug. 11.

By the order of the day of August 13 for the Third Army Corps, the reports of the regiment in general were praised, and those of Captain Brix in particular were characterized as most exhaustive and very much to the point.

The sentence in reference to it in the corps order, dated Falkenberg, 12.20 a.m., August 13, runs thus:—

> "The last report of Captain Brix from the outposts gives me an opportunity of saying that the 15th Uhlans, during the time they have been in touch with the enemy, have distinguished themselves by many detailed and accurate reports."

Captain Brix himself had some time afterwards the honour of being, for his reports, personally thanked by the Chief of the General Staff, General v. Moltke saying to him, "Your reports have guided us from the Saar to the outskirts of Metz."

The regiment had fully carried out its duty by sending out numerous patrols, by pressing forward with complete squadrons on the enemy, who in consequence was retiring quickly, without suffering serious losses.

Chief points to be noticed in the action of the 15th Uhlans.

The patrols had everywhere, as we saw, shown extraordinary boldness, which made the greatest impression on the enemy.

What an effect would have been obtained on the already demoralized enemy if the divisions had here followed up with their artillery! Ah! would

Aug. 11. that the cavalry in this campaign had only been properly put in. The example of Colonel v. Alvensleben had far-reaching results.

The spirit of the leader reacts on no troops as quickly and as markedly as on the cavalry. It is here "Like leader, like troops." But the spirit of the troops is soon extinguished by an inactive leader.

The cavalry leader represents half the value of the troops.

For this reason cavalry which is moderate, so far as the education of man and horse are concerned, under an excellent leader is preferable to an excellently developed one under a moderate leader—*L'homme c'est tout.*

The directing staff of the French army, left in ignorance of the strength of the German troops that were following them, by reason of the faulty reconnaissance work of their cavalry, did not know that they were followed by only weak detachments of cavalry. The skilful leading of these few squadrons rather confirmed the enemy's belief that strong bodies of troops were in close pursuit, and not only hastened their retreat to Metz, but also kept them in perpetual anxiety, caused them needless alarms, long halts under arms, and fatiguing night marches.

If results such as these were gained by four squadrons, how much greater would have been the effect, especially in a material sense, of a cavalry division provided with artillery!

There is no mention in the war records this day of reports from the 6th Cavalry Division. The regimental diaries, too, give no account of any particular occurrences. It was impossible that the service of patrolling, as ordered, could lead to a meeting with the enemy.

A gap of 7½ miles occurred this day between the First and Second Armies, which was covered only by the cavalry of the Third Army Corps. Aug. 11.

The Head Quarters' Staff of the Tenth Army Corps had issued the following in the 9 p.m. disposition for August 11, with reference to the 5th Cavalry Division:— The Tenth Army Corps and 5th Cavalry Division.

> "The enemy appears to have retreated behind the Mosel, or at least behind the Seille. The 5th Cavalry Division will advance to the line Remilly-Delme with its main body, and push patrols as far forward as possible towards the enemy. The Falkenberg to Metz railway forms the northern limit in their advance."

After the issue of this order the reports from the division, and the despatch from General v. Rheinbaben, arrived.

The commanding general was as little capable of being satisfied with the results of the services of the division as he was of understanding it being kept in rear, as intended by the divisional leader. The following memorandum, August 11, 4. a.m., gives clear expression to this:—

> "My view is that, though you may not reach Remilly, you should approach as near the enemy as possible. Outposts on the Nied from Han a. d. Nied to beyond the Metz-Château Salins road, thence enterprising officers forward. You can also extend into the country north of the railway if the cavalry of the Third Army Corps is not yet up. I expect officers to push forward to-day to the Mosel, in the vicinity of Pont à Mousson. Have the Metz-Nancy railway cut at one or more points. I am detailing Lieutenant Neumeister, R.E., to proceed to General v. Redern for the purpose. But to meet with success, such attempts must be made in several places. Try to make prisoners, intimidate the enemy and the inhabitants, enforce respect of our cavalry from the enemy. *This is a time when the greatest activity must be required of the cavalry.*" *

* Underlined in the original.

Marginalia:
- Aug. 11.
- 6th Cavalry Division operates behind the 5th.
- Pressure by the Head Quarters' Staff, Tenth Army Corps, on the 5th Cavalry Division.

Comparing the orders given to the 6th Cavalry Division by the Third Army Corps, and those to the 5th Cavalry Division, it is clear that the divisions were operating *in the same direction, the 6th behind the 5th*, the former with their outposts behind the main body of the 5th. The map for this date also shows this. Similar situations might be easily repeated, even without the mistakes being referred to the directing Corps' Head Quarters, if the divisions are not, as here, subject to a unified control.

A memorandum, accompanying the above to General v. Rheinbaben, was sent at the same time by Lieut.-Colonel v. Capriri, chief of the staff of the Tenth Army Corps, written by his own hand, to General v. Redern.

In it he informed him of the instructions issued to Rheinbaben in brief, announced the appointment of Lieutenant Neumeister, and emphasized "that the brigade was authorized to undertake such enterprises independently." As can be seen, everything was done by the Corps Head Quarters to induce the cavalry division to decisive action. It sadly disturbs a cavalryman's spirit that any commanding authority should be compelled to use compulsion of that sort to bring to the needful pitch of activity regiments which themselves desired above all else to be led against the enemy, and showed themselves worthy of their old renown wherever they came into action.

The remark of Lieut.-Colonel Capriri, in his memorandum to General v. Redern, is certainly apt. The cavalry leader of any rank should not ever wait for orders if he can fulfil any useful object.

Cavalry is the arm of initiative *par excellence*; and any man who is afraid of taking upon himself

CAVALRY ON SERVICE 179

a good deal of responsibility when necessary has no right to belong to it. The resolution to act independently was made very easy for General v. Redern by the fact that he found himself on the wing which lay nearest to the passages of the Mosel, and also that he had been detached. Had he found himself, like General v. Barby, under the direct orders of his divisional leader, he would naturally have needed some arrangement with him before undertaking enterprises of any magnitude. As for the rest, the above discussion has only general instruction as its object, and should not in any way be taken as a slur on the character of General v. Redern, an excellent officer, who frequently showed, on August 15 in particular, that he was by no means lacking in initiative.

On receipt of the "Dispositions" from the Corps Head Quarters, General v. Rheinbaben issued the following on the evening of the 10th:—

Aug. 11.

> "The 13th Uhlans will march to-morrow to Remilly, and push patrols as far as possible towards Metz and the Mosel. The 19th Dragoons will occupy Han a. d. Nied; the 4th Cuirassiers, Wallersberg; the Brunswick Hussars (who return to General v. Redern's command), Lucy and Thimonville. General v. Redern will move to Viviers, cover the Château Salins-Delme road, and send patrols and single reconnoitring officers to the Mosel. It would be regarded as highly satisfactory if the railway from Metz to Pont à Mousson was rendered useless in any place."

Rheinbaben's orders.

The arrangements of the Corps Head Quarters were merely formally complied with by this order; and the way for wider action was thereby opened.

It would have been advisable, however, to emphasize more strongly in the order the necessity of cutting the railway, as it was of the greatest

Aug. 11. importance at this time in hindering the transport of troops to Metz. It would also have met the requirements of the case if the divisional leader had taken personal charge of the arrangements for it, and had detailed the duties himself. There are, moreover, no material reasons for limiting the stretch to be destroyed, by the place Pont à Mousson on the south; the destruction of the stretch between Pont à Mousson and Frouard would have had the same importance as on the northern part.*

General v. Redern issued the following order from Landorf, August 11, 10 a.m. :—

Redern's orders.

"The 11th Hussars will advance by Brülingen and Lucy to Viviers, will leave two squadrons there, move with two squadrons to Delme, and place outposts on the road to Metz and towards Aulnois a. d. Seille. Captain v. Kotze, 10th Hussars,† will start at once with his squadron, and ride by Oron and Lémoncourt to Aulnois a. d. Seille, where he will remain and protect himself towards Noményy. Lieutenant Neumeister, who will accompany him for the purpose of cutting the railway, will be given an escort from this point for his further march to the Mosel. The 10th Hussars will move by Baronweiler and Oron to Fonteny, and send a squadron to Laneuville and officers' patrols by Jallaucourt to Manhoué, as well as to the Nancy-Château Salins road. The 17th Hussars will march by Brülingen to Lucy, where a squadron will remain. From there two squadrons will proceed to Morville a. d. Nied, and one squadron to

---

* Colonel Cherfils holds the view that already on this day a cavalry corps could have crossed the Mosel on a broad front with its leading bodies. That may be right, but then it must not be lost sight of that such an operation was not and could not be thought of as long as a decisive battle east of Metz was anticipated, where a cavalry corps could not willingly be spared. The withdrawal of the enemy from his position on the Nied became known to Army Head Quarters only on the following day (p. 202). In such a case we have to content ourselves with sending individual squadrons which will serve as support for officers' patrols, which must push on ahead.

† The regiment was now united.

Thimonville. Patrols are to push forward towards Metz—at least, as far as Sorebey, if not further—and by Solgne to Raucourt." *Aug. 11.*

By General v. Redern's order the requirements for reconnaissance were complied with, and the main body of the brigade was kept together within a fairly close space. But, for the important duty of cutting the railway, more should have been done; at least a second simultaneous attempt at another place should have been resolved on. With regard to bringing the troops under shelter, it is to be remarked that it was possible to manage this easily in one place, say, at Delme (the troops on outpost duty excepted); and by this the direct control of the troops would have been much facilitated. *Criticism of Redern's measures.*

If bivouacs are only chosen in urgent cases, having regard to sparing the troops, much more cramped quarters than we are used to in peace-time must often be occupied when circumstances demand it, and when in close touch with the enemy on active service, and especially in the enemy's country, where every consideration for the inhabitants disappears.

The important point is that the horses should be brought under shelter, and in places where stalls and sheds do not afford sufficient room, other spaces must be utilized, such as school-houses, churches, etc. The surrounding villages must in such a case help and contribute supplies.

The measures of the 5th Cavalry Division led to a more energetic action in reconnaissance.

On the right wing Captain v. Rosenberg, 13th Uhlans, had started from the outposts with two troops of his squadron at 4 in the morning in thick darkness and bad weather, and moved by Chanville and Domangeville towards the French Nied. At *Rosenberg's reconnaissance.*

Aug. 11. 6.30 a.m. the head of the advance guard under Lieutenant v. Wedell III. reached the strongly barricaded bridge over the Nied, N.E. of Domangeville, when they saw, straight in front of them, a large bivouac of the enemy. No outposts had been put out. Their place was apparently filled by a peasant mounted on a white horse, who took himself off in the direction of the bivouac on the approach of the Uhlans. Upon this the camp became alive, and the hostile troops, which were estimated by Rosenberg at an army corps, put themselves in motion towards Metz. After removing the barricades of the bridge, the Uhlans watched the troops from the other bank, Captain v. Rosenberg and Lieutenant v. Wedell ahead of the men, kneeling down behind a bush. A whole row of waggons did not venture to start until 2 p.m., owing to the presence of the Uhlans. Meanwhile Lieutenant v. Treskow with a patrol had been sent forward beyond Ars Laquenexy, and from here observed another march of troops, estimated at an army corps, along the Bolchen-Metz road. Captain v. Rosenberg, on his return to the outposts at Luppy, was able to report that the French had evacuated their position on the French Nied, but were still halted west of Metz. The fact that also this excellent officer completely relinquished all touch with the enemy, proves that the troops had not been educated up to this point, and that it would not be proper to throw blame on to an individual for this omission.

In consequence of these reports General v. Rheinbaben reported from Lucy at 4 p.m.—

"The division has moved into the appointed line (Remilly-Han a. d. Nied-Delme) at 3 p.m. Detachments have been pushed forward towards Metz, and up to the Mosel, from whom no reports have yet come in.

It is reported, on the other hand, that long, hostile columns are moving into camp at Laquenexy, behind Pange, and that serious delays are occurring at Pange. I have therefore sent two regiments, to see if anything can be done there. Some newspapers are forwarded herewith." Aug. 11.

Nothing seems to have resulted from this proposed despatch of troops, since it does not appear from the records, or the histories of the regiments engaged there, that any movement was undertaken. The divisional leader felt quite rightly that the appearance of a larger body of cavalry would not fail to produce its impression on the retiring enemy. But, then, it surely was his duty to cause an immediate alarm, and to lead forward in person the four regiments which were on the spot.

Meanwhile Baron v. Durant's squadron of the 13th Uhlans, on outpost duty on the Morchingen road at Remilly, had not been idle. Lieutenant v. Wedell I. had been sent from this squadron with five Uhlans towards Metz, to report how far the country was clear of the enemy. 2nd Squadron, 13th Uhlans.

The patrol had reached Ars Laquenexy unopposed, when, turning a corner in the village street, it suddenly encountered at a hundred paces' distance a party of the enemy's infantry, which faced the patrol and opened fire. The patrol at once—with Sergeant Küttler, who commanded the point, at their head—threw themselves, with lances at the engage, upon the enemy, who fired once more without hitting, and were caught by the Uhlans. One of the enemy was struck down by the sergeant's sword, another killed by a lance-thrust, and a third was taken prisoner by Lieutenant v. Wedell; the remainder fled to their comrades, halted behind the village. Another patrol from

Aug. 11. the same squadron towards Verny had the misfortune to have their retreat barred by two squadrons of mounted Jägers, and they were captured.

Result of the reconnaissances.
The 17th Hussars had also sent in valuable information, as appears from the following divisional despatch of August 12—probably in the early morning—which gives the results of the previous day's reports:—

> "Epitome of the reports. The enemy has retreated from the Nied at Pange, and the army is said to be in, and close in front of, Metz. Two officers of the 17th Hussars, who had got within $\frac{3}{4}$ of an hour from Metz, saw their bivouac fires yesterday evening. According to a report from Thimonville, these officers went forward together from Raucourt, on the road to Metz, till they spied outposts this side of Grigy. From the statement of carters, the French army lies part between the railway and the fortress, and part in Metz itself. The ground in front of Metz, they said, is mined an hour's distance into the country. No signs of the enemy were noticed in the direction of Pont à Mousson. Nancy is said, by a solicitor who came from there, to be no longer occupied. Prisoners from the 71st, 59th,* and 84th† Regiments have been taken."‡

Probably only Lieutenant Neumeister made a report direct to Corps Head Quarters about the enterprise on Dieulouard. The absurd statement of the carters about the mining of the ground, as it had been embodied in this despatch, should have occasioned an accompanying remark.

Hirschfeld's patrol.
Lieutenant v. Hirschfeld had sent in a report from Vic, S.E. of Château Salins at noon, received at 9.30 p.m.—

* 71st and 59th of Metman's Division, 3rd Corps.
† Lapasset's Brigade, 5th Corps.
‡ The original reports are dated erroneously August 10.

"Nancy and the neighbourhood not occupied. Rumour says in Lunéville 40,000 men. Telegraph destroyed in Nancy. Advanced points of Prussian troops said to be in Dieuze. Will advance with the rest of the patrol, a lance-corporal, again to Nancy."

Aug. 11.

At the same time Hirschfeld sent in newspapers and reported changes in the French ministry known through the telegraph. The destruction of the telegraph in Nancy can scarcely have produced much effect, since there were sufficient means in such a large town of replacing the wires, etc.

The statement that the patrol only consisted of one lance-corporal, proves that it had probably been too weak originally, and that it had been broken up by the previous sending off of despatch riders. Lieutenant v. Hirschfeld arrived, therefore, in sight of Nancy, accompanied by only one hussar. Hiding by day, as a rule, in the woods, or in an outlying farm, he could not venture to ride into Nancy alone; but as it was, he succeeded in capturing a French field post, the contents of which gave Royal Head Quarters important disclosures of the internal affairs of the French army. When Hirschfeld was obliged to pass through a large place he practised the ruse of ordering a great number of billets. It was only his prudence in passing through thronged streets at a walk, revolver in hand, without looking to the right or left, that he had to thank for reaching his goal unharmed. This officer's boldness will be the more admired when it is remembered that he was moving, forty-five miles ahead of any formed bodies of troops, without any support.

The absolute calm and confidence with which the few horsemen moved through the country doubtless impressed the inhabitants, who were inclined to be hostile, since this attitude probably

Aug. 11. led them to believe that strong supports were following close behind.

It must, however, be remarked that Nancy was such an important point that greater weight should have been attached to its reconnaissance. It was only owing to exceptionally favourable circumstances that so small a patrol could succeed in getting right up to the town.

Neumeister's report.
Lieutenant Neumeister sent the following report of the expedition to Metz-Nancy railway, dated Aulnois a. d. Seille, August 12, 2.45 a.m., and received at the Head Quarters of the Tenth Army Corps 1.10 p.m. :—

> "No sign of the enemy from Aulnois, Nomény, Lixières, Landremont, Ville au Val, by the Mosel Island Scarponne, on Dieulouard station. Discovered new stone bridge, which connects the Mosel Island, Scarponne, with both banks, and bridges the canal. Reached railway unseen 800 paces below Dieulouard station. Destruction of rails impossible with insufficient tools, but cut all telegraph wires, and rendered telegraphic despatch of orders and train service impossible for twelve hours."

The report closes with the remark that the passage of the Mosel could still be gained by rapid resolve and by detailing a party of infantry and artillery.

Kotze's report.
The interesting report which Captain v. Kotze sent in about the expedition may well follow here :—

> "The 3rd Squadron lay in Baronweiler on the 11th, about 7½ miles south of Falkenberg, on outpost duty, forming the left wing of Redern's Brigade, and thus the extreme flank of the Second Army, when an engineer officer (Lieutenant Neumeister) arrived with the order from the Tenth Army Corps to march at once to Aulnois a. d. Seille, and to provide him with a party from there to destroy the railway and telegraph at Dieulouard. Since the nearest way and the means of crossing the Mosel was as little known to the engineer officer as to us—for

CAVALRY ON SERVICE

no passage was marked on the map—I decided not to provide the party with only one officer, Lieutenant v. Trotha I., but also to accompany it myself. In the afternoon we reached Aulnois a. d. Seille *viâ* Delme, brought the squadron quickly under shelter, had our meal with the mayor of the place in his well-found castle, and, after commandeering crowbars, hammers, etc., from the smithy of the estate, we rode forward with twenty picked men towards Nomény. We entered the outskirts on this side of the Seille at dusk, rendered the telegraph useless, and trotted forward on the road to Pont à Mousson.

Aug. 11.

"With a couple of men in front as the advanced point, we three officers followed with swords drawn barely twenty paces behind, and the rest of the men close in rear. I had forbidden smoking and any unnecessary talking. Firearms, too, were not to be used. In this way we trotted fast along the main road, though we were in complete ignorance of the direction to take next, and met no inhabitants in the growing darkness whom we could have questioned. After we had covered barely 4 miles, we suddenly spied two horsemen a hundred paces in front, who were halted on the road, apparently vedettes.

"If we wished to surprise them, a long deliberation would not help us, so we went straight for them at a pretty good pace, and soon overtook one, a peasant, who wished to escape on a barebacked horse. Unless we would be betrayed, it was necessary to catch the other, and so forward it was as fast as the horses could gallop after him. It was not long before he parted from his horse, and disappeared in a cornfield, while we caught the horse. Our uncertain position had thus, at one turn, considerably improved. Holding a revolver to the peasant's heart, we demanded to be led to the place we named; beyond that he said he did not know the road.*

"After our guide, whose purpose in halting on the road remained a mystery to us, had resigned himself to

---

* It is no uncommon experience that the countryfolk only know the way to the next villages to their homes. It is only with gamekeepers, country postmen, hawkers, etc., that one can safely count on as guides further than that.

Aug. 11.

his fate, he led us first further along the main road, and then, soon turning off from it, to the village we had named. We knocked pretty loud on the nearest windows and doors, in our attempt to secure a new guide quickly, and there was a good deal of talk. After I had stopped all this, the occupant of the first house, an old man, was forced to come out, placed with scant ceremony on the spare horse, and, kept there by hussars to right and left, away we went into the night.

"This man could give us the name of the village which lay opposite to Dieulouard; but he also knew nothing of any bridge or means of crossing over the Mosel. Our road led us through large woods, and also through a long village, which was traversed as quickly as our guide could ride. Now the country seemed to become more hilly, we came to vineyards and hop-gardens, and at last reached the village he had named: it may have been Bezaumont. Here we found on the road a boy, half-grown up, who gladly consented to guide us to the Mosel, and to show us, to our joyful surprise, a stone bridge which had only been built this year. Leaving behind all the men who could be dispensed with, hidden between hop-poles, we hurried forward, in the hopes of now being able to attain our object. The country became every minute more hilly. Soon we began going downhill, the air became fresher, and in front of us lay the valley of the Mosel, the goal of our wishes. Deep down at our feet we heard the water rushing, and on the far side, in the valley, the traffic on the railway.

"I remained behind with one hussar on the bridge, and let the two officers, with six men, ride on to the railway. At the station there was a lively stir, trains came and went, and I saw the watchman on the permanent way examining the rails with his lantern. Suddenly the lantern went out, a few shots were heard, and the railway traffic was stopped. My excitement rose to the highest pitch. I rode to meet the troop. Then came the eight horsemen at full gallop, like the wild hunt, past me and over the bridge, throwing into the Mosel the crowbars they were swinging over their heads.

"Near the station the officers had tried to loosen

the rails with the implements they had; but they soon saw the impossibility of it, since the necessary English spanners were wanting for that purpose. When the Farrier-Corporal Karrenbach was going to cut the wires above on a telegraph pole, the railway watchman had arrived with his lantern. Trotha put his revolver to the man's breast, put out the lantern, and urged on the cutting of the wires, which they at last succeeded in doing. All this may have caused more noise than was expected—in short, suspicion was aroused at the station hard by. A few infantrymen were sent forward, and these had now, just as Karrenbach cut the last wires on the telegraph pole, tried to drive the troublesome enemy off with a few shots.

Aug. 11.

"Under these circumstances, unhappily, nothing more could be done; but an important point of passage for all arms had been found, the telegraph had been destroyed, and the railway traffic suspended for the night. The surrounding country was found peculiarly favourable for a possible occupation, since the high bank of the Mosel on this side completely commanded the railway.

"The question now was to forward an early report to the higher authorities, and to have the enemy closely watched by further patrolling.

"We returned by practically the same road we had originally made use of. The men who had been left behind joined us again, and we reached Aulnois about 2 a.m.

"From here I sent at once a written report with a sketch to the brigade, while the engineer officer hastened in person to give information of what had occurred to the Head Quarters' Staff of the Tenth Army Corps."

The enterprise had been carried out with great boldness; it was due to circumstances that it was not completely successful. At that time cavalry lacked the equipment necessary for effectively cutting railway lines. The object would assuredly have been attained with a few explosive cartridges. The question, however, arises whether, under the

Reasons for the want of success.

Aug. 11. existing circumstances, the spot for carrying out the demolition had been rightly selected. Damages at the stations are the most effective, as details in the construction can be destroyed which are very hard to replace ; but, on the other hand, the sharpest look-out is kept there, as well as a reserve supply of rails of all descriptions. In such cases, where the destruction of the line has to be carried out, the cutting of stretches of it in the open country, where it can often be successful in remaining absolutely undiscovered, will be preferable to any near the station.

According to v. Kotze's report, the squadron was brought under shelter at Aulnois, *i.e.* billeted. This may be feasible, so long as the bridges over the Seille were barricaded and occupied, and the bridges at Craincourt and Arraye carefully watched, and if the horses were stabled in " Alarm quarters " and kept saddled.

An off-saddling every six hours in turn, which admits of the horses' backs being thoroughly groomed and the blankets beaten out and freshly folded, must always be carried out, even if the order is given for the horses to remain saddled. Against an enterprising enemy, such as the French cavalry had in no wise showed themselves, this procedure, as apparently adopted by the squadron, would have been risky. Especially in the earlier part of the war, we very soon became too confident, owing to the enemy's inactivity, and later, in many cases, we received a severe lesson. A solemn warning is therefore to be applied for a future campaign, where we are bound to reckon with an enterprising enemy.

By the expedition to Dieulouard, the movement of the 6th French Corps, especially of the 10th Regiment, was delayed for many hours, the

CAVALRY ON SERVICE 191

second train being detained in Frouard, at 11 p.m., in consequence of the destruction of the telegraph. Two companies left the train and marched five miles to Marbache. From there the usual train service recommenced. This quotation shows what far-reaching consequences a thorough destruction of the railway might have had.

Aug. 11.

Early on the 12th General v. Redern forwarded a despatch from Viviers on the reports received during the night. From this despatch we may specially note that Lieutenant v. Hirschfeld had found no hostile troops at St. Nicolas, six miles south of Nancy, and had returned to the regiment on the 12th; and next, that Lieutenant Neumeister had made sure that the trains on the Nancy-Metz line were running at night at intervals of an hour and a half. That from a report of Lieutenant v. Werder, 10th Hussars, from the vicinity of Nancy, the troops being sent up along the railway belonged to MacMahon's Corps, which was certainly a mistake. That Captain v. Kotze had occupied the bridge over the Seille at Aulnois, and was going to advance again on the 12th towards Nomény, and send patrols to Dieulouard and Pont à Mousson. That Captain v. Vaerst was moving on the highroad to Metz, and that the French outposts were near Grigy, seventeen miles from Delme.

Reports that arrived at night.

On the whole, then, the patrols of the 5th Cavalry Division had sent in an abundance of valuable information on this date; but the most important duty of the day—the cutting of the Metz-Nancy line "at one or more places"—had not been taken in hand at all by the division, for the semi-successful expedition to Dieulouard had been organized by the Corps Head Quarters.

The reason why no action had been taken in this direction by the division was due, as already

Aug. 11. mentioned, to the feeble and indefinite wording of the divisional orders, which detailed the duty to no particular unit. This is again a proof how important it is that the form of the order should be to the point and clearly worded.

We shall have to refer later to a similar case, which had equally far-reaching consequences (*vide* p. 242).

There was no idea of any unified control of the service of reconnaissance by the General Officer Commanding the Division. The extraordinary dispersion of the division which occurred this day, and which is marked on the map, is most serious.

Bredow's Brigade.

The Head Quarters of the Fourth Army Corps had given orders for August 11 to General v. Bredow to maintain his general position, and allotted to him the special duty of watching the country south of Saarunion, towards Finstingen and Schallbach. Bredow pushed his left wing forward to Schallbach, and patrolled southwards, without gaining news of the enemy. This unhappy body of cavalry was kept completely in leash. Their obvious point to march upon was the important town of Nancy, which the foremost bodies of the 4th Cavalry Division did not reach till the 13th. However, to give instructions that aimed at this would have been more within the province of the Head Quarters' Staff of the Second Army.

The 5th Dragoons this day had received orders to rejoin their division, and marched off there next day.

We find in the history of the 7th Cuirassiers the remark that the more important reconnaissances were discontinued on this day "on account of the hard work of the preceding days." This may, perhaps, apply to this regiment—*i.e.* the reconnaissance on August 7 to Ingweiler—but not to

CAVALRY ON SERVICE 193

the others; indeed, the 13th Dragoons did patrol this day to Pfalzburg, Dieuze, and Marsal. They were in close touch with the Third Army, with the Würtemberg Division in particular, which had reached Rauweiler. Aug. 11.

On this day along the whole front of the First and Second Armies, the left wing excepted, close touch with the enemy had been established. Results of the day.

The altered decision of the enemy, not to halt on the French Nied, but to retire under the guns of Metz, had been noticed at once, and immediately brought to the knowledge of the Army Head Quarters.

Though here good results had been submitted, yet, as already stated, more could have been attained in the direction of the passages of the Mosel; and it can be assumed that if several more enterprises had been organized against the Nancy-Metz line, as the Head Quarters of the Tenth Army Corps desired, the cessation of the movement of the French troops on that line would by now have been successfully brought about, thanks to the energy which the cavalry displayed wherever they were employed.

The following remarks may be made here on the enemy's movements on this day:— Movements of the enemy.

The French, after occupying and fortifying a position behind the French Nied only the day before, retired of their own accord to a position in front of the forts of Queuleu and St. Julien, already selected for the event of a compulsory retreat.

The 4th Corps occupied the heights between Mey and Chieulles. Bazaine, who took over command of the newly formed Army of Metz, took up his Head Quarters in Borny, and handed over the command of his corps to Decaen; while General Aymard succeeded to the latter position.

Aug. 11. The divisions of the 3rd Corps, which had stood under arms from earliest dawn till 7 and 10 o'clock in the forenoon from fear of an attack, moved into their bivouacs in front of Borny in the afternoon. The Guard took up a position in reserve west of Borny. The transport by rail of the 6th Corps to Metz had been continued, but, as we have seen, had been subjected to a partial disturbance by the raid on Dieulouard. The 2nd Corps, with Lapasset's Brigade, moved by Peltre to the heights on both sides of the Strassburg road as far as the Seille. Lapasset occupied and fortified Mercy le Haut. The 5th Mounted Jägers occupied Peltre and Jury. The 2nd Squadron of the 7th Dragoons, advancing on the main road to Püttlingen, succeeded in capturing a patrol of three Uhlans near Sorbey. It is characteristic of the defective knowledge of their own country that the cavalry of the 2nd Corps actively reconnoitred the Seille—a stream in the immediate neighbourhood of one of their largest fortresses—to look for bridges and fords. The quotation on p. 240 shows that we had a better knowledge of France than the French Army had.

CHAPTER VI

THE cavalry divisions of the First Army, who by the night preceding the 12th had at last got in front of the army corps, continued their forward movement that day, though only performing short half-day marches. *Aug. 12. Cavalry divisions, First Army.*

The 3rd Cavalry Division reached the Nied at Bettingen, and pushed their advance guard forward over the river beyond Gelmingen. Colonel v. Lüderitz, commanding the advanced regiment, the 14th Uhlans, carried out a reconnaissance in person with the three troops by St. Barbe towards Poix. The party left Bettingen 3.30 p.m., found the strong entrenchments on the heights of St. Barbe evacuated, and only at Poix did they encounter the enemy, which they estimated at a battalion strong. At Servigny, however, a camp of a considerable body of troops was observed. Their outposts were close in front; an infantry piquet, apparently completely surprised, opened a rapid fire without doing any damage.

French cavalry, which had been seen, took no notice of the German horsemen, and did not even follow them when they retired. Colonel v. Lüderitz sent in a report of the affair from Nidingen at 8 p.m.

Captain v. Hymmen, 5th Uhlans, had been untiringly active with his party in the presence of the enemy. He sent a report from Contchen at 1.30 p.m. by Trooper Dutz, 15th Uhlans— *Hymmen's patrol.*

Aug. 12.

"At 11.30 this morning I was in Bellecroix with Lieutenant Balthasar and 40 Uhlans. About 650 yards in front of us lay the French camp, about a division strong, yet other camps seemed to stretch right back to the walls of Metz. Metz itself was in front of us. The camp was scarcely covered by outposts, though a piquet stood in front of the village of Vallières, which was only aroused by the approach of my right flanking patrol, as it rode almost into the middle of them. Beyond Bellecroix the roads from Busendorf, Bolchen, and St. Avold are unoccupied. From Bellecroix I brought in a waggon with 60 cwt. of oats belonging to the army."

This report was addressed to Army Head Quarters. At the same time an almost identical one was sent to the 3rd Cavalry Division. It is to be noticed with regard to these reports that it was very right to report not only to the division, but also to the Army Head Quarters. With important reports such a course is always advisable, even though there is no special order to that effect. Every higher authority will feel most grateful if this procedure is adopted when the occasion demands it. Both reports were transmitted, not by the men of the party, but by the 15th Uhlans. It can be assumed that this regiment provided the despatch riders, because the horses of the patrol were so done up that their employment would not have guaranteed the timely arrival of the report. Here we have a bright example of mutual assistance in the transmission of reports, as is now laid down in the "Regulations for Service in the Field." It is a point to be noticed, too, that the bearer is mentioned by name in both reports, which is very proper, especially if the men are not personally known; and, moreover, if this fact is communicated to them, it may have a favourable influence on their zeal.

Hymmen describes his experiences and impressions of this bold enterprise in a private letter dated Contchen, August 13—

Aug. 12.

"Yesterday I had the great joy of being the first in the army, who was close in front of Metz. As the French retreated the day before yesterday to Metz, I made a quick ride yesterday morning with 40 horses towards Metz, to find out where they had gone to, and came within 800 paces of the enemy's tents. My right flank patrol rode close up to a piquet (of infantry), which fired a couple of shots and was thus first alarmed. It was a supreme moment when we gained the hills straight in front of the camp, and Metz, with its walls and towers, lay before us, at least 15 miles ahead of the army with 40 horses! By the use of a dip in the ground we approached quite close. We remained still and watched the camp, till the news of our proximity reached it and a small stir took place. Then I put four horses which came from Metz to a large waggon full of oats and French saddlery, and we drove it away before their very eyes. These fellows are such limps that they didn't send a soul after me—anyway we saw no one, and returned undisturbed to our village, where we met our infantry, and I sent off reports at once to Steinmetz and Groeben. My fellows, 32 of the regiment and 27 Hanoverian Uhlans of the 14th Regiment, rode with such coolness and indifference towards the camp that I firmly believe, if I had not had the 'Halt' blown, the point would have quietly ridden in, as the flank patrol did into the piquet. Yesterday afternoon I rode over to Manteuffel, who is ten miles from here, and informed him of this ride. He was delighted, and told me he had already heard, not only from Groeben, but also from Steinmetz's Staff, what excellent reports I had sent in. When I returned I found the enclosed slip of paper awaiting me from Groeben, which, alas! called me back again for a day or two from my scouting life; I hope it will not be for more. This life is too splendid, and one feels for the first time on service that one can be of some use."

The above-mentioned note from Graf Groeben,

198   CAVALRY ON SERVICE

Aug. 12. dated Bettingen, 4.30 p.m., called the enterprising officer, to his great grief, back to his regiment, as his task was accomplished, giving him hearty thanks for his excellent reports. There he arrived on the 13th, and heard of his new appointment. On the evening of the 12th, Lieutenant v. Wallenberg, 14th Uhlans, also returned to his regiment from his patrol ride, of several days' duration, which we are, unhappily, unable to follow after the 10th.

Reconnaissance to Diedenhofen.

On the extreme right wing Lieutenant v. Voigts-Rhetz, 8th Cuirassiers, had been sent with a troop to reconnoitre towards Diedenhofen. Till he reached Stückingen he found no trace of the enemy. Here he met some dragoons, who were foraging. They fled in haste, but he succeeded in taking from them some horses and a waggon of oats. When he arrived, after a fast ride, at 2 p.m., in front of the fortress of Didenhofen, he found the gates open, and a garde mobile, who was out for a walk quite unconcernedly outside the gates, was taken prisoner. Then rang out the cry of terror, "The Prussians are coming!" and the watch, composed of the National Guard, threw away their arms and fled into the town. The patrol pressed forward to the open gates. Then a Prussian reservist, standing rigid, reported himself. He had been detained in the fortress, compelled to work in the daytime at the fortifications, and kept in confinement at night. The reservist was examined later, and gave information which justified the assumption that the fortress could be captured by a *coup-de-main*. Lieutenant v. Voigts-Rhetz had sent a report to the division at 4.30 p.m. from Kedingen, and Graf Groeben forwarded it on to the Army Head Quarters. In their reply of August 13, the ride was called a "bold and successful

CAVALRY ON SERVICE 199

performance," and the intention of a raid on the fortress was spoken of. Its startled garrison was, therefore, to be lulled into sleep, the detachments pushed forward were to be withdrawn, and the fortress watched only from a distance.

Aug. 12.

The 1st Cavalry Division had started at 6 a.m., had continued its march towards the German Nied, and reported—

Reports of the 1st Cavalry Division.

> "Division reached Füllingen 9 a.m., is bivouacking between Bingen and Rollingen, and pushed the most advanced posts to the left bank of the French Nied. There were posts of the 13th Division there.
>
> "The Nied is at present so swollen that it must be considered a real obstacle. The 15th Cavalry Brigade is reconnoitring to-day beyond Pange towards Metz. I propose to reconnoitre early on the 13th with detachments of the division so far along the Bingen - Metz road, as to effectively strike the enemy."

While the division halted at Bingen, the 9th Uhlans moved forward to reconnoitre, and to place outposts on the French Nied. Two squadrons halted at Kurzel, one squadron was sent to Maizeroy, on the left flank, and the regimental commander, Colonel v. Kleist, marched with one squadron to the hills of Puche, and from there reported—

> "Two camps on both sides of the road, and a cavalry camp south of it; no outposts out."

Lieutenant Beamisch-Bernard here made a welcome find in the castle of Urville, where Marshal Bazaine had stayed—to wit—a whole pile of French ordnance maps of the country round Metz. Under the table were found a number of envelopes with the Marshal's address, and one letter directed to him; all proofs of a hasty retreat.

If we examine the action of the two cavalry

Criticism of the

200 CAVALRY ON SERVICE

Aug. 12.
action of the 1st and 3rd Cavalry Divisions.

divisions of the First Army, the short advance of the 3rd Cavalry Division from Teterchen to Bettingen does not seem to accord with the situation.

Special orders for the cavalry divisions for August 12 had not been given. It had therefore become a question of acting according to circumstances. The 3rd Cavalry Division had only established touch with the enemy, with its most advanced patrols. Every endeavour should have been made to get up to them at last with the whole division. At the same time attempts should have been made to get around their left wing, to reach the Mosel between Metz and Diedenhofen, in order to gain a view of the valley as soon as possible, and to interrupt communication between the two fortresses. An enterprising cavalry could easily have succeeded in doing this on this day, and even without any special exertions, as Teterchen is only about nineteen miles from the Mosel as the crow flies.

If the divisional main body had only reached Antilly, three miles from the Mosel, and a favourably situated junction of roads, it would have found itself on the enemy's left flank, and could have tried the same day to throw small parties across the Mosel in order to cut the Metz-Diedenhofen railway line.

The division had done little service up till now, but had suffered severely from night marches and bivouacs in the rain. The natural desire alone to render service at last, which could compare with the actions of the sister arms, should have caused the possible consideration of "tired horses" (the usual explanation of inactivity) to be disregarded; since "it was a time when the greatest activity must be demanded of the cavalry," as the Head

… Quarters' Staff of the Tenth Army Corps had very aptly stated in writing to the 5th Cavalry Division on the previous day.

The patrols, which were already in front of the division, displayed incessant activity, but nothing further happened, as even the reconnaissance of Colonel v. Lüderitz had its origin in the initiative of this hardy leader of the advance guard.

The 1st Cavalry Division had also made but little progress, covering only about eight miles, and there is no apparent reason why they halted on the German Nied at Bingen, instead of moving with their main body the next stage forward to Kurzel.

The divisional leader says in his report that the advanced posts of the 13th Infantry Division also were on the far side of the German Nied, so the cavalry division was not yet in advance of the army, but, as the map shows, only on a line with it.

A patrol of the 8th Hussars, under Lieutenant Graf Itzenplitz, had again pressed far forward, to within five miles of the walls of Metz. In the morning he observed large camps of the enemy's infantry and cavalry near Coincy and Colombey. The news was forwarded to Royal Head Quarters, and arrived there on the morning of the 13th.

The Head Quarters' Staff of the Second Army came to some important resolutions on this date.

The reports to hand on the 11th all agreed that the enemy was establishing himself on the French Nied. Even till 11 a.m. next day no reports had been received which could shake the assumption, entertained up till now, of a probable battle on the Nied.

It was only about this hour that information came in from the Third and Tenth Corps, which gave news of the enemy's retirement from his fortified position. The transmission of the reports

Aug. 12. of the 15th Uhlans appears to have once more suffered considerable delay.

The preparations for the proposed right-wheel of the army now became unnecessary. From the fact of the French having retired to the line Peltre-Ars Laquenexy-Coincy, it was conjectured that a retreat through Metz was intended, and that this fortress would serve as a bridge head.

This, however, became doubtful again, as the bridge over the Mosel at Dieulouard was found to be intact, and in order to see clearer it appeared to be necessary to push forward larger bodies of cavalry, as soon as possible, to the plateau between the Maas and the Mosel.*

The 19th Division was to occupy Pont à Mousson as quickly as possible, as a support to the cavalry, and actually entered Delme at midnight.

The further orders of Army Head Quarters for the 13th we will give when dealing with the events of that day.

Operations of the 6th Cavalry Division.

The Head Quarters' authorities of the Third Army Corps naturally could not at all be satisfied with the activity of the 6th Cavalry Division, and in the night preceding the 12th they ordered an advance of the whole division on Pange and Laquenexy. Corps orders reached the division 2.45 a.m. on the 12th, and ran as follows:—

". . . (4) The cavalry division will march to-morrow from their cantonments with the heavy brigade, beyond the plateau Chanville-Argenchen-Vittoncourt-Voimhaut. The hussar brigade will advance beyond this position, and it is his Majesty's intention to gain more particular and definite information of the enemy. I therefore *quite distinctly demand of you*† to advance by Mont and Pange on Laquenexy, in such a manner as

* *Vide* note, p. 180. † Underlined in the original order.

to transmit precise information of the enemy's strength and disposition. I attach particular importance to receiving early intelligence. The heavy brigade will act as a reserve to the light. I leave it to the division to arrange for the disposal of the horse battery."

This order contained an encroachment on the authority of the divisional leader, which was not justified by the circumstances, as the Corps Head Quarters authorities disposed of his brigades in every detail, leaving, properly speaking, only the employment of the battery in the Duke's hands. That the very places which the division had at least to reach were laid down seems, however, the more justified, as Corps Head Quarters authorites very rightly did not place much reliance on the enterprise of the divisional commander. That same night the Duke issued this order :—

"The division will, at 6.30 a.m., be at the fork of roads to Argenchen, facing Pange. Rauch's Brigade is detailed to make a reconnaissance with the battery by Mont, Pange, and Laquenexy towards Metz. Grüter's Brigade will follow towards Berlize in support. If necessary, the 6th Infantry Division will advance to Hemilly. In preparation for the reconnaissance a squadron of the 3rd Hussars will move at once on both sides of the Nied, by Remilly and Lemud on the one side, by Anserweiler and Bazoncourt on the other, towards Pange and Laquenexy. It will send back reports as soon as possible on the road to Argenchen, and will consider itself as the most advanced point of Rauch's Brigade, which is advancing on Metz."

Rauch's Brigade, by a verbal order, was to move, in the first instance, to Pange with its main body, and there await the reports of the squadrons advancing by Laquenexy, Pange, and Mont, towards Metz, Grigy, Colombey, and Flanville.

Grüter's Brigade was to advance to Chanville,

Aug. 12. remain there in reserve, and push forward a squadron to the front towards Verny and the line Sorbey-Remilly, to connect up with the 5th Cavalry Division. [Graf Hardenberg's squadron of the 3rd Uhlans carried out this task.] A second squadron was to advance in pursuit of a squadron of African Jägers, found near Sorbey by Captain v. Buggenhagen, 3rd Hussars.

Duke William betook himself to a hill near Berlize, situated between the two brigades, and he transmitted the reports as they arrived by relay posts to Falkenberg.

If these arrangements are subjected to criticism according to the measure of our modern (present day) views of the course to be taken, we are struck by the general tendency in vogue in the employment of cavalry divisions to split up these units and to detail separate tasks to them, and thus destroy all unified control.

It was the 5th Cavalry Division in particular which displayed this tendency during the whole campaign, and especially during the first part of it on August 15 and 16, so that if their movements are followed the divisional commander never really personally led it, in the proper sense, during the whole course of the campaign.

In the 6th Cavalry Division also, on the 12th, in consequence of the direct interference of the corps, the Duke had not any part of the division under his personal orders.

The task assigned to Rauch's Brigade would have been carried out better by the division under the immediate direction of the Duke; and on meeting the enemy he would have had to make a personal reconnaissance in front of the troops, just as Colonel v. Alvensleben did a few days previously in so brilliant a manner. It is absolutely necessary that the divisional leader should see for himself in reconnaissances of this description. This personal seeing and judging, which is worth striving after even for the commander of a piquet, must be regarded as the rule for all cavalry leaders. Every despatch sent in from his own observation by a leader of division—that is to say, an officer of particular intelligence and acquainted with the whole situation—will naturally be regarded as of considerably higher value than reports of officers' patrols. In the above case the leader had contented himself with sending off from a point four miles behind the front of the advanced brigade these reports, the accuracy of which he could not even once prove. It is also impossible to approve of Grüter's Brigade being kept so far back in rear. If Rauch's Brigade had become engaged, the former could not have rendered it timely assistance; it could only, at most, in case of a disaster, have served as a rallying-point. But it should not come to such a disaster, and therefore troops should be kept so close at hand that immediate and timely support is assured.

Aug. 12.

The immediate despatch of Buggenhagen's squadron must be regarded as proper. The reconnaissance was thus well prepared. It is by the reports of an advanced squadron such as this, a patrol, as it were, ahead of the point, that sometimes the stronger reconnoitring bodies are put on the right track on which important observations become possible.

Rauch's Brigade reached Pange at 8 a.m. The Duke reported the measures taken by him at 8.45 a.m. from the "road between Chanville and Berlize." A further report from there at 10.45 a.m. runs thus:—

"(1) Rauch reached Laquenexy by way of Pange,

Aug. 12.

and was fired on there. He is bringing his guns up to help him to advance. Three squadrons of Chasseurs were noticed N.W. of Laquenexy.

"(2) Communication established with Rheinbaben—that is to say, with the 13th Uhlans, who are just passing through Remilly, in the direction of Courcelles, with guns."

In the first part of the report the statement "was fired on" occurs, without any more definite information being given. This statement is to be found in a very great number of reports from patrols during this war.

If an insufficient report like this is to be forbidden for patrols, how much more is censure called for if such a statement is made by a reconnoitring brigade? No one should ever be content with a statement of this description.

If a patrol is fired on, it is a piece of information from the enemy that he is in front of us; and it is only then that the patrol's true duty commences. A report such as that just quoted serves no good purpose whatever. The patrols from the brigade had meanwhile discovered a large camp between Coincy and Ars Laquenexy. The battery threw a few shells into the latter village, and the enemy thereupon evacuated it. The advanced squadron followed as far as that village. Lines of skirmishers moving out from the adjacent wood, followed by several columns of infantry, compelled the head of the brigade to withdraw behind Villers Laquenexy, while the battery was sent back to serve as a rallying-point behind the Nied.

At 11 o'clock General v. Rauch had sent the report from Ars Laquenexy to the 6th Infantry Division at Hemilly that "the enemy were advancing in large bodies towards Pange and north of it." [Compare order, p. 203.]

The Duke reported at 11.45—

Aug. 12.

"Rauch is beyond the Nied with his brigade. Main body at Ars Laquenexy. One squadron going by Ogy has reached Coincy. They were heavily fired on by infantry at Ars Laquenexy and Coincy. The guns fired a few shots on strong infantry columns, two to three regiments, on the Ars Laquenexy-Villers Laquenexy road. One company only is on the Coincy-Ogy road. Rauch is retiring slowly over the Nied, keeping the enemy in view."

Colonel v. Ziethen, commanding 3rd Hussars, who were at the head of the brigade, sent the squadrons forward in a "fan-like fashion," as the regimental history has it. The result was a number of reports from the patrols of the regiment.

Captain Krell, who had ridden towards Flanville, found about two divisions in camp there, and also discovered several large camps at Servigny.

Lieutenant v. Byern, who rode to the hills of Noisseville, observed several corps encamped on the plateau of St. Barbe, and numerous bodies of cavalry and artillery in front.

Captain v. Buggenhagen had found only cavalry of the enemy at Sorbey (*vide* above).

Captain Graf v. Hardenberg, 3rd Uhlans, moving by Anserweiler on Orny, found some mounted Jägers there, and gained touch with the 5th Cavalry Division.

Colonel v. Schmidt, who saw the 3rd Hussars actively engaged with the enemy in front, but had also observed that the reconnaissance towards Ars Laquenexy was checked, went northwards of the main road by Marcilly to Coincy, with the approval of the brigadier, in order to "better carry out the purpose of the reconnaissance," as the regimental diary puts it. There, under repeated infantry fire, by which three horses were

Aug. 12. hit, the regiment observed in the open ground in front the numerous and widely extended camps of the enemy at Flanville, Montoy, Colombey, Aubigny, Borny, and Grigy.

The Duke made a further report—

"West of Chanville, 12.50 p.m.

"Heads of the detachments of hostile infantry which had advanced against Rauch have halted on the Nied. Captain v. Thümen, who had been sent forward by Mont towards the Metz-St. Avold road, found that place unoccupied, but encountered the enemy's outposts behind it, and their reserve also advanced against him. There is a camp behind Coincy. I shall now order General Rauch to leave a regiment at Pange, with the duty of establishing a line of outposts on the Nied between Kurzel and the road leading from Metz to St. Avold; of patrolling towards Metz; and of retiring into cantonments with the four squadrons and the battery (Berlize-Sanry-Bazoncourt and Villiers-Stoncourt). A squadron of Uhlans remains for the present in front of Lemud, to keep up communication with the 5th Cavalry Division, and to patrol towards the Seille. The divisional staff is at Villiers-Stoncourt."

The measures taken by the Duke on the completion of the reconnaissance must be noted as eminently suitable. Above all, the leaving of a regiment at Pange guaranteed the certainty that the observation of the enemy would not be broken off.

The Duke sent a final report from Chanville at 4 p.m. (only received at Falkenberg at 8 p.m.)—

"Result of the reconnaissance: Outskirts of Metz to within $4\frac{1}{2}$ miles in advance of the main *enceinte* occupied by hostile infantry and cavalry. Between Ars Laquenexy and Colombey is a small camp. Between Colombey and the imperial road a larger one, the larger one north of the imperial road at Vantoux. Strength estimated at more than one corps. Last night troops (infantry) camped at Ogy, and to-day retired beyond Colombey. No general movement forward has been observed. The inhabitants assert, on the contrary, that movements to the rear have taken place again to-day. Yesterday the Nied was said to be still occupied, and the Guards, according to the people, to be at Metz."

<small>Aug. 12.</small>

The reports from the division to-day were abundant and to the purpose. The reconnaissance had completely succeeded in its object. The French cavalry, concentrated as they were in large bodies, rendered the task of the division easy, in a way, for which we have hardly a decent expression. The impression is that the regiments collected here lacked any enterprise. The German cavalry encountered only the infantry of the enemy. When these retired, the cavalry did not once venture to follow.

<small>Criticism of the operations.</small>

It would have been an easy task for the French to make Rauch's isolated brigade severely smart.

The 6th Cavalry Division, for all that, had done good work in this day's reconnaissance, and deserved recognition by the Head Quarters' authorities of the Third Army Corps. It was therefore a downright insult for the divisional commander that (as the diary of the division expressed it)—

<small>Head Quarters of the Third Army Corps does not believe the reports.</small>

"Corps Head Quarters deemed the reports untrustworthy, and suggested that the appearance of infantry (more than one army corps was reported) near a fortress could not point with certainty to the existence of an unusually large force."

Corps Head Quarters were therefore of opinion that the French army had already crossed the Mosel, and could not be converted from this preconceived idea even by reports to the contrary.

It cannot be assumed that the authorities would have given expression to scepticism of this sort

P

Aug. 12. if the divisional leader had been in a position to begin the report with these words: "*I have seen with my own eyes,*" etc.

The reports of the 6th Cavalry Division reached Army Head Quarters 5 p.m., with the remark—

> "Corps Head Quarters do not attach special importance to the reports, and will take no further action in consequence of them, since the infantry moving forward seem only to have the intention of driving back the advancing cavalry."

The reconnaissance came to an end at 3 p.m., and the division put out outposts on the line Ogy-Courcelles-Sorbey. [The outposts thus were posted in front of those of the 1st Cavalry Division.] A squadron of the 3rd Uhlans was to keep touch with the 5th Cavalry Division on the line Courcelles-Remilly, and to patrol towards the Seille.

The 2nd Dragoons, who marched to Pange (see the events of the 13th), had sent Graf v. Bruges there in advance.

Treacherous ringing of bells. He made the parson and burgomaster there prisoners, because they had announced the approach of the regiment to the enemy by ringing the bells. It must be noted that this action on the part of the inhabitants is to be regarded as akin to espionage. Sometimes, in the flat country on the Loire, signals were given by columns of smoke from high chimneys. The Germans, as a rule, were very easy-going in the punishment of such hostile actions, which were capable of causing considerable amount of harm.

Orders from the Tenth Army Corps for the 5th Cavalry Division. The General Officer Commanding Tenth Army Corps had issued the following instructions to General v. Rheinbaben, August 11, 10 p.m.:—

> "I desire your etc., as will appear from the attached

disposition, to remain in your position to-morrow, but to occupy the day as far as possible in minor enterprises against the enemy, and to send me frequent reports. Apart from the larger operations, which you, perhaps, have in view, I desire you to have Captain v. Rosenberg (13th Uhlans), v. Kleist (10th Hussars), v. Vaerst (11th Hussars), and Brauns (17th Hussars), despatched independently with their squadrons against the enemy, and to inform them that I expect them to succeed in gaining news of the enemy, in disturbing them, and in capturing prisoners.* Please place at the disposal of the bearer, Captain v. Thauvenay, 20 to 40 men, for a reconnaissance ordered by me towards Pont à Mousson."

Aug. 12.

The General Officer Commanding in this order encroached on the authority of the divisional leader, but he thought, not without reason, that such a course was necessary if proper action was to be expected from the division.

Criticism of the encroachment on the divisional commander's authority.

In the German Army the principle is rightly accepted that every commanding authority should preserve absolute independence within its command, and that within these limits it should keep its initiative and freedom of decision.

Frequently, therefore, where the situation demands, it is preferred to give *general instructions* instead of *distinct orders*. On the other hand, it must be borne in mind that the *method of giving general instructions*, which leaves to the officer detailed the widest and fullest scope in the mode of action, *must be applied* if the circumstances under which the officer has to act are not sufficiently known to the superior authorities for them to add more definite instructions, and *that it is advisable* to act thus if the firm conviction

* The officers detailed were personally known to the general, partly as belonging to the army corps under his command in peace-time, and partly from the name they had made when at the riding establishment.

212 CAVALRY ON SERVICE

Aug. 12. exists that the general instructions are sufficient to admit of proper action being taken that meets the case.

For self-reliance leads to that *initiative* with which each individual contributes his quota to the success of the whole. But, after all, the main point is that the object in view should be attained. The method of attaining it is a matter of indifference; and from this point of view it may often be needful to insert in the order instructions also about the method of action, regardless of whether the officer's powers are encroached upon or not. Sticklers are no good in any sphere of life, least of all in the military. I am speaking here only of active service. In peace manœuvres there is nothing at stake; there every one should learn, and be trained, to form independent resolutions. Under peace conditions, therefore, one must avoid encroaching on the authority of subordinates, and, moreover, the estimate of them by the superiors is only possible if freedom in decision is left them.

In accordance with the above corps orders, the divisional staff issued this order from Lucy to General v. Redern:—

Order of the division.

"Early this morning Captain v. Rosenberg, v. Kleist, v. Vaerst, and Brauns are to be sent out with their squadrons, independently, against the enemy, to disturb them and make prisoners."

Here the order of the Corps Head Quarters is simply reissued—a method which cannot be approved of. It was the duty of the divisional leader to detail the roads and the general direction of advance of the reconnoitring squadrons, since the intentions of the higher authorities, and the general situation as regards the enemy, must have been better known to him than to the brigadier. If possible, the divisional general should also have given more precise verbal instructions to the squadron leaders.

Let us next follow the squadrons detailed for special duty in their action.

Captain Brauns, with the 4th Squadron of the 17th Hussars, had been told off to cut the railway.

On the afternoon of the 11th, at Lucy, he was given this task—

Aug. 12.

Enterprise to destroy the railway at Frouard.

> "To reconnoitre the line of the Mosel next day, and, if possible, to cut the railway line."

Captain v. Heister, general staff officer to the cavalry division, handed over this task to Captain Brauns, with instructions that it was to be kept a secret.* At the same time he was informed of the duties assigned to Rosenberg, Kleist, and Thauvenay.

He was given Dockhorn, the sacristan of the division,† to act as an expert in the destruction of the railway. That evening the squadron was ordered by their captain to be ready 6.30 a.m. next day at the western exit of Lucy for church parade; the necessary tools were also requisitioned in the smithies. The next day, when the squadron was drawn up, the proper workmen were selected from the squadron; they were then equipped with tools and formed in one troop. At 7.30 the squadron trotted forward, accompanied by the general staff officer, Captain v. Heister, with the general's consent. It advanced with proper precautions by Lemoncourt and Jallaucourt over the Seille at Manhoué.

* Raids of this sort must always be kept secret till the very last moment, especially in the enemy's country, otherwise the inhabitants may easily overhear a word or two and the warning be given.

† The man was a railway official in civil life, and had a MacMahon's spanner in his possession.

Aug. 12.

To avoid any delay in examining the country, which was rather close, Captain Brauns, with a map and a good glass, and accompanied by a N.C.O. and two hussars, kept far in advance, spying the country and using the two hussars for pointing out the way to the squadron. Between Eceuille and Lay the squadron met a N.C.O.'s patrol of the 10th Hussars, which was riding on to Nancy.

They had thus far noticed as little of the enemy's troops as the squadron. A private carriage, which met the latter here, was seized, and made to follow it. We shall see how profitable this turned out later on. It is most useful to have waggons available, if possible, in enterprises of this nature. I can vouch for the value of it from my own experience. During a reconnaissance the squadron I commanded would certainly have lost a few men as prisoners, who had had their horses shot, if I had not rapidly succeeded in getting hold of a waggon. In raids on railways waggons will often be required to carry away rails, etc., that have been removed. A waggon commandeered like this one at the last moment does not encumber the troops, as it can be simply dropped at any moment.

At Bouxières aux Dames the valley opened out (see map, p. 217), and a stone bridge spanned the Meurthe, on the left bank of which, before it joins the Mosel, lay Frouard, with its railway station.

A high-road lined with poplars led southwards from the bridge to Champigneulles.

To the north-west, between the Meurthe and the railway embankment, stretched a meadow, which was very narrow at the spot which the squadron had to pass to reach the station.

Lieutenant Ernst with his troop was left <small>Aug. 12.</small> behind on the Meurthe bridge, to hold it with carbines, and keep it open for the squadron. He had to reconnoitre towards Champigneulles. It is to be assumed that he left his horses on the right bank under cover as much as possible in the village, and pushed skirmishers beyond and in front of the bridge, so as to sweep the canal bridge at Champigneulles, as well as the rails to the station, with their fire.

A detachment which has to keep a passage open for parties pushed further forward must be regarded as a kind of bridge-head, and secure the access to the bridge sufficiently far *in advance*—that is to say, at a distance in front, which depends on the lie of the country, on their strength, and that of the party to be covered. A defence from the near bank is only made if the passage is to be denied to the enemy.

A French infantry N.C.O. was taken prisoner on the bridge, but he could not be induced to give any information about the enemy. He had been on his way to his parents in Bouxières, and now took a seat on the commandeered carriage. The rest of the squadron, with Lieutenants v. Bernewitz, v. Luneburg, and Schweppe, crossed the bridge at noon. The party provided with the tools halted at the place indicated on the sketch. Under the sacristan's direction, the rails of the line from Nancy were torn up, the telegraph poles cut down, and the arrangements for working it destroyed.

The rest of the squadron, in a long thin column, galloped up between large trains of coal to the station, which they entered, completely surprising the enemy.

On the platform they found twenty infantrymen belonging to different regiments, and fast

Aug. 12. asleep, their chassepots piled near them. "We galloped," said Brauns in his report, "straight over the platforms and rails, all among these men, and took the greater part of them prisoners."

They were tied up with head-ropes. Officers who came up hastily made off. The telegraph apparatus was destroyed by Lieutenant v. Luneburg after he had, in the presence of Frenchmen, sent misleading telegrams to Chalons.

The leader now wished to cut the Frouard-Chalons stretch of line, and was galloping off himself with one troop, when a train came steaming in from that direction.

Another party hunted the fleeing Frenchmen between the station buildings.

Infantrymen, without their arms, got out of the train, which stopped 100 yards from the station, and were at once fired on by the hussars.

As soon as they had seized their rifles an action began, in which the squadron was outmatched. The situation became critical. Providentially the French shot badly, and, besides, the coal-waggons afforded some cover. The retirement through the station was effected quietly, and the horses remounted. The hussars lost one man and five horses killed, including the captain's, and two men wounded. The men behaved splendidly. "When I," writes Brauns, "was slowly retiring on foot under cover behind a train that was standing there without an engine, I was escorted by two hussars, who kept firing back on the enemy without intermission."

Twelve of the twenty prisoners escaped, the other eight were brought along. The men, whose horses had been hit, held on to their comrades' stirrup-leathers, and the wounded were brought back as well.

CAVALRY ON SERVICE 217

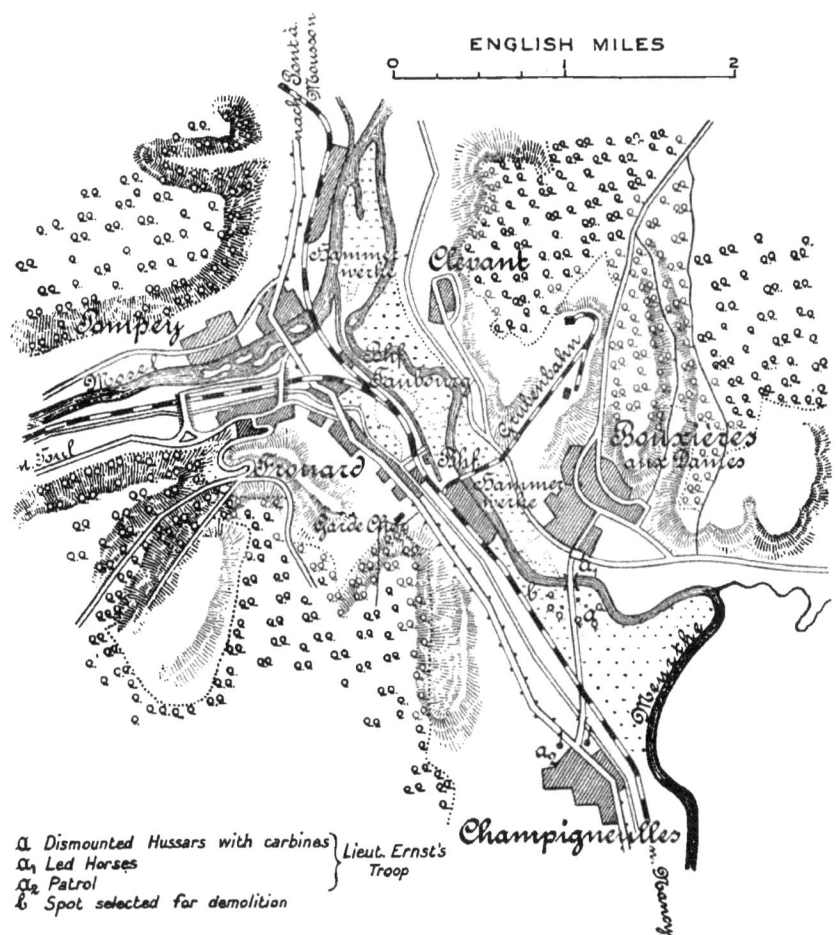

a Dismounted Hussars with carbines ⎫ Lieut. Ernst's
a₁ Led Horses   ⎬ Troop
a₂ Patrol   ⎭
b Spot selected for demolition

Aug. 12.

As the squadron reached the Meurthe bridge they were fired on again, but the shots went much too high.

The patrol sent to Champigneulles had met infantry at least a battalion strong there; and these ran into the houses at once, and opened so hot a fire at 100 yards' range that two of the twelve men of the patrol, which Lieutenant Ernst himself commanded, were severely wounded. At 1.30 p.m. the squadron retired, the wounded and two hussars, who had lost their horses, finding seats in the carriage. For the dismounted hussars and the prisoners a country waggon was requisitioned. At 11 p.m. the squadron arrived without further incident at Lucy. Captain v. Heister had, in the retreat, brought back the last men whose horses had been shot.

Comments.

The destruction of the railway at Frouard was a gallant action most prudently carried out. The difficult retirement, effected with iron nerve and without loss, proves, above all, the excellent spirit which pervaded Braun's squadron. The enterprise would have had its complete effect if only the destruction of the rails in the direction of Chalons had been successful; for this was the stretch of line which the 6th (French) Corps was using at that time. Naturally the captain could not have been aware of this. The destruction of this part of the line was peculiarly difficult, because it was protected on the east by the waters of the Meurthe and the Mosel, and would certainly have been impossible if the bridge had been destroyed, or, at any rate, occupied.

It is one of the many unintelligible items of the French arrangements that the station guard at Frouard had not occupied the bridge. It would naturally have been advisable for the squadron to have cut the line just beyond Frouard, where the Chalons line had already joined the one from Nancy, so that one operation would have broken the communication with both places; but the squadron hardly had a choice in the matter, for it had first to pass the station to dispose of the garrison there.

In the arrangements of the squadron, which were in other respects proper and well thought out, patrols along the line to Metz and by Frouard towards Liverdun were omitted; but the station in the hands of the French barred the approach at first, and later it could no longer be done, because the fight began soon after. The train, which had been stopped by the raid, carried portions of the 28th Infantry Regiment of the Line. It had left Paris at 2.30 p.m. Reports were rife in Liverdun that Uhlans had cut the line at Frouard. So the train stopped two miles out of Frouard, the troops alighted, and the fight began. The train was considerably delayed, and only reached Metz at 3.30 p.m. A company remained in the station as garrison. A second troop train passed the stretch of line in the evening, and ran into Metz at 10 p.m. (The French, moreover, confirm that the destruction—thanks to the sacristan—had been carried out rapidly and with great skill.)

Captain Brauns forwarded a long report to the Corps Head Quarters on the course of the raid, dated Lafraincourt, 5.15 p.m., from which the above account is partly taken.

Captain v. Heister added to the report a memorandum, in which he spoke in high terms of the daring and adroitness displayed that day by the whole squadron, and continues—

"Captain Brauns' whole plan was conceived with great skill, carried out with dash, and brilliantly

Aug. 12.

concluded in spite of the difficulty of the situation. At the head of his men, he had his horse shot at close range; his officers behaved irreproachably, and the men all displayed unquestioned gallantry. Dockhorn, the divisional sacristan (a railway official), who accompanied me, supervised the work of destruction under the enemy's fire. The prisoners—a sergeant from the 26th Regiment,* two from the 18th, one from the 27th, one Turco from the 1st Regiment, two from the 16th Jäger Battalion—have been examined."

All honour to the bold Brunswickers. Our material was really splendid.

Raid on the line at Pont à Mousson.

The attempt to cut the line at Pont à Mousson did not run so smoothly as this one.

Captain v. Thauvenay, 13th Uhlans, orderly officer at the Head Quarters of the Tenth Army Corps, had command of the raid on Pont à Mousson.

A combined squadron was told off for the purpose, two troops of twenty men each from the 17th Hussars, under Lieutenants Cox and v. Hodenberg, and one officer, Baron v. Toll, with thirty-two men of the 19th Dragoons.

The detachment reached the bridge over the Mosel at 11 o'clock in the morning, found Pont à Mousson apparently unoccupied, so went through it and reached the station to commence the demolition here. But just at this moment a train full of French infantry of the 6th Corps had arrived, one company of which got out and opened fire on the German horsemen, and they had to evacuate the town with the loss of two men and three horses of the 17th Hussars. Under these circumstances Lieutenant Cox wished to abandon the enterprise, but Captain v. Thauvenay ordered the men to turn about beyond the town, and, after

* The 26th Regiment had passed in a train along that line a few hours previously.

the departure of the train had been observed, they once more moved forward through the town to the station; a resolve which must meet with complete approval, and shows great energy. Aug. 12.

In the further course of events a good deal of mystery exists in several points with regard to the half-squadron of the 17th Hussars, which cannot be cleared up.

But the following seems certain. The combined squadron moved to the station, the hussars seem to have destroyed the line towards Metz pretty quickly, and only hastily, and then retired again over the Mosel bridge. In the first house on the right beyond the bridge, Lieutenant Cox ordered his horses to be brought into an open shed in the yard to unbridle and to feed.*

The Oldenburg Dragoons had begun the demolition of the line on the Nancy side, and Baron v. Toll had been told by Captain v. Thauvenay, on the second advance to the station, that the hussars would remain on the right bank of the river. Perhaps this was the case as far as one troop was concerned. Lieutenant v. Toll therefore thought that he was protected to his rear. Past the station the road leads to St. Mihiel, and crosses the line at a point where a good view can be obtained, especially towards Metz.

Here v. Toll posted a trumpeter as a look-out post, a vedette was placed further forward on the road that leads to St. Mihiel and soon begins to ascend; a patrol sent towards Metz, and another, under Sergeant Westphal, along the line towards Nancy. The dragoons now devoted themselves to the work, took off their jackets, tied their horses to the station railings, and began to shift the rails,

* According to the "History of the War," even to off-saddle (p. 441).

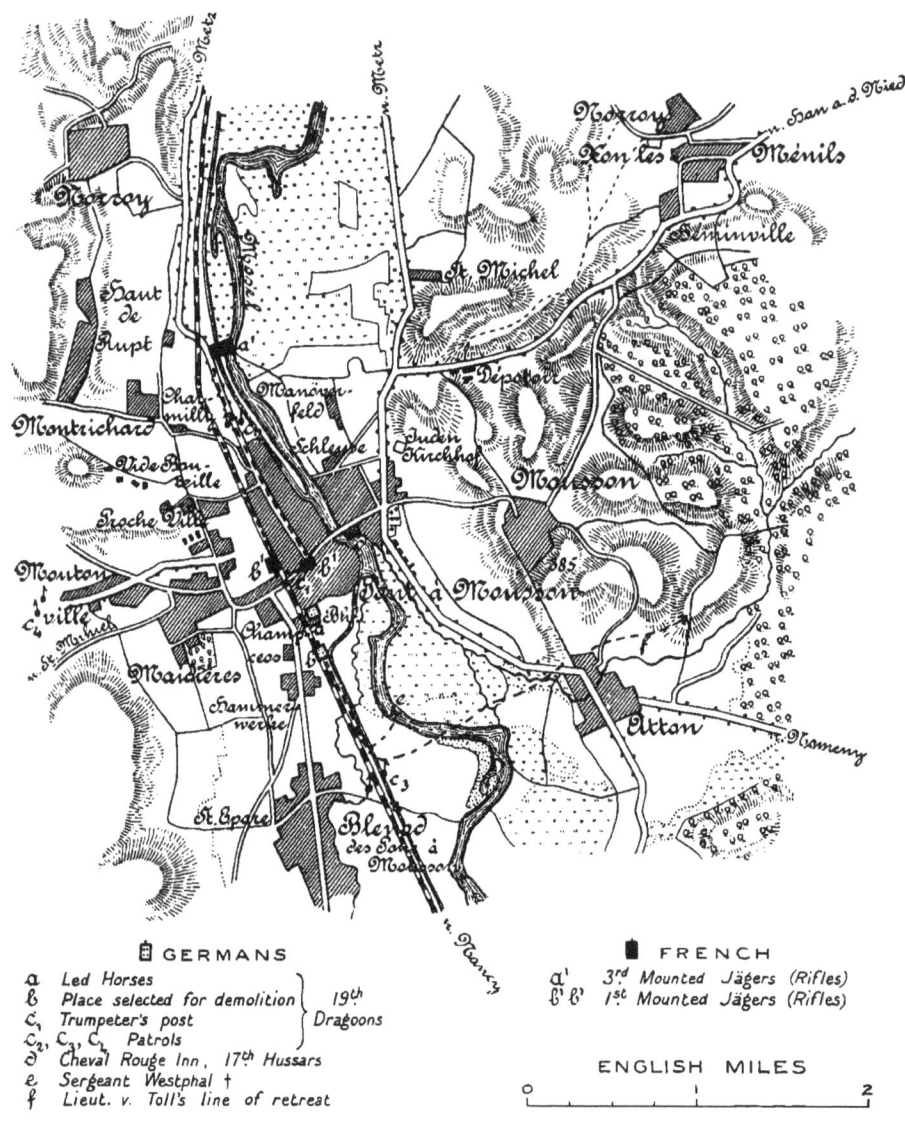

but proceeded very slowly, owing to the unsatisfactory tools which they had at their disposal and their want of practice. Captain v. Thauvenay stayed most of the time in the station buildings and wrote reports. One of them, dated 2 p.m., is to hand—

Aug. 12.

> "Pont à Mousson is not occupied by the enemy. The bridge over the Mosel is in good repair. I am occupying the station, and sending a reconnaissance towards Metz on the left bank of the Mosel."

It is noticeable in this report that no mention is made of the previous meeting with the enemy's infantry and the passing through of the troop-trains. Also, the reconnaissance towards Metz was not carried out in the sense that the report implied, since the patrol of three dragoons which v. Toll sent off in that direction can scarcely be counted as a reconnaissance. The prompt despatch of a strong officer's patrol was clearly called for.

The enemy, it is true, was to be expected from every direction; but Metz, which was known to be strongly occupied, was nevertheless the point to which special attention must be directed, and had been, according to the report sent in.

News of the appearance of the German cavalry in Pont à Mousson had been brought into Metz by the earlier train; and Marshal Bazaine ordered General Margueritte to reconnoitre towards Pont à Mousson with his brigade (the 1st and 3rd African Jägers). An hour after receipt of the order the brigade was starting on its march from St. Martin. At a fast pace the long stretch of sixteen miles was covered in a couple of hours. On the way, the general obtained information from the country-folk of the state of affairs in the town. Before

Aug. 12. entering it, he let the horses have a few minutes to get their wind;* then, leaving the 3rd Regiment in reserve in front of the town, he himself, with two squadrons of the 1st Regiment, dashed down the main street, and sent the other two along the railway line to the station.

The trumpeter of the 19th Dragoons, posted as a look-out, gave the men timely warning by signal of the danger that threatened them from the railway line.

Retreat, for which there seemed ample time, was to be effected through the town. But while the dragoons were in the act of mounting, the other squadrons of the enemy met them, coming from the town, and driving the patrol of dragoons in front of them.

Two of this patrol of three men were killed. It seems, alas! pretty clear that the blame for the disaster which occurred must be attributed to these men; for according to French accounts, two German horsemen, "who were probably on reconnaissance duty," were surprised in a public-house on the high-road in front of the town.

The dragoons could now no longer mount their horses in time, which were thrown into confusion by the enemy's fire, with the result that some broke loose and galloped away.

Those men that got mounted dashed southwards along the railway. A desperate struggle, hand to hand, ensued. But when the fallen telegraph poles, and the wire that lay on the top of them, had brought down a number of horses, Lieutenant v. Toll with his men, with quick decision, hurried down to the Mosel, which was in flood. A

---

* Such a rest shortly before a like action may completely jeopardize its success. If it was absolutely necessary for the horses "to get their wind," the pace must have been too fast up to that moment.

quick leap into the stream must bring death or deliverance from capture. Gallantly the horses swam forwards. Every man sat as still as possible to ease his animal.

Aug. 12.

But as the horsemen neared the other side, an obstacle gradually appeared confronting them—a stone-faced bank rose perpendicularly from the water. Would the horses touch bottom? would they have spirit to exert their strength again to overcome the obstacle? So they each wondered as the horses slowly approached the bank. Death or capture seemed inevitable. Yet, by good fortune, the horses touched bottom; one mighty leap, and the wall was passed!

After the horses had had a few minutes' breathing space, the retreat continued through thick bushes. The ground became more marshy every minute, and in a short time the little band stood again before another branch of the river, which, small as it was, formed a most undesirable obstacle by reason of its boggy edges and steep banks several feet high. When a practicable place had been found after some search, they jumped one after another into the water, which splashed high over their heads. The other bank was safely reached, only two dragoons, who were riding purchase-horses, could not induce them to jump into the water again.*

This was indeed a case where the cavalrymen might well cry, almost like King Richard of England, "A kingdom for an *obedient* horse."

* These and other unsatisfactory experiences in the last campaign with "purchase" horses, which proved unfit for special exertions, should keep us from employing such useless material in large numbers in mobilization. One must beware of this apparently popular *rage des nombres*. It may probably lead to much disappointment. Trust must not be placed in numbers which look all very well on paper, to prove mere moonshine when tested. Good wine must not be watered before it is tasted.

Aug. 12. This adventure of Lieutenant v. Toll's party does, after all, great credit to the training of the Oldenburg Dragoon horses. The men left behind on the island successfully hid themselves, escaped the enemy's search-party, and rejoined their regiment the next morning, with their horses in good condition. On leaving the railway embankment, Sergeant Westphal had been sent off to discover a ford. In this endeavour he met his death in the stream, although a strong swimmer. [*e* on the sketch, p. 222.]

Lieutenant v. Toll, with twelve dragoons, managed to reach the opposite bank in safety. Many of them found a watery grave. The dragoons lost one N.C.O. and four men killed, three men wounded, who fell into the enemy's hands, and nine men and eighteen horses missing. The dragoons defended themselves gallantly; the fallen sold their lives dearly, and many pieces of heroism are quoted in the regimental history, of the men who never returned to their regiment.

The 17th Hussars, meanwhile, were quietly resting in the "Cheval Rouge." "Patrols provided for the safety of the detachment," says the regimental diary. More exact information of the measures of security taken by the hussars is, unhappily, not forthcoming, but it may be taken for granted this was not sufficient.

That the leader should have brought the party, under the existing circumstances, into a yard in the middle of the town, let them feed in a shed, and even off-saddle, according to the official "History of the War," was an indiscretion which should have led to a heavy punishment. The two captured officers are said to have applied for a court of inquiry later, so I was informed, but this does not appear to have taken place. When the French cavalry burst into the town, the inhabitants shut the door of the yard, so that escape became impossible for the hussars.

Aug. 12.

The French, hurrying over the bridge, dismounted in front of the house, and began firing through the closed door and the windows of the neighbouring houses into the yard.

The hussars defended themselves bravely. When it was found impossible, according to French records, to master the hussars, the door was broken in. A tall officer—" un grand diable d'officier "—rushed forward to cut his way through; he fired a carbine at Colonel Clicquot, hit his orderly, and then threw himself with his sword on General Margueritte, and clove through his cap.

He was overpowered at last, and the hussars inside were captured. Their loss amounted to four hussars killed, Lieutenants Cox and v. Hodenberg, one N.C.O., fifteen hussars, and twenty-six horses missing.* The entire French loss was two killed, five wounded, five horses killed, and a large number disabled, which had hurt their feet in the chase along the railway line.

* According to the book "Campagne de 1870, L'armée de Metz et le Maréchal Bazaine," an examination took place before an officer of the general staff of the two captured officers in Metz. They stated at it that they were only one or two days ahead of the Second Army. This information was most valuable to the French, as appears from the account of the general staff officer. It can scarcely be admitted that the account is correct. Were it so, the behaviour of these officers must be strongly condemned. Dick de Lonlay, in his book, cites an episode which stands in happy contrast to this. On August 14, the 3rd Squadron of the 2nd Dragoons had surprised and attacked a Prussian infantry patrol, and had taken part prisoners. The officer in command, Lieutenant v. Goltz, had defended himself gallantly. At the appointed examination he answered, " Je suis Prussien, je peux marcher où il me plait ; " and to the questions put to him he made no reply, and refused to give his word of honour not to escape. Unhappily, I have tried in vain to discover the unit to which this gallant officer belonged, or to find out any further details of the incident from German accounts.

Aug. 12.

Some companies of the 28th Regiment of the Line, which came up in a train directly after the surprise occurred, joined in the pursuit of the German cavalry. According to Dick de Lonlay, this was the same train which Captain Brauns had held up in Frouard. After a temporary repair of the permanent way, the train continued its journey to Metz, leaving three companies behind to garrison Pont à Mousson.

The demolition had not, therefore, delayed the traffic to any extent. This can be partly attributed to the fact that the dragoons, in their hurried retreat, had left behind the rails, etc., that had been shifted, and that tools and spare material were ready to hand owing to the proximity of the station.

Comments on the enterprise.

Captain v. Thauvenay of course was responsible, first of all, for the safety of the party; but all the same his subordinates, Lieutenants v. Toll and Cox, were not thereby freed from all responsibility, and it was their duty to supplement the measures of protection, where the arrangements of the captain, who had provisional command, did not seem to be sufficient.

The duty to be discharged was a double one—to cut the railway at Pont à Mousson, and to reconnoitre towards Metz. This reconnaissance had primarily to be directed down the valley of Mosel, and on the left bank, since the leader, being orderly officer at Corps Head Quarters, must have been aware that reconnaissances from other directions on Metz and on Nancy were being carried out by other parties. Information is wanting as to the details of orders which the leader issued. In any case, there was not sufficient care taken for the safety of the detachment. It will be worth while, perhaps, to represent the measures which should have properly been taken. [See map of August 12.]

It must be remarked, in the first instance, that

the detachment seems to have been too weak in comparison with the importance of the undertaking; at least, a complete squadron should have been detailed.

Aug. 12.

The detachment moved forward on the main road leading from Han an der Nied by Vigny to Pont à Mousson. This is the shortest route, which favoured a rapid advance.

Reconnaissance and protection towards Metz would have been best met by sending a sufficiently strong officers' patrol—say, eight men—by Goin, Sillegny, on Arry during the forward movement. From this village, lying 1320 feet above the sea-level and close to the Mosel, a clear view is obtained, as the map shows, as far as the gates of Metz and over the hills on the left bank. When the patrol reached this vantage ground the officer would have done well to hold this post of observation with some of his men, and send only smaller patrols further forward as required.

On nearing Pont à Mousson the conical hill of Mousson becomes at once a conspicuous object, 1283 feet in height, which commands the town and affords a view far in the direction of St. Mihiel and southwards, as well as down the Mosel valley. A post placed here, with a signal agreed on which could be seen from the station, as well as communicating posts, would have prevented any surprise of the party, and rendered unnecessary any of the smaller posts and patrols, such as those sent out by the Oldenburgers. Single posts with a good view over the country form the best protection in enterprises such as this. They are preferable to patrols, as these easily betray our presence, and bring the enemy down on us; they are also less adapted for keeping a large area under constant observation.

Aug. 12.

In the measures adopted here strict adherence was kept to the pattern laid down—outposts to front and flank. This, however, was a case in which a post stationed in rear of the party would have rendered better service. If, in addition, a patrol moving down the Mosel valley had established communication with that sent to Arry, and little parties had scouted the woods which come close down on the left bank, all the measures necessary for observation and protection would have been taken.

Once arrived at the town, a dismounted troop should have been left on the bridge to guard it and keep touch with the post on the Mousson hill. The detachment numbered 70 men, and would then have been distributed as follows: patrol to Arry 8, post on the Mousson 4, patrol down the Mosel 4, two small patrols 4, troop on the bridge 20, leaving 30 men for the work at the station. It is clear that the detachment was rather too weak to carry out its double duty. Nowadays, however, 30 cavalrymen properly equipped would be more than sufficient to effect a thorough demolition within a reasonable time.

It may be doubted whether the place for the demolition was rightly chosen. The task was rendered more difficult by the fact that the line to be destroyed was protected by the river; and the retreat of the party would have been endangered by being any further distance from the bridge.

If demolitions are effected near a station, it must always be borne in mind that the enemy has material for repairs ready to hand. A patrol furnished with explosives would probably have chosen for its object the bridge over the Ache, which lies further south. Only an examination of

CAVALRY ON SERVICE 231

the place and the position could lead to a definite opinion on this point.

Aug. 12.

For the direct reconnaissance on Metz, Captain v. Rosenberg, 13th Uhlans, was detailed. Early in the morning he trotted forward with 60 picked horses and Lieutenants v. Treskow and v. Wedel (III.) by Sorbey and Mécleuves on the Strassburg-Metz main road. Near Jury he saw that the heights north of Peltre, on the far side of the Metz-Remilly railway, were occupied by strong bodies of the enemy, who had apparently a camp

Reconnaissance of Rosenberg's squadron and Vaerst's.

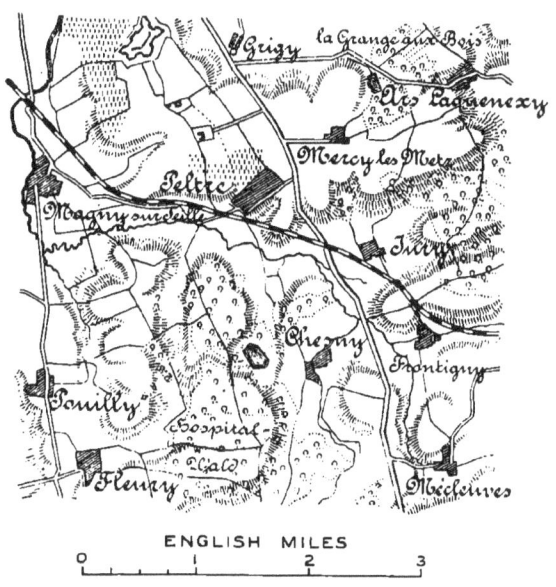

there. To gain a nearer view he continued his march in the direction of the railway embankment. [In explanation of the ground it may be noted that it falls from Chesny towards Jury. Between these two places flows the St. Peter stream, a well-known obstacle in the Metz drag-hunt. Behind the stream the country rises again towards Jury and Frontigny. On this slope runs the railway. See the sketch.]

Aug. 12.	A squadron of mounted Jägers came towards him and opened fire with their carbines. In a short encounter he overcame them, and pursued them to the embankment, taking one or two of them prisoners. Here he came under fire from dismounted cavalry; and artillery, too, opened fire with shell. The detachment had to be withdrawn out of fire as quickly as possible. From hot pursuit the leader gave orders to turn about, and at full speed the party took cover behind the nearest rise, where they dropped into a walk, and faced about again. The small force was so completely in hand that its leader could exercise complete control at the fastest pace.

Now—any mention of place is wanting, probably it was near the road on a level with Chesny—Rosenberg sends the following report:—

"No. 1.
"12 noon.

"The squadron advanced by Sorbey to Mécleuves on the Buchy-Metz road. On it we encountered a squadron of the enemy. We attacked and it turned about on our cry of 'gallop.' We chased it back to where the railway cuts the road. At the embankment we came under a hot fire (from dismounted cavalry) and retired some distance from it. The chaussée beyond the embankment is at this moment completely occupied, as well as the hills beyond, and the road in particular, leading from the chaussée to Frontigny (by artillery). An advance is impossible, and I therefore intend to take the road which goes by Pouilly, in order to get information about the enemy from there."

This last intention was certainly to the point. The detachment could not advance any further to their front; a circuit to the left, which could, moreover, be effected through the Hospital wood, screened from view, might well result in a closer insight.

Meanwhile the situation had changed, as the following report shows:—

"Report No. 2.

"No place named—1 p.m.

"After the first report had gone, the squadron came under a hot artillery fire, and at the same time the cavalry regiment from Peltre trotted up to the Chesney wood.* I therefore could not remain there. Nor could I venture into the Fleury* wood, for I guessed the regiment would have cut off my retreat. The hills of Peltre and Jury were occupied by artillery. They shot well, but the shells did not burst. I did not myself see any infantry. Some men declared they saw some, but I scarcely believe it. I could not attack the artillery, I regret to say, even after the cavalry regiment had trotted off, as I can only advance by the railway crossing, and so be placed in a serious predicament by the troops which possibly lay behind the hill."†

Captain v. Rosenberg now retired to Lemud, and does not appear to have left any patrols in touch with the enemy.

It must be remarked of the reports, that they contained much which might properly have been included in a later despatch, and was of no immediate interest to the superior authorities. In the present-day arrangement of the report forms, it would have been of special value, after a reconnaissance of this kind, and easily done, to sketch the enemy's position with a few strokes, which would also save a lot of explanations. The squadron had only one man killed and two horses hit.

According to the French account by Dick de Lonlay of this skirmish, a troop of the 6th Squadron of the 4th Mounted Jägers made a feigned attack on v. Rosenberg's detachment, to draw them under hostile fire, which was quite successful. This seems not improbable. Such a scheme can easily succeed,

* Parts of the large Hospital wood.
† It cannot be imagined that the artillery was isolated in a situation like this.

Aug. 12. if the firing party keeps well hidden and the enemy allows himself to be carried away by an ill-considered pursuit.

The French party (whether a troop or a squadron is doubtful),* according to Rosenberg's report, did not wait for his attack. But the scheme was unsuccessful, as Rosenberg had his men perfectly in hand, and soon found cover behind a sheltering slope of the hill. It is necessary for the retiring troops who carry out the feint, not to fall back direct on the firing line, but to incline to one side, otherwise they mask the fire.

The same morning v. Vaerst's squadron of the 11th Hussars advanced from Delme to reconnoitre towards Metz, and, going by Solgne, reached Chesny on the main road, where it met Rosenberg's detachment. It is curious that Rosenberg in his report does not mention the 11th Hussars. The assumption seems a fair one that they only met, after Rosenberg had written his last report. The following report from v. Vaerst appears to confirm this too :—

"August 12, 2 p.m.

"Arrived at the Metz-Saarbrücken railway, without meeting the enemy. Engaged enemy there on foot towards the railway embankment. Impossible to advance further, as embankment strongly held by all arms. Was fired on by artillery."

It is, anyhow, certain that the two squadrons operated together for some time, as the diary of the 11th Hussars states that v. Vaerst's squadron joined a squadron of the 13th Uhlans. The French account, too, speaks of two squadrons which pressed

* With the swift appearance of cavalry detachments and the rapid progress of the fight, it is often very difficult to estimate numbers correctly.

I have myself taken two troops of lancers which appeared on the field for two squadrons in column of troops.

CAVALRY ON SERVICE 235

forward on the afternoon of the 12th from Pontois to within 1¼ miles of Jury, supported by infantry. The "infantry" was a troop armed with carbines, which had dismounted, and by v. Vaerst's orders skirmished opposite the embankment of Jury, on the hill south of it. It received the regiment of Jägers as they came trotting up with so hot a fire that they thought they had infantry facing them and retired. The French also began to shell v. Vaerst's Squadron, upon which he retired to Solgne, fed his horses there, and then went back to Aulnois on the Seille.

Aug. 12.

Kleist, sent with his squadron to Nancy, arrived there by way of Chateau Salins without incident.

Kleist's reconnaissance to Nancy.

In the first town he levied a contribution of 8900 francs, and in Nancy 50,000 francs. The railway at Nancy was also thoroughly demolished, though this could scarcely affect the enemy in the present situation. That a single squadron could levy a contribution on a populous town like Nancy was a proof of the energetic action of its leader, and the want of spirit of the French.

At 9.45 on the morning of the 12th, the General commanding the Tenth Army Corps sent to the 5th Cavalry Division this more detailed order in continuation of the arrangements of the evening of the 11th. (It arrived at 11.45 a.m.)

Fresh corps orders.

> "Start at once with the troops you have with you, so as to reach Solgne this afternoon. Advanced troops must be posted towards Metz with their right wing on the Nied, where touch must be kept up with the Third Army Corps. General v. Redern is ordered direct to proceed to Noményy, and thence five miles further forward on the road to Metz. He is to send two to four squadrons to Pont à Mousson, to cut the railway there, and patrol as far as possible along the left bank of the Mosel."

Aug. 12.

Redern's advance on Pont à Mousson.

In accordance with his orders received direct, General v. Redern marched with the main body of the brigade by Nomény to Raucourt, while Major v. Garnier, 11th Hussars, was detailed to advance towards Pont à Mousson with the 2nd Squadron of the 11th and the 3rd of the 10th Hussars. The major, on his way thither, met Captain v. Thauvenay returning. As the squadrons neared Pont à Mousson, detachments of infantry, accompanied by cavalry, left the town and moved towards the Hussars, who, leaving out scouts, retired. In the firing, that sounded very heavy, the enemy had three men wounded, the Hussars none, although the bullets whistled over their heads in hundreds. The Brigadier directed the major to retire behind the Seille to Eply, and put out outposts. He sent the following report from Raucourt, 9.45 p.m. :—

"In accordance with orders, received 2.30 p.m., to proceed to Raucourt and send a detachment towards Pont à Mousson, I sent thither Major v. Garnier with two squadrons (one from 11th Hussars, one from 10th Hussars), and continued my march on Raucourt. Between 6 and 7 p.m., shortly before reaching Nomény, I received word from Captain v. Thauvenay that Pont à Mousson had been surprised, and was occupied by troops of all arms.* I deemed the two squadrons sent towards Pont à Mousson sufficient to protect Captain v. Thauvenay, and directed the major to fall back on me. Three squadrons of the 11th Hussars now only amount to three troops in strength.† Four squadrons 17th Hussars and a horse battery are at Solgne."

On the same day General v. Redern, in accordance with fresh orders from Army Head Quarters

---

* The exaggeration in the report can only be explained by the excitement consequent on the events.

† It is shown by this fact how exhausting the kind of patrolling duty is as was carried out by Redern's Brigade in those last days.

(see under August 13), received an order direct from Corps Head Quarters, dated Landorf, 3 p.m., to start at once to Pont à Mousson; secure the passage over the Mosel that very night; push patrols to the left bank of the Mosel, and leave only weak posts of observation on the Delme-Metz road. The order concludes with: "The matter is highly important." He was informed at the same time that Pont à Mousson would be occupied next day by the infantry of the corps.

General v. Redern acknowledged at 9 p.m. receipt of the order from Army Head Quarters to proceed forthwith to Pont à Mousson, and stated that he had, at the same time, received the report that 200 to 300 infantry were advancing against Major v. Garnier's outposts, and that he had with him only four weak squadrons.

This statement was perhaps exaggerated, but the order reached Redern's brigade so late that its execution had to be deferred till the following day. Moreover, it is not clear what the brigade could have effected in the dark.

The enemy could be perfectly well kept under observation from Eply. The measures taken by General v. Redern and Major v. Garnier that evening seem quite sufficient, and the position of the outposts at Eply well chosen.

The G.O.C. Fourth Army Corps had issued orders for the 12th to Bredow's brigade to proceed from Finstingen to Burg-Altdorf (18 miles), to place outposts on the line Dordal-Gebling, Vergaville, and push patrols forward to Conthil and Genesdorf. This movement was carried out without anything particular happening. The diaries do not mention any incidents.

The extraordinarily short distance covered by the patrols cannot be understood.

Aug. 12.

The 3rd Guard Cavalry Brigade had moved forward to Oron, and from there sent Captain Graf Westarp's squadron (3rd) of the 1st Guard Dragoons to cut the railway at Pont à Mousson.

On his way the leader learnt—how, it is not known—that the demolition had already been carried out, and he stayed behind in Noményi.

He sent a troop under Lieutenant Graf Schwerin to Pont à Mousson, who confirmed the news and found the place clear of the enemy. This last statement must strike one as remarkable after the events described above and those of the following day; but as Pont à Mousson had no permanent garrison, it can easily have been clear of the enemy on the night of the 12th.

Measures taken by the enemy.

With regard to the measures taken by the French, the important resolution adopted in the council of war must be given prominence—that the army should retreat to Chalons, and that this movement should begin on the 14th. Bazaine received the instructions as the then Commander-in-Chief. Meanwhile the bridges over the Seille at Magny and Marly, the two bridges at Ars, and the one at Pont à Mousson were prepared for demolition, but were not blown up. The bridge at Novéant seems to have been forgotten.

No change occurred this day in the positions of the French. The 6th Corps continued the movement of its troops by rail from Chalons. In spite of the line being broken by the German cavalry, the trains that had been dispatched reached Metz, though considerably delayed. It is clear that the various attempts on the line did not have any vital effect. The cause was solely the faulty equipment of the German cavalry in material for railway demolition, and their want of practice in the work.

CHAPTER VII

ROYAL Head Quarters had issued the following order:— {Aug. 13. Royal Head Quarters.}

"August 12, 4.30 p.m.

"As far as reports received show, the main force of the enemy is in retreat over the Mosel through Metz.

"His Majesty directs—

"The First Army will move to-morrow, the 13th, towards the French Nied, the main body on the line Tennschen-Pange, and will secure the railway station of Courcelles. The cavalry will reconnoitre towards Metz, and cross the Mosel below it. The First Army will thus cover the right flank of the Second Army.

"The latter will march on the line Buchy-Chateau Salins, push outposts to the Seille, and endeavour, if possible, to secure the passages over the Mosel, of Pont à Mousson, Dieulouard, Marbache, etc. The cavalry will reconnoitre beyond the Mosel.

"The Third Army will continue their advance towards Lunéville."

The order of His Majesty the King, which led to the famous movement to the left of the Second Army, and the great decisive battles west of Metz, had to be quoted here word for word, to gain a full insight into the task that devolved on the cavalry. {Measures for crossing the Mosel.}

To give effect to these instructions, General v. Steinmetz issued the following order to the 3rd Cavalry Division:—

"The 3rd Cavalry Division will proceed to Avancy, press forward towards Metz and Vigy, and try to push detachments across the Mosel, to see what there is on the far side."

Aug. 13. Simultaneously with the above order from Royal Head Quarters, instructions were issued to Army Head Quarters "for the use of the cavalry" about the "points of crossing the Mosel between Metz and Diedenhofen," together with most exact details of the passages, the state of the banks and the approaches. To show how precise and accurate these details were, it need only be quoted that allusion was made to two rope ferries at Hauconcourt and Ay-Hagedingen. In reference to the last named, it is mentioned that "the banks close in so much that if the water is low, a bridge 40 paces long is sufficient; if it is high, it must be 100 to 120 paces in length." Further, other crossings are described, namely one at Bettingen as a rope ferry, and at Illingen-Uckingen as a flying bridge.

The order of the General Officer Commanding 3rd Cavalry Division for August 13, dated 11.15 p.m., August 12, ran as follows:—

> "The division will start at 5 a.m. The 7th Uhlans, forming the advance guard, will march by Bettingen-Gommelingen, through Avancy, to 2½ miles beyond that place towards Metz. It will cover the division in the direction of the fortress, and detach one squadron towards Vigy to watch the road to Diedenhofen. The outposts will endeavour to join up—on the *left*, by Tennschen, with the outposts of the First Army Corps; on the *right*, towards Vigy, with the detached squadron.
>
> "Patrols are to be sent towards Metz and Diedenhofen, and attempts made to throw detachments over the Mosel, to see what troops there are on the opposite side."

On the afternoon of the same day, the 12th, General v. Steinmetz received from the Head Quarters of the Second Army a memorandum, dated 2 p.m., which informed him of the operations in view for the 13th, and of the duties allotted to

CAVALRY ON SERVICE

the cavalry divisions. [Further details are below.] At the end of the memo it says—

Aug. 13.

> "A similar movement of the cavalry of the First Army, which we assume will be initiated, would, in four or five days, completely isolate Metz."*

The intelligence shows what great importance Royal Head Quarters attached to a movement of the cavalry of the First Army on the left bank of the Mosel; and it is clear, from the events of that day till the 18th, how valuable it would have been if the cavalry of the First and Second Armies had joined hands west of Metz on the French line of retreat.

Prince Frederick Charles had recognized the significance of such a combined movement, as his despatch to the Head Quarters of the First Army shows, but, unhappily, General v. Steinmetz did not, and so the result of the action suggested by those in highest authority was deplorable.

If we examine the quoted orders of the First Army and 3rd Cavalry Division, we notice at once that the matter was not urged forward at all energetically.

The First Army insufficiently complies with the directions from Royal Head Quarters.

While the order from Royal Head Quarters ran thus: "The cavalry will cross the Mosel," the terms of this direct order were weakened in that of the order from the First Army, as it ran: ". . . and will try to push detachments across the Mosel." A sentence which was copied word for word by the division in the order for the advance guard.

The regiment forming the advance guard felt that enough had been done when a reserve officer with a few Uhlans had reached the left bank, and, hugging it closely, had remained there for a short time.

* *Vide* also the order of the prince, p. 258.

Aug. 13.
Comments.

If the Head Quarters of the First Army had recognized the significance of the instructions, the order would have been more precisely worded, and might have been expanded, to point out that the communication between the two fortresses might be permanently broken by the demolition of the railway and telegraph between Metz and Diedenhofen.* The whole division should have been detailed to cross. The railway, too, was of vital importance, as it connected the camp at Chalons with Metz; its destruction was therefore just as necessary as that of the line south of Metz, against which the cavalry of the Second Army were directing their energies. It is remarkable that the former stretch, which was much the safer,† was made very little use of by the French for the conveyance of troops, but, in point of fact, a battery arrived at Metz from Chalons, on the line by Diedenhofen, even on the 14th according to Dick de Lonlay, and communication was open as late as the 18th!

If we allude to the want of precision in the orders issued by Head Quarters of the First Army, we must also note that it should have been obvious to attach a pontoon train to the cavalry division for purposes of crossing. It would have been a question then, not of making a bridge, but only of forming rafts for crossing.

With reference to the general commanding the cavalry division, he ought certainly to have given more detailed instructions for crossing the river. The unit, its strength, and the points where detachments were to be thrown across to the other bank, should have been specially named in the

---

* This seems to have been thought of later, after crossing (see the report, p. 245), but no serious measures were taken.

† Protected as it was by the fortress of Diedenhofen and the river which was not bridged then.

CAVALRY ON SERVICE 243

order, and their duties on arrival on the other side laid down; and information given that south of Metz the cavalry of the Second Army would cross the river, and that attempts must be made to open up communication with them.*

Aug. 13.

The case was too important to admit of every further detail being left to the advance guard,

If the performance of the task were to be seriously taken in hand, immediately on receipt of the order detachments ought to have been sent towards the river in various directions, in order to seize all the materials for crossing which could be found on the right bank. It is certain that such material was available, because a patrol of the 7th Uhlans, under Lieutenant Schultz of the Reserve, was able to cross by the ferry at Hauconcourt. In the absence of a solid bridge, a more convenient means of crossing than a large rope ferry cannot be imagined. A peculiar allusion to this is made in the official "History of the War," on p. 451—

"Another patrol of the 7th Uhlans, which had reached the other bank of the ferry at Hauconcourt, returned without having met the enemy.† The larger reconnaissances ordered by Royal Head Quarters had to be abandoned, because all means of transport across the river had been brought by the enemy into safety."

In the concluding sentence the reason given stands on such shallow footing in comparison with the fact alleged in the previous sentence, that one is evidently meant to see in the description a most transparently obvious criticism of the action of the Head Quarter authorities involved.

* We shall see later that the cavalry of the Second Army was given orders in conformity with that purpose.

† This handful of men scarcely went beyond the village.

Aug. 13. According to information, procured at my request by an officer of the Metz garrison, the ferry then in use at Hauconcourt was built of wood, and 45½ feet long by 13 feet wide.* The crossing only occupied six to ten minutes, according to the state of the weather, so four crossings could be made per hour, including embarking and disembarking.

At my request trials were made by a squadron, which produced the following results : fifteen horses can be taken over together on a ferry of the dimensions quoted above, given the necessary buoyancy. Therefore in two and a half hours, assuming four journeys per hour, a squadron could be taken over. The transport of two vehicles is included in this, as only five horses remain over for the last journey.

With a regular ferry like this one, three horses could swim across by the side, their saddlery being placed in the boat, so that the squadron, without waggons, could have been put across in two hours. As the division started at 5 a.m., and had to cover eighteen miles to the Mosel, if we assume that patrols crossed meanwhile to reconnoitre, and the troops reached the ferry by a roundabout way— although the Royal Head Quarters had designated the points for crossing—two squadrons, at any rate, could have reached the opposite bank the same day. Now, it can be assumed with certainty that at the time when this ferry-boat was discovered, other means of crossing, such as punts, were available. For if the enemy secures all the means of transport, he surely would begin with the ferries before others, and at every ferry there

* It was sunk during the investment of Metz, and carried away by the water. The present boat dates from a later period, is 50 feet long and 14½ feet broad. It may also be noted that the place at Hauconcourt, on account of the favourable state of the banks, is used by the garrison of Metz as a favourite place for practising swimming across.

are always a few boats, alongside which horses could be conveyed across by swimming.

In concluding these remarks, the report may well follow, which Graf Groeben sent to his Army Head Quarters on this point, dated Vry, August 14, 10 a.m. :—

Aug. 13.

Groeben's report regarding the crossing of the Mosel.

> "Yesterday, at Ogy my patrols met hostile infantry. At Vrémy a horse of the 7th Uhlans was wounded. Under-officer v. Schierstaedt and Lieutenant Schultz of the same regiment, with five men, crossed the Mosel in a boat, and reached the exit of Hauconcourt. Nothing was seen there of the French troops. Inhabitants stated that there were no French soldiers beyond Maison Rouge, on the left bank of the Mosel. All ferry-boats are said to have been taken to Metz and Diedenhofen. Lieutenant v. Pfannenberg, who was to cut the railway and telegraph from Metz to Diedenhofen in the night, was no longer able to cross the Mosel. No further attempt in the same direction was made, as Captain v. Groeben, R.E., is to carry out the destruction of the line by direction of Army Head Quarters. The latter has been given eight Uhlans for the purpose of reconnoitring. No change has been discovered in the position of the enemy in front of Metz."

According to the official records, this report was not forwarded to Royal Head Quarters, so they remained in ignorance of the fact that their order to throw detachments of cavalry over the Mosel had not been carried out.

The report does not agree with the official "History of the War," the history of the 7th Hussars, or with their war diary, as in these accounts a ferry is mentioned as the means of crossing used, whereas Graf Groeben speaks of a boat. Since the difference is important in criticizing the measures taken, and since, in the report, Lieutenant Schultz is named as the leader of the patrol, I have procured information, with the help

Aug. 13. of the regiment, which shows that a ferry, and not a boat, was used, and that Lieutenant Schultz, and not the under-officer, reached the other bank. Lieutenant Schultz, now a manufacturer of sparkling hock in Rüdesheim, on being questioned, gave the following account of the incident: "I recollect pretty well the occurrence spoken of. I crossed the Mosel at Hauconcourt with my patrol—I think there were five men—all at one time, of course, in a ferry; in a boat it would have been impossible. I patrolled the immediate neighbourhood without finding any of the enemy, and returned to the other bank in about half an hour. During this time I had the ferryman watched by a Uhlan, pistol in hand, so that he could not escape. Soon afterwards I met under-officer v. Schierstaedt, who intended also to get to the opposite bank, but he did not succeed, as there was no longer any ferryman available to bring him across. I think the same thing happened to Lieutenant v. Pfannenberg either the same evening or the night following."

Lieut. Schultz's report.

It seems clear from this that there was not so much a want of means of crossing as of people to ferry men across.

It is characteristic of the helplessness of the cavalry of that period, that they did not know how to help themselves without the aid of ferrymen. Besides, some energetic pressure on the village authorities would have produced a sufficient number of men knowing how to manœuvre a ferry.

No thorough examination of the bank for means of conveyance seems to have been made, since the term used in the report, "all ferry-boats are said" to have been taken to Metz and Diedenhofen, can only imply that this news came from the information of inhabitants.

It can generally be assumed, if means of crossing

are wanting on the near bank of a river, that they are still to be found on the far one; and that, if even a single patrol succeeds in getting across, it will procure them on the opposite bank.

At this point all attempts to carry out the orders of Royal Head Quarters came to an end. The serious engagement on the 14th had turned attention to another direction, and the matter seems to have been entirely forgotten, though even on the 15th, if only one squadron had succeeded in getting across, it would have rendered most valuable assistance. How accurate and easy the location of the extent of the French right wing on the 18th would have been, if only German cavalry had pressed on westwards of Hauconcourt. The distance from Hauconcourt to Roncourt is only 7½ miles.

A patrol of the 7th Uhlans, under Lieutenant v. Müller, got up to Diedenhofen again on this day. The leader reported from Metzeresch, 3 p.m., that he had found a sentry line four hundred paces in front of the fortress, and had had two volleys fired on him by infantry. The garrison of the fortress had been proved to be on the alert. Any prospect of a surprise had therefore disappeared. Yet the enterprise which had been planned against the fortress was taken in hand the next day. But the attempt to take it by surprise, as we know, completely failed.

From the hills above St. Barbe the 3rd Cavalry Division had reported a large camp of huts on the far side of the Grimont wood (the 4th Corps), which extended to the St. Avold road, and appeared to stretch right over the Strassburg chaussée; also smaller camps at Chieulles, and outposts on the line Failly-Poix-Servigny. Their dispositions produced the impression that it was intended to act on the defensive there.

Aug. 13.

The 8th Uhlans' attempt to charge French cavalry.

The 1st Cavalry Division had received orders to advance on the line Mécleuves-Orny, and so formed the left wing of the First Army. The division marched on the right bank of the French Nied by Maizeroy and Pange on Domangeville. In Pange the 8th Uhlans received orders to incline to the right, and seize the high ground on the left bank of the French Nied, to act as a right flank guard to the cavalry division, which was advancing under cover of an advance guard through the deep valley of the Nied on Domangeville. In accordance with this order, the 8th Uhlans, sending the 1st squadron, Major v. Blankensee's, forward as advance guard, took up the new direction along a field way to the right of the Pange-Coligny high-road.

As soon as Lieutenant v. Rohr with the advance troop got halfway to the high ground, he suddenly perceived, 600 to 700 paces in front of him, two French squadrons deployed in line right across the road. The squadron leader, who had ridden to the front, at once had the "gallop" sounded, deployed into line, and advanced to charge. The enemy, who had remained halted, fired two ineffective volleys, which wounded only one horse, then turned about and fled back to Metz, without stopping or giving any chance of being overtaken. Colonel v. Below had meanwhile deployed his regiment for action, but the attempt to get on terms with the enemy failed. The only trophy which the regiment secured in the pursuit was a pointer, whose brass collar bore an inscription which showed that he belonged to a lieutenant in the 10th Dragoons. Thus the regiment learnt what unit was in front of them, and this fact, which might prove of value to the higher authorities, is, we will hope, mentioned in the report. At Marsilly the advance-guard squadron rejoined the regiment. In the open

CAVALRY ON SERVICE 249

ground the advanced patrols got within a few hundred paces of the section of ground about Colombey, and, being fired on here in a feeble way, reported that large hostile camps (3rd French corps) were on a level with Borny, and that the Colombey section was occupied.

Aug. 13.

Later, when the Uhlans moved into the outpost position, which the dragoons of the Third Corps had hitherto held (*vide* pp. 251 and 252), Lieutenant v. Besser remained in observation on the far side of Ogy, on a small ridge, with his troop behind him under cover, and was able to supplement the reports. Writing under fire, he reported a large camp of 70,000 to 80,000 men, on the southern slopes of St. Julien.

The leader of the advance-guard squadron of the 8th Uhlans had acted with dash and with proper perception, that he would have to provide room to debouch on the edge of the valley for the succeeding regiment, which was still on its way up the fairly steep incline, and was galloping on as it heard the firing.

Comments.

If the French squadrons, who had observed the Uhlans approaching, had only advanced to the edge of the plateau and occupied it with carbines, they could have engaged with success, not only the advanced-guard squadron, but even the whole regiment, and prevented them, badly armed as they were, from gaining the plateau at this place. The fact of the squadrons receiving the enemy at the halt with volleys, which was a common practice with the French,* shows that their training was two hundred years behind the times.

The division, meanwhile, continued its march by Villiers Laquenexy to Mécleuves, and, in

* *E.g.* when the 1st and 6th Uhlans were charging them at Orléans, December 4, 1870.

Aug. 13. accordance with orders, relieved the outposts of the 6th Cavalry Division on both sides of the Metz-Strassburg chaussée.

Reconnaissance by the 4th Uhlans.

The 4th Uhlans had received orders at Courcelles, on the right flank,

> "to advance towards Jury, to clear up the situation of the enemy there and at Mercy."

The regiment trotted through Frontigny to the Delme-Metz road, and halted in a hollow 500 paces from the railway embankment (see sketch, p. 231). Here v. Köppern's squadron was ordered to send a troop on the main road, and half a troop through Jury, to rush the enemy's outposts, and, where possible, to break through them. The main body of the squadron was to follow west of the road. The half-troop, under Lieutenant of Reserve Menger, trotted through the railway arch at Jury, through that place, and, beyond it, was fired on by about 100 infantry, at 270 yards from the wood near Mercy, from which, according to the Regimental History, "it was concluded that the wood was strongly held."

The half troop had no casualties, and returned to Jury. The 2nd troop, Ensign v. Kleist, advanced on the main road to within 100 paces of the railway arch, was then fired on from the embankment by dismounted Jägers, as well as by infantry, and returned to the squadron. The casualties were one man and two horses wounded, and one man killed. The squadron retired slowly without loss, in spite of the enemy's fire at 500 paces, as their shots all went too high. Six of the enemy's squadrons followed to the railway east of Jury. The enemy's camp was excellently shielded by the rising ground west of Mercy, and very difficult to overlook. The alarm, however, which was sounded in the enemy's camp on drum and bugle in consequence of the slight disturbance, gave authority for the deduction that an army corps or more was to be dealt with there.* The regiment retired to form the outposts at Chesny.

Aug. 13.

The reconnaissance was carried out with enterprise, and achieved the best results. Often, where, as here, no insight into the enemy's disposition can be gained in consequence of the absence of view, the only course will be to strike the enemy with small independent parties, and compel him to open fire and disclose his strength, although the losses may probably be greater than they were in this case, as we shall scarcely have to deal with an enemy who shoots as extraordinarily badly as the French did then.

Comments.

That the French allowed a few squadrons to manœuvre in front of them undisturbed is a proof of their extreme weakheartedness at that time. It is also a bad sign of a nervous disposition, when, as here, a whole army corps is aroused because a few troops of cavalry come in contact with the outposts.

The Head Quarters of the Third Army Corps had issued the following order :—

Formation of a corps cavalry.

"August 12, 4.45 p.m.

"The two infantry divisions will retain only one squadron for minor duties, and will place the other three of each regiment under the orders of Colonel v. Drygalski,† who will concentrate these six squadrons in the position at Argenchen and Chanville, hitherto occupied by the Hussar Brigade of the 6th Cavalry Division, and relieve that brigade. Duke William will march to-day towards the left, his front towards the Metz-Nomény-Nancy road, general direction Jouy aux Arches.

* As a rule, the French, in their camps, made an undue use of signals, which it would have been far better to restrict as much as possible.

† Commanding the 2nd Dragoons.

Aug. 13. He will, however, wait till relieved by Colonel v. Drygalski. Scouting parties should very soon reach Chateau St. Blaise, which affords a commanding view; from there the roads leading to Metz must be watched.* During the 13th the Mosel must be reached and crossed. It is desirable that the advanced parties should reach the Seille to-day."

Here we have the interesting example of the formation of a corps cavalry brigade. If infantry divisions are, as here, in close touch, and their strategical and tactical reconnaissances are found direct by the corps, there can be no doubt that one squadron will be quite sufficient for "minor duties," *e.g.* despatch riders, orderlies, and patrols communicating with the cavalry in front. The combination of the two regiments of divisional cavalry has this advantage, that the service of reconnaissance can be directed in unison. Now this combined brigade performed the duty of observation and protection in front of the corps which had hitherto been assigned to the 6th Cavalry Division. As every one knows, there exists in the French army the arrangement of Corps Cavalry Brigades, which has this undoubted advantage, that the cavalry divisions are thereby relieved from any consideration of the particular needs of the corps that follows them as regards observation and protection, and are able to devote themselves wholly and independently to their strategic duty.

Since the order had been given to wait for Colonel v. Drygalski, their march to the left could not commence on the 12th, as they were only relieved at 1 a.m. on the 13th. The cause of the delay was, that the bearers of the order had spent

* Army Head Quarters had laid stress on the importance of this place, which, during the investment of Metz, became most valuable as a post of observation.

far more time than had been estimated in their night ride along the very miry roads. This shows that the possibility of such delays by weather must be considered in the issue of orders.

Aug. 13.

The Colonel forwarded at 8.30 a.m. from Berlize the intelligence gained by two patrols.

Lieutenant v. Lützow had struck hostile outposts at Coincy, and had discovered a camp consisting of several army corps east and south of Metz.

Lieutenant v. Watzdorf had encountered only weak detachments of infantry and cavalry beyond Ogy.

The 6th Cavalry Division had received orders at 8.30 p.m. on the 12th from the Head Quarters of the Second Army Corps to march to the left front towards the Metz-Nomény-Nancy road with a general direction towards Jouy aux Arches, in order to gain news of the enemy from there; to push advanced parties with Grüter's Brigade up to the Seille on the 12th; while Rauch's Brigade was to make a further advance on the 13th. In consequence of the lateness of the hour, orders were given for Grüter's Brigade to concentrate at 4.30 on the morning of the 13th south-west of Anserweiler, and Rauch's Brigade at 5 a.m. at Sorbey.

Orders to the 6th Cavalry Division.

However, at 3.30 a.m. on the 13th the following Corps order arrived, dated Falkenberg, 12.10 a.m.:—

"The 6th Cavalry Division will send the Hussar Brigade on the line Sorbey-Orny-Pournoy la Chétive-Corny, one Hussar regiment between the Seille and the Nied, the other between the Seille and the Mosel. The left wing will gain touch with the 5th Cavalry Division, which has already crossed the Mosel, and the right with the First Army. The heavy brigade will canton in rear—at Verny, Goin, and Pagny—act as support to the light brigade, and send patrols across the Seille towards

Aug. 13.

the Mosel. The two Dragoon regiments, the 2nd and 12th, will rejoin their divisions."

This order arranged again in detail for the employment of the 6th Cavalry Division; so little remained for its leader to arrange.

These frequent orders from the Corps Head Quarters show how little reliance was placed on the initiative of the 6th Cavalry Division. The Corps Cavalry Brigade, just formed, was again broken up, as the regiments of the 1st Cavalry Division were brought up into their position (see p. 249).

By a Corps order from Bechy, Liéhon was appointed as an alarm station for the 6th Cavalry Division, "in view of an offensive movement anticipated from Metz." Corps Head Quarters were evidently convinced that the flank march of the army would be disturbed by a hostile attack.

Duke William's measures.

Duke William issued the following order :—

"Chanville, August 12, 10 p.m.

"In accordance with Corps orders, the division will cross the Seille and Mosel above Metz, to reconnoitre the enemy.

"Grüter's Brigade, with the horse battery, will be at Anserweiler at 4.30 a.m., Rauch at Sorbey at 5 a.m. Both brigades will proceed to Verny, whence Grüter will at once reconnoitre the Seille, and send patrols across the river. Rauch will send a right-flank detachment by Orny and Fleury. I expect to see both brigades concentrated at Verny soon after 7 o'clock."

In accordance with corps orders of 12.10 a.m., the Duke altered the above order at 3.45 a.m. General Rauch was instructed not to proceed to Verny, but to take up a position facing Metz, and occupy the line Sorbey-Orny-Fleury with the

3rd Hussars, their main body at Orny, and the line Fleury-Fey-Corny with the 16th Hussars.* Aug. 13.

Verny was properly chosen as the point of concentration for the division, as its chief duty, besides the reconnaissance of Metz and the roads leading thither from the west and down the Mosel valley, lay in the protection and screening of the left-flank march of the Second Army. It is noticeable that no patrol was specially directed to Chateau St. Blaise, in spite of Corps orders to that effect. It can, however, be assumed for certain, by the position of the outposts which were pushed within a few miles of the place, that it was reached by patrols in the course of the day. In the afternoon the Duke at Chérisey ordered Pournoy la Chétive to be occupied by two troops of Cuirassiers. The place is on the Pont à Mousson-Metz road, and covers the passage of the Seille.

The 16th Hussars were sent by General v. Rauch through Orny to Fleury as a right flank detachment. The regiment was then to place outposts towards Metz between the Seille and the Mosel on the line Fleury-Corny, keeping touch on the right with the 3rd Hussars, whose outposts were on the line Courcelles-Pouilly; and on the left they were to open up communication with the 5th Cavalry Division across the Mosel, while the 3rd Hussars did the same with the 1st Cavalry Division. The 16th Hussars marched through Mécleuves, whence hostile camps were discovered near Jury and Peltre, and proceeded through the Hospital Wood to Fleury. Here Buggenhagen's squadron encountered a foraging party of French dragoons, which they drove back and pursued through Pouilly to Magny, where they were 16th Hussars.

* According to the faulty wording of this order, both were to occupy Fleury.

Aug. 13. checked by French infantry, who opened fire. The Hussars had only two horses wounded, while they killed two dragoons and captured two horses and several waggons filled with hay. In consequence of this occurrence, Colonel v. Schmidt had called out his regiment and marched forward. The 3rd Squadron scouted beyond the outposts by Novéant to Gorze and Thiaucourt, but was unable to gain touch with the 5th Cavalry Division; which is not to be wondered at, as only patrols from the Division reached those places. The account in the staff diary of the 14th Cavalry Brigade states, however, that the 6th Cuirassiers succeeded in gaining touch with the 5th Cavalry Division, but does not state where it was effected. The 3rd Squadron, which had become engaged in Corny, left there in the afternoon, and the 4th left Fey. It was a hostile reconnoitring party, which retired at once when the rest of the regiment and a squadron of Cuirassiers came up in support.

The outposts resumed their old positions. The reconnaissances of the division discovered forces of the enemy estimated at two or three corps beyond Peltre, Jury, and Laquenexy, and observed three camps on the Mosel.

Corps Cavalry.

The commander of the Corps Cavalry Brigade had reported from Berlize, 1.15 p.m., that he had taken over the outpost line; also that Lieutenant v. Lützow, 12th Dragoons, had discovered French outposts at Coigny, and estimated the enemy south and east of Metz at several corps. Lieutenant v. Watzdorf, 2nd Dragoons, had seen weak parties of infantry and cavalry beyond Ogy.*

The Third Army Corps does not

It is surprising to find the following sentence in Army Orders, dated Delme, August 14, 6 a.m.:

* A troop under Lieutenant Graf Bruges had skirmished near Pange with hostile horsemen, who retired.

CAVALRY ON SERVICE 257

"From the cavalry brigades of the 6th Cavalry Division, which have been pushed towards Metz, no information whatever has been received either yesterday or to-day. Intelligence must be forwarded to-day as early and often as possible."

Aug. 13. send on important reports.

And yet the following report of the 6th Cavalry Division occurs in the records of the Head Quarters Third Army Corps:—

"Chérisey, 7 p.m.

"Colonel v. Schmidt, 16th Hussars, reports, 'Communication established with 5th Cavalry Division at Coin.* Enemy's trenches at Chateau de la Grange (on the Metz-Cheminet road). Yesterday two French Cuirassier regiments advanced from Metz towards Pont à Mousson, to gain touch, it is said, with McMahon's Corps, but were unsuccessful. Numerous infantry patrols of the enemy in the vineyards of Corny and Augny. Jouy is not permanently occupied by infantry. Enemy's cavalry posts between Augny and Marly. According to trustworthy information, infantry are at work on the railway at Montigny. Patrols to the left bank of the Mosel have seen nothing of the enemy. Information just arrived that a picket at Corny is attacked by the enemy."

The above minute report was not forwarded on by the Third Army Corps.

The Commander of the Second Army had forthwith correctly appreciated the situation, now changed by the sudden evacuation of the position on the Nied; and in particular perceived that a further insight into the intentions of the enemy was possible only if a view was obtained of the roads leading westwards towards Metz, and that this again was possible only if large bodies of cavalry were pushed forward on to the high ground between the Maas and the Mosel. With this object in view, the

Measures of the Second Army to push the cavalry to the country between Mosel and Maas.

---

* Apparently patrols of both divisions had met there.

S

Aug. 13. following order was issued to the Head Quarters Tenth Army Corps :—

"August 12, 3 p.m.

"As the enemy has evacuated the position behind the Nied, your Excellency will order Lieutenant-General v. Rheinbaben, with his two cavalry brigades, which I shall direct Bredow's Cavalry Brigade to join as soon as possible, to move to the Mosel in the direction of Pont à Mousson and Dieulouard this same day.

"General v. Rheinbaben is to cross the Mosel, gain the high ground between the Mosel and the Maas, and advance northwards towards the Metz-Verdun road, in order to find out for certain whether the enemy is retiring from Metz on this road. If, as is supposed, a similar advance across the Mosel below Metz takes place on the part of the cavalry divisions of the First Army, the enemy's army in Metz will be cut off from all communication with France within three or four days.*

"Your Excellency will please impress on Lieutenant-General v. Rheinbaben the extreme importance of this object. Early to-morrow an infantry division, preceded by an advanced guard sent quickly forward, will start towards Pont à Mousson, to occupy this important point, and uphold communication with General v. Rheinbaben."

These were indeed important and brilliant tasks which the highly gifted commander of the army appointed for his cavalry.

It may be remarked, in reading the orders, that it would have been better to speak, not of the Metz-Verdun road, but of the roads leading westwards from Metz, since there were three; *i.e.* by Mars la Tour; by Conflans (the latter separating from the former at Gravelotte) and by Briey-Fléville, the northern one. There was a danger in the above wording, that by the "Metz-Verdun road" only the nearest and most southernly would be understood.

* Compare what is stated on p. 241.

As already seen, the movements had been Aug. 13.
initiated as early as the 12th by the commander of
the Tenth Army Corps, and the 19th Division,
detailed as the infantry advance guard, had already
started on its march to Delme that same day, and
reached Pont à Mousson late on the afternoon of
the 13th.*

The 5th Cavalry Division continued its march Orders to
to the left. General v. Redern received the General Redern.
following order:—

"Solgne, August 12, 7.15 p.m.

"In accordance with the Army Order just received,
I request you to concentrate the brigade at daybreak at
Pont à Mousson, and to send a regiment at once from
there to Thiaucourt, which will push patrols in various
directions as far as the Metz-Verdun road, and to wait
with the rest of the brigade at Pont à Mousson till I
myself arrive with Barby's Brigade. I shall move the
Brunswick Hussars, with the battery, early to-morrow
to Pont à Mousson.

"The enemy is said to have left the line of the
Mosel, and it has become of great importance to cause
him loss on the Metz-Verdun road, but it must be
ascertained first whether he is really retreating from
Metz to Verdun. Barby's Brigade will watch the Metz-
Pont à Mousson-Pagny road with a detachment."

The 10th Hussars had by 4 a.m. again sent a
troop under Lieutenant v. Trotha from the outposts
at Eply to Pont à Mousson. A report of Captain v.
Kotze to the division stated that the ruins of
Mousson and also Atton had been found unoccupied. Leaving the troop behind in the ruins,
Lieutenant v. Trotha and Captain v. Ploetz,† who
accompanied him, rode forward to reconnoitre Pont
à Mousson, and found the vineyards occupied by

* This infantry division had covered 47 miles in 41½ hours. See map of August 11.

† Of the 2nd Guard Dragoons, adjutant at Head Quarters of Tenth Army Corps.

Aug. 13. hostile infantry. From here word was sent to Redern's brigade that was marching up, and the orders received from it were, to discover in what strength the town was held.*

On this the troop advanced within rifle range of the town. Lieutenant v. Trotha, with a N.C.O. and a trumpeter, rode through the place to the bridge, found none of the enemy, and heard from the inhabitants that a battalion of infantry was on the point of starting by rail to Metz. Lieutenant v. Trotha rode at once over the bridge to the station, and found it deserted. Many articles of equipment lying about testified to the hasty departure. The rails in the direction of Nancy, up the line, had been torn up, and the important parts of the points removed. Trotha reported at 9.45 a.m. from the town—

> "Have ridden with one N.C.O. through the town. Enemy no longer holds this bank, and has retreated across the bridge. Just sent the troop into the town to hold the exits. I will barricade the bridge."

Lieutenant v. Trotha had acted shrewdly and to the point. Captain v. Ploetz reported to the Tenth Army Corps at 11 a.m. that Pont à Mousson had been evacuated at 9.30 by a battalion and a squadron of the enemy,† and that Redern's Brigade was just coming in. Redern reported his occupation of the town at 11.30 a.m.

The brigade had met with some resistance, as its advance guard had been fairly hotly fired upon from the vineyards, most probably by stragglers.‡

* Such an order should have been really superfluous.
† Probably a mistake as regards the squadron.
‡ Compare the measures of the French, given later on. The shots may have been fired by some men escorting the hospital train.

CAVALRY ON SERVICE

The 3rd Squadron, 10th Hussars, cleared the outskirts with their carbines, and after half an hour's delay the regiment entered the town. The 2nd Squadron occupied the station and completed the demolition of the telegraph and railway in both directions.* The 1st Squadron provided protection towards Metz and Nancy, the 3rd Squadron did the same to the west. The vedettes were frequently fired at by Franctireurs.

The 11th Hussars had been left on the right bank, and held the bridge in the town. In the evening two squadrons occupied the cavalry barracks there, and two others provided the outposts at Pagny in the direction of Metz, from which patrols were pushed on to Gorze without seeing anything of the enemy. The 10th Hussars started at 8 p.m. towards Thiaucourt, and on the way had their advance guard fired on by mounted Jägers.

General v. Rheinbaben entered Pont à Mousson with Barby's Brigade at 1.15 p.m.† In his report he emphasized the need for the occupation of the town by infantry.

To Redern's report on the distribution of his troops, General v. Rheinbaben added the information that he had instructed him to send detachments to Thiaucourt, Pagny, and Dieulouard immediately on the arrival of the infantry that were expected. The 1st Squadron of the 10th Hussars, detached to Nancy, had had the contribution levied on the town and other requisitions conveyed by two troops to Château Salins.

Aug. 13.

---

* As it was still doubtful at this moment whether the place could be occupied permanently, this demolition seems justified; but it would have been better to ask for permission.

† It would have been more advisable if the divisional commander had arrived in front of this important place with his leading brigade, in order to make *personal* inquiries and to make the first arrangements *in person*.

Aug. 13. Despatch riders, which had been sent during the night to the 5th Cavalry Division, had been unable to find the divisional staff, so the squadron leader despatched an officer direct to the Head Quarters of the Tenth Army Corps. This shows how necessary it is for all Head Quarters authorities to appoint a collecting station for reports and make it known to all detached parties.

Light Guard Cavalry Brigade before Dieulouard.

The Light Cavalry Brigade of the Guards, attached by army orders to the 5th Cavalry Division, had been sent to Dieulouard. The brigade had started from Oron at 6 a.m. The 3rd Squadron of the 1st Guard Dragoons rejoined them in Nomény (see p. 237). The advanced squadron (4th) of the 1st Guard Dragoons found the Mosel bridge at Dieulouard partly blown up; but the repair of it was an easy matter, and the bridge was crossed by the brigade in single file.

While the 4th Squadron was occupied in thoroughly demolishing the railway, patrols reported that two trains were coming from Frouard. As the demolition was complete, the trains had to stop. A brief engagement followed, in which one dragoon of the picket was wounded. The French, convinced by the carbine fire of the dragoons that the passage was already held by strong bodies of infantry, made no attempt to drive them off, and steamed back. The battery (Captain v. der Planitz) attached to the brigade was able to send a few shells after them. Here at last the transport by rail of the 6th French Corps was finally checked, and a thorough destruction of the railway was effected. Towards evening Dieulouard was occupied by a battalion of the Alexander Regiment, which had been hastily brought up, and by a battalion of the 16th Regiment.

Orders reached the Fourth Army Corps on the

12th that Bredow's Brigade was to join the 5th Cavalry Division on the 14th at Pont à Mousson or Dieulouard. By orders from the corps the brigade was to reach Jallaucourt on the 13th and start at 5.30 a.m. This was a march of nineteen miles, which seems to have been very arduous owing to bad weather and bad roads. The corps followed it. Complaints are made in the diary of the corps that Bredow's Brigade, entrusted with the reconnoitring of the roads, had told off orderlies instead of officers as guides to the troops, and they were not acquainted with their duties.

Aug. 13.

Bredow's Brigade, during their attachment to the Fourth Army Corps, had not been in a position to render any real service; this is the evil consequence of distributing army cavalry to the corps. We have already seen that the Fourth Army Corps did not know what to do with its numerous cavalry. These splendid squadrons were thus practically useless.

May every leader, who has cavalry allotted to him, ever bear in mind that this arm is too expensive to do nothing.*

It is only in this sense that that unhappy expression, "the expensive arm," should be used.

Of the measures of the enemy, there is little worth mentioning; the troops had another "rest day," and no changes took place in their position. The troops were much exhausted by their previous marches in execrable weather, the feeding of them was difficult, and the obtaining of it caused an immense waste of power. The men were disturbed by constant contact with the German patrols and the consequent alarms. Rousset says, "The perpetual sniping, which was heard in all directions, without the reason being known, kept rousing the

Measures of the French.

---

* The saying of General C. v. Schmidt.

Aug. 13. men and disturbing their rest." This is indeed a great testimony to the enterprise of the German cavalry patrols.

The movement by rail of the 6th Corps was continued. Trains arrived at one, two, and four o'clock in the morning. The last named, with the 9th Regiment on board, was the one which had been harassed by Lieutenant v. Trotha's troop of the 10th Hussars, and the occupants of which had opened fire from the vineyards. One more train followed it conveying transport and ambulances, the last to enter Metz. The whole of the 2nd Division, the above-mentioned 9th Regiment excepted, had to remain behind at Chalons. It is inexplicable why the troops were not conveyed by Diedenhofen, where the communication, according to French accounts, remained open till the 18th. The French cavalry carried out various reconnaissances this day, which led to small skirmishes, like that at Pange, between the 2nd Dragoons and a combined squadron of mounted Jägers, but had no special results. The following incident shows what little enterprise the enemy's cavalry possessed. German cavalry were reported in Jouy aux Arches. At 2 p.m. the 3rd and 4th Squadrons of the 9th Dragoons advanced towards the place, and half an hour later the 1st and 2nd followed. The inhabitants said there were 400 to 500 horses in the main road.* " Prince Murat, the leader, not knowing whether he had infantry or cavalry in front of him, and as night was coming on (!) retired to Montigny, which the regiment re-entered at 5 p.m. (!) "

We shall see again, later on, that this general did little credit to the name of his illustrious ancestor.

* At this time only a patrol of the 16th Hussars could have been in Jouy aux Arches, according to the situation already described.

CHAPTER VIII

His Majesty the King issued the following order:— Aug. 14.

"Herny, August 13, 9 p.m.

"According to intelligence received, large bodies of the enemy are halted this morning on this side of Metz, near Servigny and Borny. His Majesty directs that the First Army shall remain to-morrow, the 14th, in their position on the French Nied, and, by means of advanced troops, *watch* whether the enemy retires or advances to the attack. In view of the latter event, the Second Army will send the 3rd Corps *for the present* only as far as Pagny, and the 9th Corps on Buchy, where they will remain ready, at a distance of five miles, by a well-timed move, to engage in a decisive action in front of Metz. On the other hand, the First Army is in a position to check any advance of the enemy to the south by a flank *attack*.

Order from Royal Head Quarters.

"The remaining corps of the Second Army will continue their advance to the stretch of the Mosel between Marbache and Pont à Mousson. The 10th Corps will occupy a position in advance of Pont à Mousson.

"The cavalry of *both* armies will be pushed forward *as far as possible*, and must harass any possible retreat of the enemy on the road from Metz to Verdun." *

In accordance with these instructions General v. Steinmetz, on the 14th at 2.30 a.m., briefly ordered the separate units of the First Army to remain in their present positions. The 1st Cavalry

The cavalry of the First Army.

---

* The words given in italics here are underlined in the original order of His Majesty. Prince Frederick Charles, the day before, in his order to the Tenth Army Corps, had given expression to the idea which is contained in this last sentence (see p. 258).

Aug. 14. Division received information of the instructions given by Royal Head Quarters to the Second Army, together with orders to direct their attentions in particular on Metz. No fresh orders were issued to the 3rd Cavalry Division as to crossing the Mosel, which alone could have satisfied the requirements given in the concluding sentence of the Royal order. There is little to be told of the action of the cavalry divisions of the First Army on this date, on which the battle of Colombey was fought.

When the battle began, the 3rd Cavalry Division was alarmed at 5 p.m., and going by St. Barbe took up a position of readiness behind the right wing of the fighting line at Retonfay. The battery alone of the division took part in the battle. Patrols from the division, according to the official "History of the War," reported at 4 p.m. that Chieulles and the camp near the wood of Grimont had been evacuated. The 1st Cavalry Division, specially charged with watching the enemy near Metz, had discovered, at 12.30 p.m., the retrograde movement of the enemy. General v. Hartmann, about this time, reported from the hills north of Mécleuves that the enemy still occupied Peltre and the wood south of Mercy le Haut, but that they had withdrawn already large forces from the camps under observation, between Mercy and Metz; and he soon afterwards stated that the retirement of troops of all arms from Mercy had been plainly going on since 1.45 p.m.

The 4th Uhlans.
The 4th Uhlans, which had posted outposts towards Chesny to cover the division already in bivouac at Pontoy, advanced at 6 a.m. by Frontigny to the railway to clear up the situation. (See map on p. 231.)

To admit of the regiment crossing the railway,

CAVALRY ON SERVICE 267

which was covered by fire from a railway cabin, at the request of the regimental commander, Colonel v. Radecke, to Captain Baron v. dem Busche of the 15th Infantry Regiment, a patrol of eighteen men was sent from their picket in front of Frontigny to advance along the railway and cover the cabin with their fire. One troop of Uhlans meantime moved through Jury, and another up to the railway cabin. The French deployed their infantry, as on the previous day, at the wood of Mercy le Haut, and opened a hot fire, whilst the cavalry of the outposts, perhaps a squadron and a half, retired out of range down the high-road. The camp was alarmed, but only one cavalry regiment moved out.

Aug. 14.

"This fact, as well as the whole conduct of the enemy in the camp—there was far less movement in it than on the previous day—gave evidence," says the regimental history, " of the retirement of large bodies of troops. As no larger development on the part of the enemy took place, the regiment returned at 1 p.m. to its outpost line." There is no report from the regiment to be found in the records. It is, to say the least, doubtful whether the conclusion, which the regimental history gives, was, or could be, arrived at from the observations made, since, as already stated, no view of the plateau behind Mercy could be obtained either from Jury or the railway embankment, and it is not clear that any reconnaissance to the flank was made. It is interesting to note in this reconnaissance the support which the infantry afforded to the advance of the Uhlans, by bringing fire to bear on the railway cabin which checked their progress. The adoption of a similar line of action, by undertaking the *rôle* of infantry with men armed with carbines, is strongly to be recommended, in order to assist patrols to reach an important place. Sometimes it may only be

Aug. 14.

Stumm's patrol.

necessary to divert the enemy's fire for a few minutes.

The first and most valuable information was sent in this day by the divisional cavalry, namely, by Lieutenant Stumm, 8th Hussars whose exceptional services on the 6th and 7th we are already acquainted with. This officer, according to the official "History of the War," sent in at 10.45 a.m. the first information of the retirement of the French. It will be of special interest to follow his movements this day, somewhat in detail.

At 6 a.m. General v. der Goltz, commanding the advance guard of the Seventh Corps, rode forward with the 3rd Squadron of the 8th Hussars towards Colligny to reconnoitre the enemy's position. Lieutenant Stumm was sent forward with a troop on the line Ogy-Laquenexy, to establish the communication that was wanting between the line of infantry outposts and the posts of the First Corps north of Colligny, in the neighbourhood of Puche. General v. der Goltz gave him personal instructions. He was to advance and reconnoitre as quickly as possible towards the fortress of Metz, in order to ascertain, above all, whether the enemy's main forces still lay on this side of the Mosel, or whether they had already moved or were moving to the left bank. The troop galloped towards Marsilly, and halted close behind the village. In posting his vedettes Lieutenant Stumm was fired on several times by infantry. Some peasants who were seized gave information about large bodies being on the move in front of Metz, at Grimont, Vallières, Nouilly, Borny, Colombey, etc.; that French troops were everywhere about on this side of the Mosel, that the camps were alarmed, and that the movement of troops to Metz had commenced early in the morning.

Lieutenant Stumm rode alone far beyond Coincy, and with his telescope convinced himself of the truth of these statements. He had meantime established communication with the outposts of the First Army Corps. When riding back to Marsilly he discovered some cavalry vedettes between Ars Laquenexy and Chateau Aubigny. A large detachment appeared to lie hidden behind a small copse. In order to make sure what force stood opposite him, he collected his troop and rode fast out of Marsilly straight towards the enemy's cavalry. The troop had barely shown itself on the hill west of Marsilly when a long line of horsemen in open order pressed forward to meet him, followed by a detachment of at least two squadrons in close order.

Lieutenant Stumm made his troop incline a little to the north. This movement was scarcely completed when he was compelled by a rapid infantry fire to retire hastily behind Marsilly. A hostile squadron followed him to Marsilly, but speedily turned about when met by a few well-directed shots from the infantry posts.

The troop suffered no actual loss from the enemy's infantry fire. Lieutenant Stumm got a bullet between his knee and the saddle-flap; one of the horses had a graze on the crupper, and another bullet twisted up the beard of Sergeant Paul, which hung down covering his chest. A second advance due west was out of the question, so there remained only the possibility of slipping round by Coincy. Lieutenant Stumm, accompanied by his sergeant and two orderlies, rode to Coincy and examined the country in front through his glasses, unnoticed.

The report below gives the result of this reconnaissance; the writing of it was begun in the saddle south of Coincy, in the presence of the enemy, and

Aug. 14. could only be finished on arrival at the picket, after the advance of a hostile squadron had again compelled a hasty retreat.

Report of Lieutenant Stumm's troop of the 1st Westphalian Hussar Regiment, No. 8—

"After the attack of the two squadrons of Cuirassiers, all is quiet again. I have taken up a position behind the village of Marsilly. The vedettes occupy their old places. I am in permanent communication with the dragoons of the First Army Corps. The enemy's picket is still at Puche. There is no longer any infantry in front of us. Ars Laquenexy also is clear of infantry, but now occupied by Cuirassiers. One squadron of Cuirassiers has withdrawn further north, towards Colombey. Patrols from this squadron are constantly disturbing us. I have reconnoitred towards Metz, and got a view of the whole position. It is as given below—

"*Position near Metz.*

"Fort St. Quentin, beyond Metz, on the opposite side of the Mosel, is strongly defended, and enormous entrenchments have been freshly built there.

"Fort Grimont (St. Julien), to the north, is also strongly defended. The fort lies between Mey and Nouilly; the road from St. Barbe and Servigny leads past it into Metz. At the foot of Fort Grimont lies a main camp of the enemy. The enemy remains still in camp, but some troops seem to have already left it, and to have retired to the fort and into the fortress. The camps close to Flanville, Montoy, and Noisseville are mostly deserted, and only occupied by cavalry detachments.

"The cemetery of Flanville, on the main road to Metz, is occupied by a small infantry detachment. A larger detachment has thrown up a small entrenchment somewhat nearer Metz, about Montoy, on the main chaussée, and has occupied it. Further on lies the main camp.

"At Vallières there are said to be large bodies of troops; they are probably those which retired this morning from in front of our outposts.

CAVALRY ON SERVICE 271

"In advance of Fort Grimont, on the heights of Mey and Nouilly, freshly made entrenchments can be seen.

Aug. 14.

"Colombey and the camp there, that was still occupied this morning, have been evacuated by the infantry.

"A slow retirement of the whole line (Ars Laquenexy, Vantoux, Lauvallier, Coincy, Noisseville) seems to be the only conclusion. The enemy alone still visible there is the Cuirassier Regiment. A detachment of infantry could easily compel the cavalry to retire from here. Flanville itself is unoccupied.

"I shall watch the further retreat of the troops from Fort Grimont, and will at once report.

"Written at Marsilly, in front of Coincy, August 14, 10.45 a.m.

"STUMM, Lieutenant." *

Once more Lieutenant Stumm rode through Coincy and gained a well-advanced point of rising ground, commanding a wide view, right in front of the alarmed enemy.

Though the enemy's infantry kept creeping closer and closer, though a squadron of Chasseurs rode up and threatened the rear of the isolated patrol, with the obvious intention of cutting it off, yet Lieutenant Stumm, with his trumpeter and four men, jumped down from their saddles, took cover behind some old walls covered with bushes near the road, and opened fire on the enemy. The latter may have thought they had infantry also opposed to them, and checked for a minute, previous to a further advance.

But these few moments were enough to

---

* The transmission of this first and most valuable information is clear from the following remarks, which are written in pencil on the original:—

"read 14. viii. 70. /11.30 a.m. . . . v. der Goltz (adv. guard).
ditto 14. viii. 70. /12.55 . . . v. Glümer (13th Divn.).
arrived Eighth Army Corps. 14. viii. . . . 2 p.m.
arrived First Army in copy . . . 2 p.m.
(Telegraphed with the later despatch to the king, 3.30 p.m.)"

Aug. 14. convince Lieutenant Stumm that the long dark lines of men were moving slowly westwards between the easily recognizable poplar trees. The nearest French skirmishers were barely 200 paces distant, and the French squadron was just beginning to gallop, when the hussars seized their horses, bent low in the saddle, dashed back at full tilt behind Marsilly. The enemy did not follow.

Lieutenant Stumm made out the important report in no time, and sent it at the gallop to the main body of the advance guard. It ran as follows :—

"Report from Lieutenant Stumm.

"All the French forces of Fort Grimont have left the camp, and are retiring in long columns on the roads 'St. Barbe,' 'Nouilly,' and 'Mey' to Metz. Country people who were stopped state that the whole army is about to retreat to Nancy.

"The Cuirassiers, who were in front of me, have gone back, to be relieved by dragoons (Chasseurs).

"Coincy, August 14, 3 p.m.
"Signed: STUMM.
"2nd Lieutenant, 8th Hussars."

The report went on by telegraph at 3.30 to His Majesty the King.

On this report, and on those of the other patrols collectively, which all coincided, General v. der Goltz immediately made his dispositions for attack.

Any discussion on Lieutenant Stumm's procedure seems superfluous. The reader will gain sufficient instruction from the account given. But the example presented here also shows what a profound and significant influence a report can have on the most important resolutions of the commander of an army, and what honours lie at the feet of the young cavalry officer who succeeds in transmitting in good time invaluable information to the Commander-in-Chief.

Aug. 14.

It is to be hoped that in future campaigns a more adequate visible reward than has hitherto generally been the case will be granted for such services, which equal in importance great and certainly more conspicuous feats, such as the capture of a battery.

The 1st Dragoons, who were on outpost duty on the right of the 8th Hussars, were also in continuous close touch with the enemy. The enemy's dragoons, with their long-range carbines, kept our vedettes and patrols constantly under fire.

1st Dragoons.

From them, too, reports of the retreat of the enemy came in, the accuracy of which it was, however, difficult to confirm on account of the action of the enemy's outposts. Captain v. Duncker, with a detachment, then drove a troop of the enemy's dragoons back near Montoy, in order to gain a clearer view, and was thus able to assure General v. Manteuffel, who had ridden into the outpost lines, of the truth of the reports received of the enemy's retirement. On this, at 2 p.m., the general issued orders to his corps.

The Third Army Corps occupied the position, Louvigny-Pagny-Vigny, to cover the parts of the Second Army which were crossing the Mosel.

The 6th Cavalry Division had remained in their position in front of the Third Army Corps, their task had not been changed.

Their commander issued the following order from Chérisey, 5.15 a.m. :—

"The division will remain in its position at the head of the Third Army Corps, to cover the march of the rest of the corps across the Mosel.

"Between 7 and 8 a.m. the hussars will be relieved on outpost by the Uhlans. The most vigilant

T

Aug. 14.

observation and especially active patrol service is demanded to-day."

Some satisfactory reconnaissances were this day made by the division.

Colonel Graf Groeben's reconnaissance.

Graf Groeben, colonel of the 3rd Uhlans, made a personal reconnaissance with a patrol * to the commanding situation of Château St. Blaise. He reported from there at 1 p.m. :—

"1. Entrenchments on Mount St. Quentin—on the eastern slope towards Metz, and the western towards Lessy.

"2. Camp of about one brigade at the railway bridge, on the right bank of the Mosel.

"3. Another, strength unknown, behind Montigny.

"4. A new earthwork midway between Augny and Montigny, and near it small camps.

"5. A considerable camp east of the road (where ?).

"6. Other camps not recognizable.

"7. No troops on the roads from Metz to Corny, Augny, or Verny.

"8. No camp and no troops on the opposite side of the Mosel.

"9. It seems as if the main forces are no longer at Metz.

"A reconnaissance to St. Julien, near Metz, would be advisable."

Graf Groeben had already stated, in a report from the outpost line at Pournoy at 10.15 a.m., that he had pointed out in several reports, no longer to hand, to the 6th Cavalry Division that the retreat of the enemy from Metz on Paris, or on Pont à Mousson, was more than probable.

The colonel had come to this conclusion from the fact that the troops visible at Metz seemed

---

* This patrol of ten Uhlans was led by Lieutenant v. Lange, now Lieut.-General v. Lange (retired).

few in proportion to the three army corps at least which were known to be collected there.

In the above report it is to be noticed that, from the colonel's point of observation, the country behind Ban St. Martin, where considerable numbers of the French were camped, could not be looked into on account of the interposing Mount St. Quentin, and that, for that reason, he evidently recommended that a view of the country should be gained from St. Julien.

The 3rd Uhlans had relieved the 16th Hussars on outpost; v. Leipsiger's squadron (5th) had occupied the country between Fey and Corny, and established communication with the 5th Cavalry Division. A patrol on the left bank of the Mosel was surprised in Ars a. d. Mosel by marauders and inhabitants, a corporal was killed, and two Uhlans wounded and captured. The squadron had to protect the bridge at Corny. The protection of this important passage by one squadron, not even armed with carbines, must be considered insufficient; and if an enemy more enterprising than the French had stood opposite, a serious punishment might have resulted. The patrols from the regiment displayed great activity and reached Magny and to within 400 paces of an earthwork in course of building east of Frescati. A report of the squadron leader has been kept—

"Corny, 8 p.m.

"Under-officer Leopold rode through Bayonville, Onville, Villecey, without seeing any troops. In Chambley he found 1st and 4th Squadron of 11th Hussars, and the other squadrons in Buxières and Gorze. Near Les Baraques he encountered patrols of Chasseurs, and followed them to the wood, where he was fired on apparently by a picket.* The 5th Cavalry Division is in

* This N.C.O. may well serve as a pattern to our N.C.O.'s as patrol leader.

Aug. 14.

Thiaucourt, with one brigade in Beney. Other patrols went by Jouy to where the Nancy-Metz railway crosses the Mosel. There they struck the infantry outposts. Behind the railway embankment was a battalion of infantry, which opened fire. The patrols advanced again later on, and discovered considerable camps close to the railway—perhaps four regiments of infantry and one squadron."*

The 15th Uhlans. Reconnaissance by Colonel v. Alvensleben.

The 15th Uhlans had put out outposts at Orny, and sent patrols towards Ars Laquenexy.

The regiment was placed in the outpost line assigned to it, so far from the enemy that its duty "to reconnoitre diligently" gave the enterprising leader the welcome opportunity of searching out the enemy's dispositions under the most difficult conditions. Colonel v. Alvensleben at once established communication in person with the 1st Cavalry Division, which was met on the right out in front near Mécleuves, with its outposts towards Peltre and Mercy le Haut. The high ridge, on which these places stand, prevented any view into the main position, as long as the enemy occupied it. Only now and then (in the forenoon) were movements of small detachments towards Metz seen against the sky; and none in the opposite direction.

General v. Hartmann, commanding the 1st Division, attributed these movements to reliefs and fatigue duties, like fetching water, etc., thus proving the French forces had remained on the right bank.

* The most important duties of the squadron were a regular system of patrols and the protection of the bridge; yet a large proportion of men had always to be employed as outposts in the country that it was impossible to see over; an officer remained with the picket, and only one regular officer and quite a junior reserve officer remained available for patrolling. One N.C.O., with ten men, guarded the bridge, where the squadron leader, too, was usually to be found. It is clear what a weak force the squadron had at its disposal for their important task. [Taken from notes of Captain, now General of Cavalry, v. Leipziger (retired).]

As Colonel v. Alvensleben was unable to share this view, he continued his reconnaissance beyond the right flank of the 1st Cavalry Division, and found close, south-east of Mercy le Haut, an excellently sited but already abandoned abatis facing the wood, which aided an approach. This proved that there had been an intention to defend the heights of Mercy le Haut. He found also a double vedette that was not on the alert at the eastern entrance of the place; and soon after struck the head of the 7th Jägers as they were marching from Ars Laquenexy up to Mercy le Haut.

General v. der Goltz followed with the battalion and H.R.H. Prince Adalbert, who had joined the advance. [We have already seen him on August 7 in close touch with the enemy. *Vide* p. 66.]

The general, when asked the reason of his advance, replied in the best of humour, "I have been seeing the enemy retiring the whole day, and want to give the rest a tickling up before they disappear into their earthworks." *

His whole brigade was soon engaged, and so began the battle of Colombey. The freedom with which the French took up the battle, procured constant reinforcements from Metz, and prevented any special progress, made the attack of the 18th Division most effective. The division had marched towards the sound of the guns, had appeared late in the afternoon on the right flank of the 15th Uhlans' outposts, and was led against the enemy's flank at Peltre by Colonel v. Alvensleben in person at the head of the 36th Fusilier Regiment. The country on this flank absolutely prohibited any attack by the cavalry.

Lieutenant v. Werthern, 16th Hussars, had led

* This well-attested remark is an important contribution to the criticism on the intention of the general on this day.

Aug. 14. a patrol by Augny, and, north of it, and had discovered French camps, which were actively astir; entrenchments were being thrown up, and trains kept frequently coming in. Spahis had been seen at Ancy and Ars.

Reconnaissance of the outpost squadrons.
To ascertain the reason of the constant activity in the French camps—a reconnaissance to the south had been made from one of them—the 3rd Squadron from the 15th Uhlans, and the 1st from the 6th Cuirassiers, advanced together in the afternoon from the outposts to Fleury, and beyond.

Captain v. Ploetz, 15th Uhlans, had left the 4th and 5th troops of his squadron behind as a picket in front of Chérisey. The regiment had collected all the "registered" horses into a fifth troop in each squadron, which seemed most practical, because it was often possible to spare these animals which were not yet used to saddle-work; and also because the troop at full war strength is an unwieldy body, as long as the squadron is pretty well up to strength. The squadrons got close up to Metz, and drove in a whole regiment of mounted Jägers. The railway put an end to any further advance, and, besides this, the left flank was threatened by infantry, which opened a hot fire on the patrol, and severely wounded a N.C.O. of the Uhlans with a shot in the leg. In the reconnaissance, Peltre, Mercy le Haut, and the earthworks there were found to have been abandoned. To judge by the still visible tracks, the enemy must have marched off towards the sound of the guns, the thunder of which came from Colombey.

Colonel v. Schmidt had reported: two squadrons dismounted between Magny and Marly; Novéant on the left bank clear, but Spahis at Ancy and Ars. Captain v. Grimm reported from Crepy

(Peltre) pickets of the enemy's infantry, and behind them larger bodies of troops.

The above account shows that the 6th Cavalry Division had successfully performed their task of observation and reconnaissance towards Metz, and thereby covered the flank march of the Second Army; their patrols had been active and enterprising.

This must have made it more annoying for the commander, that the reports transmitted by the division to the Third Corps were continually received with doubt. Colonel v. Voigts-Rhetz, chief of the staff of the Third Corps, according to the divisional diary, in speaking to the general staff officer of the division on the 14th, said "that all the reports of the division pointed to a delusion, that there was nothing at Metz, and that the troops reported were only the outposts of the fortress" (see p. 209). In the evening an officer from the staff of the Second Army arrived at Chérisey to ask what was the matter, "since no reports from the division had reached His Royal Highness." Now, what had become of these reports, numbers of which had certainly come in from the division? There is no doubt whatever that the Army Corps Head Quarters considered them valueless * (see p. 257).

Owing to the remarks of the Army Corps staff on the reports of the division, the Army Head Quarters apparently considered it necessary to

Aug. 14.

Reports of the 6th Cavalry Division regarded as untrustworthy by Head Quarters of Third Army Corps.

---

* According to a verbal communication from Major-General v. Treskow, at that time first adjutant of the 6th Cavalry Division, Army Corps Head Quarters, on inquiry from Major v. Schoenfels (general staff officer of the division), remarked that the reports of the last few days were looked upon as "utter rot" ("Tartaren-Nachrichten"). In a letter of the G.O.C. Third Army Corps to Prince Frederick Charles —handed in at 3 p.m.—it is expressly stated: " . . . Also yesterday's reports were unimportant; I have desisted from forwarding them to Y.R.H., because I did not think they were right."

Aug. 14. demand from the division a report of their movements on these dates, especially on the 12th.

The result of the reconnaissance on the 12th was given in the despatch from Chérisey, 10 p.m., viz.—

> "The definite assurance that the country for 4½ miles in front of Metz was occupied in force by troops of all three arms, that there were camps at Grigy, Colombey, Vantoux, and Montigny, and that the corps of Frossard, Bazaine, and the Guard stood, according to the prisoners' account, at Metz. Anyhow, the number of troops seen were larger than those usually stationed in front of fortresses, and to this effect the division had clearly given information in five separate reports to the Corps Head Quarters."

We know the reports from the division were substantially accurate, and subsequent events confirmed them.

5th Cavalry Division crosses the Mosel. Prince Frederick Charles had already issued for the 14th his own orders, which were in entire agreement with the views of the Commander-in-Chief.

Part of the order to the 5th Cavalry Division ran thus—

> "The 5th Cavalry Division will advance to the plateau between the Mosel and the Maas to Thiaucourt, and point their advanced troops northwards to watch the Metz-Verdun road. Les Baraques, east of Chambley, and the plateau north-west of Gorze both afford a view of that road."

The general commanding the Tenth Army Corps, in a supplementary order, also directed that a relay post should be stationed in Regniéville, and that the division should watch as far as the Mosel on the right, and gain touch with the cavalry of the Guard on the left.

General v. Rheinbaben already on the 13th had

ordered the advance on Thiaucourt (p. 259), and further directed in brief— Aug. 14.

> "The two squadrons in Pagny will advance towards the Metz-Verdun road as far as Gorze-Chambley, to a suitable point, as Les Baraques, east of Chambley, and the plateau of Gorze are said to afford a view of that road.
>
> "The four squadrons in Thiaucourt will advance to St. Benoit en Woëvre, and push their advanced parties by Woël-Hadonville* towards the Metz-Verdun road, while seeking to gain touch with the two squadrons at Chambley.
>
> "The remaining squadrons of Redern's Brigade will follow with the horse battery to St. Benoit.
>
> "Barby's Brigade will proceed to Thiaucourt, and send one squadron from Pont à Mousson to Pagny, two squadrons to the left, to Flirey, on the Pont à Mousson-Commercy road, in order to keep touch with the Guard-Dragoon-Brigade, which has its right flank at Novéant aux Prés. It will establish a relay post at Regniéville, and send patrols to the Mosel, on the right, and to Essey, on the left.
>
> "The 12th Cavalry Brigade will reach Pont à Mousson.
>
> "The advance will start at 7 a.m. Report to be furnished as soon as the Metz-Verdun road comes into view.
>
> "The advance guard of the infantry, which will, in any case, occupy Vandières, in the Mosel valley, will halt where the road from Pont à Mousson separates to Thiaucourt and to Flirey."

General v. Redern ordered the 17th Hussars to march to Beney, to push the outposts to St. Benoit, and to send forward officers' patrols with strong covering parties in the directions named, "to ascertain whether the enemy is withdrawing large bodies of troops from Metz."

---

* It would have been more correct to say "by Woël and Hadonville."

Aug. 14.

A troop was to be sent forward to Dommartin-la-Chaussée, or Charey, to open communication with Chambley.

The 5th Cavalry Division accordingly continued the advance on Thiaucourt commenced on the 13th by the 17th Hussars. The regiment had, however, on the 13th, as Lieut-Colonel v. Rauch reported at 4 a.m. from Regniéville, not proceeded beyond that place, as it was constantly harassed by the enemy on the march, and as the woods near Thiaucourt were occupied by the enemy's cavalry.*

The squadrons moved out of Pont à Mousson at 7.30 a.m., and General v. Bredow started from Jallaucourt at 4.30.

The 11th Brigade reached Thiaucourt, and the 13th Brigade Beney, with their outposts at Benoit en Woëvre.

Captain v. der Mülbe, 2nd Squadron, 17th Hussars, reported from the outposts (which was received at 8.15 p.m.)—

"That Lieutenant v. Münchhausen, patrolling from Latour en Woëvre to Hannonville, on the high-road to Metz, left his men and horses in Jonville, and, creeping up behind a hill, observed a battalion of pioneers on the march, going from Metz to Verdun. On questioning the inhabitants of the other villages, he was told that many small detachments had passed through, and that it was commonly stated that the troops were going to retire from Metz."

The brigade sent on the news at 8.30 p.m.

1st and 4th Squadron 11th Hussars, on the Gorze plateau.

The 1st and 4th Squadron 11th Hussars, who had slept the night at Pagny, reached the plateau of Gorze according to orders, but they saw nothing

---

* The French cavalry possessed, in their chassepot carbine, a weapon far superior to our needle carbine, and they were far more accustomed to use it than the German cavalry, both on foot and on horseback.

of the enemy, who, in consequence of the battle of Colombey, had stopped their march westwards. Aug. 14.

Captain v. Vaerst reached Les Baraques 11.30 a.m., and reported from there that he had seen nothing of the enemy on the Metz-Verdun road.*

General v. Rheinbaben forwarded his report at 8 p.m., and it reached the Second Army "late at night."

Vaerst had reached the high-road by Buxières, and had ordered his patrols to press on to the forts west of Metz, without their having come in contact with the enemy. At the time of sending off the report the country as far as the forts was indeed still clear, but two cavalry divisions came up there late in the afternoon (*vide* p. 285). The records do not contain any further reports from the hussars.

The squadrons passed the night in alarm quarters in Chambley with outposts on the line Buxières to the stream north of Chambley.

Two squadrons of the 13th Uhlans had been sent to Flirey. One (the 4th) had advanced by Ancy along the Mosel valley to the hills near Dornot. Shortly before this a patrol of the 9th Dragoons had been surprised by the inhabitants in Ancy, and some of them carried off to Metz. As the inhabitants showed themselves unfriendly, threw stones, and poured pitch out of the windows, Captain v. Rosenberg was compelled to take some of them with him as hostages. He reported at 6.30 p.m.— Attacks by inhabitants of Ancy.

"Place?

"Lieutenant v. Treskow advanced with one troop to the heights of Jouy aux Arches. From there he could clearly see that only quite small bivouacs still remained

* According to the diary of the regiment, the report was received by its colonel at 1.30 p.m., being directed "by St. Benoit, thence on Dampoitoux." The reason for this roundabout way is not apparent. The brigade forwarded the report 2.45 p.m.

Aug. 14.

on the right bank of the Mosel. The newly commenced forts on the left bank at Scy and Ban St. Martin are half finished. The whole country seems deserted. The country-folk say that long columns have marched westwards to-day from Metz."

This report was sent to Corps Head Quarters at 8.45 p.m. According to the regimental history, the patrols sent to the north-west also ascertained that movements of the enemy were taking place west of Metz. The records make no mention of this. The account is so vague that no special weight could be attached to it. According to the above report, founded on the statement of the inhabitants, it must be doubted whether the patrols themselves saw these movements or not. In the evening the squadron returned to Pagny.

A despatch from General v. Rheinbaben, which reached the Corps Head Quarters the same day, and reached the Second Army Head Quarters at midnight, ran as follows:—

"Thiaucourt, 8 p.m.

"Since, according to the report of the 13th Hussars, the 3 p.m. report has gone astray, I again report that Captain v. Vaerst saw nothing from Les Baraques at 11.30 a.m. on the Metz-Verdun road, and nothing of the enemy anywhere. According to the statement of an inhabitant here (Rheinbaben's host), whose brother-in-law is a brigadier in Metz, and seems well informed, the enemy will fight in front of Metz . . ."

Comments.

It cannot be said that the results of the reconnaissance of the 5th Cavalry Division had been very satisfactory, although individual patrols had brought in valuable information, nor that the general of division had properly performed the important task entrusted to him. The division certainly did not advance far enough forward towards their objective. The main body covered a march of less than 15

miles from Pont à Mousson to Thiaucourt. So
slow a rate was not in accordance either with the
importance of the duty, or with the order issued to
the cavalry by His Majesty (see p. 265). Two roads
led from Pont à Mousson to the most southernly
road from Metz to Verdun; the one by Gorze in
the Mosel valley, which, owing to its being a defile,
was unsuited to the movement of large bodies of
cavalry; the other by Thiaucourt was a high-road,
which joins the Metz-Verdun road at Fresnes en
Woëvre. Good roads, however, led from Thiaucourt
by Chambley and Xonville more direct there. It
does not seem unreasonable to expect that 25
miles should be covered on this day, and that the
main body should thus have reached the line
Chambley-Xonville. The outposts could then have
rested at night on that most important road.

Aug. 14.

Although the French in their movement westward did not get very far this day, yet Forton's Cavalry Division, the advance guard of the 2nd Army Corps, reached beyond Gravelotte at 7.30 p.m. and put out pickets towards the woods of Gorze, where, according to Dick de Lonlay, Prussian patrols had been observed. The same authority relates that Colonel Juncker was wounded by a shot while visiting the outposts in the night.

Lost reports.

Du Barail's Reserve Cavalry Division, which had to reconnoitre the northern road by Conflans to Verdun as advance guard to the 3rd and 4th Corps, arrived at their camp at Malmaison on Forton's right as early as 5 p.m. According to French accounts, there is no doubt that German patrols, probably the 3rd or 13th Uhlans, came into contact; but where are their reports?

The Guard Dragoon Brigade had continued to move on the left of the cavalry of the Second Army, and sent v. Trotha's squadron of the 2nd

The Brigade of Guard Dragoons.

Aug. 14. Guard Dragoons to reconnoitre towards Toul, and to cut the railway between the fortress and Frouard. Another party of half a squadron, under Lieutenant Graf Hue de Grais, had to go to Frouard and cut the railway there.

Two reports contain the result of these expeditions, which were sent on by Graf Brandenburg from Rogéville at 6.30 p.m.—

Report of the patrol of Graf Hue de Grais—

"Frouard.

"I reached Frouard 10 a.m. without meeting the enemy. 400 to 500 French troops are said to have been in Frouard yesterday; they retired by Toul to Paris. I have taken up a position in front of Frouard on this side of the Mosel. Have torn up the rails on the Frouard-Toul and Frouard-Strassburg lines."

Report of the patrol to Toul; handed in at 2 p.m.—

"1. Railway lines on the bridge at Gondreville, south of Villiers-St. Etienne, torn up. Only small patrols of the enemy seen.

"2. The squadron came within a mile of Toul without seeing anything of the enemy. Some mounted Jägers showed themselves at the exits, and were followed by the 4th troop. I then followed into the town with the 2nd and 3rd troops, leaving the 1st as a reserve in front of the town. We chased the enemy into the middle of the suburb. An officer and several men were either shot or cut down. The squadron came under so hot a fire from the houses, from infantry and cavalry, that I left the town. The squadron had no casualties: one N.C.O. was scratched. I drew up the squadron in front of the town, and sent Lieutenant v. Wagenhof back into the town to demand its surrender. This was unsuccessful.

"Signed: v. TROTHA."

Added verbally—

"The commandant said, 'Repassez si vous voulez.

CAVALRY ON SERVICE 287

The sluice gates below the town were opened, to drain the water out of the fortifications." Aug. 14.

While the squadron demolished the railway, v. Trotha learnt that he was close to the sluice gates which kept the ditches round Toul full; so he forthwith undertook their destruction.

The detachment of mounted Jägers which the squadron had followed into the town was thirty or forty strong. The inhabitants had said the garrison of Toul consisted only of Gardes Mobiles, which explains the attempt to procure a surrender, and the officer with the flag of truce had threatened them with bombardment within four hours if they did not surrender.

This expedition of v. Trotha's is a capital bit of cavalry service. Would that our cavalry will always show a fancy for such bold measures!

The advance of the Guard Dragoons on this day, five miles, from Dieulouard to Rogéville, is remarkably short.

The position of the enemy on the evening of the 14th is not easy to determine, as the French, for the most part, after the battle were on the march westwards during the night.* *Movements of the French*

The departure of the 3rd and 4th French Corps had been delayed twenty-four hours by the battle on the 14th. The 3rd Army Corps, command of which had been given to Marshal le Boeuf in place of General Decaen, killed, was on the march during the night of the 14th–15th. The divisions passed through Metz in the night, and only reached their camp on the left bank of the Mosel at Plappeville Devant les Pont, and opposite the island of Chambières, on the morning of the 15th.

* What is shown on the map is meant to depict only the general situation.

Aug. 14. The 4th Corps also marched right through the night. On the morning of the 15th, Cissey's Division arrived at Woippy, Grenier's at St. Eloy, Lorencez at Lorry, and Legrand at Woippy le Sansonnet.

The Guard Corps was also on the march through the night. On the morning of the 15th, Deligny's Division reached the neighbourhood of Moulins, Picart's reached Longeville, and the cavalry division Ban St. Martin.

Of the 2nd Corps, Bataille's Division reached Scy at the foot of Mont St. Quentin at 4 p.m.; Vergé's Division came into camp there at 9 p.m.; and Laveaucoupet's was directed to form the garrison of Metz. Valabrègue's Cavalry Division and the artillery of the corps took the entire night to traverse Metz, as they could not use the pontoon bridges. They took nine hours to cover less than four miles.

The cavalry division, which had started from Mercy le Haut at 1 p.m., had halted for hours in the plain of the Seille at Sablon till 9 p.m., and only arrived greatly fatigued at St. Hubert at 5 a.m. on the 15th.

Forton's and Du Barail's Cavalry Divisions, as we have seen (p. 285), reached the neighbourhood of Gravelotte and Malmaison in the afternoon.

CHAPTER IX

By an Army Order, dated Herny, August 14, 6 p.m., issued before news of the battle east of Metz had been received at Royal Head Quarters, and when the possibility that the main portion of the French army was still on the right bank had to be considered, His Majesty the King had given directions for the right wing of the Second Army (IIIrd, IXth, XIIth Corps) to concentrate, and for the IInd Corps to continue its march. The first line of the First Army (Ist and VIIth Corps) was to maintain its original position, and the VIIIth Corps to be brought forward to Bazancourt, in order to assist the proposed move to the left, and to bring the First Army nearer to the right wing of the Second Army.

Aug. 15. Order of H.M. the King.

To clear up the situation on the enemy's side, the Second Army was instructed to send the whole of its available cavalry to the left bank of the Mosel against the enemy's communications between Metz and Verdun, and to support it, in the direction of Gorze and Thiaucourt, by whichever corps was the first to cross the Mosel. For this purpose the Third Corps was to prepare a bridge below Pont à Mousson on the 15th. It was expressly stated that the forward movement of the 3rd Cavalry Division was not restricted by any previous instructions.

As soon as His Majesty, on riding over the battlefield, became personally convinced that there could be no large bodies of troops east of Metz,

Aug. 15. the orders previously issued were altered, in so far as it was now intended to cross the First Army also over to the left bank as quickly as possible.

Thus the Eighth Corps was directed on Orny; General v. Steinmetz drew the First Corps to Kurzel and the Seventh to the country between Pange and the Courcelles railway station; ordered the cavalry divisions on the flanks of the army to watch Metz from Avancy and Verny. Prince Frederick Charles regained the use of the several corps on the right wing, especially of the Third Corps, which His Majesty had hitherto retained at his own disposal.

3rd Cavalry Division remains this side of the Mosel.

The 3rd Cavalry Division received no new instructions to attempt to cross the Mosel. The orders from Royal Head Quarters with reference to it were not complied with. These orders seem to have been completely forgotten, since in the order for the 16th, which directed the flank march of the army, it was brought from the Mosel banks to the country between Courcelles and Mécleuves. The division, by special orders, had searched for wounded on the battlefield during the night to the 15th, and their patrols had pressed forward to Fort St. Julien.

At 9 a.m. the division went into bivouac at Vry, and the 7th Uhlans were sent ahead to Vremy and Avancy.

The 1st Cavalry Division had never received the order to proceed to Verny. In accordance with previous orders, they reached the vicinity of Marsilly and went into bivouac later at Courcelles on the Nied behind the outposts of the Seventh Corps.

Patrols to the forts of Metz.

The 1st Dragoons patrolled actively towards Metz. Lieutenant v. Bernhardi got beyond Bellecroix with a patrol, without striking even the outposts of the enemy.

CAVALRY ON SERVICE 291

An officers' patrol from the 8th Hussars went even further, and reached the farm of Les Bordes, which lies close in front of Metz, at 6.30 a.m., where the first hostile posts were discovered. Lieutenant v. Bassewitz, 15th Hussars, got close up to Fort Queuleu and brought in seven pioneers who were at work in the ditches there.

Aug. 15.

Another officer of the same regiment, Lieutenant v. Wilamowitz, who had been detailed to gain touch with the First Army Corps, and on his way met the 1st Dragoons trotting to Bellecroix, rode up to the closed gate of the Les Bordes fort without meeting a single French soldier.

We thus see that the reconnaissance of the divisional cavalry of the First Army—these patrols are almost all mentioned in the official "History of the War"—was far more spirited and productive than that of the cavalry divisions.

During the gradual advance of the right wing of the Second Army towards the Mosel the 6th Cavalry Division continued their observation of Metz, and, keeping their position between the Mosel and the Nied, pushed forward on both banks of the Seille as far as the outskirts of the town. On the east they kept touch with the Hessian Cavalry Brigade.

6th Cavalry Division watches Metz.

Duke William issued the following order mainly as the result of Graf Groeben's reports of the previous day :—

"August 15, 1 a.m.

"1. Colonel Graf Groeben, with two squadrons of his regiment, with the Cuirassier squadron on the Seille, and with a section of horse artillery, will start from Pournoy la Chétive at daybreak (4 a.m.), and reconnoitre by Augny towards the Nancy road, and, if possible, across the Mosel towards the Verdun road.

"2. Major v. Hessberg will march at 4 a.m. with a squadron of Cuirassiers, a section of horse artillery,

Aug. 15.

and, joined by the advanced squadrons of v. Plötz and v. Knobloch, will proceed by Pouilly on both sides of the main road to Metz, and on the left of it, if possible, to St. Privat.* A squadron of the 15th Uhlans will move by Chesny, to keep touch with the 18th Division. These detachments, after a thorough reconnaissance, will leave smaller observation parties out, and report as soon as possible to Verny and Chérisey."

Groeben's reconnaissance.

Graf Groeben's despatch, given below, gives clear information of the performance of his task.

"The Cuirassier squadron (v. Heuser) and the two guns reached camp at Pournoy only at 4.30 a.m. The march was commenced at once by Augny towards Metz, with a right flank party moving by Cuvry, Marly, and Magny. The 2nd squadron of the regiment, on outpost, was brought to Augny in support, and a troop of the squadron at Corny was sent forward by Jouy les Arches towards Metz.

"A mist aided our advance. Beyond Augny the atmosphere cleared, but a thick cloud still covered Fort St. Quentin, and hid any view from it.

"Uhlan patrols moved towards the considerable earthworks on the Augny-Metz road, and found them empty.

"Three troops of Cuirassiers followed along the Augny-Metz (Montigny) road, and, past the earthworks, the advanced troop of the two Uhlan squadrons (3rd and 4th). The remainder of the two Uhlan squadrons, two guns, and a troop of Cuirassiers followed at a trot to Bradin's Farm, where they took up a position under cover.

"The advanced troop of the Uhlans and that of the Cuirassiers reached Montigny and rode through it. The Uhlans took four prisoners and captured a supply waggon with oats. It was only at the further exit of the place, close to the fortifications, that hostile infantry was met.

"Meanwhile, from the junction of the Nancy and Thionville railways, I observed a large camp of the

* A farm 2200 yards north-east of Frescati, which has now disappeared.

enemy on the left bank between Longeville and Moulins b. Metz, where absolute silence still reigned. According to the inhabitants, all the camps on the right bank had been abandoned in the night, and the troops were said to have marched away for the most part towards Verdun.

Aug. 15.

"Though the reconnaissance on the right bank had gained its object (an advance across the Mosel was not feasible, and the reconnaissance on the left bank had been entrusted to v. Leipziger's squadron in Corny), I could not resist the pleasure of disturbing the peacefulness of the camp at Longeville. The two guns came into action west of Bradin's Farm, and opened fire on the camp. The effect was most amusing. Shouts and confusion everywhere. It was some time before the still veiled Fort St. Quentin began to fire in the direction of Bradin's Farm. When the mist cleared, the artillery on our side stopped fire, and the main body of the detachment was withdrawn towards Augny, behind the cover of a wood.* The advanced troops remained facing Montigny. The troop sent on the Metz-Nancy road destroyed the railway at the junction as best they could, and cut some telegraph wires.

"The troops in the camp meanwhile assembled behind the covering thicket at Moulins, and detachments ascended Mount St. Quentin; but detachments also began to march towards Ancy. The earthworks on the Metz-Augny road were found to be only partially completed. This, as well as the completely passive attitude of the enemy, the march of troops on the far bank observed by myself, and the unanimous statements of both prisoners and inhabitants, confirm the intention of the enemy not to leave their main forces concentrated in Metz. A further proof is that the railway bridge over the Mosel was blown up at 10 a.m. The section of two horse-guns fired 48 shells at ranges of 2200 and 2800 paces.

"The fort fired three shells.

"Signed: GRAF GROEBEN."

---

* Doubtless the little wood of Frescati, on the drill ground, so well known to the garrison of Metz.

Aug. 15. Graf Groeben sent the following reports in the course of his expedition:—

"Montigny Railway Station, 9.45 a.m.

"Camp at Montigny shelled with effect. Enemy at Moulins. Various detachments retiring to Mount St. Quentin. Artillery fired on us from there without result. Four prisoners from the 12th, 88th, and 100th Regiments sent back, among them a young officer from St. Cyr. They state they belong to Canrobert's Corps, which came from Chalons four days ago. Enemy quite inactive. Infantry have occupied the railway bridge on the left bank of the Mosel."

"Redoubt, south end of Montigny, Time (?).

"Am right in front of Montigny, with two squadrons Uhlans and the guns.

"One troop Uhlans and three troops Cuirassiers are reconnoitring Montigny.

"All the camps south of Montigny evacuated during the night, as well as the partly finished redoubts. Inhabitants say that French troops are marching to Verdun.

"The patrols on the left bank of the Mosel met enemy's infantry beyond Ancy, and could not reach the Metz-Verdun road."

Influence on the enemy.

This skilful and bold reconnaissance, which gave the Commander-in-Chief very valuable information, produced a considerable effect on the enemy.

The same morning Tixier's Division of the 6th Corps, which had passed the night of 14th to 15th under arms at Montigny, marched over the railway bridge at 6 a.m., reached Longeville les Metz, and went into camp there. The troops were enjoying the rest they so much needed, when the first shells from Groeben's detachment burst among them.

The first dropped among a group of officers, of whom three were killed, while one officer and eight men were wounded. An indescribable confusion ensued; every one ran wildly about shouting. The other shells did no further damage. The 9th Jäger Aug. 15. Battalion hurried to take up a position on the heights, and Fort St. Quentin opened fire. Napoleon's Head Quarters on this date were at Longeville. This surprise had such an effect on Marshal Bazaine that he gave orders for the demolition of the railway bridge of the Metz-Diedenhofen line mentioned in the despatch above —an absolutely purposeless order.

The bridge, which was covered by the fire of the fortress and was of the utmost value to the French for traffic between one bank and the other, had two piers destroyed by the explosion; these were repaired later during the investment.

We most certainly approve of Graf Groeben Comments. employing his guns here. Apart from the actual damage which such a surprise produces, the moral influence on the troops surprised is much more lasting. The man who has once experienced such an occurrence will always have the feeling that his commander has made a slip, and that the enemy is his superior. The French infantry, however, soon regained their *morale* after such experiences, as the battle of Beaumont also shows. The action of Graf Groeben this day instinctively invites comparison with the action of the 5th Cavalry Division early on the 16th, when they surprised Forton's Cavalry Division in camp, and opened fire with their guns. Graf Groeben acted wisely, while the action on the 16th was a mistake. Graf Groeben, quite apart from his small force, and with a river between him and the enemy, could not even think of an attack with the *arme blanche*. But on the 16th the Prussian cavalry ought to have made an attack, which promised certain success, and, leaving other things alone, was, moreover, favoured by the lie of the ground.

Aug. 15. The results would have been incalculable. Not only would the enemy's cavalry division have been dispersed, but a great effect would have been produced on their infantry and artillery camped in rear, through whom the Prussians and the routed French cavalry would have ridden in a mass. It would have been the best possible preparation for the subsequent attack of the Prussian infantry.

The batteries naturally created a great impression on the cavalry division. It fled in utter rout and had some loss, but as it was not pursued it collected again after a time, and regained its effectiveness for action in the course of the day; so the impression was by no means a lasting one.

The infantry were in no way affected by the occurrence; on the contrary, the thunder of the Prussian guns gave them the promptest information of the advance, so that they were fully prepared to receive the Prussian infantry when they advanced.

The cavalry leader must always consider that his guns are only an *auxiliary* weapon, though a very precious one, and must therefore never allow his command to play the simple *rôle* of escort to the guns, as the Prussian cavalry did on the morning of the 16th.

Reconnaissance by Hessberg's detachment. Major v. Hessberg, with 5th and 3rd Squadron 6th Cuirassiers, 3rd Squadron 15th Uhlans, and two horse artillery guns, had started from Verny as early as 5 a.m. The 5th Squadron of the 6th Cuirassiers had provided the outposts facing Metz, and had already ascertained during the night that the village of Marly, hitherto strongly held, had been evacuated. The squadron, now acquainted with the country, formed the advance guard, sent one troop to the left flank, and advanced along the main road by Magny. The main body sent one troop to the right flank to gain touch with the First Army. The leader of the detachment endeavoured to reach the wide plateau rising south of Metz on the left bank of the Seille, although the only passage across the Seille, which rendered this possible, to the north of Magny, was within effective range of Fort Queuleu. Favoured by the rising morning mist, as well as by the careless watch kept by the garrison, the detachment was successful in debouching unobserved from Magny, and in gaining the plateau, filing through the abatis on the road. Camping grounds of all arms were found there, which had apparently been abandoned only the evening before, or during the night at any rate, in consequence of the successful action of the First Army.

Aug. 15.

A large star fort had been built on the eastern slope of the hill, commanding Magny, in which the entrenching tools were found still there.* While the main body took up a position under cover, the 5th Squadron advanced towards Sablon. Lieutenant v. Bredow's troop crossed the railway bridge, though received near it by a hot fire from some houses, and compelled the riflemen to retire. The advanced party dashed through Sablon, and arrived within 1200 yards of the outworks in the neighbourhood of the station. Here, however, they were forced by infantry fire to retire. Meanwhile the alarm was sounded in the forts, and infantry moved out and established themselves in a railway train. The guns of the detachment now came into action, and with a few shells drove the enemy out of the waggons. The guns had unlimbered within 800 paces of the station; they then retired to 1300 paces, and threw shells at that range into the town.

* Fort St. Privat, now called Prince August von Württemberg.

Aug. 15. Altogether twenty-four shells were fired. As other riflemen in the neighbourhood kept the guns constantly under fire, and Fort Queuleu now commenced a fire mostly ineffective, and, moreover, as the object of the reconnaissance had been attained, the detachment withdrew under cover and waited to see if the enemy would perhaps march on and follow with larger bodies of troops.

When the detachment advanced north of Marly and left the main road, a troop was sent along it to reconnoitre as far as possible towards the fortifications. The troop advanced as far as a barricade, held by guns, which barred the road in Sablon. The enemy were so startled by the appearance of the troop there, that the gun detachments failed to fire a single shot at the men as they retired down the road. Lieutenant v. Buch then stationed himself at the railway crossing.

After the detachment had ascertained for certain that the enemy were not advancing across the railway, it retired to Verny, and moved into bivouac there at 1 p.m.

Major v. Hessberg sent in the following report, which reached the 6th Cavalry Division at 9 p.m., and the Third Corps on the 16th at 7.30 a.m.—

"Place (?), 7.30 p.m.

"Advanced by St. Privat across the railway to Sablon. Met no enemy except small infantry patrols. The camps deserted, many entrenching tools being left behind. Inhabitants of Sablon opened fire from the houses and railway trains. Earthworks and camps there partly built. Only a camp on the left bank of the Seille, near Montigny, still occupied. Fortress alarmed; commotion in all directions."

This reconnaissance, pushed close up to the strong works of the fortress, was also carried out with skill and boldness, and materially assisted in throwing light on the situation of the enemy.

CAVALRY ON SERVICE

The Prussian cavalry, as was the case whenever they were employed, displayed great dash and enterprise.

Aug. 15.

According to instructions, the 1st Squadron of 15th Uhlans advanced by Chesney towards the south front of Metz. In the thick mist it got so close to the fortress that, when the mist lifted, it found itself facing Fort Queuleu, a strong earthwork, where work was still going on.

The 6th Cavalry Division left their position at noon to march to Corny, by order of the Third Army Corps, in consequence of its further advance to Novéant. Two squadrons of the 3rd Uhlans— v. Leipziger's and Bothe's—remained on outpost duty facing Metz, and reported from there, according to the division's war diary, "large masses of the enemy on the march west of Metz on the left bank of the Mosel." The division went at first into bivouac at Pommerieux, and then into quarters at Coin a. d. Seille.

6th Cavalry Division.

Prince Frederick Charles intended to reach the Mosel with his whole army on the 15th, in order to cross the river and then continue operations with his united forces; in these the 5th Cavalry Division was given, as we saw, an important *rôle*.

During the night of the 14th–15th two important despatches had been received, as we know; one, Captain v. Vaerst's, 11th Hussars, from Les Baraques, stated that no enemy had been seen either on the Metz-Verdun road or anywhere west of Metz. Two reports (Lieutenant v. Treskow's and Captain v. Rosenberg's, 13th Uhlans), from the hills near Jouy aux Arches, stated that there were only small bivouacs in front of Metz and on the right bank of the Mosel, and that on the 14th long columns, as it was alleged, had already marched from Metz to the west.

300 CAVALRY ON SERVICE

Aug. 15.

Where was the Rhine Army?

These reports were contradictory. Where was the enemy, who had till now been camped in front of Metz?

The news of the battle on the 14th, which was conveyed to General v. Moltke by a telegram received by him August 15, 6.45 a.m., with the additional sentence, "pursuit on the Metz-Verdun road is important," increased this uncertainty still further. As we now know, the contradiction is explained by the fact that, of the enemy who had disappeared from the camps in front of Metz, part had hurried eastwards to the battlefield, part had collected in the town, and part camped behind Mount St. Quentin, and were on the march westwards from there. In the morning, however, when v. Vaerst wrote his message from Les Baraques at 11.30, they had not yet come far enough to be discovered by the patrols.

We see from this how difficult sometimes the problems are which may confront the leader, even if the reports he gets are perfectly accurate.

The above-mentioned order from Royal Head Quarters for the 15th (dated 6 p.m. August 14) arrived in Pont à Mousson about midnight.

Measures by the Head Quarters of the Second Army.

It was of vital importance for the Commander-in-Chief of the Second Army to obtain information. The whole Tenth Corps with the 5th Cavalry Division, which had been strengthened by the Guard Dragoon Brigade, was to serve this purpose.

The following order was therefore issued, which reached the Tenth Corps 9 a.m. :—

"Pont à Mousson, 7 a.m.

"Information must be obtained, by an advance on the left bank of the Mosel with the troops that are ready, as to whether the main force of the enemy's army have already withdrawn from Metz, or whether they are in the act of retiring."

CAVALRY ON SERVICE

Barby's and Redern's Brigades were to be employed in the first line, and with horse artillery to march as quickly as possible in the above-mentioned direction, till they gained an insight into the situation. At the same time they were to seek to the northward for communication with the cavalry of the First Army. The two infantry divisions of the Tenth Corps were to be pushed down the Mosel valley and to the north-west, to serve as support to the advanced cavalry, and a general advance was to be made down the Mosel valley for the purpose of reconnoitring and obtaining information in the direction of Metz.

Aug. 15.

The order of His Majesty issued on the 15th, which has been mentioned, and giving back the disposal of the IIIrd, IXth, XIIth Corps to the Prince, contained an additional remark to the effect "that the French were probably already in full retreat to Verdun."

Meanwhile the Tenth Corps had sent General v. Rheinbaben this order at 8 a.m.—

Orders by G.O.C. Tenth Army Corps to Rheinbaben.

"I send you herewith a report, the contents of which agree with other intelligence received, that the enemy's forces leaving Metz are on their retreat to Verdun.

"I request you to start at once for Fresnes en Woëvre in strength, and to try to bring the enemy to a halt.

"Thiaucourt will remain occupied by one regiment with carbines, as a supporting point.

"I have informed Army Head Quarters of these measures."

The report accompanying the above order is practically identical with the following important one, which the Tenth Corps sent to Army Head Quarters at 8 a.m. The contents of it originated from Lieutenant v. Willich, adjutant at Head

Aug. 15. Quarters of the Tenth Corps, who had reconnoitred towards Metz on the right bank, and reported from Corny at 6 a.m. (where he had a conversation with Captain v. Leipziger) as follows:—

Willich's report.

"Corny is occupied by a squadron of the 3rd Uhlans. Captain v. Leipziger states that a serious engagement took place yesterday afternoon east of Metz, etc. Rumbling of waggons has been heard since 1 o'clock last night. An officers' patrol, which nearly reached Gravelotte, struck the enemy's outposts there about 2 o'clock this morning,* and the officer heard the sound of troops moving in the direction of Verdun.

"A patrol was hotly fired on by a section of infantry north of Ancy at 5.30 a.m.

"The 3rd Uhlans are reconnoitring beyond Augny towards Metz.

"Signed: v. Willich." †

Captain v. Leipziger afterwards received special thanks from Prince Frederick Charles for his excellent reports on the 14th and 15th August. Later, when the order from Army Head Quarters arrived, the general commanding Tenth Army Corps issued his second disposition, 9.30 a.m., for the 15th, which supplemented the original order to General v. Rheinbaben, and said—

"The regiment left behind in Thiaucourt will be sent after him as soon as other troops come up. He will turn from Fresnes en Woëvre towards Metz, and will march along the Metz-Verdun road towards Metz till he gains a view of the situation. He will, on his left, seek to gain touch with the cavalry of the First Army."

* Forton's Reserve Cavalry Division.

† General of Cavalry v. Leipziger has told the author that on the evening of the 14th, and during the night to 15th August, a great number of reports had been sent by the squadron, which all spoke about the noise of heavy transport, and later on also of troops marching. Among these reports the one mentioned above was found almost verbatim.

General v. Bredow had received orders to start Aug. 15.
at 5 a.m. and march to Thiaucourt. The orders
were clear. It is plain from the direction ordered—
Fresnes en Woëvres—that the French were assumed
to be considerably further westwards than was
actually the case, an assumption which was not
justified according to the negative reports of the
14th. But the direction given to the general to
move from Fresnes en Woëvre towards Metz was,
in any case, bound to bring him in contact with the
enemy.

The measures taken by General v. Rhein- Measures by Rheinbaben.
baben are given in a despatch to Army Corps
Head Quarters, which arrived at 12.30 p.m.—

"Thiaucourt, 10 a.m.

" General v. Redern, with the two hussar regiments *
and the battery, has reached La Chaussée; the 4th
Cuirassiers, Dammartin.

" Captain Brauns, 17th Hussars, got beyond Latour
en Woëvre, and v. Knobelsdorf, 11th Hussars, beyond
Hannonville, without seeing anything of the enemy.

" The 19th Dragoons are to follow at once. I shall
remain behind to collect the squadrons detached to
Pagny and Flirey.

" A report has just arrived from the 4th Cuirassiers
that there is a French dragoon regiment at Puxieux.
Under these circumstances, I shall go forward myself to
take further measures."

The measures stated here show how faulty the Comments.
leadership of the division was, as unhappily it was
in other situations in the course of the campaign.
Instead of leading the division forward in person
with forces united, we see it completely split up
into squadrons, so that directly Redern's Brigade
(the nucleus of the troops moving against the
enemy) encountered the French, it numbered only
four squadrons and a horse battery, three of the

* He had orders to leave one regiment in Beney.

Aug. 15. 17th Hussars and one of the 11th Hussars, and the two advanced squadrons of the 11th Hussars soon joining them. Yet the general had eighteen squadrons at Thiaucourt at his immediate disposal. [See map, distribution of the 5th Cavalry Division, 9 a.m.]

Out of these squadrons, it is true, four had by Army Corps orders, to wait in Thiaucourt for the arrival of Bredow's Brigade, so that only fourteen squadrons could advance at once. The general's intention, however, to remain in Thiaucourt " in order to collect the squadrons detached to Flirey (1st and 2nd Squadrons 13th Uhlans) and Pagny " (4th Squadron 13th Uhlans) remains quite inexplicable.

General v. Rheinbaben had thirty-six squadrons and two batteries under his command, so it certainly was not his business to personally take charge of the bringing up of three squadrons. Nor is the order intelligible to leave a regiment in Beney, when the 19th Dragoons had been left behind to occupy Thiaucourt. This precautionary measure, in view of the general situation, and especially the fact that Bredow's Brigade had received orders to proceed at 5 a.m. from Pont à Mousson to Thiaucourt, eleven miles, seems entirely superfluous.

An advance on a broad front was certainly advisable, as one had to look for the enemy on the Metz-Verdun road, and expected to find them on the piece between Gravelotte and Fresnes en Woëvre. But there was therefore the more reason for keeping the bulk together, as it was highly probable that an engagement would occur, and the task " of bringing the enemy to a halt " could not be carried out without doing so.* From this point

---

* With reference to the criticism given here, I must draw special attention once more to what was said in the " Preface."

of view it would have been desirable for the general to have advanced with the squadrons he had on the spot against about the centre of the appointed line.

Aug. 15.

The right was the exposed flank. It was known from the information given by Army Corps Head Quarters that there were outposts of the enemy at Gravelotte.

If, therefore, special measures of protection were necessary on this side, from the fact of these outposts of the enemy being still reported in the morning, strong forces of the enemy could hardly be expected as yet on the other side.

On his right flank the general knew that there were two squadrons 11th Hussars, which had moved by Pagny and Les Baraques. Of course he could not tell exactly where they were at the moment. But if the other two squadrons of the regiment had been sent after them under their colonel, with the task of proceeding towards Rezonville on the right flank, sufficient measures would have been taken to secure this side.

On the left flank, officers' patrols to Fresnes en Woëvre, Harville, Suzemont, would have been sufficient, followed by a squadron as support, which could have moved by Woël.

With some such distribution of troops, the general could have had fifteen squadrons and twelve guns to lead forward together, and the co-operation of the 11th Hussars in any fight on the Metz-Verdun road, as well as the speedy arrival of Bredow's Brigade, could have been reckoned upon in addition.

Let us now look at the actual events as they can be ascertained from the sources available.

Redern's advance.

General v. Redern had orders, as we saw above, to advance with two regiments and Schirmer's

x

Aug. 15. horse battery in the first instance to La Chaussée, and from there he was to reconnoitre the Metz-Verdun road with strong detachments. He detailed the 10th Hussars to remain in Beney; they had only three squadrons, as Kleist's was still detached.

Starting at 5 a.m. in thick mist—it cleared at 7—and having reached La Chaussée, Brauns' squadron, 17th Hussars, was sent on Latour en Woëvre, and v. Knobelsdorff's, 11th Hussars, on Hannonville.

These squadrons had reported at 8.30 that the French were not marching on the Metz-Verdun road.* Immediately afterwards shots were heard in front, and reports announced that large bodies of French cavalry were on the march in the direction of Puxieux. As the 1st and 4th Squadrons of the 11th Hussars were at this time moving about on the plateau north of Gorze, the general had with him only the battery and three squadrons of the 17th Hussars and the 5th of the 11th. The 4th Cuirassiers had been directed on Dommartin to cover the right flank.

Vaerst's and Prince Salm's squadron.
Captain v. Vaerst, Prince Salm, and the 4th Squadron 11th Hussars had been ordered to reconnoitre towards Rezonville. They started at 5 a.m., and after an hour's ride struck four hostile cavalry regiments south of Rezonville; it was Forton's Reserve Cavalry Division, which was moving on Mars la Tour, and had the 1st Dragoons in advance.

General Prince Salm gave the author the following account of what occurred:—

* The regiment soon after had a waggon with saddlery, which had started from Chambley, and several lame horses, taken by a party of the enemy's cavalry, while the escort took to flight in the woods, and rejoined their squadron later. No other particulars are given.

"To deceive the enemy as to our strength, and aided by the mist, we formed our two squadrons into four of single rank, and sent word at once of our position, and of what we had seen, to Redern's Brigade, which we knew to be on the march by Beney and St. Benoit en Woëvre. The enemy's cavalry, which had with them, or brought up soon after, two batteries, formed to attack us. As soon as they were formed up and ready, we disappeared behind a hill, and appeared again on their flank. This manœuvre was repeated several times, to gain time and to deceive the enemy. They did not, however, make up their minds to attack. Meanwhile, our patrols were reconnoitring towards Metz, towards the Yron stream by Mars la Tour, and to the north."

<small>Aug. 15.</small>

Retiring gradually before the enemy's superior force, the squadrons succeeded in capturing nine scouts in the face of their regiment.* The French fired a great deal, but without effect. The action of the squadrons was particularly clever and bold; the deception of the single-rank formation could only be successful with the help of the mist, with an enemy so near. As events proved, the French horsemen displayed considerable dulness and little resolution.

Lieutenant v. Salis, of the 4th Squadron 11th Hussars, at this time proceeded to Bruville with a patrol, and had a separate skirmish with a patrol of the enemy.

A report from the Tenth Army Corps, which reached Army Head Quarters at 6 p.m., of the occurrence appears in their war records, and reads as follows:—

"Report of Lieutenant v. Salis.

"Place (?) Time (?)

"The squadron had camped at Chambley, and started at 7 a.m. (?) to the Metz-Verdun road, and

<small>Salis-Podbielski's report.</small>

---

* According to a report of the Tenth Army Corps to Army Head Quarters, arriving there at 6 p.m., four prisoners of the 1st Dragoons had been handed over to them.

Aug. 15.

towards Mars la Tour in particular. In Rezonville the squadron came under infantry fire. Lieutenant v. Salis' troop proceeded to Bruville, which was held by Mounted Jägers. On the Metz-Etain road he noticed infantry detachments halted, and cavalry patrols between them. Pressed by Chasseurs à Cheval, he retired on Mars la Tour, but now found that place also occupied. Both he and his horse were wounded here, while an officer of the enemy was struck from his horse, and his horse was brought along. He met the adjutant of the regiment south of Mars la Tour, who told him that one of the guns of the horse battery had lost five horses, as five of the enemy's batteries were engaging it.

"Certified correct,
"v. PODBIELSKI, Lieutenant."

Lieutenant v. Salis, while on patrol, had noticed near Mars la Tour a French officer riding fast. He at once rode off to him, and as he had a very fast horse, was soon beside him, far in front of his men.

He attacked him, bent his sword crooked (perhaps against a chain-mail shirt) trying to run him through; while the Frenchman fired six shots from his revolver, one of which wounded Lieutenant v. Salis in the right thigh, and another hit his horse in the neck. Meanwhile the rest of the party had come up, and a carbine bullet laid low the French officer Driant, a Lieutenant of Dragoons. French cavalry now threw themselves from all directions on the patrol, who narrowly escaped capture, and brought away the horse of their wounded officer. In Xonville Lieutenant v. Salis was placed in a waggon and sent on further. He met Lieutenant v. Podbielski, of the general staff of the Tenth Corps, and gave him the information repeated in the above report.

The Prussian squadrons gather

In Xonville the two hussar squadrons joined Redern's Brigade, which had without hesitation moved forward to meet the enemy. The French

CAVALRY ON SERVICE 309

1st Dragoons, which had gained a long distance in front of the division, now went back, and the whole of Forton's Division took up their position at Mars la Tour. The Prussian horse battery opened fire, which was replied to by the two horse batteries of the enemy. <small>Aug. 15. around Redern.</small>

The 4th Cuirassiers had received orders to start at dawn, march to Dommartin, bivouac there, and push detachments to reconnoitre along the Metz-Verdun road. The 4th Squadron was detailed for the latter duty. At 9.15 a.m. it reported that it had met the enemy and begged for support. The regiment moved out at once by Chambley to Puxieux. The 4th Squadron, meanwhile, had joined Redern's Brigade, so that general had seven squadrons at his disposal when his guns engaged the enemy's artillery. The Prussian battery is said to have fired 120 shots. After an hour's duel the superiority of the enemy's guns was so decisively proved that the Prussian squadrons retired behind Puxieux. The rest of the Cuirassier regiment and the remaining squadrons of Redern's Brigade—three squadrons 10th Hussars, which had hurried from Beney to the sound of the guns, and one squadron 11th Hussars—now appeared on the scene, so the cavalry under Redern totalled fifteen squadrons.

The regiments had, on their own initiative, partially made good the mistake of their divisional commander.

We will look at the situation on the enemy's side up to this point.

Forton's Reserve Cavalry Division had left their bivouac at 4.30 a.m. for Mars la Tour, where hostile cavalry had been reported. The first hostile squadrons which were encountered retired, and the 1st Dragoons, who were the advanced regiment, followed them up quickly. Colonel de Torceville <small>Action of the enemy.</small>

Aug. 15. reported the state of affairs to Prince Murat, his brigadier, who was following in second line with the 9th Dragoons, but he "ne suit avec le 9me dragons qu'avec une extrême lenteur"; * otherwise, according to the French accounts, a great success could have been gained.

The French followed the Prussian squadrons to beyond Puxieux, and then they saw Redern's Brigade coming up. The artillery duel began. Prince Murat sent an orderly back with a message. This man fell into an ambush of ten Cuirassiers, who pressed on him from out of a wood, "avec des cris de bêtes fauves," wounded him severely, and took his horse; but they were driven off by some dragoons, who killed two Prussians and wounded the officer.†

Meantime, General Forton had moved forward with the 7th and 10th Cuirassiers and two batteries on Mars la Tour, whence a party of Prussian hussars were making their exit, and extended his Cuirassier Brigade, just in front of the village, on the left of the road, followed by his battery and the Hussar Brigade.

Artillery fight.

At 10.30 the artillery engagement began, in which the French batteries fired thirty or forty rounds per gun, of which ten were shrapnel, and after a short time gained the upper hand. The Prussians retired, and Forton spent three hours with watering his horses at Mars la Tour.

This cannonade, lasting for hours, had no object. If a body of cavalry does not attack, the bringing up of the batteries is often a move to hide irresolution. At any rate, the firing had one good effect,

* According to Dick de Lonlay, compare p. 264.

† This can only refer to the skirmish which Lieutenant v. Salis' patrol had about this time with the French cavalry. The only important mistake in the French account occurs in the description of the Prussian unit.

as it summoned the Prussian squadrons, which hastened up with most praiseworthy zeal. {Aug. 15.}

General v. Redern, with his strength, as we have seen, increased to fifteen squadrons, decided to attack when the enemy's guns ceased firing, and his patrols had even reported the withdrawal of a part of their artillery to Metz. {Redern decides to attack.}

The 10th Hussars leading, an advance was made at a fast trot towards Mars la Tour. On the hills above the village the hussar scouts came under a hot fire from two of the enemy's squadrons, while the other French regiments had taken up a position at the eastern exit of the place. It was just 1.30 p.m. The horse battery unlimbered again to prepare for the attack, but the Divisional General, who had just arrived, forbade any further advance, because, as the official "History of the War" expresses it, "with the apparent superiority of the enemy it seemed to him to offer no hope of success." "Meanwhile," it continues, "the remaining regiments of Barby's Brigade assembled at Puxieux, and, half an hour later, Bredow's Brigade came in at Xonville, so that after 2 p.m. thirty-four Prussian squadrons and two horse batteries were available in the neighbourhood of Mars la Tour." The moment had arrived to bring off a great coup, and, in driving back the enemy's cavalry, to execute the reconnaissance which the army leaders so urgently required. However, the leader of these splendid and keen-spirited regiments failed; the Prussian cavalry went into bivouac after the enemy had retired to Vionville. {Rheinbaben's interference.}

General v. Rheinbaben sent the following despatch, received at Army Head Quarters at 6 p.m.:— {The 1 p.m. despatch.}

"Tronville, 1 p.m.

"Arrived at Tronville at noon with five regiments and one battery. Met the enemy's cavalry and a superior

Aug. 15.

force of artillery, which presently withdrew to Metz. The light cavalry is advancing closer to Metz. Bredow's Brigade will probably soon follow up. I propose to remain in Tronville, or in front of that place in the direction of Metz.

"Communication with the First Army not yet established."

The G.O.C. Tenth Army Corps, forwarding this despatch, added—

"The officer who brought this despatch thinks he heard infantry fire after he had left."

Comments on the number of both sides.

Major Kunz, in his account, has pointed out so forcibly that a great success could have been scored here, that I can omit any investigation, and shall only quote the following as the result of that admirable historian's researches—

"Soon after 2 p.m. thirty-four Prussian squadrons, comprising 4250 sabres, were concentrated. Opposite them stood General de Forton's fifteen squadrons of 1680 sabres. Perhaps an hour later ten squadrons of Du Barail's Reserve Cavalry Division, numbering 1200 sabres, could have joined in the fight, on the flank or possibly even in the rear of the Prussians. Half an hour later, again, fifteen squadrons of Valabrègue's Cavalry Division could have taken part in the fight with 1500 sabres. The Prussians numbered thirty-four squadrons of 4250 sabres, which were *concentrated*. They had opposed to them forty squadrons of 4380 sabres, *i.e.* only 130 sabres more. These 4380 sabres were, however, *not concentrated*, but originally only consisted of 1680 ; then, an hour later at the earliest, 1200 sabres more, and after a further half-hour 1500 sabres could hasten to support them."

If the excuse of "tired horses" is alleged as justification for this regrettable omission, it must be mentioned, on the one hand, that the enemy's

CAVALRY ON SERVICE

horses were by no means fresh; and on the other, that this is the invariable and time-worn excuse for the inaction of cavalry. Blücher's words may well be called to mind *à propos* of this—

Aug. 15.

"*No attention should be paid to the objections of the cavalry, for when such an object as the destruction of the whole of an enemy's army can be attained, the country can well spare the few hundred horses which may die of exhaustion.*"

The words of Blücher.

The fact was, that on the Prussian side the enemy's strength was not properly observed, and the constant clouds of fresh dust rising on the skyline from the approaching bodies of cavalry warned the Divisional General to consider the wisdom of an attack. The only means to be used here are patrols of very well-mounted officers, who must be placed at the disposal of the cavalry leader. In the high church tower of Mars la Tour, which they occupied, the French possessed an important point for a reconnaissance to a distance, and were more easily able to overlook the scene of action.*

Moreover, every attack undertaken on horseback involves a risk. Whoever avoids it will always find some excuse for not having made the attack.

If the Prussian leading failed here, that of the French was no better. I can only agree with a well-respected and authoritative French Service paper, *Journal des sciences militaires*, which points out that at the moment when de Forton's Division met General v. Redern's six squadrons, the earliest reinforcements for the German cavalry were ten miles off, Bredow's Brigade was nineteen miles off, and that therefore it would have been easy for the French cavalry "to clear up the dangerous mystery on the left flank."

Action of the French.

* The possession of a coign of vantage like this may be valuable even in the fight itself.

Aug. 15.

Since the French army was intended to march to the Maas, the important task for their cavalry lay on the left flank, from which direction alone their movement could be disturbed. Only through the faulty action of the French cavalry was it possible that the demonstration of General v. Rheinbaben had the result of checking the retreat of the French.

Reconnoitring means after all fighting.

General v. Rheinbaben, by his "demonstration"—it amounted to nothing more—had been successful in checking the retreat of the French, yet the mere presence of the totally inactive French cavalry hindered him from observing the French army and gaining information.

He should have considered his task fulfilled only after he had established contact with the enemy's forces of all three arms.

Reconnaissance after all means fighting, for which preparation must always be made, even in the dispositions made for the advance.* This principle was not then established in the minds of cavalry leaders. They had not been educated up to it. This must be taken into consideration in a subsequent criticism of events.

So the Prussian cavalry went into bivouac. Nothing had as yet been done in the way of reconnaissance. Let us see what arrangements were then made for the purpose.

General v. Rheinbaben first sent a message from Puxieux, 3 p.m., in which he stated that six regiments and three batteries had faced him, and he continues—

> "I am placing outposts west of the Dame wood,† the right wing pushed forward towards Puxieux, the

---

* It is hardly conceivable that even to-day well-known military authors—it is true they do not belong to the arm—have no clear conception of the importance of this requirement.

† The name—Bois de la Dame—is not on the map. The wood

left beyond the Metz-Verdun road. I am unable to advance further, because there is no water. I remain at Sponville."

Barby's Brigade bivouacked at Puxieux, Redern's at Xonville, Bredow's at Suzemont, facing Mars la Tour.

The 2nd and 3rd Squadron of the 19th Dragoons formed the outposts of Barby's Brigade. Scouts were sent forward close to Mars la Tour to watch the enemy.* Continuous firing went on. The bivouac of Barby's Brigade was made so unsafe by the long-range French carbines that it was shifted further back the same evening.

Redern's Brigade had posted v. Kotze's squadron (3rd) of the 10th Hussars on outpost at the Mariaville farm, three-quarters of a mile south-west of Mars la Tour.

Two officers' patrols, under Lieutenant v. Hirschfeld and Lieutenant of Reserve Dietze, went forward from here at 5 p.m. They found Mars la Tour and Puxieux unoccupied, but observed bodies of the enemy's troops on the heights west of Rezonville, who were busy cooking. Their strength was estimated at 20,000 men. The report, according to the information to hand, never reached either the Tenth Army Corps or the Head Quarters of the Second Army. Where it got to cannot be discovered. It must be taken for granted that if this report had reached the division it would have

margin: Aug. 15.

margin: Captain Kotze's report.

which had stood west of Puxieux, and which was still marked on the ordnance map, by which Rheinbaben made his dispositions, had been already cut down by 1870.

* Bonie in his "Campaign of 1870, La Cavalerie Française," says: "The enemy always kept touch with us by a cloud of scouts; and followed our smallest movements." An honourable proof that the troops did their duty. The disposition of the bivouac so close to the enemy was most unnecessary. Troops that are resting should always camp at a reasonable distance from the enemy. There are other means than this of keeping contact.

316   CAVALRY ON SERVICE

Aug. 15. given occasion for further reconnaissance, and that a more accurate estimate of the enemy would then have been formed.

Opinions of Head Quarters' Second Army. This report was not calculated by itself to shake the assumption at Army Head Quarters, which had been further strengthened by Groeben's and Hessberg's reports, and the events of the 14th, that the French, under cover of darkness, were in hurried retreat on the three roads leading to the west. It could not be anticipated that the staff arrangements of the French for passing through Metz and for crossing the Mosel would be so faulty that most vexatious delays would occur, or, on the other hand, that the Commander-in-Chief would renounce the use of the third, the most northern road. It was quite clear why Prince Frederick Charles had demanded all haste, for the army before reaching the enemy had to effect another crossing and climb a steep ascent. Those 20,000 men, which had been reported, might well form a strong rearguard, which, starting early on the 16th, could hardly be overtaken this day by an equal force of the Second Army.

Rheinbaben's 1 p.m. despatch, the only one of the reports referring to the hostile forces between Metz and Verdun, which had reached Army Head Quarters on the 15th, might on closer consideration have led to the view that that body of cavalry was an advance guard, but not the expected rear guard. Even then it was not so forcible as to be calculated to change the previous and apparently deep-rooted opinions to the exact opposite.

1st Squadron 16th Uhlans tries to gain touch Thus far no measures were taken to gain touch with the cavalry of the First Army. It was only natural that no detachments would be made as long as the enemy's cavalry were still in front of them.

Men cannot reconnoitre as long as they have to fight.

Aug. 15, with the First Army.

Captain v. Wulffen, with 1st Squadron 16th Uhlans, was now detailed by General v. Bredow

> "to advance by Mars la Tour to Jarny, and from there to seek for the cavalry of the First Army by means of patrols."

The squadron trotted without stopping to the wood, which begins a mile south of Jarny, and the advance troop scouted through it. The troop then went on to Jarny, passed through, and turned to the right on the road to Metz, while a foraging party, of one N.C.O. and eight men, went off to a farm in the wood.

When the squadron had passed the wood the leader discovered on some low ground to his right a bivouac of the enemy, which he estimated at one battalion and two squadrons (in point of fact the transport of Du Barail's Reserve Cavalry Division and two squadrons of African Jägers were camped there).

At the same moment the advanced troop, which was led by a young officer of the reserve, suddenly struck the enemy's outposts, which received him with a hot fire. After passing the wood, the troop must have ridden on without taking necessary precautions, otherwise this surprise could not have occurred.

Skirmish at Jarny.

Captain v. Wulffen turned off to the Yron brook, and directed Lieutenant Freytag, the leader of the advance guard troop, to follow. He dashed back, pursued by the African Jägers, and in passing through Jarny was attacked by the inhabitants, who not only opened fire, but even tried to seize their horses by the bridle. The foraging party was surprised by a company of infantry; at their

Aug. 15. approach the farmer had quickly closed the gate, and the Uhlans only opened it by riding at it at a gallop. The squadron came out of it all right, although they had to cross the Yron brook by a small stone bridge in single file. Going across country they reached Hannonville, watered there, and rejoined their regiment at 9 p.m. The losses amounted to four men killed, nine men and eighteen horses missing.

Comments. The cause of the disaster must be attributed to the careless reconnaissance of the advanced guard troop, the charge of which, as it seems, had unfortunately been entrusted to an entirely inexperienced officer, and to the insufficient measures of protection of the foraging party, who let themselves be shut up in the farm by the peasant. One cannot judge now whether Lieutenant Freytag was compelled to retire through Jarny. If it is questionable for small parties in the enemy's country, under conditions such as these, to pass through inhabited villages when going, it is, of course, still more risky to do so on their return journey, when pursued by the enemy.

To carry out this important duty under the conditions that prevailed, one squadron does not seem sufficient; a whole regiment should have been detailed for it.

Important news from a traveller. When at 7 p.m. the 1st Squadron had not rejoined the regiment, the 2nd Squadron were ordered to proceed to Tronville and support the 1st Squadron on their return march. The squadron, v. Porembsky's, reached a point north of Tronville, and from there patrols were sent to Tronville, Vionville, and into the Tronville coppice. The coppice was clear, but the patrols were fired on from the Tronville-Vionville road; there was also much movement on this road, and alarm signals

CAVALRY ON SERVICE 319

were heard in Vionville and the villages that lay beyond. Aug. 15.

It had by now grown too dark for any personal observation, and by chance the patrols captured a travelling artisan coming from Metz, who was on his way to Verdun.

On being questioned, he stated that "all the places between Metz and Vionville were crowded with troops; at least 100,000 men were said to be there. Napoleon had been in Metz that evening, but he thought that he had gone away from the army. Bazaine was in Gravelotte." According to the regimental history, the man was sent back to the brigadier. Strange to say, there is no criticism or mention of the affair either in the official accounts or in the description of the events of the day.

Where did this man go to? He brought the most valuable intelligence of the whole day, which completely cleared up the situation.

I have taken pains to make further investigations, and, through the 16th Uhlans, was most kindly provided with this information by the squadron leader of the time, now Lieut.-Colonel on the retired list. The report is being lost.

Herr v. Porembsky writes as follows:—

> "The account in the regimental history of the travelling artisan is quite correct. On the evening of the 15th he was taken by my squadron during a reconnaissance from the bivouac towards Vionville.
>
> "I was astonished to find in the official "History of the War" that the strength of the French army was still unknown on the 16th, in spite of the statement of the artisan. The importance attached by me to the statement is shown by the fact that after my first examination of the man I called up a N.C.O. of the squadron, whom I directed to take charge of him, and made the man repeat the whole statement. It was impossible to write in the open, as it was dark. The artisan, who I

Aug. 15.
think was a shoemaker, said that, as the whole French army was going to Verdun the next day, he would find no more work in Metz, and wanted to look for some in Verdun. He was a German. The whole French army, under Marshal Bazaine, were encamped between Metz and Vionville. Napoleon had been in Metz till early in the morning (August 15), but the artisan had heard he was to have left Metz that morning to go to Verdun. I sent the N.C.O. with the prisoner back into bivouac to the regiment, and they sent him on, as they said. I specially impressed upon the N.C.O. that the report was important."

Comments.
There is no doubt that the man disappeared, perhaps while on his way to the regiment. It can well be imagined that in the darkness he evaded the N.C.O. who was escorting him, as the affair must have seemed to him serious or at least unpleasant. Herr v. Porembsky does not appear to have received any chit from the N.C.O., and the latter, feeling guilty, may have held his tongue. The stupendous events of the next day have buried the matter in oblivion.

There are several lessons to be learnt from this affair.

1. The man's statement ought at once to have been taken down in writing by the captain. If it was dark, the squadron surely had a lantern with them, which ought to form part of the field equipment of every officer, as the means of writing despatches after dark should certainly be always handy. The escort would have to hand over the written statement together with the man, so that it could be compared with any later statement of his.

2. The N.C.O. should have been accompanied by a Uhlan, especially if it was already dark.

3. Measures should have been taken to prevent the man's escape. If he walked loose by the side

of the N.C.O.'s horse, a leap into the bushes or over a ditch was all he had to do to escape in the darkness. Precaution is often necessary even with people who are apparently inclined to be friendly, and especially when the matter is as important as in this case.

<small>Aug. 15.</small>

General v. Rheinbaben sent the following reports to the G.O.C. Tenth Army Corps on the afternoon and evening of the 15th:—

<small>Rheinbaben's further despatches.</small>

> "According to a report just received, infantry are advancing in the direction of Tronville-Puxieux. It would be most desirable to send infantry from Thiaucourt towards Dommartin. A reconnaissance has shown that the enemy's vedettes are at Vionville, and that a large camp of all arms is somewhere near Rezonville.*
> "Xonville. 15. viii. 70—5 p.m.
> "Sd.   v. RHEINBABEN.
> "Received 15. viii. 70—5.30 p.m."

Details as to strength are wanting in the despatch. As the camp had been discovered, further details should have been ascertained by every possible means.

> "Evening. Mars la Tour is occupied by us. A squadron has been sent to Jarny, to gain touch with the First Army. According to Rosenberg's report, there are hostile infantry and artillery at Ancy. I beg for some artillery and a field hospital. There is apparently no enemy visible on the line from Metz." (?)

---

* The news of the enemy in the foregoing despatch is the result of a personal reconnaissance by Captain v. Heister, general staff officer to the division. He had ridden forward accompanied by an orderly, south of the main road, on Vionville, at the conclusion of the artillery engagement, and after the retirement of the French cavalry; and, halting north-east of and beyond Tronville, had discovered behind the cavalry division the camp of a large corps of the enemy. When he reached a squadron of the 19th Dragoons halted under cover on the further side of Tronville, he was informed by their colonel that a man had been hit by a rifle bullet at long range, and that the squadron was therefore to withdraw further back. [Information given by General of Cavalry (retired) v. Heister, see p. 315.]

Aug. 15.

"Xonville, 7.45 p.m. Have tried to gain touch with the First Corps, but hostile squadrons and an infantry battalion were met with. The outposts are being constantly fired on by infantry, so I intend, if necessary, to retire in the direction of Verdun."*

Lyncker's detachment.

The Tenth Army Corps, as we know, had received instructions to push its infantry divisions forward on the 15th into the Mosel valley, and towards the north-west, to support the 5th Cavalry Division.

In accordance with these instructions, Lehmann's Brigade—four battalions, 4th Squadron of the 9th Dragoons, and one battery—and later on the rest of the 19th Division, had been directed on Thiaucourt. Further, a detachment under Colonel v. Lyncker, consisting of two infantry battalions, 1st, 2nd, and 3rd squadrons 9th Dragoons, and one battery, were sent down the Mosel valley to Novéant.

The 3rd Squadron of the 9th Dragoons patrolled actively down-stream, being constantly fired on by the inhabitants of the villages which lay in the hills.

Colonel v. Lyncker reported at 7.45 p.m. from Novéant his arrival there, and that he was sending a larger reconnoitring party by Ancy to Ars. He also forwarded the following report:—

"Report of Captain v. Blumenthal.

"A schoolmaster, just met with on the road from Metz, states that the French army, 50,000 strong,

* We see that the transport of Du Barail's Cavalry Division gradually increases to a corps. It is a well-known fact that detachments which have suffered a blow, like the 1st Squadron of the 16th Uhlans, are inclined to exaggerate the strength of the enemy.

The firing emanated evidently not from infantry, but from the long-range carbines of the French cavalry. As regards the choice of a bivouac, see p. 315. According to the despatch of the Tenth Army Corps on the battle of the 16th, this report did not reach the G.O.C. till early on the 16th, at Woël, while riding to the battlefield [a further proof of faulty staff work], but it caused the general to turn northwards at once to get nearer the scene of action.

marched out of Metz at 6 p.m. last night, *viâ* Longeville, Moulins, St. Ruffine, the Route impériale, Gravelotte, Rezonville, Vionville, Mars la Tour. He has been arrested, and is handed over herewith."

Aug. 15.

Colonel v. Lyncker sent the man on to the 19th Division, and at 10 p.m. sent a further report thither—

"The two troops of Major v. Studnitz's squadron have advanced to Vaux, on the left bank of the Mosel, and have observed the French troops marching away from Metz, past Moulins, on the Verdun road. French infantry patrols appeared at Jussy."

Major v. Studnitz was wounded on this occasion.

Colonel v. Lyncker, in the 7.45 p.m. report, had also stated that portions of the Third Army Corps from Corny were moving towards Metz, a battalion of the Leib-Regiment was quartered in Dornot; and he added, " Under these circumstances the detachment is unnecessary, and begs for employment elsewhere." An hour later the colonel reported from Novéant that the 5th Division was crossing the Mosel, and was going into bivouac round his cantonments. In the margin of the 10 p.m. report, quoted above, is the pencil note—

Brm. s. p. r. Referred to Army Corps Head Quarters Staff for decision (*vide* enclosed).

Thiaucourt. " 16. viii. 70—1 a.m.
 " By order : v. Scherff, Major."

All the above reports were therefore transmitted simultaneously, and the first and most important one was thus much delayed. They are in the records of the Tenth Army Corps, but there is nothing to show that they were forwarded to the Army Head Quarters.

The Guard Cavalry Division was moving in a

Aug. 15.

Guard-Uhlan Brigade.

more westerly direction on the left flank of the Second Army.

The Brigade of Guard Uhlans, hurrying on in front of the Guard Corps, had reached Mesnil la Tour on the morning of the 15th. Captain v. Platow commanding 1st Squadron of the 1st Guard Uhlans, received instructions there

> "to advance at once to Commercy and reconnoitre it, to gain touch with the Guard Dragoon Brigade at Beaumont, to procure information about the passages of the Maas and the railway at Foug, and, lastly, to requisition in Commercy 10,000 kilos of oats and 8000 kilos of bread."

The squadron carried out its task fully. The railway and telegraph were destroyed. The French had evacuated Commercy, and only a few much-exhausted 4th Cuirassiers were found there. Touch with the Guard Dragoon Brigade could not be established, as they were no longer in the neighbourhood of Beaumont.

The 2nd Squadron of the 3rd Guard Uhlans, under Captain v. Rosen, were given a special duty at Mesnil la Tour

> "to reconnoitre the fortress of Toul and the railways leading thence to Nancy and Commercy."

The reconnaissance was carried out right to the very walls, in spite of a hot fire from the fortress, and Lieutenant Prince Hohenlohe was sent in with a flag of truce. He was fired on, and received an answer from the commandant that he awaited a regular siege.

Lieutenant v. Strantz meanwhile destroyed the telegraph on the Toul-Commercy railway line; and Lieutenant Graf Rantzau did the same on the Toul-Nancy line.

The Guard Dragoon Brigade had arrived west

CAVALRY ON SERVICE 325

of Beaumont, and put outposts out towards St. Mihiel and Commercy, when orders arrived to march at once to Thiaucourt. The dragoons arrived there at 4 p.m. Furthest away on the left flank, v. Kleist's squadron of 10th Hussars was still engaged.

When the 4th Cavalry Division arrived in Nancy on the 14th, the squadron went to St. Nicholas that same day, and crossed the bridge at Pont St. Vincent on the 15th.

As regards the movements of the enemy, the following remarks are made to supplement the map:—

Aug. 15.

Movements of the French.

The 3rd Corps had continued its march west. Montaudon's Division camped at 7 p.m. south of Amanweiler; Metmann, after a long night march, at Plappeville at 7 a.m.; Castagny, at Verneville at midnight. Aymard had reached Devant les Ponts at 2 a.m., continued the march at 3 p.m., but could not proceed owing to the block on the road, and bivouacked at Ban St. Martin. The cavalry camped close to the left bank of the Mosel, and under the ramparts, part during the night awaiting the order to advance with their hands on the bridle, part trying to move forward; but they made little progress.

Of the 4th Corps, which had also been on the march during the night, Cissey's and Grenier's Divisions reached the neighbourhood of Woippy; Lorencez reached Lorry, and the cavalry Woippy early in the morning.

The 2nd Corps reached Gravelotte. Valabrègue's Cavalry Division had started at 7 a.m. When its head passed through Rezonville the report arrived that Forton's Division was seriously engaged. When Valabrègue, hurrying forward, reached the first houses of Vionville, he learned that the action

Aug. 15. had finished, and so he went into bivouac there. The infantry of that corps, hearing the sound of guns, had prepared for action, and made some advance on Vionville.

Tixier's Division of the 6th Corps reached Longeville les Metz at 6 a.m., as we saw, when they were greeted by the shells from Groeben's detachment. They marched on at 8 a.m., and camped at 11 p.m. at St. Marcel. The 9th Line Regiment, the only one of Bisson's Division which had joined the corps, reached Rezonville at 5 p.m. La Font's Division camped in the evening 4000 yards in front of Gravelotte on the Vionville side, and Levassor's camped at 4.30 p.m. in front of Gravelotte towards the Bois des Ognons.

Of the Guard, Deligny's Division had camped in the morning near Tixier's Division at Longeville, and reached their camp between St. Hubert and Point du Jour at 2 p.m. Picard camped at Gravelotte; so did the Guard Cavalry, whose advanced parties had left Ban St. Martin at 2 p.m., and reached the plateau of Gravelotte towards 7 p.m.

The experiences of Forton's Cavalry Division have already been spoken of. They camped for the night at Vionville, with their outposts facing Trouville and Mars la Tour. Dick de Lonlay asserts that in consequence of the day's events the divisions were "in high spirits."

Du Barail's Cavalry Division had just arrived at Jarny, when Forton's request for support reached it. Leaving the baggage under the protection of two squadrons of Mounted Jägers at Jarny, the division turned southwards at once, and formed for attack near La Grange farm. The action was already over when Du Barail arrived, so he moved by Jarny, where the skirmish with the 16th Uhlans' 1st

Squadron had meantime occurred—out of this the French concocted a great story, " de toute cette escadron allemande il ne s'échappent que trois hommes "—and camped for the night at Doncourt.

Aug. 15.

If we look back at the service of reconnaissance of the German cavalry on the memorable August 15, we reach the conclusion that, apart from the failure of the 5th Cavalry Division to attack, they did all that could be expected. If the information sent in from the right and from the left is all pieced together, it will give a clear impression of the enemy's situation.

Review of Aug. 15.

The First Army ascertained that the enemy had abandoned the ground immediately east of the fortress. The 6th Cavalry Division gave similar information with regard to the south side, and accounts in general pointed to the march of the enemy to the west.

The 5th Cavalry Division and the 9th Dragoons confirmed the latter intelligence, as they separately reported a large camp of troops of all arms, and the appearance of 20,000, 50,000, and 100,000 men on the plateau west of Metz. From this the conclusion could be drawn that the Second Army could overtake the main portion of the enemy's forces on the very next day; only the smaller portion could perhaps have turned off along the two northern roads.

Even this doubt could have been set at rest if the 3rd Cavalry Division, in accordance with orders from Royal Head Quarters, had sent detachments across the Mosel.

The Guard Cavalry had made it certain that no troops of any importance had retired to the line of the Maas, St. Mihiel-Commercy.

If the results of the reconnaissances had only come to the knowledge of the commander of the

Aug. 15. Second Army on that same day, all doubts on the situation would have been settled, and a clear insight would have been gained. The enemy would not have been supposed to be far to the west, or even in part already *on* the Maas, as appears from the order dated Pont à Mousson, 7 p.m., for the 16th. This states that the idea was that only moderately strong bodies of the enemy—his rearguards—would be encountered on the southern road to Verdun, and that arrangements would have to be made to "follow him" across the Maas.

We have seen, however, that not one of the most important reports, even v. Kotze's, reached Army Head Quarters on the 15th. Whether the news came in before or after the issue of orders at 7 p.m. would not have mattered much, so long as they arrived early enough in the night for alterations in the orders to reach the units they referred to.*

This occurrence, which is of the most far-reaching significance, leads us to the following conclusions :—

---

* We have already shown (p. 279) on August 14 that the 6th Cavalry Division was unfortunate enough to have its reports considered as valueless by Head Quarters of Third Army Corps. This prejudice, which can only be explained by the preconceived notions about the enemy's measures, had not yet vanished in that quarter on the 15th ; this is proved by the following incident, which happened to Captain v. Leipziger at the bridge of Corny. General v. Leipziger gives the following notes on it :—

"On the 15th, when the Head Quarter Staff of the Third Army Corps crossed the Mosel bridge, I reported myself to General v. Alvensleben, who did not know me personally. Major v. Kretschmann, of the General Staff, called the G.O.C.'s attention to the fact that I was the captain who had constantly reported about the departure of the French in a westerly direction. General v. Alvensleben thereupon addressed a few words to me, from which I gathered that he had attached no value to these reports, and he then rode on. It was only on August 17, at a review of the troops by H.M. the King, that I heard from Prince Frederick Charles that these reports had contributed very much to throw light on the situation at Royal Head Quarters."

It is, of course, sad for the cavalry, if all its efforts meet with so little confidence as they met with at the Head Quarters of the Third Army Corps. The recognition of this must naturally end in the killing of all enterprise.

1. The reconnoitring cavalry must transmit their information *as early as possible*, if it is to be made use of on the next day in the operations of a large army. It follows that cavalry must not only observe, but, under the circumstances, observe quickly. This may sometimes be the reason for resolving to attack. If General v. Rheinbaben had attacked on the 15th, the news (which gathered subsequently by patrols never reached Head Quarters) would have been received early enough for them to be made use of on the next day.

2. The arrangements for the speedy transmission of reports must be most carefully prepared; to that end all possible means must, in certain cases, be designedly employed. The course of events, as well as the official accounts, prove that arrangements were not satisfactorily made on the 15th; that important despatches were, some of them, entirely lost, or remained unduly long in the hands of the intermediate authorities. The field telegraph, bicycles, and other means give us nowadays additional material for organizing the service more effectually. It is only a question, therefore, of making the proper arrangements. That these do not always come into existence of themselves is shown by the events we have described.

APPENDIX I

DISPOSITION OF THE CAVALRY OF THE FIRST AND SECOND GERMAN ARMIES IN THE WAR OF 1870–71.

First Army.

DIVISIONAL CAVALRY.
  Seventh Army Corps:
    13th Division—8th Hussars: Lt.-Col. Arendt.
    14th Division—15th Hussars: Col. v. Cosel.
  Eighth Army Corps:
    15th Division—7th Hussars: Col. Baron v. Loë.
    16th Division—9th Hussars: Col. v. Wittich.
  First Army Corps:
    1st Division—1st Dragoons: Lt.-Col. v. Massow.
    2nd Division—10th Dragoons: Col. Baron v. der Goltz.

CAVALRY DIVISIONS.
  First Cavalry Division: Lt.-Gen. v. Hartmann.
    Officer of General Staff: Major v. Saldern.
      Adjutants: Capt. Baron v. Eichstedt-Peterswaldt.
      Lieut. Graf zu Eulenburg.
  1st Cavalry Brigade: Major-Gen. v. Lüderitz.
    Adjutant: Lieut. v. Jerin.
    2nd Cuirassiers: Col. v. Pfuhl.
    4th Uhlans: Lt.-Col. v. Radecke.
    9th Uhlans: Lt.-Col. v. Kleist.
  2nd Cavalry Brigade: Major-Gen. Baumgarth.
    Adjutant: Lieut. Dallmer.
    3rd Cuirassiers: Col. v. Winterfeld.
    8th Uhlans: Col. v. Below.
    12th Uhlans: Lt.-Col. v. Rosenberg.
    1 Battery R.H.A.: Capt. v. Selle.
      (24 squadrons.)

APPENDIX

Third Cavalry Division: Lt.-Gen. Graf v. der Groeben.
    Officer of General Staff: Capt. Graf v. Wedel.
    Adjutants: Capt. Baron v. Rosenberg.
        Lieut. v. Klüber.
    6th Cavalry Brigade: Major-Gen. Mirus.
        Adjutant: Lieut. v. Meyerfeld.
        8th Cuirassiers: Col. Graf v. Roedern.
        7th Uhlans: Lt.-Col. v. Pestel.
    7th Cavalry Brigade: Major-Gen. Graf Dohna.
        Adjutant: Lieut. v. Holtzenbecher.
        5th Uhlans: Lt.-Col. v. Reitzenstein.
        14th Uhlans: Col. v. Lüderitz.
        Battery R.H.A.: Capt. Schrader.
        (16 squadrons.)

SECOND ARMY.

DIVISIONAL CAVALRY.
  Guard Corps:
    1st Guard Infantry Division—Guard Hussars: Lt.-Col. v. Hymmen.
    2nd Guard Infantry Division—2nd Guard Uhlans: Col. H.H. Prince Henry of Hesse und bei Rhein.
  Third Army Corps:
    5th Division—12th Dragoons: Col. Pfeffer v. Salomon.
    6th Division—2nd Dragoons: Col. v. Drygalski.
  Fourth Army Corps:
    7th Division—7th Dragoons: Col. Baron v. Schleinitz.
    8th Division—12th Hussars: Lt.-Col. v. Suckow.
  Ninth Army Corps:
    18th Division—6th Dragoons: Lt.-Col. Baron v. Houwald.
    25th (Hessian) Division—25th Cavalry Brigade: Major-Gen. Baron v. Schlotheim.
        Adjutant: Lt.-Col. Baron v. Gemmingen-Hornberg.
        1st Reiter Regiment: Col. v. Grolman.
        2nd Reiter Regiment: Major Baron v. Buseck.
  Tenth Army Corps:
    19th Division—9th Dragoons: Lt.-Col. Graf v. Hardenberg.
    20th Division—16th Dragoons: Col. v. Waldow.

APPENDIX

Twelfth Army Corps (Royal Saxon):
  23rd Division—1st Reiter Regiment: Col. v. Sahr.
  24th Division—2nd Reiter Regiment: Major Genthe.

CAVALRY DIVISIONS.
  Guard Cavalry Division: Lt.-Gen. Graf v. der Goltz.
    General Staff Officer: Major v. Ostau.
    Adjutants: Major v. Saldern-Ahlimb.
              Lieut. v. Britzke.
    1st Guard Cavalry Brigade: Major-Gen. Graf v. Brandenburg (I).
      Gardes du Corps: Col. v. Krosigk.
      Guard Cuirassiers: Col. Baron v. Brandenstein.
    2nd Guard Cavalry Brigade: Lt.-Gen. H.R.H. Prince Albrecht of Prussia.
      Adjutant: Lieut. Graf zu Eulenburg.
      1st Guard Uhlans: Col. v. Rochow.
      3rd Guard Uhlans: Col. Prince Frederick William zu Hohenlohe-Ingelfingen.
    3rd Guard Cavalry Brigade: Lt.-Gen. Graf v. Brandenburg (II.).
      Adjutant: Lieut. v. der Schulenburg.
      1st Guard Dragoons: Col. v. Auerswald.
      2nd Guard Dragoons: Col. Graf. v. Finkenstein.
      (24 squadrons.)
  Fifth Cavalry Division: Lt.-Gen. Baron v. Rheinbaben.
    Officer of General Staff: Capt. v. Heister.
    Adjutants: Capt. v. dem Knesebeck.
              Lieut. Graf v. Plettenberg-Lenhausen.
    11th Cavalry Brigade: Major-Gen. v. Barby.
      Adjutant: Lieut. v. Marschall.
      4th Cuirassiers: Col. v. Arnim.
      13th Uhlans: Col. v. Schack.
      19th Dragoons: Col. v. Trotha.
    12th Cavalry Brigade: Major-Genl. v. Bredow.
      Adjutant: Lieut. v. Klitzing.
      7th Cuirassiers: Lt.-Col. v. Larisch.
      16th Uhlans: Major v. der Dollen.
      13th Dragoons: Col. v. Brauchitsch.
    13th Cavalry Brigade: Major-Gen. v. Redern.
      Adjutant: Lieut. v. Goetz.

APPENDIX

10th Hussars : Colonel v. Weise.
11th Hussars : Lt.-Col. Baron v. Eller-Eberstein.
17th Hussars : Lt.-Col. v. Rauch.
1 Battery R.H.A. : Capt. Bode.
1 Battery R.H.A. : Capt. Schirmer.
(36 squadrons.)

Sixth Cavalry Division : Major-Gen. H.H. Duke William of Mecklenburg-Schwerin.
Officer of General Staff : Major v. Schoenfels.
Adjutants : Capt. v. Treskow.
Lieut. v. Usedom.
14th Cavalry Brigade : Major-Gen. Baron v. Diepenbroick-Grüter.
Adjutant : Lieut. von und zu Schachten.
6th Cuirassiers : Lt.-Col. Graf zu Lynar.
3rd Uhlans ; Col. Graf v. der Groeben.
15th Uhlans : Col. v. Alvensleben.
15th Cavalry Brigade : Major-Gen. v. Rauch.
Adjutant : Graf Ross.
3rd Hussars : Col. v. Zieten.
16th Hussars : Col. v. Schmidt.
1 Battery R.H.A. : Capt. Wittstock.
(20 squadrons.)

Twelfth Cavalry Division : Major-Gen. Graf. zur Lippe.
General Staff Officers : Capt. Reyher.
Capt. v. Kirchbach.
Adjutant : Lieut. v. Koenneritz.
23rd Cavalry Brigade : Major-Gen. Krug v. Nidda.
Adjutant : Lieut. v. Boxberg.
Guard Reiter Regiment : Col. v. Carlowitz.
17th Uhlans : Col. v. Miltitz.
24th Cavalry Brigade : Major-Gen. Senfft v. Pilsach.
Adjutant : Lieut. v. Hönning O'Caroll.
3rd Reiter Regiment : Col. v. Standfest.
18th Uhlans : Lt.-Col. v. Trosky.
1 Battery R.H.A. ; Capt. Zenker.
(16 squadrons.)

APPENDIX II

Examples of a Few Schemes

which may help to a further study of the duties of cavalry on the basis of the accounts and criticisms given in the book.

The following examples pick up the thread of the situation as it was at the moment generally, but here and there, though based on it, certain assumptions are made which change it a little.

Problems, set thus, will be productive of more proper views on war than those which are founded on pure invention, and they have the additional advantage of promoting the study of military history, and of making that study more useful.

The reader will soon recognize that the following examples are far from exhausting the use that can be made of these historical events; the schemes can be multiplied indefinitely, and continued on the groundwork of the original data.

In case the attached ordnance and other maps, which take in the whole country under discussion, are not sufficient to solve the problems, the sections, "Saarbrücken," "Metz," "Pfalzburg," and "Nancy," of Reimann's map are recommended for use.* The map in the official "History of the War"—"Environs of Metz"—is also recommended.

Problem I. For August 6.

(*Reconnaissance.*)

The 3rd Cavalry Division is concentrating at Lebach on the morning of August 6. At 8 a.m. the following order arrives there from Head Quarters of the First Army :—

* One shilling each.

"Tholey, August 6, 6 a.m.

"The enemy appears to have resigned the offensive at Saarbrücken, and the town is clear. According to a report from the commandant of Saarlouis, his outposts are in touch with the enemy on the line, Ueberherrn-Ittersdorf. A strong body of enemy's cavalry is reported at Sierck.* Large hostile bodies are said to be concentrating in the vicinity of Busendorf, Tromborn, and St. Avold.

"I request you to cross the Saar to-day and reconnoitre towards the line Busendorf-St. Avold, protecting the right flank of the army.

"(Sd.) v. STEINMETZ."

(1) As G.O.C. 3rd Cavalry Division, appreciate the situation, with regard to the tasks, which might devolve on the division in the next few days.

(2) Outline the orders for the division on the morning of August 6.

(3) When the main body of the division at 11 a.m. is on the point of crossing the river at Saarlouis, the thunder of guns is heard, from the direction of Saarbrücken, which soon grows heavier. During the advance, the report had already come in to the G.O.C. from the advanced patrols that the enemy's outposts are no longer at Ittersdorf, and that unmistakable signs pointed to their departure in the direction of Busendorf. Give the decisions arrived at by the G.O.C.

A further problem can be made out, based on the destination reached by the 3rd Cavalry Division on August 6, and the results of the battle of Spicheren.

I will not make it out here, in order not to anticipate the resolutions to be arrived at for the solution of the previous problem.

PROBLEM II. FOR AUGUST 7.

(*Reconnaissance.*)

The commander of the 3rd Cavalry Division, which is concentrated at Saarwellingen on August 6, had received information of the successful issue of the battle of Spicheren that evening. (See map for that day.) He had been informed of the situation to his immediate front by the report of Lieutenant v. Ramin [*vide* pp. 9–12], and had got news of the enemy at St. Avold (p. 12, *et*

---

* Twenty miles N.W. of Saarlouis.

APPENDIX

seq.) from Captain v. Hymmen, who (as is assumed) had met the 1st and 2nd Squadrons of the 19th Dragoons returning from the reconnaissance on St. Avold. He had also learnt from the commandant of Saarlouis that Sierck was once more clear of the enemy, who had moved off southwards.

(1) As G.O.C. division, appreciate the situation, and give his views concerning his task on the extreme right wing of the German army.

(2) The Head Quarter Staff of the First Army had added to the telegram reporting the result of the battle the instructions—

"Information of the enemy's disposition on the line Busendorf-St. Avold is urgently required."

(3) Outline the divisional orders for August 7.

PROBLEM III. FOR AUGUST 7.

(Pursuit and reconnaissance.)

The commander of the 6th Cavalry Division reached the Exerzir-Platz at Saarbrücken at 4 a.m. on the 7th, with Grüter's Brigade, and found his division concentrated there.

The Commander-in-Chief of the First Army placed three squadrons—one from the 8th, 9th, and 15th Hussars respectively—and a horse battery at his disposal, and requested him to take up the pursuit of the enemy, to ascertain his line of retreat, and in particular to clear up the situation at St. Avold.

He was informed at the same time that the 5th Cavalry Division was being employed in a southerly direction towards the Blies.

Give an outline of divisional orders.

PROBLEM IV. FOR AUGUST 7.

(A critical moment in the pursuit.)

The 6th Cavalry Division had reached the neighbourhood of Kochern in its pursuit, through Forbach, at 11 a.m. on August 7; and is halted in column of regiments between there and Thedingen.

The battery in action at the railway station is shelling a supply column under strong escort on its way to St.

Avold, *via* Merlenbach, which is held by the enemy's infantry.

The Zieten Hussars (15th Cavalry Brigade) have been pushed forward to Pfarrebersweiler, and have sent one squadron to Dieblingen. The regiment reports the advance of a strong force of the enemy from Genweiler and Cappel at 11.30 a.m.

The force advancing from Genweiler is estimated at one division, and the one advancing from Cappel, at one cavalry division; the latter apparently followed by infantry.

A little later the squadron leader reports, direct from Dieblingen, strong columns of the enemy on the road from Saargemünd—probably more than one division with a small force of cavalry, the head of which reached Iplingen at 11 a.m.

(1) What should the G.O.C. do?
(2) Give his orders to the division.
(3) Make out the reports.

PROBLEM V. FOR AUGUST 7.

(*Reconnaisance of a Cavalry Corps.*)

The French have been defeated on August 6, at Spicheren. It has been discovered that a small portion has retreated on St. Avold, and that their main body retreated on Saargemünd, which is strongly held by troops of all arms.

The Cavalry Corps of the Second Army—the 5th and 6th Cavalry Divisions—has concentrated behind the Blies, on and east of the Habkirchen-Saargemünd road.

The 12th Cavalry Brigade is watching the enemy at Bitsch and Rohrbach.

The Divisional Cavalry, composed of the regiments which took part in the battle, are engaged under one commander in the pursuit of the enemy, who are retreating from Spicheren.

The 3rd Cavalry Division is advancing on Bolchen-St. Avold.

The G.O.C. Cavalry Corps of the Second Army receives orders to leave the 12th Brigade behind and advance by Saaralbe on Metz.

(1) Appreciate the situation, as G.O.C. Cavalry Corps.
(2) Outline his orders for August 7.

APPENDIX

PROBLEM VI. FOR AUGUST 7.

(Regaining the touch which has been lost, and checking the enemy in his advance.)

The disposition of the cavalry of the left wing of the Second Army on the evening of August 6 is given in the map for that day.

The 10th Hussars and the 5th Dragoons, as well as a battery of horse artillery, have been handed over to the commander of the 12th Cavalry Brigade.

Early on the 7th, the news of the result of the battle of Wörth, and the retreat of the main body of the defeated force, apparently on Bitsch, have come in.

Intelligence is received at the same time that the enemy immediately in front has disappeared from Bitsch and Rohrbach, and that all touch has been lost.

General v. Bredow receives orders on the morning of the 8th from Head Quarters of the Fourth Army Corps to reconnoitre in the direction of Lorentzen-Saarunion; Lorentzen-Pfalzburg, Ingweiler and Niederbronn; and to inflict as much damage as possible on the enemy, supposed to be moving on Bitsch; at any rate to delay him, as Prince Frederick Charles intends to place himself, with superior numbers, across his path at Rohrbach on the 8th.

At the same time, the G.O.C. informs the Brigadier that the Army Corps is to reach a point south of Wolmünster in the afternoon, and will push forward mixed detachments to support the cavalry and to keep the garrison of Bitsch under observation.

(1) How should the Brigadier carry out his task?
(2) Give Brigade Orders for August 7.

PROBLEM VII. FOR AUGUST 8.

(Pursuit; reconnaissance; establishment of communication.)

The 5th Cavalry Division is distributed as shown in the map for August 7. The G.O.C. is acquainted with the information about the enemy that has up till now come in (see p. 39, etc.). On the evening of the 7th the division received the following communication from Army Head Quarters:—

"Bliescastel, August 7, 8 p.m.

"I request you to cross the Saar to-morrow with the division, and—

"1. To overtake the enemy, who has retired from Saargemünd and Saarbrücken on Püttlingen ; to do him as much damage as possible, and to ascertain his whereabouts.

"2. To establish communication with the Third Army in the direction of Pfalzburg, and to permanently destroy the railway west of the fortress.

"3. To push patrols as far forward as possible by Saaralbe towards Nancy, to discover whether the news in the French papers are correct, that a strong corps concentrated there has commenced to march eastwards to join the army of the Rhine.

"The 6th Cavalry Division, reinforced by artillery and the Divisional Cavalry, has orders to take up the pursuit to, and beyond, St. Avold.

"(Sd.) FREDERICK CHARLES."

(1) How should the G.O.C. carry out his task?
(2) Give his orders for August 8.

N.B.—The detachments of the 5th French Corps which were at Rohrbach and Bitsch on August 6 may be disregarded.

PROBLEM VIII. FOR AUGUST 9.

(*Reconnaissance and raid on the railway.*)

On August 8 the 3rd Cavalry Division received the reports about the enemy from the patrols which they had pushed forward—some of these reports, as we know, were not correct.

The commander receives on the evening of August 8 the following communication from Army Head Quarters:—

"Völklingen, August 8, 6 p.m.

"The army remains to-morrow in its present position. I request you, however, to cross the river to-morrow at Saarlouis, and to advance westwards across the Nied as far as possible.

"The 1st Cavalry Division moves forward by Kreutzwald, Ham, and Bolchen. Your task is to reconnoitre the fortress of Diedenhofen and the Mosel between that place and Metz; and to arrange to cut the Diedenhofen-Metz railway.

"The next duty of the division will probably be to push forward reconnoitring patrols across the river, at the same time securing itself towards the north.

"(Sd.) V. STEINMETZ."

(1) How should the G.O.C. carry out his task?
(2) Give his orders for August 9.

APPENDIX

PROBLEM IX. FOR AUGUST 9.

(Operations on the enemy's flanks. Events consequent on the enemy's attack.)

The 1st Cavalry Division received, on the evening of the 8th, the following communication from the Head Quarters of the First Army :—

"Völklingen, August 8, 6 p.m.

"The army will remain to-morrow in its present position.

"St. Avold is still strongly held by the enemy, whose left wing is assumed to be at Buschborn.

"You will advance to-morrow by Kreutzwald and Ham in the general direction of Bolchen. Your task will be to locate the enemy's left wing, to threaten his flank, and to reconnoitre to the north side of Metz.

"The 1st Cavalry Division will advance towards Diedenhofen and the Mosel, and will cross the Nied at Busendorf.

"The 6th Cavalry Division, followed by a portion of the Second Army, will endeavour to seize St. Avold.

(1) How should the G.O.C. carry out his task?
(2) Outline his orders for August 9.
(3) When the division reaches Kreutzwald at 10 a.m., heavy firing of artillery from the neighbourhood of St. Avold is heard, and simultaneously the report arrives that Karlingen is occupied by hostile infantry, estimated at more than one battalion strong.

What does the G.O.C. decide to do?

PROBLEM X. FOR AUGUST 10.

(Reconnaissance; demolition of the railway; establishment of touch.)

The distribution of the 5th Cavalry Division on August 9 is given in the map for that day. The information which the G.O.C. possesses about the enemy can be gathered from the account in the text. It is assumed that the united division was placed under the direct orders of the commander of the Second Army.

On the evening of August 9 the following communication reaches the leader of the division :—

"Saargemünd, August 9, 6 p.m.

"I request you to advance to-morrow with the division, far enough in the direction of Gross-Tänchen and Han a. d. Nied at least, to regain the lost contact with the enemy. You will at the same time reconnoitre towards the south side of Metz; and keep in view a reconnaissance of the Mosel between Metz and Pont à Mousson, as well as the demolition of the railway on the left bank.

"It is of vital importance to destroy the railway as soon, and as permanently as possible. The division will also keep touch with the Third Army and reconnoitre towards Nancy.

"The 6th Cavalry Division will reconnoitre towards the eastern side of Metz, on the line Falkenberg-St. Avold. The Guard Cavalry Division will move from Achen, by Saaralbe, on Mörchingen.

(1) How should the G.O.C. carry out his mission?
(2) Outline his orders for August 10.

PROBLEM XI. FOR AUGUST 11.

(*Measures for attack on the battlefield.*)

The reports of the cavalry on the 10th had indicated that the enemy was making preparations to hold a position on the French Nied. The Head Quarters of the Second Army concluded, in consequence, that the French would accept battle on the eastern side of Metz.

The measures which Prince Frederick Charles took for August 11 are given on p. 168, etc. It is assumed that the 5th and 6th Cavalry Divisions have been placed under the direct command of the Prince. Their dispositions are given on the map for August 10.

(1) How should this body of cavalry be employed on August 11?

(2) Give the orders to be issued from Army Head Quarters to the commanders of the divisions.

(3) Outline the orders to the 5th and 6th Cavalry Divisions by their respective G.O.C.'s.

PROBLEM XII. FOR AUGUST 12.

(*Reconnaissance; demolition of railway.*)

On August 11, the 11th and 13th Cavalry Brigades, with the two batteries of horse artillery, under the command of the G.O.C. 5th Cavalry Division, had reached the French Nied, south of the Falkenberg-Metz railway. [See map for August 11.]

APPENDIX 343

The G.O.C. Tenth Army Corps issues the following order on August 11 :—

"All the information received indicates that the enemy has retired from the front of the corps behind the Mosel. The division will march at dawn to-morrow, will reach Pont à Mousson, and make every endeavour to destroy the Frouard-Metz railway permanently at various points. It will reconnoitre towards Metz from the south, will send patrols to the left bank of the Mosel and a detachment on Nancy.

"The 19th Infantry Division will reach Delmé to-day; the 2nd Guard Cavalry Brigade intends to advance to Aulnois a. Seille."

(1) How should the G.O.C. carry out his task?
(2) Give his orders for August 12.

Problem XIII. For August 13.

(Reconnaissance and crossing of a river.)

The 3rd Cavalry Division receives at Bettingen on the evening of August 12 the following communication from Head Quarters of the First Army :—

"Head Quarters, Buschborn, August 12, 6 p.m.

"The further retreat of the French from the entrenched positions on the French Nied, as well as the rumours said by prisoners to have spread through the army, make it probable that the enemy is preparing to retire across the Mosel. Information of his intentions can only be gained by reconnaissances to the left bank of the river.

"I therefore request you to cross the Mosel north of Metz with the division to-morrow, and (1) to permanently interrupt the communication between this fortress and Diedenhofen; (2) to watch the north and north-west side of Metz, as well as the roads leading from there to Briey and Conflans; (3) to gain touch with the cavalry of the Second Army, which will also cross the Mosel to-morrow and advance towards the Metz-Verdun road.

"The 1st Infantry Division is going to-morrow to Antilly, and will place a battalion at your disposal to support you at the point of crossing.

"(Sd.)   v. Steinmetz."

For the solution of the problem it may be assumed that—

(a) The cavalry divisions were armed and equipped with the materials for crossing rivers as the cavalry of the present day are.

(b) No material for crossing was available on the right bank. Ferries had existed at Illingen-Uckingen, at Bettingen, Ay-Hagedingen, and at Hauconcourt.

(c) The news of the enemy on the other bank was in accordance with the reports of the commander of the division (p. 245).

(1) How should the G.O.C. division carry out his task?
(2) Outline his orders for August 13.

PROBLEM XIV. FOR AUGUST 13.

(*Screening duties.*)

The 6th Cavalry Division, after its reconnaissance on August 12, had retired behind the French Nied. The Head Quarters were at Berlize. In the evening the following order arrived from the G.O.C. Third Army Corps:—

"1. The Second Army is to march to the left to-morrow in the direction of Pont à Mousson. The 5th Cavalry Division is to cross the Mosel there to-day.

"2. The 6th Cavalry Division will proceed to the country on both sides of the Seille on the line Hospital Wald-Fleury-Corny, and hold the bridge at the latter place.

"It will send patrols towards Metz and on the left bank of the Mosel, and protect the proposed operations from the enemy's interference and observation.

"The division will keep touch on the right with the 1st Cavalry Division, which is covering the line from the Hospital Wald to the French Nied.

"3. The 6th Infantry Division will place two battalions at your disposal—to be ready at Chanville at 6 a.m., where a battery of the 3rd Field Artillery Regiment will also come under your orders.

"4. Reports to be sent to the central despatch station, to which place relays of orderlies are to be provided."

(1) Appreciate the situation as G.O.C. division.
(2) Give divisional orders for August 13.
(3) Give the orders to be issued by the Brigadiers, based on your divisional orders.
(4) As the main body of the division reaches Sanry at 8 a.m. on August 13, it receives information from the right flank that strong hostile columns of all arms are marching on the roads by Montoy and Ars Laquenexy, and the

APPENDIX

troops on the two roads are estimated at more than a division.

What does the Divisional Commander decide to do?

Problem XV. For August 14.

(Reconnaissance; engagement. Events consequent on the enemy's attack.)

On the evening of August 13 the 6th Cavalry Division in Verny receives the following communication from the G.O.C. of the Second Army, under whose direct command the division had again been placed (assumed):—

"Head Quarters, Delmé, August 13, 8 p.m.

"The 5th Cavalry Division, their main strength being assembled at Pont à Mousson, will advance to-morrow by Thiaucourt in the direction of Mars la Tour towards the roads leading westward from Metz.

"The 3rd Cavalry Division will cross the Mosel to the north of Metz at Hauconcourt.

"Your Highness is ordered to cross the Mosel to-morrow at Corny-Novéant, to reconnoitre by Ars towards Rozérieulles and Metz, and gain the plateau of Les Baraques with your division.

"From there Your Highness will reconnoitre the roads leading from Metz to Verdun, and endeavour to gain touch with the 3rd and 5th Cavalry Divisions. On establishing communication with the latter division Your Highness will place yourself, until further orders, under the command of Lieut.-General Baron v. Rheinbaben.

"Should you encounter French troops retiring from Metz, their march must be delayed at all costs.

"The 12th Cavalry Division will move to a position between the Seille and the Mosel, and occupy Corny.

"(Sd.) Frederick Charles."

(1) How should the G.O.C. division carry out his task?

(2) Outline his orders for August 14.

(3) When the division reached Corny, and one regiment had already crossed the existing suspension bridge (in single file), it receives from the 12th Cavalry Division a report to the effect that hostile troops of all arms are advancing from the south side of Metz on the roads to Jouy aux Arches and Cuvry, and that they are driving the outposts of the division back.

What does the G.O.C. 6th Cavalry Division decide to do?

N.B.—The division is armed and equipped as in Problem XI.

PROBLEM XVI. FOR AUGUST 14.

(The investment of a fortress.)

The commander of the Guard Cavalry Division at Bréhain receives the following communication on the evening of August 13 from Head Quarters of the Second Army:—

> "The main body of the 5th Cavalry Division is concentrated at Pont à Mousson, and will advance to-morrow by Thiaucourt towards the roads from Metz to Verdun.
>
> "Patrols sent out by the 3rd Guard Cavalry Brigade, who arrived to-day in front of the fortress of Toul, have reported that the town is only weakly held by 'Gardes Mobiles,' and gathered from the state of affairs there that if the town were surrounded by cavalry and shelled by field guns, this would suffice to force it to surrender. You will start to-morrow, as early as possible, by way of Dieulouard to Toul, and attempt to procure the surrender of the fortress.
>
> "The 3rd Guard Cavalry Brigade, which is at present with its main body in Dieulouard, will rejoin your command.
>
> "The G.O.C. Guard Corps has been directed to hand over the mounted batteries of the Guard Artillery to you for this purpose (*i.e.* three batteries of six guns each).
>
> "According to the French newspapers, troops by rail are expected in Commercy from Paris.
>
> "(Sd.) FREDERICK CHARLES."

(1) How should the G.O.C. Guard Cavalry Division carry out his task?

(2) Give his orders for August 14.

PROBLEM XVII. FOR AUGUST 15.

(Reconnaissance and engagement.)

The general situation in front of the Second Army on the evening of August 14 is as described in the text.

The orders issued to the G.O.C. 5th Cavalry Division, and the reports received about the enemy, are given on p. 300, etc.

The disposition of the division on the evening of the 14th are shown on the map for that day.

(1) As G.O.C. 5th Cavalry Division, appreciate the situation.

(2) Give the necessary orders for the movements of the division on August 15.

INDEX

OF THE MOST IMPORTANT OF THE DUTIES OF CAVALRY DISCUSSED IN THIS BOOK

A

Artillery, employment of Horse   295

B

Bells, sounding of may mean treachery of inhabitants . . 210
Billets, in the neighbourhood of the enemy, sparing horses, security . 102, 181, 190, 226
Billetting, in closest quarters even if necessary . . . 181
Bodies of cavalry, when separated, their junction towards the front 76

C

Cavalry, marching behind other troops 144
Cavalry, in difficult country . 39
Cavalry commanders, duty of initiative of . 57, 92, 178, 200, 313
Cavalry commanders, duty of, to reconnoitre personally . . 205
Cavalry commanders, importance of giving personal instructions 213
Cavalry corps, their formation . 111
Cavalry divisions, attached to army corps . . 105, 110, 178
Cavalry divisions, communication between them while advancing 153
Cavalry divisions, necessity of unified control . 5, 77, 110, 303
Cavalry divisions and divisional cavalry, their different tasks 5, 111, 263
Cavalry divisions and divisional cavalry when armies are in close touch 169
Cavalry divisions, on the flanks of an army 169
Cavalry divisions, their frontage when reconnoitring . 110, 304
Cavalry divisions, organization while advancing . . . 303
Cavalry divisions, employed as a kind of reserve cavalry . 35, 144
Cavalry divisions, number of roads to advance on . . 112
Cavalry divisions, strategical employment of . . 5, 33, 76, 171
Cavalry divisions, uniting several under one commander . . 5, 34
Commanders of troops, resolution of, when reports contradict each other . . . 300
Communication between large bodies of troops . . . 153
Control, at telegraph offices, of transmission of reports . . 117
Crossing a river 240

D

Defile, defence of . . . 215
Despatch-riders, numbers of, to be sent 20
Detachments, time when to send them out 316
Direction of enemy's march, report on . . . 18, 105, 158
Dismounted action . . 215, 235
Dismounted action, deception of the enemy, who thinks it is infantry 262

INDEX

Distance at which reconnoitring cavalry is to be sent forward . 110
Divisional cavalry, employment of . . . 4, 53, 54, 63, 252
Divisional cavalry, strength of 4, 124

E

Equipment, officer's, necessity of being provided with a lantern 320

F

Feint, attack 233
Fords, making use of . . 71
Formation of a corps cavalry brigade 251

G

General instructions and orders, issuing of 211
Guides, country people as; their usefulness 187
Gun-fire, march to the sound of distant 311
Gun-fire, proper and improper use of 295
Gun-fire, as a means of reacting favourably on distant actions . 26

H

Horses, saving of . . 137, 138
Horse Artillery, their employment 295

I

Information, by inhabitants; its value 18
Information, by papers left behind in orderly rooms . 174, 200
Information, by searching abandoned camps, billets, hospitals 130, 151, 173
Information, by enemy's stragglers; its value . . . 117
Initiative, by a cavalry leader 57, 177
Initiative, of subordinate leaders in correcting omissions by superior commanders . . 309

L

Lance, its effect. . 119

M

March, directions of enemy's columns on the march; difficulty of determining it . . 122
Masses of cavalry, employed as divisional cavalry, disadvantages 263

N

Night, duties of patrolling during; necessity for practice . 28

O

Observation, necessity of keeping the enemy, when discovered, under . . . 12, 95, 161
Observation, with field-glass . 11
Observation, by special posts . 12
Off-saddling, even if ordered that horses should remain saddled . 190
Orderlies, as guide-posts . . 263
Orders, encroachment on the authority of subordinates 16, 203, 211, 254
Orders, importance of being precise in . . . 254, 258
Orders, disadvantages of vagueness in . . . 179, 192, 239
Orders, consequences of weakening the terms used in . . 241
Orders, or general instructions . 211
Outpost-squadrons, following up the enemy without orders . 151

P

Patrol, effect of first appearance of a 15
Patrols, attacking a superior enemy 119
Patrols, when the traces left by the enemy branch off in different directions . . . 89
Patrols, entering an inn; consequences 224
Patrols, falling into an ambush . 125

INDEX

Patrols, firing in support of a reconnaissance . . . 271
Patrols, their instruction by the divisional commander 10, 18, 150
Patrols, mixed, of infantry and cavalry 27
Patrols, preparing reconnaissance for larger bodies. . . . 172
Patrols, in pursuit of hostile ones 90
Patrols, their quarters during night . , . . 90
Patrols, rest-day for . . . 87
Patrols, in rear of the enemy . 25
Patrols, their relief . . . 47
Patrols, their strength . 25, 186
Patrol-leaders, instruction of, by the sender . . . 10, 150
Patrolling duties, continual; causes loss of horses . . 236
Prisoner of war, how to act when taken 133, 227
Provisions, requisitioning of, by patrols. 12, 87
Pursuit, arrangements for . . 76

Q

Questioning prisoners . 320

R

Railway, demolition of; choice of spot 190, 218
Railway, demolition of; principle . . . 80, 139, 261
Railway, demolition of; marking the spot 139
Railway, demolition of; measures of security 228
Reconnaissance, procedure when feelers have to be pushed far ahead 137
Reconnaissance, necessity of attacking to gain timely information 329
Reconnaissance, what to do when civilians are brought in with important information . . 320
Reconnaissance, its undivided control 4, 77, 137
Reconnaissance, by enveloping . 232
Reconnaissance, after all, means fighting 75, 314
Reconnaissance, support by rifle fire 267

Reconnaissance, by turning the flanks 232
Reconnaissance in a fog . . 57
Reconnaissance, knowledge alone begets bold resolutions; ignorance begets anxious delay 85, 116
Reconnaissance, ascertaining names of places when on . 157
Reconnaissance, at night by strong bodies of cavalry . . 237
Reconnaissance, its final object . 107
Reconnaissance, of a place which is occupied 26
Reconnaissance, merely by outposts 172
Reconnaissance, value of personal 205, 210
Reconnaissance, by the point . 14
Reconnaissance, by the relief of outposts 126
Reconnaissance, by several squadrons, of a place which is occupied 98
Reconnaissance by telegraph . 44
Reconnaissance, importance of timely results of . . . 329
Reconnaissance, importance of transmitting information as early as possible . . . 329
Reconnaissance, unsatisfactory results of; cause of it . . 284
Reconnaissance, of a wood . 10
Registered horses, classification of 278
Registered horses, objections against their use . . . 225
Reports, collecting station; necessity for such 262
Reports, contradictory; cause . 128
Reports, exaggerated . . 236
Reports, to the highest quarters in the first instance . . 43
Reports, worthy of imitation 25, 41, 43, 61, 99, 101, 123, 127, 130, 134, 151, 156, 173, 174, 186, 196, 208, 270, 272, 286, 291, 298, 307
Reports, importance of rapid transmission by intermediate authorities . . 42, 116, 329
Reports, means for ascertaining their loss 148
Reports, expediency of simultaneous despatch to different authorities 42
Reports, support from other troops in transmission . . 196
Reports, control of their transmission at telegraph offices . 117

350 INDEX

Reports, consequences of wrong 91, 116
Reports, wrong, owing to withdrawal of outposts and departure of transport . . 128
Requisitioning, measures of security when 318
Requisitioning, measures of security against treachery of inhabitants when . . . 21
Reserve, its meaning with cavalry 52, 205
Resting, troops; their distance from the enemy . 61, 68, 322
Return, choice of road to, after reconnaissance . . . 317

S

Securing important crossings . 275
Security, measures of, by occupying commanding points in rear 230
Security, measures of, by posting vedettes in rear . . . 230
Seeking communication with distant portions of the army . 108
Similar sounding names of places in France 92
Single rank, effect of forming a squadron in 307
Sluice-gates, of fortresses; importance to destroy such . 287
Squadron, as a patrol in advance of the point 205
Squadrons, sent forward fan-like 207

Strategical and tactical reconnaissance 252
Strength, of divisional cavalry . 124
Support, of advanced points, by closed bodies . . 36, 120, 121
Surprise, by dismounted cavalry 194
Surprise, disadvantages of a halt shortly before its execution . 224
Surprise, causes of a successful . 236

T

Telegraph, destruction of . . 189
Touch, capturing stragglers does not mean having gained . 106
Touch, lost . 12, 17, 95, 123, 136
Touch, lost at night by outposts 28
Training, advantages of good horse- 225
Transmission of orders, paying attention to the possibility of delays in the 252
Transport, importance of proper directions for . . . 113, 145

U

Uniform of the enemy's troops, necessity of being acquainted with 172

W

Waggons, provision of, in raids . 214

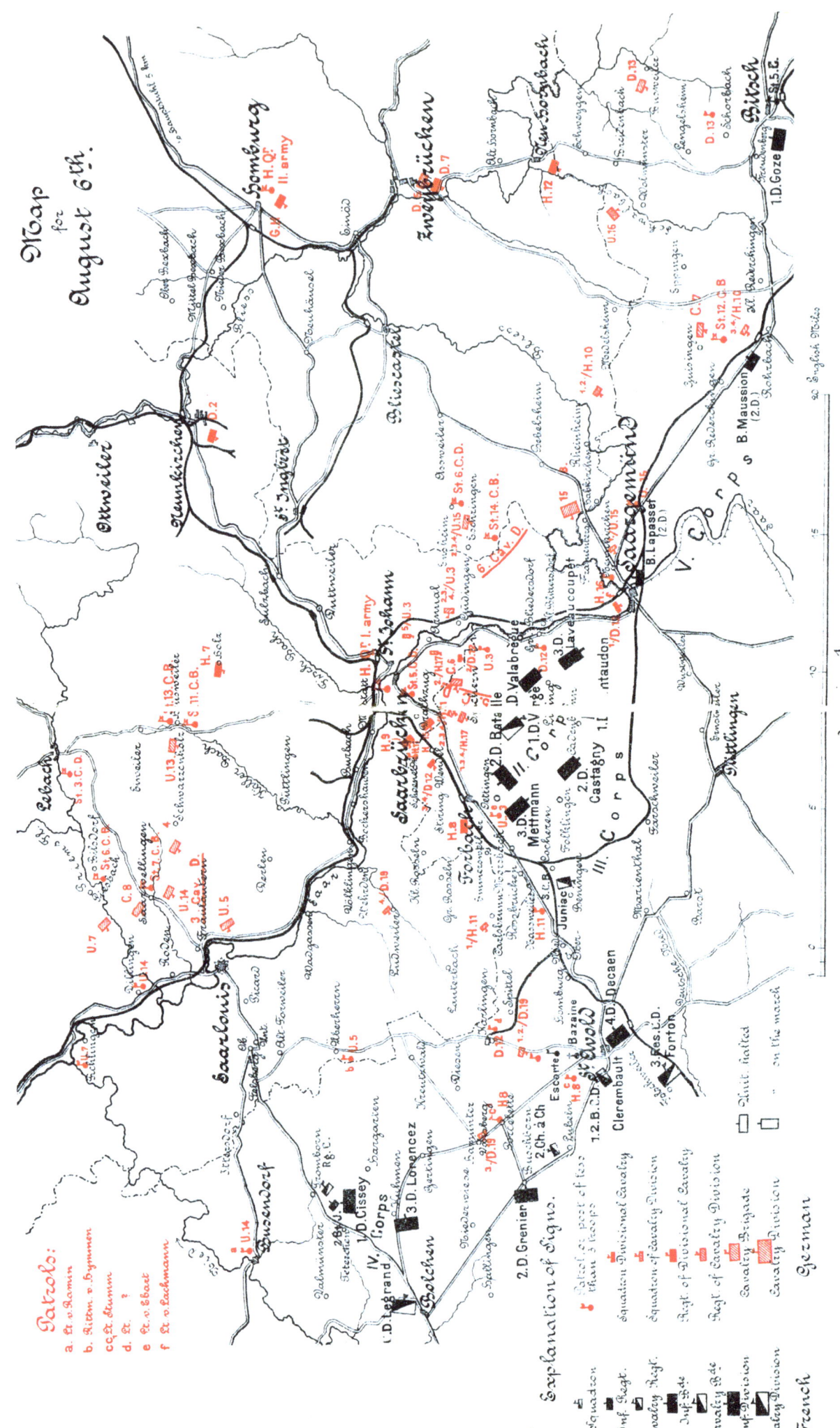

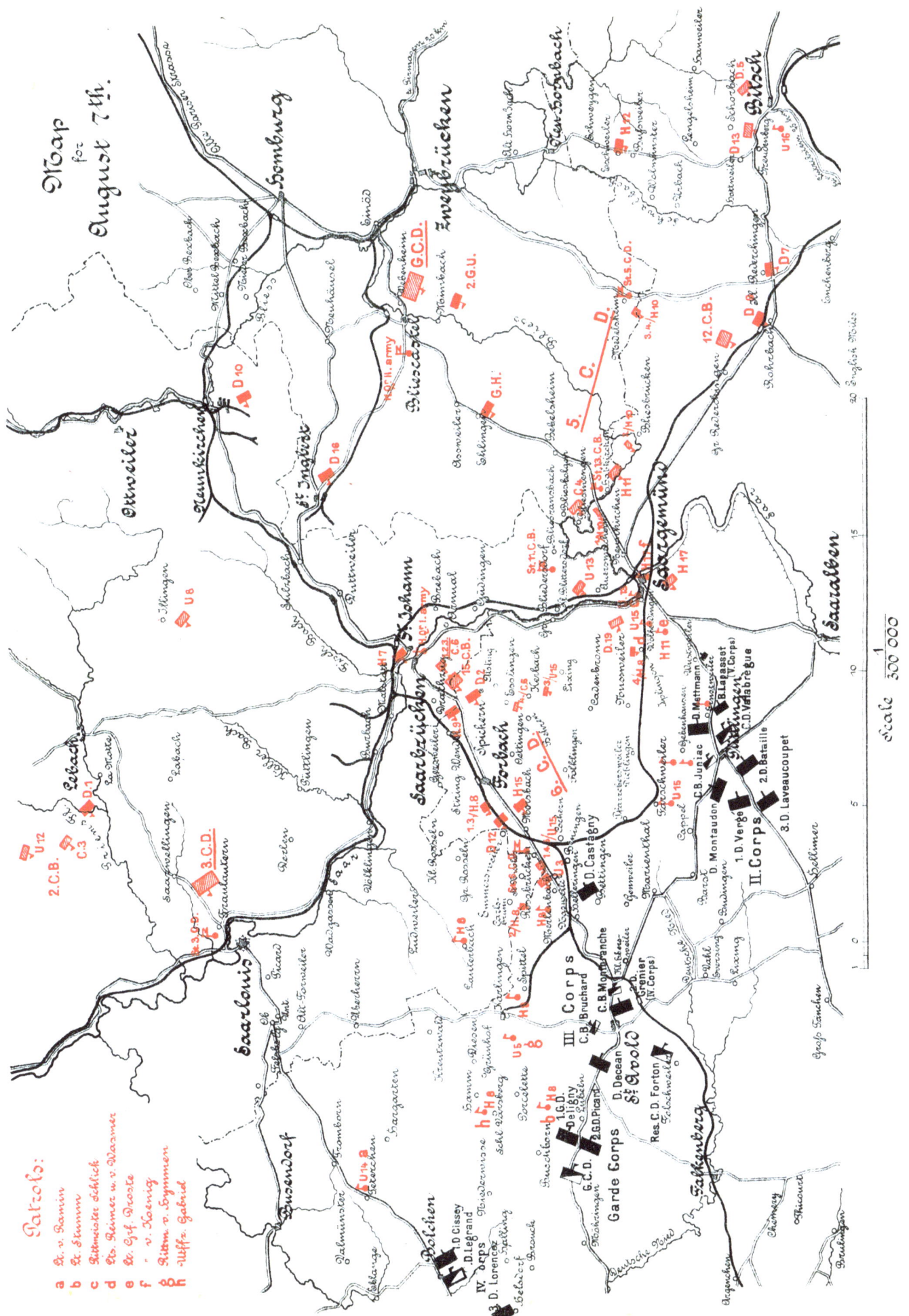

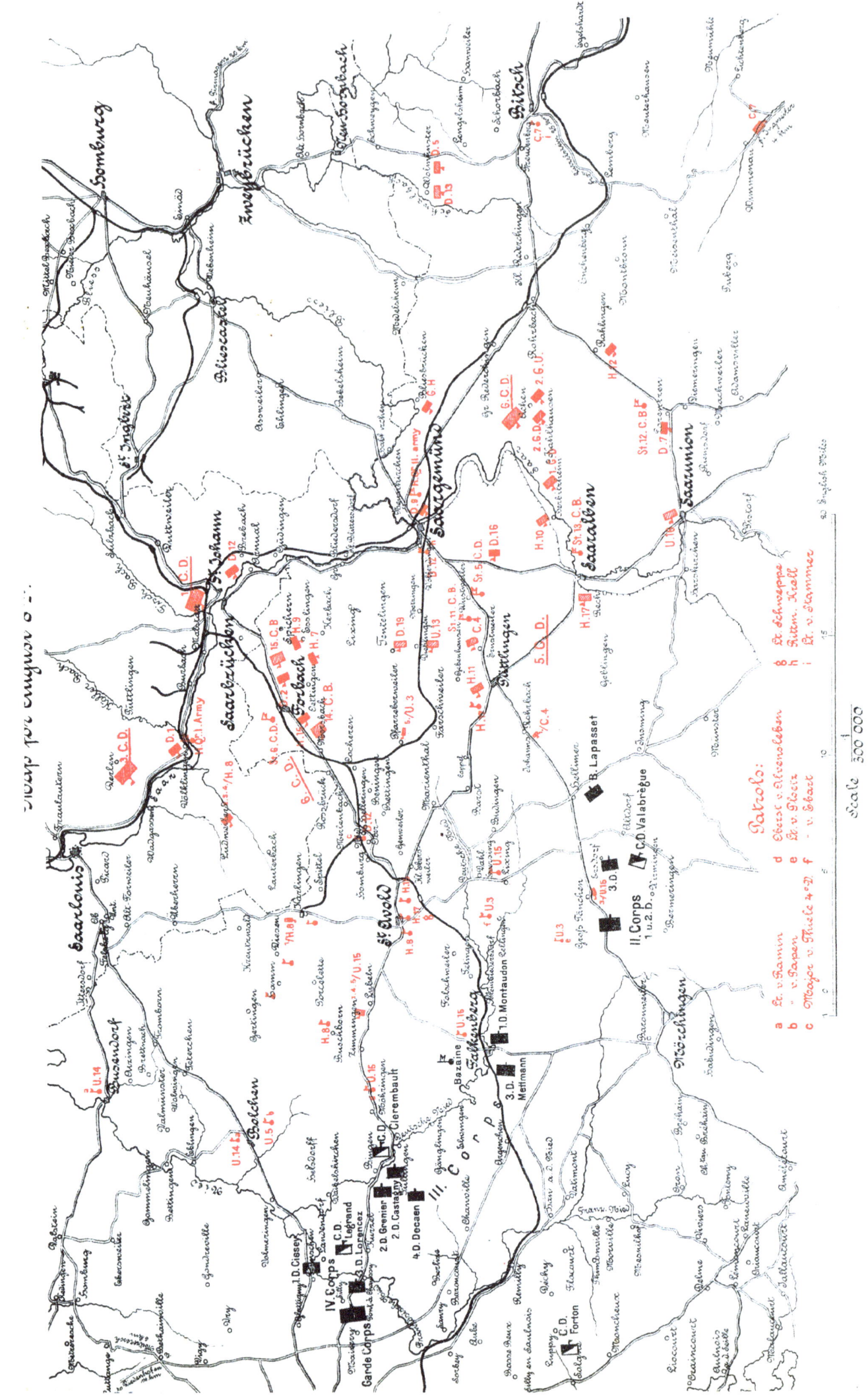

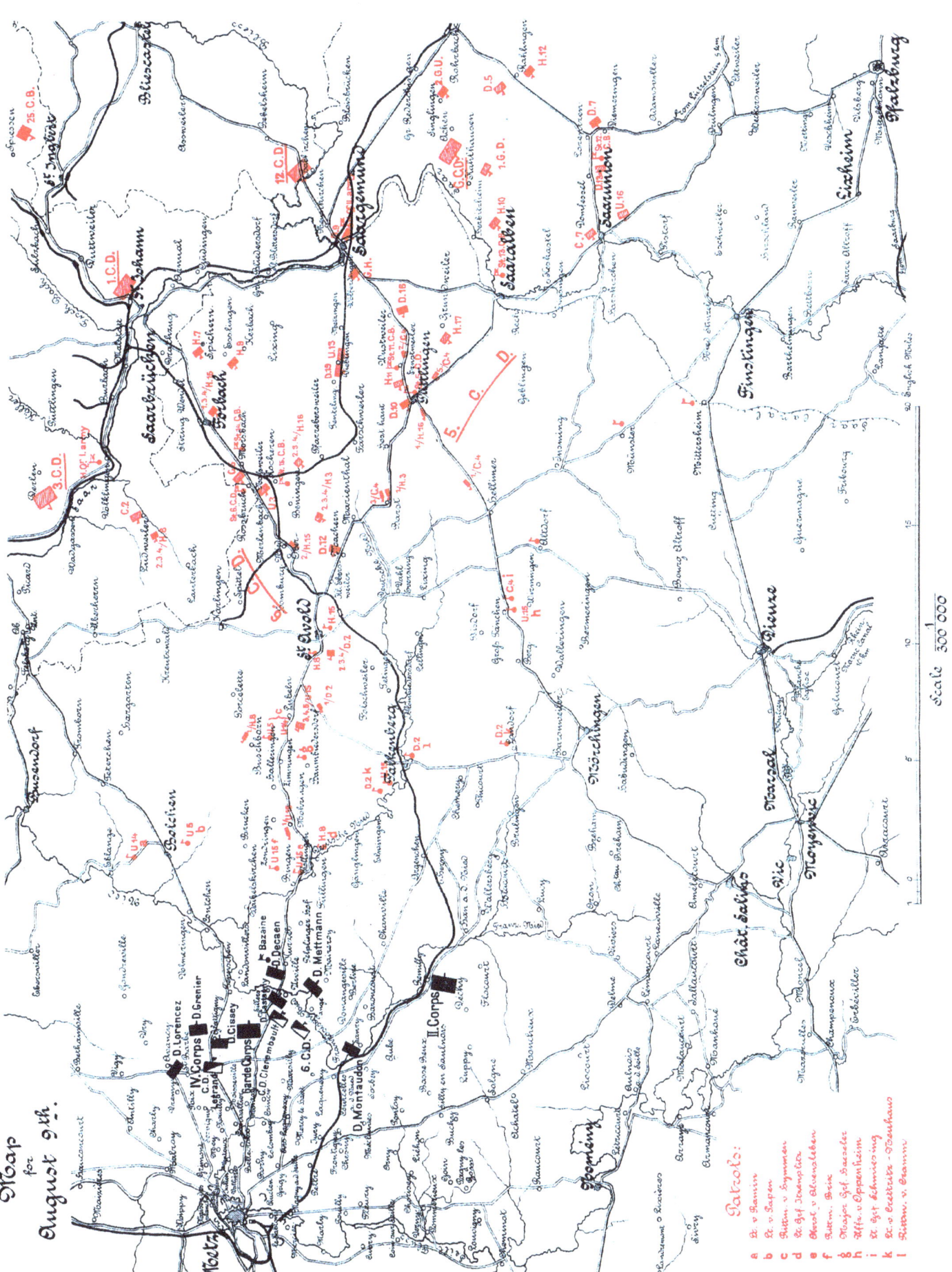

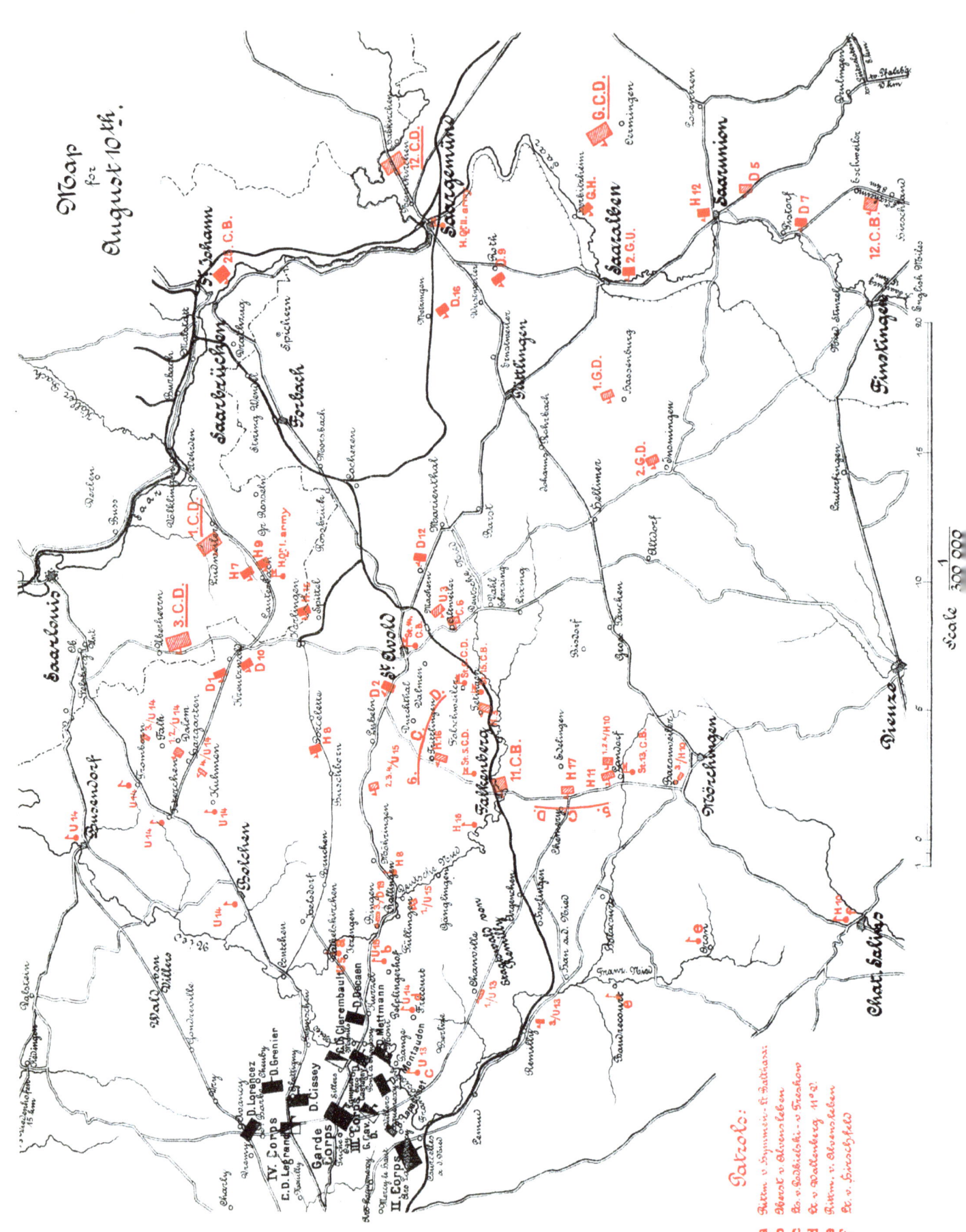

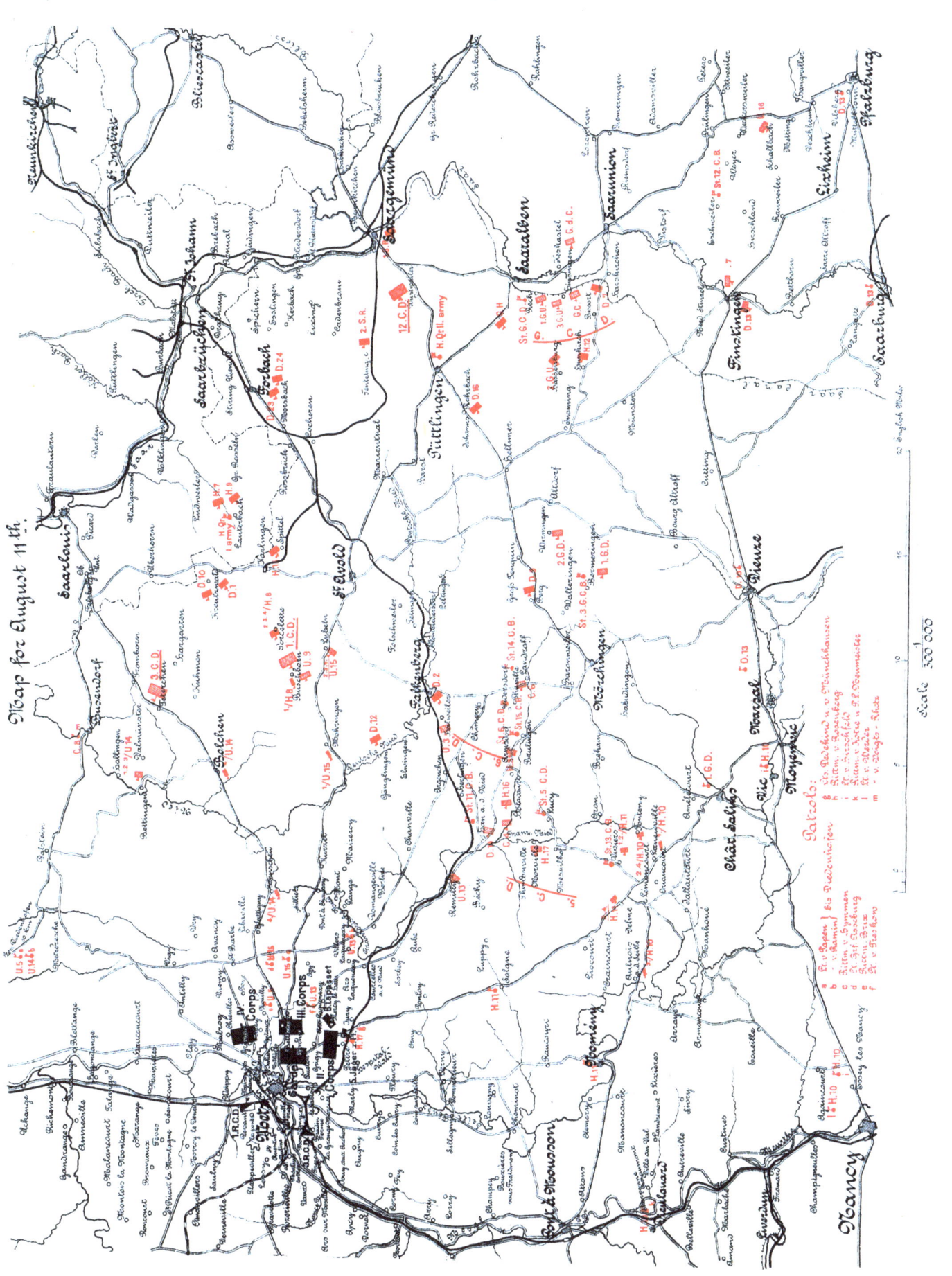

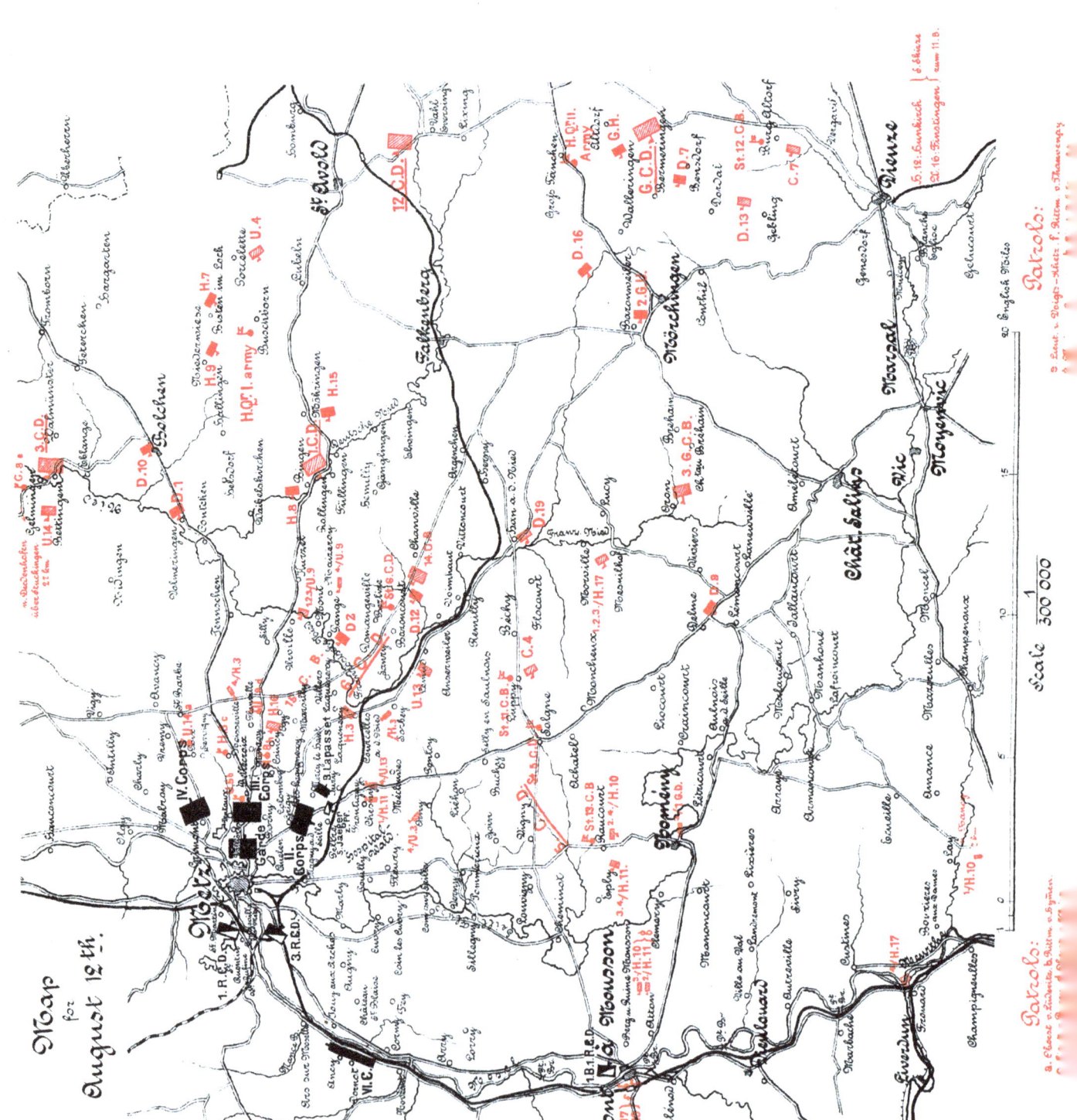

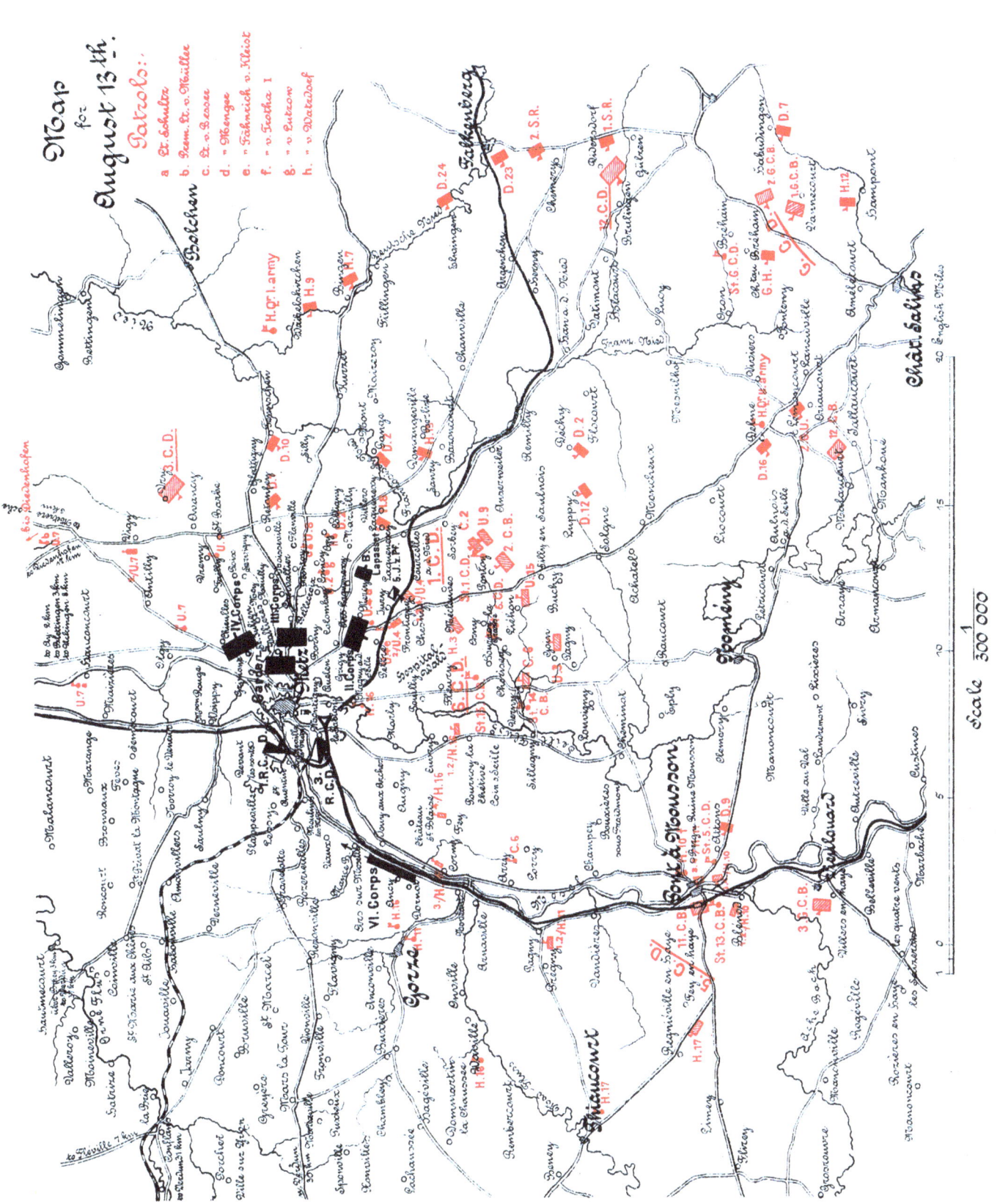

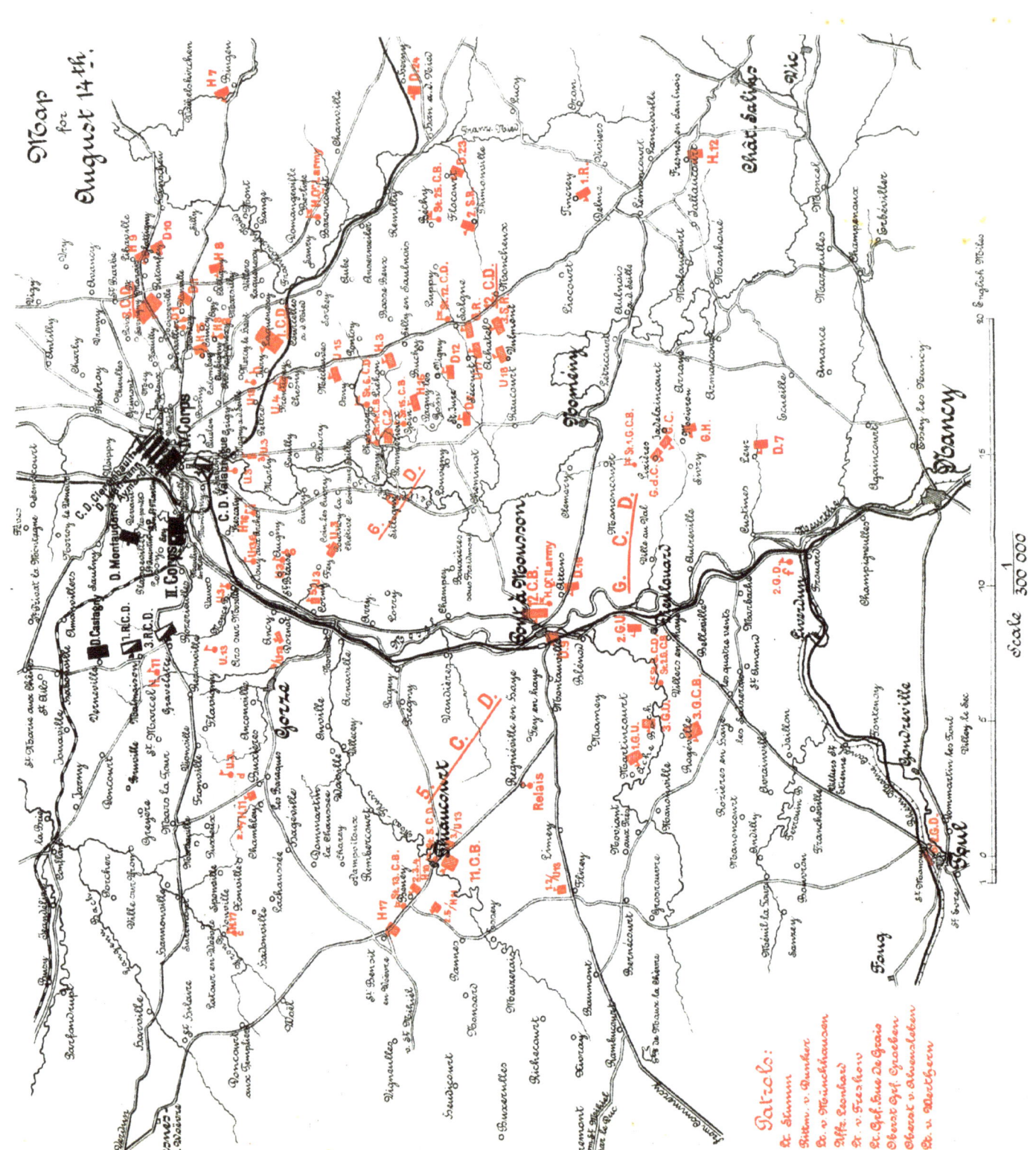

The Distribution of the Vth Cav: Div^n on Aug. 15th.

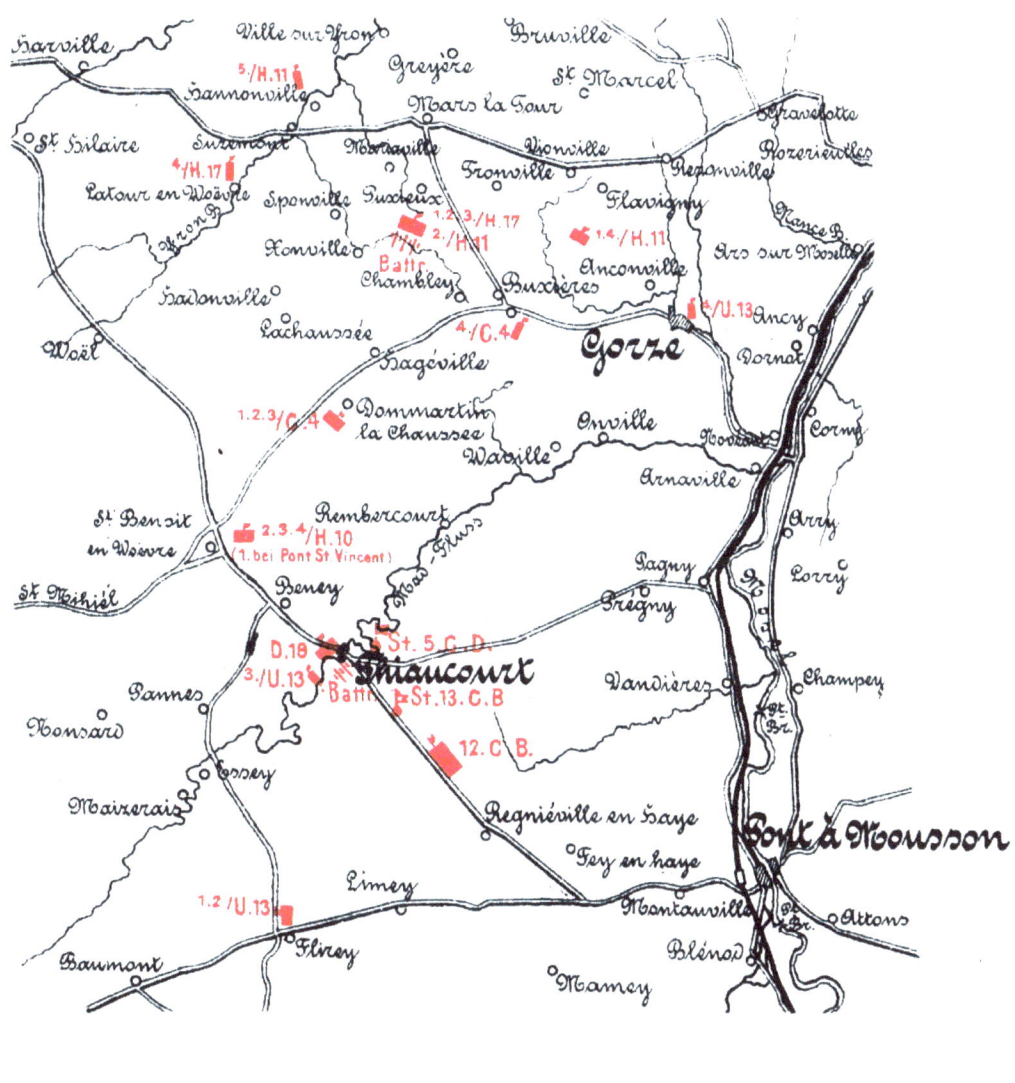

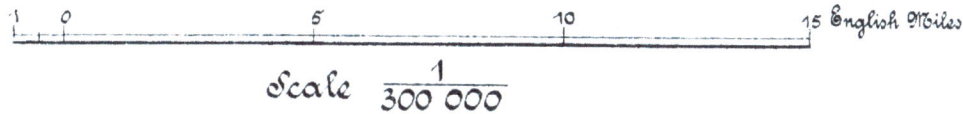

Scale $\frac{1}{300\,000}$

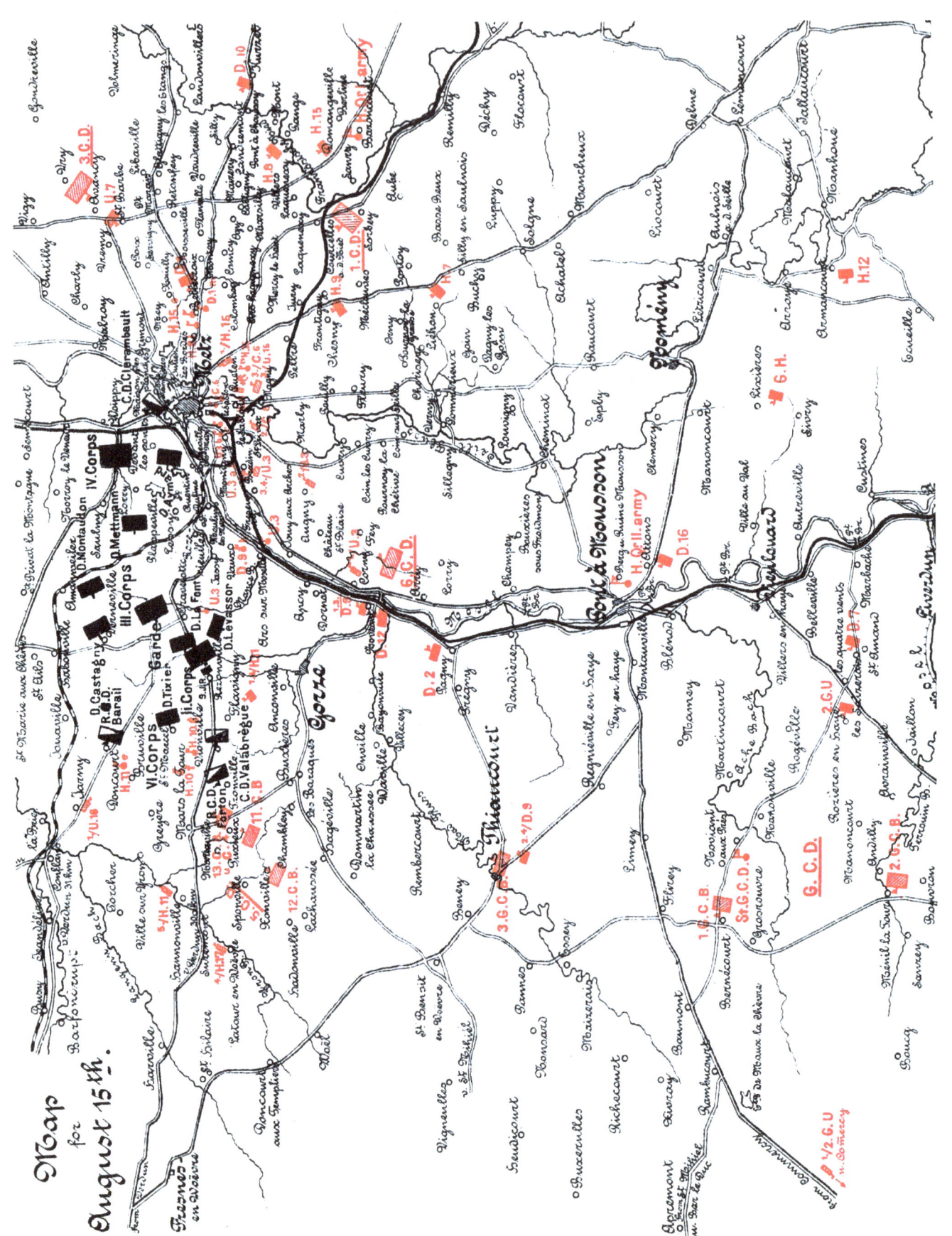

The Country between the Saar and the Nied.

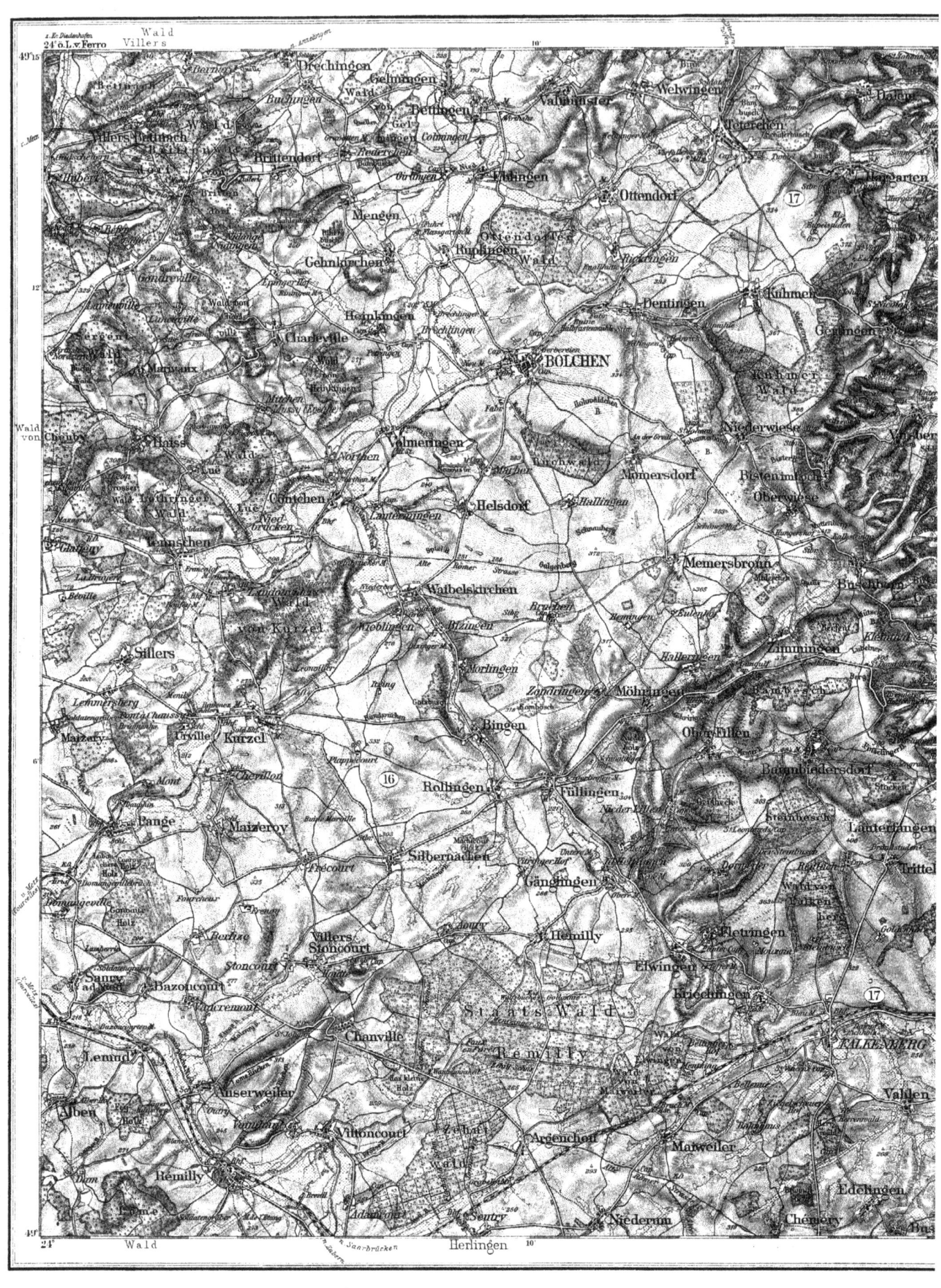

Scale $\frac{1}{100\,000}$

Explanation of a few terms used on Map.

n. = to (direction of road)   Str. = road
v. = from " "   Weg = road or path
Bhf = railway station   a.d. = on the
Khf = churchyard   Wald = wood

The Numbers give the heights above datum
Mean-level of the Baltic at Swinemünde
is 0.7 inches below datum.

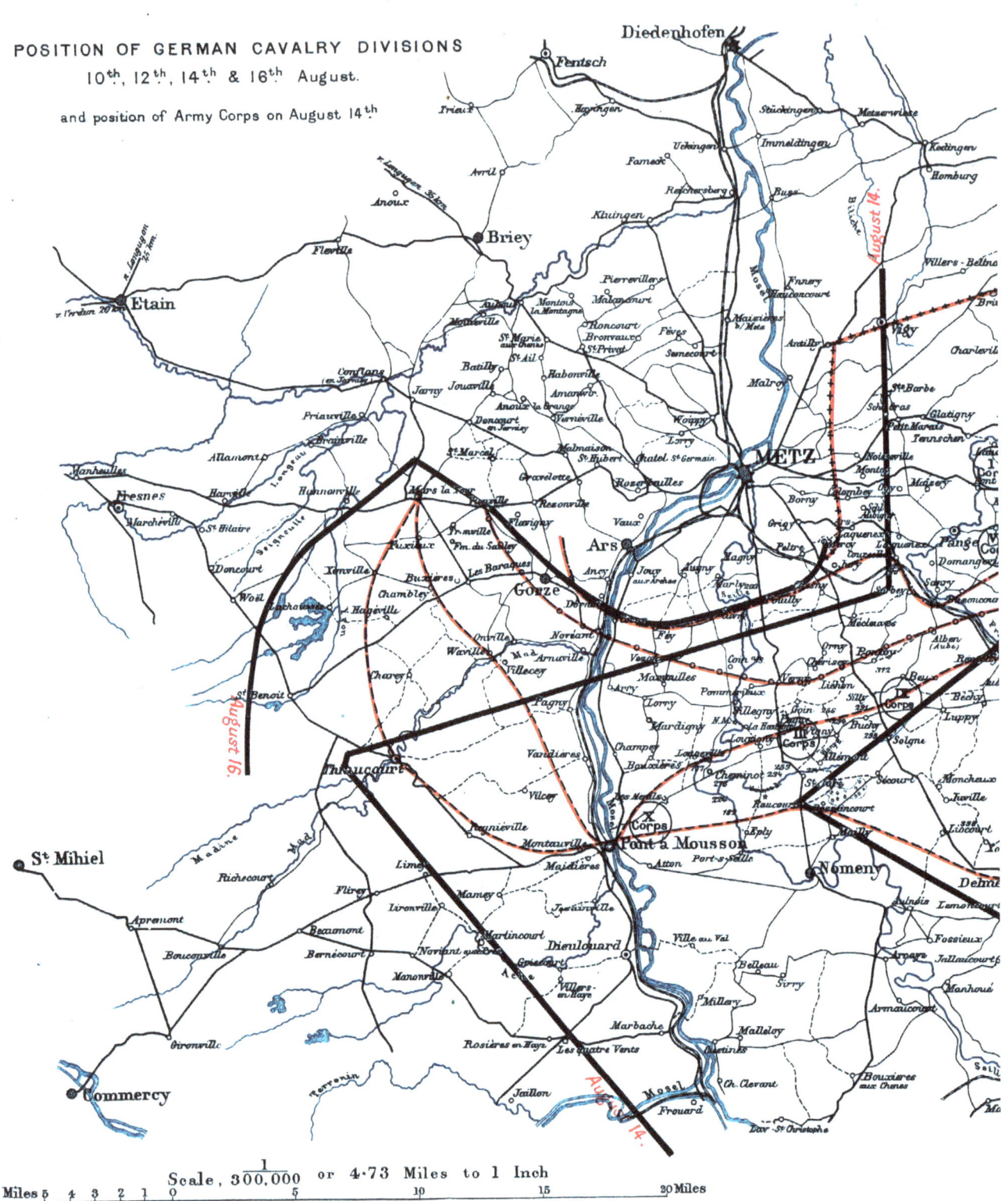

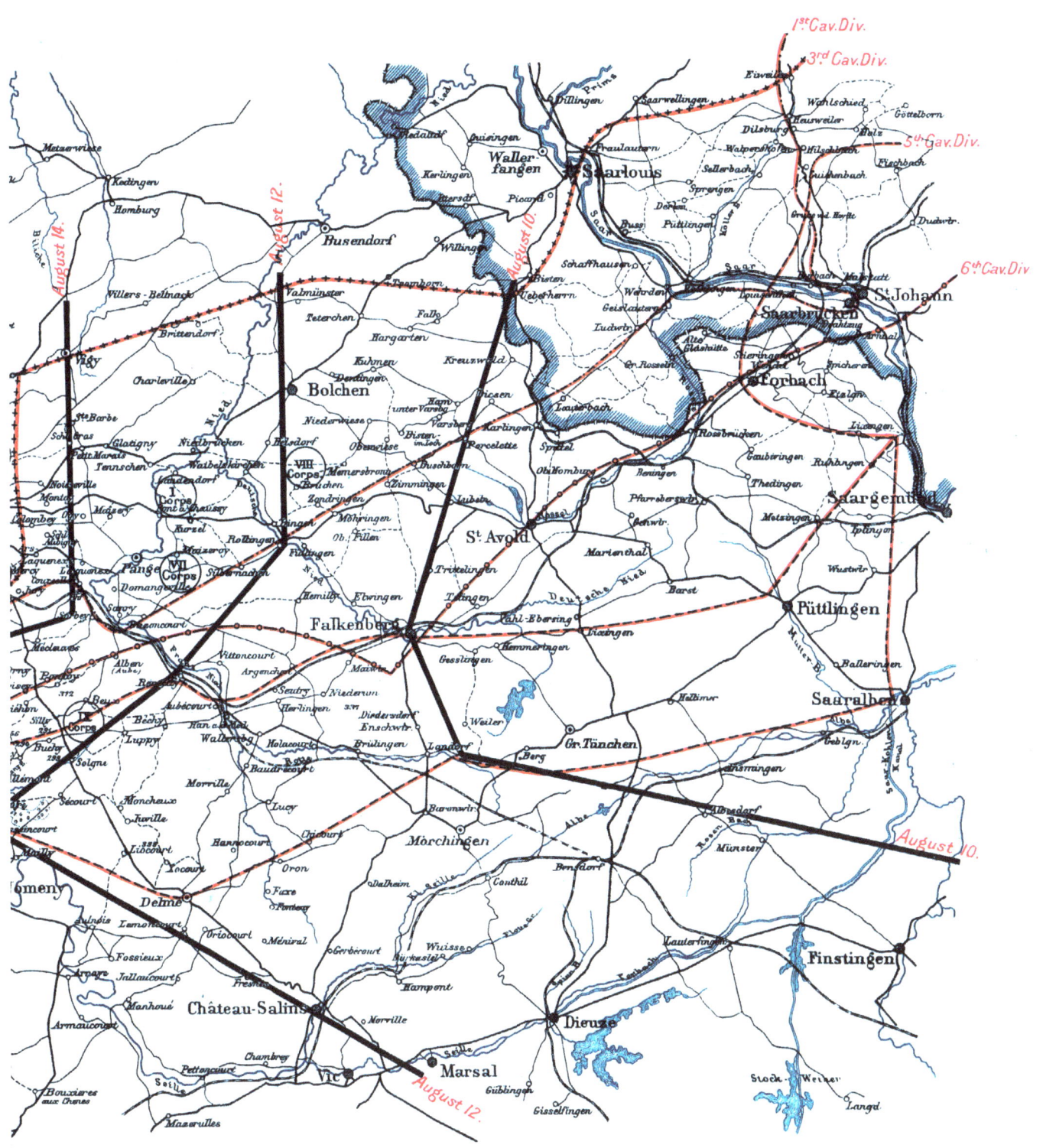

www.ingramcontent.com/pod-product-compliance
Lightning Source LLC
Chambersburg PA
CBHW041703290426
44108CB00027B/2839